Runways to God

Runways to God

the psalms as prayer

By

paschal botz, o.s.b.

the liturgical press

collegeville   minnesota

Cover: Design by Brother Placid, O.S.B.
Frontispiece: woodcut by Sister Photina, C.S.J.

First printing: January 1980
Second printing: November 1980

Library of Congress Cataloging in Publication Data

Botz, Paschal, 1905-
    Runways to God.

    1. Bible. O. T. Psalms—Commentaries. I. Title.
BS1430.3.B67   223'.2'077   79-24756
ISBN 0-8146-1059-5

Dedication

To the Authoress of the greatest Psalm

Contents

Preface   ix
Psalms 1 to 150   1
The *Magnificat*   341
The *Benedictus*   343
Nunc Dimittis   345
Suggested Psalms for Various Occasions   346

Preface

The title *Runways to God* suggests flying. Taking off in a plane as it speeds down a runway is thrilling. As one rises into the wide open sky, the perspective changes. Objects and people on the ground do not shrink, but they look smaller. There is danger in not getting off the runway or in flying too low. Likewise, *Runways to God* suggests rising with mind, heart, and body through prayer into the great realm of God. Not to give our whole self to the Godward thrust means dragging one's feet, clinging to things less than God. Flying and praying are far from arbitrary actions. Reason and science govern the one, revelation and faith the other.

God's Word offers little direct help on the technology of aviation, but it gives every norm on the art of going to God. Our response to God's speaking is faith, the wholehearted acceptance of His known will. The ancient encounters with God's Word and Deed are the Psalms, prayer records of faith in every situation of life and death. While their literal meaning reflects the past, they are alive and crucial in their Christ-meaning of the present. To assist men and women of faith and prayer to become "Psalm happy" in some small way is the purpose of this book. The Psalms must become contemporary to the People of God today as in times past. If Christ made them His prayer book during His life on earth, He is doing so again now in His Holy Spirit of prayer, unless He left us orphans in this important life function.

To suggest the Psalms as authentic and solid spirituality is saying the obvious. If this were a scholarly work, the title might be *From Sinai to Sion*. My purpose is not scholarly, to elucidate all about the historical sense. Others have done this; the reader can find competent commentaries in libraries, private and public, to discover the inspired literal sense. As a lifelong student of the Psalms, I have tried to do the same in order not "to go off the deep end" in my prayer comments. Praying the Psalms means more; it means going beyond the literal sense to the fuller meaning intended by God for Christ and His Church. The task is enormous: comparing the world of the old order with the World of Christ. Here in these brief remarks I can only try to point out the way.

Scholars will find much to criticize in this volume: readings chosen, comments made (or not made), interpretations adopted, and more. My only concern is to serve the reader with something pertinent to prayer, as it rises from each Psalm. If the day will ever come when specialists agree on text and interpretation, then another volume like this, a better one, will appear. Meanwhile, decisions have to be made and people led back to the rich traditional prayer of Christ and His Church. The Vatican II and post-Vatican voices constantly urge this return, and God's People are ready and anxious for that true discipleship of Christ in prayer. We discern it as the work of the Holy Spirit who is tracing the "roads to Zion" in their hearts. Most of the Psalms are immediately intelligible, but not in their christological significance.

Each Psalm is a unique spiritual creation. This is important for learning to "sow them in the heart," for pondering them, for making them our own, for "becoming the author of each Psalm." Those baptized in Christ Jesus are destined for discipleship and holiness of life. All who share the divine life are endowed with powers of instinct (gifts) that make them sensitive and eager to catch the divine message intended for them in each Psalm. God still speaks to His People in these inspired sung-prayers, sacramentals of divine light and grace, lessons of the moral law, carriers of holiness. "Holy is his Name" and holy are all "born of God." In a never-ending movement of godliness, prayer of the Psalter will "enlarge the hearts" by expanding our capacity to love God and man. And in the process we solve our problem "with the music of the harp" (Ps. 49:5).

The pattern of this commentary is simple. First, each Psalm is presented in its Old Testament framework of origin, literal meaning, and purpose, with a minimum of space given to its classification and the interesting points that fill other commentaries. The first reading of a Psalm usually yields valuable spiritual insights for prayer. God and the human author meant the poetic character of the Psalter for the purpose of prayer; likewise the community (corporate) and personal values, the past events and foreign imagery of a distant world. Bygone situations can have a normative lesson for us latecomers who have to work hard at sifting out the perennially valid message of faith. A common spirituality pervades the Old Law and the New when it comes to themes of revelation: God as Creator and Savior, the very concepts of God and man, truth and justice balanced by mercy and love, and always the theme of trusting praise. The literal sense should fire the spirit of man with the inspiration of God's Spirit. The repetitions that occur are an obvious reflection of the Psalms themselves.

Second, the commentary interprets this literal reality (including the difficult parts of the Psalms) in the light of Christ and the New Testament. The entire Old Testament prepares for Him and His Kingdom. Therefore to seek the fulfillment sense is not a minimum law (applicable to a few verses), but a maximum one (Cardinal Newman). The Psalms are forward-looking. They speak about Christ. His sacred Blood flows through the whole Psalter (Thomas Merton). "Everything written about me in the law of Moses and the prophets and *Psalms* must be fulfilled" (Lk. 24:44). The search for this final sense of the Psalms has occupied the Church in every generation; it must engage our best efforts in comparing one spiritual world with another, with the help of God who is Author of both. The "voices" in the Psalmody are both old and new.

The brief comments here about each Psalm do not exhaust the challenge of this task of faith. Countless attempts have been made to relate every Psalm to the New Testament. In one of the earliest documents (*The Apostolic Tradition*, about 210 A.D.), the Psalms and hours of prayer have reference to Christ's passion, death, and rising. The word "symbolize" occurs in a discussion of the Old Testament's relation to the New. Early bishops preached on the Psalms; for example, St. Augustine wrote his great work on the Psalms as pointing to Christ. Even now the Church, during Holy Week, points out the imprecations that fell on Him, the innocent Lamb-Victim: "Christ redeemed us from the curse of the law, having become a curse for us" (Gal. 3:13). Faith requires us to relate the Psalms to Christ. But I do not want to anticipate the Church's final decisions regarding interpretations of Psalms and wish to make no claims that conflict with the living Voice. The reader will take many of the suggested relations as theological accommodations which stand or fall with the way the praying Church interprets them.

We pray each Psalm the way Christ did and still does. Just as He devoted precious moments of His life to them, so now He enters into their world of prayer, of suffering and rejoicing, of battle and victory, or teaching and guiding, always giving the literal meaning a new turn and fulfillment. His salvation and Kingship, His sentiments of mercy and kindness, His love of enemy, His prior concern for the poor, all is new revelation that gives the Psalms a new dimension. God is still the God of justice, and presumption is as dangerous as ever. Retribution still belongs to God and sin still is enmity with God, but the Savior taught us to refrain from revenge. He laid down His life for sinners at the hands of sinful men, and He prayed for them. He rejected the prince of this world and the impenitent. Consequently, we apply all the harsh things of revenge to Satan and his world of darkness. The devil manipulates evil in the world. Sin and evil came to mankind through one man. The Lord recognized evil more clearly than we do. In Samaria, enemy country with people who would not receive Jesus and the disciples, He rebuked the "sons of thunder" for wanting to call down fire from heaven (Lk. 9:54). That is a clear but hard lesson for us to learn!

There is more than spiritual continuity between the two Testaments. When we pray with the Body of Christ, the Church, and exercise our discipleship, we renew and relive and reenact Christ's Mysteries in our midst. We are joined to the salvation action of the Lord. When we participate in the Psalmody of the Church, Christ is saying, "Today this scripture has been fulfilled in your hearing" (Lk. 4:21). We do not simply "read" the Psalms as historical and literary masterpieces, like paging through a cherished family album, interesting but past. No, we have an "instant replay," a breakthrough of Christ praying and praising, except it is far more real than TV can replay an event. Christ the Lord comes in sacred Sign, not only in and through bread and wine, anointing and water, but also He is the Voice of Psalmody in the Church's sacramental order. We lack words to describe His presence of this spiritual order and the greatness of liturgical Psalmody. That can lead to a mysticism of the sacramental order, affirmed by the Fathers of Vatican II in the Constitution on the Sacred Liturgy:

> Christ is always present in His Church, especially in her liturgical celebration. . . . Lastly He is present when the Church prays and sings. . . . From this it follows that every liturgical celebration, because it is an action of Christ the Priest and of His Body, which is the Church, is a sacred action surpassing all others (No. 7). . . . For the goal of apostolic endeavor is that all who are made sons of God by faith and Baptism, should come together to praise God in the midst of the Church (No. 10).

The living Voice has spoken. All this is possible because Jesus is glorified at the right hand of the Father. It is implied in Jesus' answer to the Jews who questioned the Eucharist: "Then what if you were to see the Son of man ascending where he was before?" (Jn. 6:62). The power of the Holy Spirit is the key to all liturgy, which is the Divine in human and material form, where Christ lives, prays, works, heals, battles, forgives, teaches, blesses families. We have found Him of whom Moses, the prophets, and the Psalms wrote (Jn. 1:45). Our pilgrim hearts are full of joy as we renew the Savior's "sacrifice of praise." Our vocation is praise. That is our sanctification, as the Spirit of the Psalmody enters open hearts and lets us penetrate deeper into the Mystery that is Christ.

The Psalms must be fulfilled in our generation and the age to come (Eph. 1:3-14). If this is true, if the Psalmody is symbolic and typical of the great Christ-Reality, then we must sing and pray in the Spirit to the Father with the Heart of Christ. Considering these matters this work can be called liturgical. Much more needs to be said about prayer, most of all about the Psalms in the liturgy. Besides providing suggestions on how to pray the Psalms, this book points out where a given Psalm occurs in the Liturgy of the Hours (weeks I, II, III, and IV refer to this official book of prayer). Praying seriously and lovingly teaches prayer. Praying in community teaches prayer. Singing the Psalms will "enthrone God on the praises of Israel" in the diocese, parish, and home. There the enemy is "legion" and needs to be pushed back "to go to his own place."

The text adopted here is the Revised Standard Version/Catholic Edition (RSV approved for ecumenical use). The Vulgate numeration of a Psalm stands in parenthesis. The kind generosity of De Rance, Inc. makes this book possible at a popular price.

Paschal Botz, O.S.B.
St. John's Abbey
Feast of the Immaculate Conception, 1979

Psalm 1

Blessed is the man
who walks not in the counsel of the wicked,
nor stands in the way of sinners,
nor sits in the seat of scoffers;
²but his delight is in the law of the LORD,
and on his law he meditates day and night.
³He is like a tree
planted by streams of water,
that yields its fruit in its season,
and its leaf does not wither.
In all that he does, he prospers.

⁴The wicked are not so,
but are like chaff which the wind drives away.
⁵Therefore the wicked will not stand in the judgment,
nor sinners in the congregation of the righteous;
⁶for the LORD knows the way of the righteous,
but the way of the wicked will perish.

The Blessed Man

God calls that person blessed who delights in the law of the Lord. In contrast the wicked chooses his own will as law, and that selfishness reaps the "Begone!" judgment that Christ foretold. Created with free will, everyone has to make the decision which way to go. Highways run in opposite directions, and happiness lies in choosing the right one.

Easy to understand, this Psalm, the only one written in prose, serves as a moral prelude to the whole Psalter and teaches the same basic lesson as the Gospel. Human happiness lies in doing God's will. More than that, it consists in meditating on it day and night and fulfilling it with eager delight. The Lord gave us the parable of the divine seed that bears fruit (Mt. 13). The one who hears the Word of God, reflects on it constantly, makes sacrifices to carry it out, is like a tree near running water that bears its fruit in due time. "The company of the scoffers" stands in opposition to "the assembly of the just." God's family is made up of the men and women who are followers of Christ on the way, on the pilgrimage to heaven. God watches over them, because Christ is the Way.

In order to identify with this Psalm in prayer, we should know that the empty chaff represents the wicked, useless persons whom

1

God rejects in the final judgment. This judgment is like the winnowing process of the harvest floor: the farmer tosses the harvest into the air with his fork. The heavier grain drops down and is kept, while the wind blows away the light, empty straw and chaff, which is eventually burned (Mt. 13:42 and 3:12). We have it in this Psalm as well as in the Lord's parables: the divine verdict will separate the good from the bad. True success in life belongs only to the just, those who prosper in God's eyes.

Praying this Psalm then means making a decision for Christ, who revealed the right way, the will of God the Father. He will welcome His own in words similar to our Psalm: "Come, blessed of my Father, inherit the Kingdom" (Mt. 25:34), while on the contrary He will reject the evildoers, "Depart from me, you cursed, in the eternal fire. . . ." The wicked walk the broad and easy way that leads to doom, and they are many (Mt. 7:13). Even now we can judge a tree by its fruit; the day of judgment will tell if there has been a conversion. The Church takes this first Psalm for her hour of readings during Easter week, again on the II Sunday of Easter and Sundays.

Psalm 2

Why do the nations conspire,
and the peoples plot in vain?
²The kings of the earth set themselves,
and the rulers take counsel together,
against the LORD and his anointed, saying,
³"Let us burst their bonds asunder,
and cast their cords from us."

⁴He who sits in the heavens laughs;
the LORD has them in derision.
⁵Then he will speak to them in his wrath,
and terrify them in his fury, saying,
⁶"I have set my king
on Zion, my holy hill."

⁷I will tell of the decree of the Lᴏʀᴅ:
　He said to me, "You are my son,
　　today I have begotten you.
⁸Ask of me, and I will make the nations your heritage,
　　and the ends of the earth your possession.
⁹You shall break them with a rod of iron,
　　and dash them in pieces like a potter's vessel."

¹⁰Now therefore, O kings, be wise;
　　be warned, O rulers of the earth.
¹¹Serve the Lᴏʀᴅ with fear,
　　with trembling ¹² kiss his feet,
　lest he be angry, and you perish in the way;
　　for his wrath is quickly kindled.

Blessed are all who take refuge in him.

Praise to the Messiah King

This Psalm is messianic. That means it refers directly to Jesus, the "anointed One," the King. Speaking of an earthly royal descendant of David, the author has in mind also the ardently awaited One, the great climax of the line of David. Christ Jesus alone is the final fulfillment of God's prophetic decree, and no other. Dramatically, this ancient hymn opens with a challenge to all kings and nations who revolt against God and His Messiah: "Why do the nations conspire and the peoples plot in vain?" saying, . . . "Let us burst their bonds asunder and cast their cords from us."

God Himself is King. Reluctantly He allowed His chosen people a visible king, an earthly representative, whom He adopted as a son, whom He would defend against all enemies, so long as he remained faithful to God. David and every successor on the throne was to prefigure the final, greatest King, the Messiah. God's promises to David are in 2 Sam. 7, and this Psalm repeats them in inspired song. Man's earthly contradiction only causes laughter in heaven, the divine derision that quickly turns into terrifying anger. If God has set up an earthly throne on Sion and in the New Kingdom has set His Son-made-man upon that throne, all human opposition He will dash to pieces like a potter's jar.

Our praying faith celebrates God's victory in Christ, first as a fact of His human Kingship, now as the ongoing triumph of His Church against all coalitions of evil, and then in His second, glorious Coming. David was a type of this Christ (see Ps. 89:3-5, 14, 27), who is the incarnation of the Son of God, the highest flowering of any royal line, who makes this Psalm clear to us. The literal meaning, which we cherish, gives only a faint insight into the total divine meaning which this Psalm unfolds in the Church's prayer.

The whole of Scripture is God's Word. God is always present to His Word. The inspired New Testament applies our Psalm to Christ. For instance, Acts 4:25f. quotes the first two verses to describe how Herod, Pilate, the Gentiles and the people conspired against Jesus. Paul at Antioch in Pisidia speaks of Jesus' descent from David (Acts 13:22f.) and quotes from Psalm 2 as prophetic: "You are my Son; this day I have begotten you" (see also Acts 13:33ff.). Again, Heb. 1:5 affirms it of the Son and denies it to angels. Priesthood as well as Kingship is Christ's according to Psalm 2 (Heb. 5:5). The Mystery of the incarnation makes Him both son of David and Son of God.

In Revelation, He rules "with an iron rod," "shattering like earthen pots" His enemies (2:27; see also 12:5ff. and 19:15f. for "the iron rod" and "blazing wrath" of the "King of kings.") Pilate crowned Him as king in derision, when Christ declared Himself as King. He died on the "King of Israel Cross" (Jn. 18:33-37). Reaping this opposition, He won immortal victory and was anointed with "the oil of gladness" (Heb. 2:8f.) and "crowned with glory." (Heb. 2:10 speaks of "bringing many sons to glory" as the prize of suffering.)

We are "the sons of glory" as we share in His Kingship. We are His followers on Calvary and Olives and share His warfare against "the prince of this world," against the powers of hell active in our world. Confidently we pray this Psalm with Christ present in the Church (on Christ the King, the Annunciation, Good Friday, Tuesday after Easter, II Sunday of Easter, Exaltation of the Cross, February 2, I Sunday lauds, and feasts of Martyrs). We do well to meditate often this crucial Psalm.

Psalm 3

O LORD, how many are my foes!
Many are rising against me;
²many are saying of me,
there is no help for him in God.

³But thou, O Lord, art a shield about me,
   my glory, and the lifter of my head.
⁴I cry aloud to the Lord,
   and he answers me from his holy hill.

⁵I lie down and sleep;
   I wake again, for the Lord sustains me.
⁶I am not afraid of ten thousands of people
   who have set themselves against me round about.

⁷Arise, O Lord!
   Deliver me, O my God!
For thou dost smite all my enemies on the cheek,
   thou dost break the teeth of the wicked.

⁸Deliverance belongs to the Lord;
   thy blessing be upon thy people!

Morning Prayer

Here we picture King David fleeing for his life before his own son Absalom, who led a revolt and sought the throne. Surrounded by hostile subjects, who were increasing into the thousands, David went with bowed head amid the taunts of the godless. God had raised him up to be king; now it looked hopeless, as the scoffers shouted, "There is no help for him in God" (see 2 Sam. 15-18).

But David trusted the more in God. He turned to the holy place where God dwelt and cried out in hope to the Lord, his shield and glory. This trust enabled him to rest anywhere, to lie down and sleep securely, and to awaken with new confidence. It is a small thing for the Lord to protect His own against all enemies, and experience in trust is the best teacher. To rise from sleep is an image of rising to the new day of God's help. God Himself will take care of any opposition (smiting on the cheek is a human way of saying that divine justice deals with calumny and blasphemy). Even in his suffering, David, like Christ after him, had a blessing for the people (last verse), thereby giving the example and going beyond his personal feelings.

Salvation is always from the Lord, and we need it more than safety from temporal enemies. The Church puts this Psalm on the lips of the suffering, dying Savior. He bowed His sacred head in apparent defeat, while His enemies boasted, "Will God save Him now? Come down from the Cross, if You are the Son of God!" Jesus prayed "with loud cries and tears to God, who was able to save him from death, and he was heard because of his reverence" (Heb. 5:7). His prayer was heard in the resurrection to glory.

We rise daily from hopeless situations to serene trust, as we learn to pray this Psalm. The Church is more conscious than ever of spiritual enemies surrounding her, and she prays constantly for her enemies, as Jesus did. The Lord, who promised persecution to His Church (Jn. 15:18-20), also promised victory. Every day He enacts His passion and death and victory anew in the Body of His Church. We, who are clothed with Christ, are His members suffering. As the Church prays Psalm 3, especially on Easter Thursday, on the II Sunday of Easter, and as morning prayer on I Sundays all year, our faith perceives how actual it is today.

Psalm 4

Answer me when I call, O God of my right!
Thou hast given me room when
I was in distress.
Be gracious to me, and hear my prayer.

²O men, how long shall my honor suffer shame?
How long will you love vain words, and seek after lies?

³But know that the LORD has set apart the godly for himself;
the LORD hears when I call to him.

⁴Be angry, but sin not;
commune with your own hearts on your beds, and be silent.

⁵Offer right sacrifices,
and put your trust in the LORD.

⁶There are many who say, "O that we might see some good!
Lift up the light of thy countenance upon us, O LORD!"
⁷Thou hast put more joy in my heart
than they have when their grain and wine abound.
⁸In peace I will both lie down and sleep;
for thou alone, O LORD, makest me dwell in safety.

Evening Prayer

The text as it stands tells of a man retiring at night with a heavy heart and turning to the Lord in his distress. Be it a court case, be it some other worry, he takes a stand against men of influence, those who pursue illusions and falsehood (idols) and set the pace for less notable persons. The just man finds himself straightened on all sides, and recourse to God sets him free, at large, and puts him at rest. This is the story and lesson for men and women today: their first recourse for settling their problems is turning to God with a true religious spirit. New confidence is needed every day, at every turn. Turning to God means conversion and surrender.

God hears every sincere prayer, accompanied by right living and legitimate offerings of sacrifice, in opposition to idol worship. The fear of God makes him tremble who lives in sin. Shedding tears of compunction on one's bed is contrition, a first condition for the praise of God. The Lord alone gives peace to the troubled heart. Turning with the eyes of faith, in humility, to the Savior will reap a rich reward of peaceful sleep. It is the way out of all troubles. Peace of heart is greater joy than an abundant harvest of grain and wine.

Those who long for better times should purify their own lives and wait for the Lord to show His provident care. This is also the message of Christ's Sermon on the Mount (Mt. 5-6, especially 6:19-34). Quiet, peaceful sleep is the time for God's working. Trust in Him is the condition for His speaking to the listening heart.

"Shine the light of your countenance upon us, O Lord," is a familiar Old Testament prayer. When Moses asked to see the face of God once more, He said, "My face you cannot see" (Ex. 33:20), but He answered the prayer in another way, a secure and wonderful way. That way was the Divine Presence in the Ark and cloud, in the priesthood and ritual sacrifice. That was to be the "face of the Lord" for centuries to come (Ex. 40:34-38). Generation after generation the faithful Jews pilgrimaged to Jerusalem to see the "face of the Lord," which meant not only His presence, but victory and wonders and answer to their prayers. No other nation was so privileged.

We can make this our constant plea, "Lord, show us Your face," in our private lives as well as in our public worship. In the New Testament, in the Church, the sacraments and prayer of the hours are the face of Christ. All the liturgical signs contain God's (Christ's) special presence, as other Psalms will predict in a more forceful way. Revelation is light. Faith is light, even if it is night, and we rest in the security of the Lord who called Himself the Light. "Walk as children of light" (Eph. 5:8). The Church prays this Psalm with Christ on Holy Saturday, as well as in her night prayer (compline) on Sundays and solemnities.

Psalm 5

Give ear to my words, O Lord;
   give heed to my groaning.
2Hearken to the sound of my cry,
   my King and my God,
   for to thee do I pray.
3O Lord, in the morning thou dost hear my voice;
   in the morning I prepare a sacrifice for thee, and watch.

4For thou art not a God who delights in wickedness;
   evil may not sojourn with thee.
5The boastful may not stand before thy eyes;
   thou hatest all evildoers.
6Thou destroyest those who speak lies;
   the Lord abhors bloodthirsty and deceitful men.

7But I through the abundance of thy steadfast love
   will enter thy house,
   I will worship toward thy holy temple
   in the fear of thee.
8Lead me, O Lord, in thy righteousness
   because of my enemies;
   make thy way straight before me.

9For there is no truth in their mouth;
   their heart is destruction,
their throat is an open sepulchre,
   they flatter with their tongue.
10Make them bear their guilt, O God;
   let them fall by their own counsels;
because of their many transgressions cast them out,
   for they have rebelled against thee.

11But let all who take refuge in thee rejoice,
   let them ever sing for joy;
and do thou defend them,
   that those who love thy name may exult in thee.
12For thou dost bless the righteous, O LORD;
   thou dost cover him with favor as with a shield.

Plea at Dawn

Every Psalm is a gem, inspired by God, written for a different situation, usually in a class by itself. We have here the personal prayer of a just man, in close friendship with God, contrasting his right faith with the faithlessness of people that cause him great suffering. To protest his love for God means taking a stand against evil. He hates the company of evildoers and wants to be on God's side. If he is being falsely accused of idolatry, one can understand why he calls on God to vindicate him.

Filled with reverential fear, he enters the sacred Temple to worship, pray, and listen to the Lord. His love for God's house and visible ritual prepares us for the Christian world of sacraments. Confidence and trust come from the Altar, where God gives security and refuge from all His enemies. "The boastful may not stand before thy eyes" recalls the Savior's judgment against the Pharisee boasting in the Temple (Lk. 18:10ff.). Taking refuge in God means to divest oneself of self-merit and self-righteousness.

There are phrases and ideas well worth remembering in this Psalm: "my King and my God," "sing for joy," "guests of God" (in other versions), "entering thy house," loving God's holy Name. Whosoever loves His Name, loves God. The ending is beautiful, as the divine protection with a shield reminds us of Christ the Good Shepherd. But there is more that recalls the Savior.

Jesus at His trial stood before false witnesses. No one was more aware than He of evil in man, more conscious than He of spiritual falseness. He used language very like our Psalm to stigmatize the Pharisees, and He called the devil a liar from the beginning (Jn. 8:44). Every sin is a kind of lie and boasting. Jesus went to a victim death for the defeat of all treachery, for the victory of goodness and truth. He sent His disciples as sheep among wolves. "Watch!" "Make thy way straight before me." Even among the apostles there was a betrayer, and St. Paul speaks of "false apostles" (2 Cor. 11:13).

We must learn from Christ how to pray this Psalm. He condemned sin and died to save the sinner. To learn this distinction is absolutely necessary for the Christian. Our stunted moral sense often makes us love the very things we should hate, evil in ourselves, attachments to sin and lying. Again, we may condemn sin in others and tolerate it in our own lives. Ultimately, we cannot see the guilt in others as we do in our own lives. Only He who died for us sinners can help us, lest we become impenitent and die in our sin.

The Church appropriately prays Psalm 5 for ultimate victory at dawn on I Tuesdays. Dawn is the hour of resurrection.

Psalm 6

O LORD, rebuke me not in thy anger,
    nor chasten me in thy wrath.
²Be gracious to me, O LORD, for I am languishing;
    O LORD, heal me, for my bones are troubled.
³My soul also is sorely troubled.
    But thou, O LORD—how long?

⁴Turn, O LORD, save my life;
    deliver me for the sake of thy steadfast love.
⁵For in death there is no remembrance of thee;
    in Sheol who can give thee praise?

⁶I am weary with my moaning;
    every night I flood my bed with tears;
    I drench my couch with my weeping.
⁷My eye wastes away because of grief,
    it grows weak because of all my foes.

⁸Depart from me, all you workers of evil;
    for the LORD has heard the sound of my weeping.
⁹The LORD has heard my supplication;
    the LORD accepts my prayer.

¹⁰All my enemies shall be ashamed and sorely troubled;
    they shall turn back, and be put to shame in a moment.

Grief in Sickness and Sin

Here we have the first of the seven penitential Psalms (6, 32, 38, 51, 102, 130, and 143). It contains the characteristic Old Testament view that God punished sin with sickness. The author is in deep physical and spiritual distress. Was sin the cause of his malady? Sometimes there existed a mysterious interweaving of the two, and also today there is an undeniable connection (as when reckless driving brings physical grief).

The Savior saw this and a deeper relation between suffering and sin. At times He cured persons by saying, "Go, sin no more." Or again, "Your sins are forgiven, arise!" It is in this vein that St. Paul writes, "The wages of sin is death," meaning the sin of Adam. "Therefore, just as through one man sin entered the world, and with sin death, death thus coming to all men inasmuch as all sinned . . ." (Rom. 5:12, also 1:18; 5:5-9; 6:12). Furthermore, sickness and death are pictures of sin, which is spiritual evil.

But Christ also disagreed with those who, like the "friends" of Job, see in every ailment and accident a punishment for personal sin (read Jn. 9:1-3; 11:4; Lk. 13:1-5). He advanced revelation by His word and example. The cure of death ultimately is His rising from the dead, His great victory over suffering and death (see Rom. 8:35-39). And that is the final proof for the forgiveness of sins. Jesus took upon Himself pain and death, but not the guilt of sin.

God is not angry like men are. That is a human way of speaking which pictures for us His justice. "Sheol" is the realm of death, the "nether world" of the Hebrews. There are many words for it in the Psalms: the dark pit, the grave, the abode of the dead, etc. There men led a shadowy existence, and little was known about it. Sacred writers dreaded it as a place where there was no praise of God. Also on this Christ enlightened us, as it is the limbo into which He descended first, after His death on the Cross, to bring redemption to the faithful ones of the Old Testament.

Let us cling to the certainties of faith and not follow the religion of fear by pointing the finger of guilt at those who suffer. Just as the Savior suffered and died for the salvation of sinners, and gave His Church the sacrament of healing, the Holy Anointing of the Sick, and left her the power of forgiveness of all sin, so we must be present to the sick and sinners in a special way. We must weep and do penance with the sinner, because of the seriousness of God's "anger" in the final judgment (see Mt. 25:41; 7:23; Lk. 13:27). As we pray for the sick, we pray for delivery from evil.

This Psalm of sorrow is also the beginning of praise. Before we can utter its words or shed tears of compunction, God will look to the heart and start the process of healing. Faith will cure the sick man in the Body of forgiveness which is the Church, for there Christ has set up the great Sign of His mercy (Jas. 5:14f; Mt. 16:19; Jn. 20:21-23). The Church uses this Psalm in her office of readings on I Mondays.

Psalm 7

O LORD my God, in thee do I take refuge;
    save me from all my pursuers, and deliver me,
2lest like a lion they rend me,
    dragging me away, with none to rescue.

3O LORD my God, if I have done this,
    if there is wrong in my hands,
4if I have requited my friend with evil
    or plundered my enemy without cause,
5let the enemy pursue me and overtake me,
    and let him trample my life to the ground,
    and lay my soul in the dust.

6Arise, O LORD, in thy anger,
    lift thyself up against the fury of my enemies;
    awake, O my God; thou hast appointed a judgment.
7Let the assembly of the peoples be gathered about thee;
    and over it take thy seat on high.
8The LORD judges the peoples;
    judge me, O LORD, according to my righteousness
    and according to the integrity that is in me.

9O let the evil of the wicked come to an end,
    but establish thou the righteous,
thou who triest the minds and hearts,
    thou righteous God.

10My shield is with God,
    who saves the upright in heart.
11God is a righteous judge,
    and a God who has indignation every day.

¹²If a man does not repent, God will whet his sword;
 he has bent and strung his bow;
¹³he has prepared his deadly weapons,
 making his arrows fiery shafts.
¹⁴Behold, the wicked man conceives evil,
 and is pregnant with mischief,
 and brings forth lies.
¹⁵He makes a pit, digging it out,
 and falls into the hole which he has made.
¹⁶His mischief returns upon his own head,
 and on his own pate his violence descends.
¹⁷I will give to the Lord the thanks due to his righteousness.
 and I will sing praise to the name of the Lord, the Most High.

God's Justice Prevails

An animated judgment scene occurs here, with an innocent man probably brought to court by unjust accusers and he appeals his case to the highest Judge, God on high enthroned over the assembly. As such, it is typical of other Psalms where the just man stands before human judges and yet resorts with desperate cries for justice to God who hears his prayer. Would that men and women would take their litigations to the divine court, as God alone can help and come to the rescue of the most desperate persons.

The world is full of oppressed people, who live and die without coming to their rights. The poor and helpless always go down to defeat and receive no justice in this world. This is a Psalm for all such, and the message is this: God will help the victims of injustice, if they trustfully appeal to Him. As the Psalmist raises his hopes to heaven, he is more sure of God's help than he is of the enemies' lies and mischief. It comforts him not only that he is aware of his own innocence but also that God will fight for him with the strongest weapons. Injustice will always boomerang. The wicked man falls into the trap he sets for others.

We must trust God to the end. If we go from this life undefended, He is the more concerned. Ultimate justice depends on Him and His judgment in the sight of all nations. Like the Psalmist, all of us stand before the great, just Judge who not only occupies the ultimate throne on high but also "tries the hearts and minds" of the lowly here below. Christ will call those blessed who suffer persecution and injustice for His Name's sake. Happy are we if we can protest innocence ("if there is [no] wrong in my hands" and appeal "to the integrity that is in me"). Happy are we if we can throw back the false accusations into the face of the real spiritual enemy. The final test will be if we "will sing praise to the name of the Lord, the most High."

But who of us is without sin? Who is not involved in some guilt? We deepen our spirituality if we turn to Christ who is without guilt, and pray our Psalm: "Who of you can accuse me of sin?" The most innocent of men, the holy One, stood patiently before a court of false accusers and waited for God's final justice (Mt. 26:52f. and 7:2). He promised the same treatment to His faithful ones (Jn. 15:19f. and 16:2f.). God intervened. He will intervene in our case (1 Cor. 15:22-26). If we pray this Psalm with Christ present (as the Church does every I Monday, at noon), it will bring us sanctification. (Additionally we can read 1 Pet. 4:17-19; 5:8-10; 2 Pet. 3:8-10.)

Psalm 8

O Lord, our Lord,
　　how majestic is thy name in all the earth!

Thou whose glory above the heavens is chanted
2　　by the mouth of babes and infants,
thou hast founded a bulwark because of thy foes,
　　to still the enemy and the avenger.

3When I look at thy heavens, the work of thy fingers,
　　the moon and the stars which thou hast established;
4what is man that thou art mindful of him,
　　and the son of man that thou dost care for him?

5Yet thou hast made him little less than God,
　　and dost crown him with glory and honor.
6Thou hast given him dominion over the works of thy hands;
　　thou hast put all things under his feet,
7all sheep and oxen,
　　and also the beasts of the field,
8the birds of the air, and the fish of the sea,
　　whatever passes along the paths of the sea.

9O Lord, our Lord,
　　how majestic is thy name in all the earth!

Praise God's Glorious Name

Psalm 8 is a favorite Psalm, often quoted. Promptly we come to the reason for praise: God's majesty in creation. Praise comes from all creatures, especially from man, the mouthpiece of the visible order. From the stars of heaven to the infants in the cradle, God receives homage. Each creature in its place raises its voice Godward, and the author lists only a few of each class. From man God craves a unique kind of worship: the conscious, freely willed adoration of which he alone is capable.

By God's creative act man is set above all things with a God-given dominion (Gen. 1:28). Man and woman in paradise represented all creation, themselves being the paragon of God's creative hand, in the visible universe. "Thou hast made [them] a little less than the angels" ("God" by some interpreters). Although mankind occupies only a tiny speck among the galaxies, they enjoy a further sign of divine favor, a "crowning with glory and honor." God crowns the "image and likeness" in man with a shared dignity of grace and divine life, and adoptive sonship, supernatural life of Christ.

This is a victory of God in the hierarchy of created beings and lends new meanings to the phrase "enemies of God" who are silenced. The Psalms are ever conscious of these enemies and the loss of glory on their part. Making men "partaker of the divine nature" (2 Pet. 1:4) in his spiritual rebirth (Baptism) foils the enemy in unsuspected ways. What is man to deserve such a destiny? What is man to destroy it (in himself, in the unborn who are called to glory)?

The praise of infants and children received special attention from the Lord, who quoted our Psalm at His glorious entry to Jerusalem (Mt. 21:15f.). "And Jesus said to them: 'Yes, have you never read: Out of the mouths of babes and sucklings thou hast brought perfect praise?' " In a different context: "Unless you turn and become like children, you will never enter the Kingdom of heaven" (Mt. 18:3). Their sung praise has power to confound God's enemies. Would that we trained children in this godly action.

The full thrust of this Psalm comes from our praying it with Christ, the Son of God, who went through the stages of infancy and childhood in His incarnation. The New Testament reveals our true greatness. "See what love the Father has given us, that we should be called children of God, and so we are" (1 Jn. 3:1). Heaven will be a sharing of Christ's glory. He, "the first-born of all creation, for in him all things were created" (Col. 1:15), received dominion over all things (Eph. 1:22), and shares His glory with His followers (Jn. 17:22). By His Cross He earned the crown of glory (Phil. 2:5-11 and Heb. 2:5-9). Those sharing with Christ will not only judge the world, but angels too (1 Cor. 6:2f.; see also 1 Cor. 15:27).

Surely an appropriate Psalm for many occasions: September 14 (office of readings), September 29 (vespers), November 1 (office of readings), Monday of Easter (noon), Ascension (noon), Trinity (office of readings), II and IV Saturdays (lauds).

Psalms 9 and 10

I will give thanks to the LORD with my whole heart;
I will tell of all thy wonderful deeds.
²I will be glad and exult in thee,
I will sing praise to thy name, O Most High.

³When my enemies turned back,
they stumbled and perished before thee.
⁴For thou hast maintained my just cause;
thou hast sat on the throne giving righteous judgment.

⁵Thou hast rebuked the nations, thou hast destroyed the wicked;
thou hast blotted out their name for ever and ever.
⁶The enemy have vanished in everlasting ruins;
their cities thou hast rooted out;
the very memory of them has perished.

⁷But the LORD sits enthroned for ever,
he has established his throne for judgment;
⁸and he judges the world with righteousness,
he judges the peoples with equity.

⁹The LORD is a stronghold for the oppressed,
a stronghold in times of trouble.
¹⁰And those who know thy name put their trust in thee,
for thou, O LORD, hast not forsaken those who seek thee.

¹¹Sing praises to the LORD, who dwells in Zion!
Tell among the peoples his deeds!
¹²For he who avenges blood is mindful of them;
he does not forget the cry of the afflicted.

¹³Be gracious to me, O Lord!
　　Behold what I suffer from those who hate me,
　　O thou who liftest me up from the gates of death,
¹⁴that I may recount all thy praises,
　　that in the gates of the daughter of Zion
　　I may rejoice in thy deliverance.

¹⁵The nations have sunk in the pit which they made;
　　in the net which they hid has their own foot been caught.
¹⁶The Lord has made himself known, he has executed judgment;
　　the wicked are snared in the work of their own hands.

¹⁷The wicked shall depart to Sheol,
　　all the nations that forget God.

¹⁸For the needy shall not always be forgotten,
　　and the hope of the poor shall not perish for ever.

¹⁹Arise, O Lord! Let not man prevail;
　　let the nations be judged before thee!
²⁰Put them in fear, O Lord!
　　Let the nations know that they are but men!

＊　＊　＊

Why dost thou stand afar off, O Lord?
　　Why dost thou hide thyself in times of trouble?
²In arrogance the wicked hotly pursue the poor;
　　let them be caught in the schemes which they have devised.

³For the wicked boasts of the desires of his heart,
　　and the man greedy for gain curses and renounces the Lord.
⁴In the pride of his countenance the wicked does not seek him;
　　all his thoughts are, "There is no God."

⁵His ways prosper at all times;
　　thy judgments are on high, out of his sight;
　　as for all his foes, he puffs at them.
⁶He thinks in his heart, "I shall not be moved;
　　throughout all generations I shall not meet adversity."

⁷His mouth is filled with cursing and deceit and oppression;
    under his tongue are mischief and iniquity.
⁸He sits in ambush in the villages;
    in hiding places he murders the innocent.

His eyes stealthily watch for the hapless,
⁹   he lurks in secret like a lion in his covert;
he lurks that he may seize the poor,
    he seizes the poor when he draws him into his net.

¹⁰The hapless is crushed, sinks down,
    and falls by his might.
¹¹He thinks in his heart, "God has forgotten,
    he has hidden his face, he will never see it."

¹²Arise, O Lord; O God, lift up thy hand;
    forget not the afflicted.
¹³Why does the wicked renounce God,
    and say in his heart, "Thou wilt not call to account"?

¹⁴Thou dost see; yea, thou dost note trouble and vexation,
    that thou mayst take it into thy hands;
the hapless commits himself to thee;
    thou hast been the helper of the fatherless.

¹⁵Break thou the arm of the wicked and evildoer;
    seek out his wickedness till thou find none.
¹⁶The Lord is king for ever and ever;
    the nations shall perish from his land.

¹⁷O Lord, thou wilt hear the desire of the meek;
    thou wilt strengthen their heart, thou wilt incline thy ear
¹⁸to do justice to the fatherless and the oppressed,
    so that man who is of the earth may strike terror no more.

Thanks and Petition

Because of their underlying unity of structure and thought, these Psalms clearly belong together as one (despite some text problems of scholars on this "acrostic," which means that a new letter of the alphabet heads nearly every second verse). Interwoven with direct prayers that God may save the poor man from the wicked, it contains:

1. Thanks to God for victory over national enemies, and His enthronement;
2. Personal cries for help for the poor man, whose faith is in the God of Zion (daughter), whose suffering comes from God's enemy, the sinner;
3. A lengthy description of the godless man, his intrigues and defiance of God;
4. Confidence in God on the part of the helpless and humble ones.

As we enter prayerfully into this Psalm, we meet God as judge and protector. The framework is far-reaching, from His universal judgment to His most personal concern for the individual. He always vindicates those who trust in Him and wait. Yet there is the repeated cry: "Arise, O God!" and "Why wait so long?" because man is feeble with impatience and thinks he can wait no longer. God seems to be silent, and man begins to grasp His greatness when he realizes his own nothingness.

All who seek the Lord, in both Testaments, belong to the "anawim," the poor. The apparent success of the prosperous wicked makes it hard to understand divine Providence. In this situation, too, firm confidence best serves the glory of God by whose mighty justice all enemies will be shattered. To understand all the Psalms, we need to see the solidarity of nation and individual, and of both with God.

The final great day of victory and judgment is called the "Day of Yahweh" in sacred Scripture. It is the Day of Christ, when there will be total justice in His final judgment (see Mt. 25:30-46; also Rev. 20:12). The poor who died without being vindicated, and the wicked who acted as if there were no God, will each reap reward and punishment, divine justice.

Suffering with Christ is training for heaven, a law of His Kingdom. The people of God live in faith and hope, depending on Him who is their King and who fulfills the role of God, Father of the poor. His love for those who wait patiently is like fire that tries the quality of silver and gold. Knowing this they live in peace as they pray for the coming of the Kingdom. While those who cannot wait act like practical atheists, and their number is legion, Jesus teaches His own the Providence of the Father by waiting. "I knew that thou hearest me always" (Jn. 11:41; see also 2 Cor. 1:8-10 and 2 Tim. 4:16-18).

The most telling attitude of the first Christians, who waited for Christ, is in their earliest prayer: "Come, Lord Jesus!" To wait with

Him "one hour" is the striking response of His faithful ones, who pray this Psalm with Him on I Mondays and Tuesdays (office of readings).

Psalm 11 (10)

In the LORD I take refuge;
how can you say to me,
"Flee like a bird to the mountains;
²for lo, the wicked bend the bow,

they have fitted their arrow to the string,
to shoot in the dark at the upright in heart;
³if the foundations are destroyed,
what can the righteous do"?

⁴The LORD is in his holy temple,
the LORD's throne is in heaven;
his eyes behold, his eyelids test, the children of men.
⁵The LORD tests the righteous and the wicked,
and his soul hates him that loves violence.
⁶On the wicked he will rain coals of fire and brimstone;
a scorching wind shall be the portion of their cup.
⁷For the LORD is righteous, he loves righteous deeds;
the upright shall behold his face.

Hearts Strong in Faith

With this Psalm we pray our confidence in God. It does not expand on the trials of the Psalmist, except that men were telling him to flee, to take refuge in the mountains. That was human wisdom in the face of dangers surrounding him. Superior forces of danger were threatening, most of all spiritual powers against which he was helpless. Instead of flight, he chose to fight with the help of God who dwelt both in His holy Temple and in heaven above. When evil prevails, when the pillars of right and wrong fall, when strong men cower, then the just man has no protection. Then the gifts of counsel and fortitude come into play.

If we, in the face of superior evil, lose trust in God, we become practical atheists. God is always present, "beholding the children of men." The Lord of heaven rests on Zion, His earthly abode. That is our place of refuge. There He shows His face and favor to all who are upright and trusting. "He who puts his faith in it [the stone of Zion] shall not be shaken" (Is. 28:16). The cult of God brings victory, pictured by figures like "coals of fire and brimstone," as in the days of Sodom and Gomorrah (Gen. 19), to describe the action of God and the destruction of the wicked.

The Savior warned us against the dangers to salvation. He overcame the evil one, sin and death. Abandoned by all, He did not take the advice to seek safety in flight, but He trusted in the Father while clinging to good. He referred to this as "drinking the cup," or the lot that would come to His followers. "Can you drink the cup . . . ?" He is present to us always, as we in turn, faithful members of His, drink the cup with Him.

As we pray this Psalm, we are walking in the light. The more we depend on the Lord as our mainstay, the more will human props fall aside. He who dwells in the heavens, lives in our midst, abides in our hearts as His home (Jn. 14:23). In living communion with Him, we grow in supernatural fortitude and hope, as we listen to His voice rather than to the false counsellors of human cowardice. "The upright shall behold his face," for the vision of God belongs to the pure of heart.

Fittingly, the Church uses this Psalm for the feasts of one martyr, as on I Mondays (vespers) and I Tuesdays (office of readings).

Psalm 12 (11)

Help, Lord; for there is no longer any that is godly;
for the faithful have vanished from among the sons of men.
²Every one utters lies to his neighbor;
with flattering lips and a double heart they speak.

³May the Lord cut off all flattering lips,
the tongue that makes great boasts,
⁴those who say, "With our tongue we will prevail,
our lips are with us; who is our master?"

⁵"Because the poor are despoiled, because the needy groan,
I will now arise," says the Lord;
"I will place him in the safety for which he longs."
⁶The promises of the Lord are promises that are pure,

silver refined in a furnace on the ground,
purified seven times.

[7]Do thou, O LORD, protect us,
guard us ever from this generation.
[8]On every side the wicked prowl,
as vileness is exalted among the sons of men.

Prayer for Truthfulness

From the consideration of human faithlessness, this Psalm rises
to divine fidelity. No age holds a monopoly on lying and deception,
but when the Psalmist wrote, lying was prevalent and "vileness exalted." Men were boasting of it, men who determined the public mores.
As usual, the poor and afflicted were the victims. They were helpless,
except in turning to God for redress. "Now I will arise," He promised,
which means that He would restore order and safety to society. God's
pure promises are set in shining contrast to the black hearts of evil men

Lying is a form of injustice. It is basic immorality. The same in
every age of mankind; it distorts the order of God's creation. Whatever its form, boasting, pretense, or the double heart, our Psalm is a
stern rebuke to those who love it. God will not tolerate any sort of it.
Many Psalms denounce this widespread evil. Today it means sinning
against truth as much as in former times. One effect is that it robs the
poor. Another, that it destroys community, for truthfulness is the basis
of trust.

To be on God's side, one must renounce lying. Christ Jesus lived
within a system that was corrupt with lying. He uttered strong denun-
ciations of the deceitful Pharisees and Scribes, all instruments of the
prince of lying, the devil (Jn. 8:44). Yet He, the Prince of justice and
truth, went down to apparent defeat at their hands and deceitful lips.
Only then did God's promise become ultimately true: "I will now arise!"
"Whatever promises God has made have been fulfilled in him" (2 Cor.
1:19f.), because "in him it is always Yes." "The promises of the Lord
are pure, silver . . . purified seven times."

Every man and woman who bears the name of Christian, stands
as a witness to truth in all its forms. He or she must not only pray for
the triumph of truth, but purify his or her life, so that the light of truth
may shine out. As we discover lying in our makeup or actions, we must
push back evil in our own life, if we are to be disciples of the Lord. On

the other hand, the Lord pronounced those blessed who suffer as victims of injustice for His sake. The demon of lying is still abroad. He causes no less devastation than in days past.

Let us not only imitate Christ to the best of our sincerity, but because of our incorporation into His body, let us depend on His victory and help. This Psalm can be our quick "Be gone, Satan!" as we are guided by the Holy Spirit of Christ and His instincts of faith. With Christ abiding in us and we in Him, we can "rightly handle the word of truth" (2 Tim. 2:15; see also 2 Thess. 8-12). This power of salvation will come to us from Christ, as we pray the Psalm with the Church on I Tuesdays (noon, lauds, and office of readings).

Psalm 13 (12)

How long, O LORD? Wilt thou forget me for ever?
How long wilt thou hide thy face from me?
²How long must I bear pain in my soul,
and have sorrow in my heart all the day?
How long shall my enemy be exalted over me?

³Consider and answer me, O LORD my God;
lighten my eyes, lest I sleep the sleep of death;
⁴lest my enemy say, "I have prevailed over him";
lest my foes rejoice because I am shaken.

⁵But I have trusted in thy steadfast love;
my heart shall rejoice in thy salvation.
⁶I will sing to the LORD,
because he has dealt bountifully with me.

How Long, O Lord?

Patience is no passive virtue. The fruit of long, positive, and active spiritual effort in the midst of insuperable difficulties, patience is part of fortitude. To sustain hope out of faith, when God does not make His presence felt and when the enemy seems about to win, is the gift of God's grace in human weakness. Clinging to God under the most trying conditions is possible only because God is really near. We cannot directly perceive the working of the Holy Spirit in us. But as we complain to the Lord, hope surfaces and we end by singing our trust in Him.

The author is on the verge of death, with what affliction of body or soul we do not know, as he utters the question, "How long, O Lord?" Recovery appears as necessary for salvation, a condition for silencing the enemy. Death may be that enemy, and God grants his plea. This is the Old Testament stage of faith. God grants visible, tangible, and temporal favors in order to engender faith in His invisible, spiritual, and future rewards. God's people took these first steps as His children to prepare for the coming maturity.

We speak of naked faith as when darkness and death take over, and yet we trust and believe in God's presence. This is the stage of revelation in Christ and the Church, the era in which we live. God often grants what we ask for, but He can also withhold it in favor of something more beneficial to us. Then we speak of darkness and the absence of God. But it is our maturity in Christ even then to wait for the Lord. If our trust is divine, if our hope is God-made, then nothing will shake us, even when things go to pieces. Even then God is the center of our existence, and Christ is present.

The motive of our prayer, then, as we pray this Psalm (and others), is the glory of His Name. That transcends our experience of the moment, and despair has no hold on us. This New Testament maturity comes from the pain and death of Jesus, who waited for the resurrection. For a short time the enemy boasted, "I have prevailed over him," when all light vanished from Him. He used a Psalm prayer on the Cross, "My God, my God, why hast thou forsaken me?" (Ps. 22:1). The risen, glorified Savior answers our complaint, "How long, O Lord?" with His revelation to His disciples, "A little while" (Jn. 16:16-20).

In the light of this faith we become adult members of Christ, ending as the Psalm does, "singing to the Lord, because he has dealt bountifully with me." In the Church's living prayer we sing this Psalm on I Tuesdays (noon).

Psalm 14 (13)

> The fool says in his heart,
>   "There is no God."
> They are corrupt, they do abominable deeds,
>   there is none that does good.

²The LORD looks down from heaven upon the children of men,
    to see if there are any that act wisely,
    that seek after God.

³They have all gone astray, they are all alike corrupt;
    there is none that does good,
    no, not one.

⁴Have they no knowledge, all the evildoers
    who eat up my people as they eat bread,
    and do not call upon the LORD?

⁵There they shall be in great terror,
    for God is with the generation of the righteous.
⁶You would confound the plans of the poor,
    but the LORD is his refuge.

⁷O that deliverance for Israel would come out of Zion!
    When the LORD restores the fortunes of his people,
    Jacob shall rejoice, Israel shall be glad.

Folly and Wisdom

A real fool is not one who excites laughter, as a circus clown who makes himself odd and grotesque, but one who acts strangely and is ridiculous in the sight of God. He is the opposite of a wise man, who directs his actions according to God's will. A fool thinks poorly and abuses his God-given nature and faculties in a stupid, irresponsible way. All sinners are fools. As long as there is sin in the world, there will be such. Our author, who is inspired, does not have modern atheism in mind, but the practical atheist, the fool who acts as if there were no God watching over him. All kinds of atheism are most impractical. They do not work. Yet the world is full of fools.

Instead of cultivating ways of prayer, men devise new perversions, new follies. The folly which the author means is exploiting the poor, "eating up my people." The prophets of old held out God's punishment for those who "ate the people" by multiplying evil deeds (e.g. Is. 5 and Jer. 5). When people lose wisdom, they increase their folly. Our Psalm was written when godless perversity was so widespread, that no one was left to take pity on the poor. Folly had become official, in high places. Only God heard their cries. In His Providence He blesses those who call on Him, just as He makes the fools come to grief. Especially in the assembly on Zion does He hear and restore the fortunes of Israel.

The New Testament continues the theme of this Psalm. Rom. 1: 18-32 gives expression to it and quotes our Psalm directly in 3:10-12. Salvation did come out of Zion, and the restoration of prosperity began with the new order of Christ and the folly of the Cross. The Holy Spirit of Christ is the Spirit of wisdom and of the gifts that renewed the face of the earth. Every generation and age finds this to be true.

While modern atheism is both "practical" and doctrinal, destroying as it does the very belief in God, its effects on individuals and society are all the worse: loss of the moral sense, shameless freedom in sinning, ever new records in folly. Sometimes, with the Psalmist, one might think there is no one left to do good, when Christians indulge in cursing the holy Names of God and Jesus Christ. In our midst are also passive fools, like atheists, who are silent and permissive of evil around them, so they enjoy a false sort of security.

One of the Lord's questions was: "When the Son of man comes, will he find faith on earth?" (Lk. 18:8). Those who pray this Psalm with the Church (on I Tuesdays, at vespers), and carry it out in their lives, are the men and women of faith and wisdom.

Psalm 15 (14)

O LORD, who shall sojourn in thy tent?
Who shall dwell on thy holy hill?

[2]He who walks blamelessly, and does what is right,
and speaks truth from his heart;
[3]who does not slander with his tongue,
and does no evil to his friend,
nor takes up a reproach against his neighbor;
[4]in whose eyes a reprobate is despised,
but who honors those who fear the LORD;
who swears to his own hurt and does not change;

[5]who does not put out his money at interest,
and does not take a bribe against the innocent.

He who does these things shall never be moved.

Integrity Before Worship

This Psalm prayer, similar to Psalm 24:5-6, gives us an important moral lesson that is wisdom for our relationship to God. "Who will dwell on thy holy hill?" means worship in God's Temple. Ascending the mountain of the Lord stands for seeing the face of God in holy ritual, eating as His guests, living with Him in His "tent." The Psalmist gives God's answer in a few verses that spell out integrity of morals, most of all justice to one's neighbor. Thinking the truth in one's heart, speaking it, and truthfulness in action to others are some of the conditions.

We cannot love evil and love God at the same time. God exercises hospitality by inviting us as His guests, but it is made dependent on our justice and charity. In the Savior's terms it means wearing the wedding garment before banqueting in His Kingdom. Fearing the Lord today is called love of His holy will. "Blessed are the pure of heart, for they shall see God." Even in this life they live before the face of God. The reprobates are those who accept bribes against the innocent, which begins with evil in the heart. The Psalm ends, like so many others, with a blessing, a "taking home" of the gift of God, the generous Host, a lasting memento of communion with Him.

To fulfill this Psalm in a literal way, the Christian crusaders built an archway of Confession on the steep ascent to Mount Sinai, a holy mountain, where Moses saw the face of God. There they stationed a father confessor to absolve pilgrims on their way up. Moral holiness then and now is still the prerequisite, along with faith, for those who aspire to be God's guests on the holy mount of His sacrificial banquet, the Eucharist. Ritual purity alone is not enough. In the Old Testament ascent to union with God, in the New Testament sacramental fulfillment, and in the final heavenly communion, God's norm is "Be perfect, as your heavenly Father is perfect."

Is. 1:11-16 asks for virtue before sacrifice. Jer. 7:21-23 calls for obedience rather than sacrifice. Jesus wants us to be reconciled with our brother before offering our liturgical gift (Mt. 5:23f.). He purged the Temple of traffickers (Jn. 2:13-18). The new Temple, the Body of Christ, must also be holy (1 Cor. 3:16f.). Moral sanctity comes from the heart. "Therefore, putting away falsehood, let every one speak the truth with his neighbor, for we are members one of another" (Eph. 4:25). Integrity of speech, as coming from the heart, is part and parcel of this law of the Kingdom (Jas. 3:2-10).

On November 1 the Church prays this Psalm (office of readings), also at I Monday vespers, and vespers for holy pastors and other men.

Psalm 16 (15)

Preserve me, O God, for in thee I take refuge.
²I say to the LORD, "Thou art my Lord;
I have no good apart from thee."

³As for the saints in the land, they are the noble,
in whom is all my delight.

⁴Those who choose another god multiply their sorrows;
their libations of blood I will not pour out
or take their names upon my lips.

⁵The LORD is my chosen portion and my cup;
thou holdest my lot.
⁶The lines have fallen for me in pleasant places;
yea, I have a goodly heritage.

⁷I bless the LORD who gives me counsel;
in the night also my heart instructs me.
⁸I keep the LORD always before me;
because he is at my right hand, I shall not be moved.

⁹Therefore my heart is glad, and my soul rejoices;
my body also dwells secure.
¹⁰For thou dost not give me up to Sheol,
or let thy godly one see the Pit.

¹¹Thou dost show me the path of life;
in thy presence there is fulness of joy,
in thy right hand are pleasures for evermore.

Happiness in God

This is a beautiful and important Psalm for Christian piety because of the author's total dedication to God, intimate joy in Him, its messianic character (prophetic of Christ's resurrection), and vision of eternal life. That a faithful Jew, perhaps also a convert to Judaism, should call on God for help, renounce false cults and even the names of so-called gods, is not surprising, for God is the source of all delights for Jew and Gentile. Without Him all life becomes empty and meaning-less. Total dependence on the Lord shines through the entire Psalm-poem.

In times past the Church used it for chosen ministers, but it applies to all the baptized who by spiritual rebirth belong in a special way to the Lord. All who are in Christ have found the pearl without price. All have the call to holiness. Every Christian can say, "The Lord is my chosen portion and my cup. I am one set apart for God. In Him my lot is most favorable. Communion with God is my future. Now already my life is filled with blessings and joy." Our lot is to be saints, as God claims us as His intimate friends. We might well call this the Psalm of Christian vocation and of various calls within that destiny. God's measuring lines are immeasurable in His infinite expanse of goodness.

With this Psalm joy in God seizes our heart and soul. Even the body is preoccupied with Him day and night. "In the night" suggests a contemplative love of the Lord God, a constant vigil with Him. After this short life of seeking Him, communion forever replaces the short-lived joys and sorrows. The imperfect runways lead to endless blessed-ness.

Surely the Psalm incites us to make constant efforts at continuous prayer. If union with God is eternal, then all our present striving is mere practice and rehearsal. Every baptized Christian must learn to sing, "I have a goodly heritage," and "God, [my] God, has anointed [me] with the oil of gladness beyond [my] comrades" (Heb. 1:9). In many ways has this Psalm gone into fulfillment in the members of Christ's Body (see Lk. 24:44f.). Jesus, who is ever intimately united to the Father (Jn. 16:32), shares this intimacy with those who will never die (Jn. 11:26 and 1 Cor. 15:20-23).

St. Peter refers our Psalm directly to Christ risen (Acts 2:25-32), and St. Paul clearly does the same (Acts 13:34-37). Therefore we must hear the voice of the risen Savior when the Church prays it on Holy Saturday (office of readings), on the Tuesday after Easter (noon), then November 1 (office of readings), II Sundays (vespers), and at Thursday compline. Our present stirrings of joy are the pledge of "pleasures at thy right hand for evermore."

Psalm 17 (16)

Hear a just cause, O Lord; attend to my cry!
Give ear to my prayer from lips free of deceit!
²From thee let my vindication come!
Let thy eyes see the right!

³If thou triest my heart, if thou visitest me by night,
if thou testest me, thou wilt find no wickedness in me;
my mouth does not transgress.
⁴With regard to the works of men, by the word of thy lips
I have avoided the ways of the violent.
⁵My steps have held fast to thy paths,
my feet have not slipped.

⁶I call upon thee, for thou wilt answer me, O God;
incline thy ear to me, hear my words.
⁷Wondrously show thy steadfast love,
O savior of those who seek refuge
from their adversaries at thy right hand.

⁸Keep me as the apple of the eye;
hide me in the shadow of thy wings,
⁹from the wicked who despoil me,
my deadly enemies who surround me.

¹⁰They close their hearts to pity;
with their mouths they speak arrogantly.
¹¹They track me down; now they surround me;
they set their eyes to cast me to the ground.
¹²They are like a lion eager to tear,
as a young lion lurking in ambush.

¹³Arise, O Lord! confront them, overthrow them!
Deliver my life from the wicked by thy sword,
¹⁴from men by thy hand, O Lord,
from men whose portion in life is of the world.
May their belly be filled with what thou hast stored up for them;
may their children have more than enough;
may they leave something over to their babes.

¹⁵As for me, I shall behold thy face in righteousness;
when I awake, I shall be satisfied with beholding thy form.

Psalm of Innocence

Here we have the typical example of a faithful Jew, falsely accused of crime (perhaps idolatry), at court "with his back to the wall" fighting for his life. It looks like a legal case, which had gone from the city gates to the highest court of appeal, the presence of God enthroned in His heavenly sanctuary and earthly Temple, where He is the final Judge. The poor man calls on Him for justice, lest he become the victim of pitiless adversaries. The prayer for help is sincere. He repeats it with desperate urgency. God, who sees the heart, will destroy lying lips. The author does not claim absolute sinlessness or complete innocence, but only freedom from the accusations of his enemies. He has been faithful to the Lord's commands. Even at night, alone with God, his heart is right.

The Lord hears his appeal for vindication. Phrases like "Keep me as the apple of the eye; hide me in the shadow of thy wings" are beautiful prayers of trust that bring peace (see also Psalm 91). On the other hand we have the men of violence and deceit, like cruel animals ready to pounce on their prey, even to kill the innocent one. They are complacent and well fed, prosperous and arrogant, greedy and secure. The author wishes them more than their fill of riches, but for himself he wants to behold God's face. God's honor is at stake, as the poor accused one cries, "Arise, O Lord!" Evil must not prevail. The enemy will never see God's face.

Our Psalm closes with a strikingly wonderful expression of faith in the afterlife, seeing God's face upon awakening from death. It is what we call the beatific vision. The reference to great joy in beholding God "as He is" bespeaks an ancient belief in Israel. That the Psalmist closes his poetic prayer-song in this way, after feelings ran high, is all the more significant. Coming from a troubled spirit, it proves that his union with God was genuine.

How shall we pray this Psalm? As Christ prayed it, with the conviction that the earthly enmity described is but a picture of the invisible, spiritual ongoing warfare. So the Church prays it (on I Wednesdays, vespers, and on the common of one martyr in the office of readings). We do well also to pray it when we do not come to our rights and for others, all the falsely accused, because the Savior prayed it when falsely accused. "For our sake he made him [Christ] to be sin, who knew no sin, so that in him we might become the righteousness of God" (2 Cor. 5:21).

Psalm 18 (17)

I love thee, O LORD, my strength.
²The LORD is my rock, and my fortress, and my deliverer,
  my God, my rock, in whom I take refuge,
  my shield, and the horn of my salvation, my stronghold.
³I call upon the LORD, who is worthy to be praised,
  and I am saved from my enemies.

⁴The cords of death encompassed me,
  the torrents of perdition assailed me;
⁵the cords of Sheol entangled me,
  the snares of death confronted me.

⁶In my distress I called upon the LORD;
  to my God I cried for help.
From his temple he heard my voice,
  and my cry to him reached his ears.

⁷Then the earth reeled and rocked;
  the foundations also of the mountains trembled
  and quaked, because he was angry.
⁸Smoke went up from his nostrils,
  and devouring fire from his mouth;
  glowing coals flamed forth from him.
⁹He bowed the heavens, and came down;
  thick darkness was under his feet.
¹⁰He rode on a cherub, and flew;
  he came swiftly upon the wings of the wind.
¹¹He made darkness his covering around him,
  his canopy thick clouds dark with water.
¹²Out of the brightness before him
  there broke through his clouds
  hailstones and coals of fire.
¹³The LORD also thundered in the heavens,
  and the Most High uttered his voice,
  hailstones and coals of fire.
¹⁴And he sent out his arrows, and scattered them;
  he flashed forth lightnings, and routed them.
¹⁵Then the channels of the sea were seen,
  and the foundations of the world were laid bare,
at thy rebuke, O LORD,
  at the blast of the breath of thy nostrils.

¹⁶He reached from on high, he took me,
he drew me out of many waters.
¹⁷He delivered me from my strong enemy,
and from those who hated me;
for they were too mighty for me.
¹⁸They came upon me in the day of my calamity;
but the Lord was my stay.
¹⁹He brought me forth into a broad place;
he delivered me, because he delighted in me.

²⁰The Lord rewarded me according to my righteousness;
according to the cleanness of my hands he recompensed me.
²¹For I have kept the ways of the Lord,
and have not wickedly departed from my God.
²²For all his ordinances were before me,
and his statutes I did not put away from me.
²³I was blameless before him,
and I kept myself from guilt.
²⁴Therefore the Lord has recompensed me according to my
righteousness,
according to the cleanness of my hands in his sight.

²⁵With the loyal thou dost show thyself loyal;
with the blameless man thou dost show thyself blameless;
²⁶with the pure thou dost show thyself pure;
and with the crooked thou dost show thyself perverse.
²⁷For thou dost deliver a humble people;
but the haughty eyes thou dost bring down.
²⁸Yea, thou dost light my lamp;
the Lord my God lightens my darkness.
²⁹Yea, by thee I can crush a troop;
and by my God I can leap over a wall.
³⁰This God—his way is perfect;
the promise of the Lord proves true;
he is a shield for all those who take refuge in him.

[31]For who is God, but the Lord?
   And who is a rock, except our God?—
[32]the God who girded me with strength,
   and made my way safe.
[33]He made my feet like hinds' feet,
   and set me secure on the heights.
[34]He trains my hands for war,
   so that my arms can bend a bow of bronze.
[35]Thou hast given me the shield of thy salvation,
   and thy right hand supported me,
   and thy help made me great.
[36]Thou didst give a wide place for my steps under me,
   and my feet did not slip.
[37]I pursued my enemies and overtook them;
   and did not turn back till they were consumed.
[38]I thrust them through, so that they were not able to rise;
   they fell under my feet.
[39]For thou didst gird me with strength for the battle;
   thou didst make my assailants sink under me.
[40]Thou didst make my enemies turn their backs to me,
   and those who hated me I destroyed.
[41]They cried for help, but there was none to save,
   they cried to the Lord, but he did not answer them.
[42]I beat them fine as dust before the wind;
   I cast them out like the mire of the streets.

[43]Thou didst deliver me from strife with the peoples;
   thou didst make me the head of the nations;
   people whom I had not known served me.
[44]As soon as they heard of me they obeyed me;
   foreigners came cringing to me.
[45]Foreigners lost heart,
   and came trembling out of their fastnesses.

[46]The Lord lives; and blessed be my rock,
   and exalted be the God of my salvation,
[47]the God who gave me vengeance
   and subdued peoples under me;
[48]who delivered me from my enemies;
   yea, thou didst exalt me above my adversaries;
   thou didst deliver me from men of violence.

⁴⁹For this I will extol thee, O Lᴏʀᴅ, among the nations,
    and sing praises to thy name.
⁵⁰Great triumphs he gives to his king,
    and shows steadfast love to his anointed,
    to David and his descendants for ever.

Lifelong Training for God

King David reviews his long struggle for faith and trust in the
Lord. It is the record of God's primacy and assistance. Two parts clearly
make up the Psalm (v. 30 is the dividing point). The author begins
by depicting God's titles in praise (the "horn" of salvation signifies
strength). The dangers and cries of distress contrast with God's majesty.
Great poetic imagery unfolds itself (vv. 7-19), and David learns to know
his own weakness and God's power. The lessons of divine love and
fidelity came to him the hard way, through tribulation and humiliation.

We find almost word for word the entire story in 2 Sam. 22:2-51.
In the latter part we have the resulting action of David in God's Name.
David fought harder than all, but he gave credit to the God on high
and in His holy Temple. The whole account reminds us of Paul's saying,
"By God's grace I am what I am" (1 Cor. 15:10). David's lifelong fidelity
and innocence is known, except for the crime of which he repents in
Psalm 51. He does not tire of repeating the praise due to God's action,
more tranquilly in the last part of the Psalm.

Significant is the statement, "Therefore I will extol thee, O Lord,
among the nations, and sing praises to thy name." That is also the message of Christ, the last of David's royal line, who brought the Old Testament order to perfection and fulfillment. "This is the victory that overcomes the world, our faith" (1 Jn. 5:4). Begotten of God in Baptism,
we too must learn the ways of battle in faith. The old order existed for
the sake of the new. First comes the literal order (of warfare, enmity,
danger, punishment, retribution), then the spiritual. Suffering and
death lead to ultimate victory (see Eph. 6:10-17), the new order of
Christ, all under God's dominion and personal help.

This describes the history of faith and its development. Through
the visible human order, we come to learn the divine. The process
repeats itself in Christ and in the way He worked and taught. He gave
the new law, "Love your enemy and do good . . ." (Lk. 6:35-38). He
told Peter, "Put back your sword into its place" (Mt. 26:52). The law
of revenge (*lex talionis*) gave way to the law of love and mercy.

The innocence of Christ, His obedience and suffering, we find literally foretold in the person of David. His great victory, the greatest of all, is His resurrection (see 1 Cor. 15:54), which we proclaim to all nations when we pray the Psalm with the Church on I Wednesdays and Thursdays (office of readings). The whole Psalm, in its original and fulfilled senses, finds its summary in the Lord's prayer, "Hallowed be Thy Name."

Psalm 19 (18)

The heavens are telling the glory of God;
and the firmament proclaims his handiwork.
[2]Day to day pours forth speech,
and night to night declares knowledge.
[3]There is no speech, nor are there words;
their voice is not heard;
[4]yet their voice goes out through all the earth,
and their words to the end of the world.

In them he has set a tent for the sun,
[5]which comes forth like a bridegroom leaving his chamber,
and like a strong man runs its course with joy.

[6]Its rising is from the end of the heavens,
and its circuit to the end of them;
and there is nothing hid from its heat.

7The law of the Lord is perfect,
  reviving the soul;
the testimony of the Lord is sure,
  making wise the simple;
8the precepts of the Lord are right,
  rejoicing the heart;
the commandment of the Lord is pure,
  enlightening the eyes;
9the fear of the Lord is clean,
  enduring for ever;
the ordinances of the Lord are true,
  and righteous altogether.
10More to be desired are they than gold,
  even much fine gold;
sweeter also than honey
  and drippings of the honeycomb.

11Moreover by them is thy servant warned;
  in keeping them there is great reward.
12But who can discern his errors?
  Clear thou me from hidden faults.
13Keep back thy servant also from presumptuous sins;
  let them not have dominion over me!
Then I shall be blameless,
  and innocent of great transgression.

14Let the words of my mouth and the meditation of my heart
  be acceptable in thy sight,
  O Lord, my rock and my redeemer.

The Sun and the Law

The sun is up. The day is here. The new light speaks of God's revelation. The perfections of God are proclaimed in eloquent silence by His created world. Without word or voice creations tells of His glory. Scientists who "discover" ever new wonders are only catching up with divine wisdom. A Palomar astronomer once closed his lecture on the new galaxies, found with the great 200-inch reflector, in the opening words of our Psalm, "The heavens are telling the glory of God." The farther man's mind penetrates the world around him, the more does that witness stagger us with His greatness and beauty.

The first six verses of the Psalm tell about the rising and setting of the sun. What we observe makes us believe we are the center of the solar system. True science says it is the other way around: the sun is the center and we course around it. We live by appearances. But there is more to it. Our vision and horizon are limited. The author uses the figure of a bridegroom and an athlete and so makes nature a joyful book in large, bright letters. As the sun unveils God's glory, so the law of the Lord reveals another world in which man walks a new path, travels a runway to his Maker and Savior.

The sun and the law both come from God and lead to God. The law lights up man's way of worship and morals. The second part (vv. 7-14) fills his path with light and his heart with joy as it gives unity to the entire Psalm. The law of the Lord is perfect, right, reliable, pure, and enduring. The abundant praise (like Psalm 119) shows how religious a man the author was. But he can be loyal to God only with God's help. "Clear me from hidden faults" and from presumption, which is a kind of idolatry. Godliness is wisdom.

Christ Jesus is the Sun of justice, who enlightens the world. From the virginal womb of holy Mary is His rising. Mary was the bridal bower and spouse of Christ before she was His mother (Dante). After her the Church, His bride, hails His glorious coming in sign as "the day-spring from on high," to bring light and salvation to those in darkness (Lk. 1:78f.). This living Sun, the personal Son of God, rises in us daily and fills us with joyful confidence to give voice to His coming to all the world. Rom. 10:18 applies this thought to the preachers who proclaim the Good News.

Jesus fulfilled the old law with the new one of love, one that will last forever (1 Cor. 13:1-13). Law is still an important function in the Body of Christ for the salvation of mankind. If the heavenly Father is solicitous about flowers, grass, and birds, how much more about man and woman (Mt. 6:26-30). We need the light of His law to find our way. His Holy Spirit guides our every effort (Gal. 5:25). Nobody needs to be in the dark. God's law is written in our hearts (Heb. 8:10). "My inner self agrees with the law of God" (Rom. 7:22), and in our weakness (Rom. 7:14ff.) God comes to the rescue, especially with the praying Church. She uses this Psalm not only on I and II Mondays (noon and lauds) but also on great feasts like Christmas (office of readings and noon), Ascension (noon), Monday after Easter (noon), John the Evangelist (office of readings), and common of apostles, virgins, and holy women (office of readings).

Psalm 20 (19)

The LORD answer you in the day of trouble!
The name of the God of Jacob protect you!

²May he send you help from the sanctuary,
and give you support from Zion!
³May he remember all your offerings,
and regard with favor your burnt sacrifices!

⁴May he grant you your heart's desire,
and fulfil all your plans!
⁵May we shout for joy over your victory,
and in the name of our God set up our banners!
May the LORD fulfil all your petitions!

⁶Now I know that the LORD will help his anointed;
he will answer him from his holy heaven
with mighty victories by his right hand.
⁷Some boast of chariots, and some of horses;
but we boast of the name of the LORD our God.
⁸They will collapse and fall;
but we shall rise and stand upright.

⁹Give victory to the king, O LORD;
answer us when we call.

God's Name a Blessing

A people's prayer around the Altar, this royal Psalm begs for the king in the Name of the Lord. Rendered ritually before battle, it reflects the spiritual unity of king and people bonded to God by an ancient covenant. The enemies that threaten Israel also threaten the promises of the God of Jacob (earlier name for Israel). The sanctuary is Zion, where they offered sacrifice on behalf of their leader while they chanted this Psalm. Almost always at war, the people of Israel, a holy nation, prayed this "standard" prayer in which worship and warfare are all one.

Striking is the verse, "Some boast of chariots and some of horses, but we boast of the name of the Lord our God." The enemy of the Jews had more "modern" weapons of war. We think of our war machines and nuclear weapons, which are always outdated and useless in the face of God's Name. The Lord has spoken His oracle in the sanctuary: He will give victory to His anointed ones from His holy place and His heavenly fortress. Once God has spoken, we know the outcome, just as St. Peter, released from prison, could say, "Now I know that the Lord has sent his angel . . ." (Acts 12:11).

"In the Name of the Lord" is a more powerful weapon than any war device. Here the blessing is officially spoken by/over the king, God's representative, by ministers of the Altar, also God's representatives, with the people's response, God's holy people. "May the Lord fulfill all your petitions" and "Give victory to the king!" The New Testament equivalent is "through Christ our Lord who lives and reigns . . . ," which we use, not only to save a king but also to save God's royal people assembled in His Name around the Altar.

The right way to pray this Psalm is not merely in time of war (even then, whose side is right?), but for the Church militant now while the. battle is on. We are responsible that the Kingship of Christ may prevail, we His mystic members by the incorporation of Baptism. We do not seek temporal or political power, but the glory of God, the victory of right over the kingdom of evil. This prayer is most powerful for the triumph over sin, death, and satan (Heb. 10:12f.). "Saul, Saul, why do you persecute me?" (Acts 9:4) proves that this is true. The great task of the Church is to extend Christ's reign on earth (1 Cor. 15:24-27, 54; Heb. 2:8; Rev. 11:15-18). "To him be glory for ever. Amen" (Rom. 11:36).

The Church avails herself of this prayer on I Tuesdays at vespers.

Psalm 21 (20)

In thy strength the king rejoices, O Lord;
and in thy help how greatly he exults!
²Thou hast given him his heart's desire,
and hast not withheld the request of his lips.
³For thou dost meet him with goodly blessings;
thou dost set a crown of fine gold upon his head.
⁴He asked life of thee; thou gavest it to him,
length of days for ever and ever.
⁵His glory is great through thy help;
splendor and majesty thou dost bestow upon him.
⁶Yea, thou dost make him most blessed for ever;
thou dost make him glad with the joy of thy presence.
⁷For the king trusts in the Lord;
and through the steadfast love of the Most High he shall
not be moved.

⁸Your hand will find out all your enemies;
your right hand will find out those who hate you.
⁹You will make them as a blazing oven
when you appear.
The Lord will swallow them up in his wrath;
and fire will consume them.
¹⁰You will destroy their offspring from the earth,
and their children from among the sons of men.
¹¹If they plan evil against you,
if they devise mischief, they will not succeed.
¹²For you will put them to flight;
you will aim at their faces with your bows.

¹³Be exalted, O Lord, in thy strength!
We will sing and praise thy power.

The Glory of Our King

Like Psalm 20, a royal Psalm and companion piece of prayer, this one mirrors the heavenly king's power and glory and blessings in His earthly royal representative for whom the author wrote it. With these inspired words we praise God for His interventions on behalf of a great king of His people. We pray that He may follow up His past actions with future assistance. In faith it all has meaning because the king's enemies are desecrating God and His people. The blessings of a successful king are many (victory, prestige and power, riches and glory, even length of days), but the greatest is the joy over God's special presence.

For an earthly king much of this strikes us as poetic exaggeration, but we must remember that in Christ all these promises find their full meaning ("most blessed for ever"). We can never praise too much the divine favors bestowed on the triumphant humanity of the Savior for whom all these symbols of kingship are intended. In a moment of self-revelation, Jesus praised the Father for all He had given His Son on earth (see Lk. 10:21f.).

Since we are co-heirs with Christ of these promises and gifts (Rom. 8:17), our joy too will be perfect (Jn. 15:11). If our prayer is a reflection of God's goodness and glory, His Kingship will be our blessing and victory. We see His presence now in faith, and it is a royal glory invisibly present (Heb. 2:9), so we celebrate His crowning and our own sharing in His royalty. The best way of celebrating the power and victory of Christ is to join the Church's use of this Psalm on I Tuesdays (vespers) and on the common of pastors and holy men (office of readings). In this communal, solemn action of praise, we have the ultimate surety of the Holy Spirit. We do well also to use it in personal, private praise.

Psalm 22 (21)

My God, my God, why hast thou forsaken me?
　　Why art thou so far from helping me, from the words of
　　　my groaning?
²O my God, I cry by day, but thou dost not answer;
　　and by night, but find no rest.

³Yet thou art holy,
　　enthroned on the praises of Israel.
⁴In thee our fathers trusted;
　　they trusted, and thou didst deliver them.
⁵To thee they cried, and were saved;
　　in thee they trusted, and were not disappointed.

⁶But I am a worm, and no man;
    scorned by men, and despised by the people.
⁷All who see me mock at me,
    they make mouths at me, they wag their heads;
⁸"He committed his cause to the Lord; let him deliver him,
    let him rescue him, for he delights in him!"

⁹Yet thou art he who took me from the womb;
    thou didst keep me safe upon my mother's breasts.
¹⁰Upon thee was I cast from my birth,
    and since my mother bore me thou hast been my God.
¹¹Be not far from me,
        for trouble is near
        and there is none to help.

¹²Many bulls encompass me,
    strong bulls of Bashan surround me;
¹³they open wide their mouths at me,
    like a ravening and roaring lion.

¹⁴I am poured out like water,
    and all my bones are out of joint;
my heart is like wax,
    it is melted within my breast;
¹⁵my strength is dried up like a potsherd,
    and my tongue cleaves to my jaws;
    thou dost lay me in the dust of death.

¹⁶Yea, dogs are round about me;
    a company of evildoers encircle me;
    they have pierced my hands and feet—
¹⁷I can count all my bones—
    they stare and gloat over me;
¹⁸they divide my garments among them,
    and for my raiment they cast lots.

¹⁹But thou, O Lord, be not far off!
    O thou my help, hasten to my aid!
²⁰Deliver my soul from the sword,
    my life from the power of the dog!
²¹Save me from the mouth of the lion,
    my afflicted soul from the horns of the wild oxen!

²²I will tell of thy name to my brethren;
    in the midst of the congregation I will praise thee:
²³You who fear the LORD, praise him!
    all you sons of Jacob, glorify him,
    and stand in awe of him, all you sons of Israel!
²⁴For he has not despised or abhorred
    the affliction of the afflicted;
  and he has not hid his face from him,
    but has heard, when he cried to him.

²⁵From thee comes my praise in the great congregation;
    my vows I will pay before those who fear him.
²⁶The afflicted shall eat and be satisfied;
    those who seek him shall praise the LORD!
    May your hearts live for ever!

²⁷All the ends of the earth shall remember
    and turn to the LORD;
  and all the families of the nations
    shall worship before him.
²⁸For dominion belongs to the LORD,
    and he rules over the nations.

²⁹Yea, to him shall all the proud of the earth bow down;
    before him shall bow all who go down to the dust,
    and he who cannot keep himself alive.
³⁰Posterity shall serve him;
    men shall tell of the Lord to the coming generation,
³¹and proclaim his deliverance to a people yet unborn,
    that he has wrought it.

From Death to Life

All men live to die. Christians die to live. They find God in suffering. The silence of God in suffering is the way of faith. Solitude and abandonment are themes of this Psalm. The hardest trial of suffering for believers is the feeling of abandonment by God, the God who has taken such good care of us from our mother's womb, the God of our happy youth, the God who answered our prayers. Sick unto death, his body wasting away, with nothing to look forward to, surrounded by enemies like hungry lions and senseless dogs, the Psalmist reaches out with his last thread of strength to the presence of God.

This moment of darkness is one of pure faith, like Psalm 88. "Be not far from me" helps one learn of His nearness. That is the meaning of the first part (vv. 1-21). It is the price we pay for sin, but also the price of glory, that is, if we may speak of "price." No brutality of bulls, lions, and dogs comes near to the wild ferocity of man to man. In bold poetic language, this is the story of millions who die abandoned, as they think. And yet God is near, ready to pick up wretched sufferers, more like worms than men.

The God who is "enthroned on the praises of Israel" in His holy place is near. He, the Glory of Israel, present to His assembly, hears the last cry of the dying. As his prayer is being heard, the Psalmist vows to spread the news of God's favors to all. He vows to offer sacrifices to the God of his fathers, even to proclaim His Name to the nations of the world. Finally, God stretches out His hand to the poor and humble and shares His own glory with the hungry at the banquet of salvation and eternal happiness.

The fulfillment of this wonderful messianic Psalm in Christ's passion and death makes it the perfect prayer of the Church for Good Friday (office of readings, and every III Friday at noon). Jesus is the Suffering Servant of Yahweh (in Isaiah), about whom this Psalm speaks, from Gethsemane to the resurrection. He literally went through the phases described: the physical pain, the anguish of spirit, the scorn of heartless enemies who wagged their heads, the silence (He did not seek vengeance), the fear and the loneliness. Even the loss of one immortal soul was enough to throw Him to the ground, not to speak of the many on the wide freeway that leads to hell. For these He suffered in vain. He reaped hatred for love.

We can never fathom the depth of His terror because our humanity is stunted, while His was sinless and sensitive to evil. No one will ever write the inner life of Him who joined our human nature to the Godhead, who loved life more than we do. Out of His pure soul, out of this dark moment, He cried out, "My God, why hast thou forsaken me?" With His dying strength He prayed this Psalm on the Cross of love, while His enemies gloated in triumph. And He thought of this hour during His lifetime (Lk. 10:50). It was the spirit of part II (vv. 22-32) that sustained Him, even as the nails pierced His hands and feet, like biting dogs. Nothing could shake His trust in the Father, no abandonment, no dry crust of human ingratitude.

The Providence of the Father promised Him glory to come, the conversion of peoples yet unborn, the universal praise to come. Victory came through death and rising. His loving will to forgive was forever crystallized at that moment, which became for us the Banquet-Sacrifice. No wonder that the genius of faith took verse 26 as a table prayer. Blessed are they who gaze on His wounds and dying Face with faith and love.

Many passages are fulfilled in our Psalm. "They shall look on him whom they have pierced" (Jn. 19:37 and Rev. 1:7), unto salvation for believers and eternal destruction for enemies. "They parted my garments among them, and for my clothing they cast lots" (Jn. 19:24). "I will proclaim thy name to my brethren; in the midst of the congregation I will praise thee" (Heb. 2:12), thus predicting the liturgical reenactment of His Word and Deed. His offering on the Cross was perfect (see Jn. 17:1-26).

The triumph of darkness (Lk. 22:53) is also reenacted today in countless victims of suffering the world over. Christ is persecuted and suffering in His members. Will they give themselves in faith to the unseen Savior-God who gave them victory and the resurrection? The answer depends on us, how we make known this Mystery "of life in God" (Rom. 6:9f.) and proclaim His victory to all nations.

Psalm 23 (22)

The LORD is my shepherd, I shall not want;
2   he makes me lie down in green pastures.
He leads me beside still waters;
3   he restores my soul.
He leads me in paths of righteousness
    for his name's sake.

4Even though I walk through the valley of the shadow of death,
    I fear no evil;
for thou art with me;
    thy rod and thy staff,
    they comfort me.

⁵Thou preparest a table before me in the presence of my enemies;
thou anointest my head with oil, my cup overflows.
⁶Surely goodness and mercy shall follow me
all the days of my life;
and I shall dwell in the house of the LORD for ever.

The Shepherd Heart

A morning prayer in the Church's office, this Psalm probably is the favorite of the whole Psalter. Not only is a nomad people on the constant lookout for grass and water, but also everybody understands how attractive God is when He calls Himself the Shepherd of My sheep (Ez. 34:11-16; see also Is. 40:11). The prophets spell out what the good shepherd should do for his sheep and what the Lord Himself will do, what the false shepherd neglects to do. God appointed the boy David as shepherd over His people. This shepherd-prince David composed our Psalm. He came from the flocks of Bethlehem and knew what tender care the sheep require, how they depend entirely on him for food, rest, and protection. Without this constant care the sheep become lean and neglected and victims of wild animals. "For his name's sake" refers to the shepherd's divine vocation.

Only a true shepherd knows when there is nothing wanting, what individual sheep need from birth till death. The sheep in turn know the shepherd better than they know each other. They will not rest unless they are fed and contented, free from danger and enemies. Green pasture and fresh water, protection when in a harsh country, simple things like these will make the flock tranquil and docile. In Palestine the sheep still answer to their name when the shepherd calls them. Rod and staff are there for their protection.

Suddenly the picture changes from God the Shepherd to God the Host at table. All at once we are guests at God's table "spread in the presence of my enemies," that is, in full view of such as want to harm the flock. Here is spiritual care and salvation under the image of plentiful food for guests who enjoy eastern hospitality, like the anointing of the head with perfumed oil (see Lk. 7:46 where Christ complained of the lack of it). A full, generous cup of wine is part of the refreshment. To the wandering Jews, God's desert hospitality provided manna, fresh meat, and cool water from the rock, besides protection from their foes.

Jesus Christ is the Shepherd and Host and Food at God's table.

"I am the good shepherd," who leads the sheep, calls them by name, feeds them with rich food, guards them even to the laying down of His life (Jn. 10:1-18). He is always with His sheep (for example, we can see the glorified Shepherd coming in Rev. 1:12-20 to John in persecution). The classic figure is Christ carrying the strayed and weak sheep in His arms. He forever reenacts the parable of the lost sheep (Lk. 15:1-7) in His sheepfold, the Church, His Body. He Himself is the way for His sheep (Jn. 8:12) and through His bishops guides us with crook and staff. He feeds His sheep at the heavenly, messianic banquet of His Body and Blood. Water in Baptism is the first necessity for entering His fold. The fragrant oil of anointing gives us the seal of the Spirit in Confirmation (2 Cor. 1:21f.) and healing in sickness. As we wander through the dark valley of tears, we look to the Shepherd-Sacred-Heart for comfort. We are satisfied with all good, while the rich go away empty.

Already we dwell in His house, also sinners who "have returned to the Shepherd" (1 Pet. 2:25). The final scene awaits us in heaven, where the Shepherd-Lamb stands on the golden altar (Rev. 21:22 and 22:1). "I know mine, and mine know me."

Psalm 24 (23)

The earth is the LORD's and the fulness thereof,
     the world and those who dwell therein;
²for he has founded it upon the seas,
     and established it upon the rivers.

³Who shall ascend the hill of the LORD?
     And who shall stand in his holy place?
⁴He who has clean hands and a pure heart,
     who does not lift up his soul to what is false,
     and does not swear deceitfully.
⁵He will receive blessing from the LORD,
     and vindication from the God of his salvation.
⁶Such is the generation of those who seek him,
     who seek the face of the God of Jacob.

7Lift up your heads, O gates!
    and be lifted up, O ancient doors!
    that the King of glory may come in.
8Who is the King of glory?
    The LORD, strong and mighty,
    the LORD, mighty in battle!
9Lift up your heads, O gates!
    and be lifted up, O ancient doors!
    that the King of glory may come in.
10Who is this King of glory?
    The LORD of hosts,
    he is the King of glory!

God's Introit

An ancient procession song, used at the solemn entry of God's
Ark to Zion, where He dwelt in His citadel (see 2 Sam. 6:12-20), this
Psalm becomes our contemporary prayer, transplanted into new,
believing hearts. We cherish the original, literal meaning for its rich
yield in Christ and His people, who likewise seek the face of God.

Opening with high praise to the Creator Lord, who is present to
His handiwork (the old popular view was that He founded the earth
on the waters), the Psalm quickly confronts us with His special dwelling
on the holy mountain. Who dares ascend to His presence? (See comments on Psalm 15.) The man of faith, who is pure of heart. Not mere
ritual, legal cleanness is called for, but inner, moral holiness. Communion with God is not for those who call themselves holy, but whom
God calls holy. God chose Zion, and He lays down the conditions for
beholding His face. All vanity is sinful, even falsity with our neighbors.

Then God knocks at the gates of the city. His carriers and ministers
demand entry. A chorus from within asks who is calling. The Psalm
takes a highly dramatic form. The King of glory is there, the supreme
Lord of heaven and earth. The gates are never high enough for Him.
The summons and answer are repeated. Then a great tide of welcome
sweeps the ancient Ark into the city, with this introit song. The Lord
of hosts is the leader of armies, heavenly and earthly. This title is now
used for His heavenly hosts (e.g. at the *Sanctus*). We deal here with
a great theophany, or appearance of God, a forerunner of the New
Testament signs that reveal Christ's coming. These sacramental signs,
like the Ark, are carriers of His living presence. The God of revelation
is even closer to us than the God of creation. He is present. He is always

coming. His Advent is now.

Christ, the King of glory, stands at our door and knocks. "Behold, I stand at the door and knock; if anyone hears my voice and opens the door, I will come in to him and eat with him, and he with me" (Rev. 3:20). What happened at Jerusalem's gates, happens at our ritual door, happens at the human heart. Christ does not take possession of us unless we open to Him, invite Him, welcome Him, as did the disciples at Emmaus. Our love for Zion is not historic awe for a city in ruins, but the active seeking of God's face. We find Him wherever He reveals His presence, not just in His creation (Col. 1:16), but in His living Body, the Church. When we seek Him, He has already seized us (Phil. 3:12).

The Savior is forever "turning the tables." For inviting Him, we become His guests. We think we have to do it all, but Christ holds the primacy. We answer His invitation. The free will of man becomes the gateway of God, and He enters when we proclaim that "Jesus Christ is Lord" (Phil. 2:11). Our Psalm finds mention in 1 Cor. 20:26. The Church prays it on Easter Tuesday, Holy Saturday, for the dedication of a church (office of readings), on the common of the Blessed Virgin Mary, on I Tuesdays (lauds) and IV Sundays (office of readings).

Psalm 25 (24)

> To thee, O Lord, I lift up my soul.
> [2] O my God, in thee I trust,
>> let me not be put to shame;
>> let not my enemies exult over me.
> [3] Yea, let none that wait for thee be put to shame;
>> let them be ashamed who are wantonly treacherous.
>
> [4] Make me to know thy ways, O Lord;
>> teach me thy paths.
> [5] Lead me in thy truth, and teach me,
>> for thou art the God of my salvation;
>> for thee I wait all the day long.
>
> [6] Be mindful of thy mercy, O Lord, and of thy steadfast love,
>> for they have been from of old.
> [7] Remember not the sins of my youth, or my transgressions;
>> according to thy steadfast love remember me,
>> for thy goodness' sake, O Lord!

[8]Good and upright is the Lord;
>   therefore he instructs sinners in the way.
[9]He leads the humble in what is right,
>   and teaches the humble his way.
[10]All the paths of the Lord are steadfast love and faithfulness,
>   for those who keep his covenant and his testimonies.

[11]For thy name's sake, O Lord,
>   pardon my guilt, for it is great.
[12]Who is the man that fears the Lord?
>   Him will he instruct in the way that he should choose.
[13]He himself shall abide in prosperity,
>   and his children shall possess the land.
[14]The friendship of the Lord is for those who fear him,
>   and he makes known to them his covenant.
[15]My eyes are ever toward the Lord,
>   for he will pluck my feet out of the net.

[16]Turn thou to me, and be gracious to me;
>   for I am lonely and afflicted.
[17]Relieve the troubles of my heart,
>   and bring me out of my distresses.
[18]Consider my affliction and my trouble,
>   and forgive all my sins.

[19]Consider how many are my foes,
>   and with what violent hatred they hate me.
[20]Oh guard my life, and deliver me;
>   let me not be put to shame, for I take refuge in thee.
[21]May integrity and uprightness preserve me,
>   for I wait for thee.

[22]Redeem Israel, O God,
>   out of all his troubles.

The Way to God

The opening of this Psalm is like a definition of all prayer: lifting up one's soul to God with complete trust, simplicity of heart, while waiting for the Lord. Surrender to God while seeking His paths must be the interior spirit of the individual who cultivates prayer. Quiet hope means longing for God's will in the midst of contrary forces. The

Psalm is strongly penitential in character and admirably fits the season of Advent, which is the time of hope.

This prayer affords strength for the way that God makes Himself known to His own, to the poor, and to sinners who look to Him for mercy and goodness. It is a path of divine love, even in the face of difficulties. It also provides wisdom for practical living, truth in action. God grants mercy and pardon for His own Name's sake. He forgets and forgives the sins of our younger days. Even the great sin of idolatry He pardons, providing we sincerely beg for it. His moral guidance brings us delivery from our enemies and dangers all along the path of life. Fear of the Lord is the way of wisdom. Our love must be so great that we are afraid of offending Him. Such is the lifelong process of lifting up our soul, hearts, and hands. It is the following of Christ, who will finally lift us up in our resurrection and ascension. Gravitating heavenward instead of earthward, going up and not down, is the way of faith, the goal of our prayer runways.

Psalm 25 describes the "way of peace" (Lk. 1:79). Related also to the wisdom book of Proverbs, it teaches us the way of detachment, which is the wisdom of Christ the Lord (St. Paul has more about this wisdom of the Holy Spirit in 1 Cor. 2:6-13.). Conscious of our spiritual enemies and suffering, we pursue hope in God with this Psalm of prayer. Jesus the Savior prayed it for a sinful world and for His Church, still battling His enemies, especially sin and guilt. He fights our "individual" battles in and for us if we abide in Him (see Mt. 4:1-11). Since there is no prayer without struggle and warfare, prayer makes us "strong in the Lord" (Eph. 6:10-18). Our Psalm then describes the folly of the Cross, which is the wisdom of Christ, opposed to the wisdom of a sinful world.

Called an alphabetic or acrostic Psalm (every verse or second line beginning with another Hebrew letter), this one is easier to pray than others with more problems. The Church prays it now on I Thursdays (noon), formerly during Advent, for which it still serves to express longing for Christ, then His ever-nearer coming, and our lifting up our whole being, all Advent themes.

Psalm 26 (25)

Vindicate me, O LORD,
for I have walked in my integrity,
and I have trusted in the LORD without wavering.
²Prove me, O LORD, and try me;
test my heart and my mind.
³For thy steadfast love is before my eyes,
and I walk in faithfulness to thee.

⁴I do not sit with false men,
nor do I consort with dissemblers;
⁵I hate the company of evildoers,
and I will not sit with the wicked.

⁶I wash my hands in innocence,
and go about thy altar, O LORD,
⁷singing aloud a song of thanksgiving,
and telling all thy wondrous deeds.

⁸O LORD, I love the habitation of thy house,
and the place where thy glory dwells.
⁹Sweep me not away with sinners,
nor my life with bloodthirsty men,
¹⁰men in whose hands are evil devices,
and whose right hands are full of bribes.

¹¹But as for me, I walk in my integrity;
redeem me, and be gracious to me.
¹²My foot stands on level ground;
in the great congregation I will bless the LORD.

Innocence on Trial

As the inspired Word of God, every Psalm is precious and deepens
our union with God. It carries blessings for us because its divine message to us is a direct sacramental. Even though we find it hard to understand, as when a man defends his innocence, this is true. In the Old
Testament Psalms, we find this rather frequently. Sometimes we are
dealing with legal court trials (as in Psalms 7 and 109). Our Psalm is
easy to understand, if we assume that the author is defending himself
before the law. The penalty was death for more serious crimes (Dt. 17:

2-13) such as idolatry. The author would not deny his general sinfulness or need for redemption or claim a perfect life for himself, but he rejects specific charges, in this case consorting with hypocrites, evildoers, and idolators.

In self-defense he renounces the assembly of false men; on the other hand, he professes his love for the house of God. In proof he follows the ritual of washing his hands (compare Mt. 27:24, Pilate washing his hands and falsely declaring his innocence of the Blood of Christ) and joining the procession around the altar of God. It all had the force of an oath declared in the holy presence of God. His sole love is for the place where God's glory dwells and for the assembly that blessed the Lord. For the sincere Jew this was the most searching test, with God present as the Judge of hearts.

This has nothing in common with the hypocrisy of the Pharisee declaring his justice, whom the Lord condemned (Lk. 18:9ff.). Our Psalm in fact has a penitential character. Christ prayed it for us. He prayed it more perfectly than any son of Adam, for He was sinless (Jn. 8:46 and Heb. 7:26) and spent His whole life doing the Father's will (Jn. 17). He took upon Himself the blame and punishment for our sins and was crucified with malefactors (Mt. 15:28).

We do well to utter this prayer in sorrow for all current forms of false worship and occultism. "For what accord has Christ with Belial? . . . What agreement has the temple of God with idols?" (See the whole passage of 2 Cor. 6:14-18.) The more we belong to Christ, the more can we declare our innocence (Rom. 8:1 and 1 Jn. 1:9f.). The praying Church uses this Psalm with Christ on I Fridays (at noon).

Psalm 27 (26)

> The LORD is my light and my salvation;
>   whom shall I fear?
> The LORD is the stronghold of my life;
>   of whom shall I be afraid?
>
> ²When evildoers assail me,
>   uttering slanders against me,
> my adversaries and foes,
>   they shall stumble and fall.

³Though a host encamp against me,
    my heart shall not fear;
though war arise against me,
    yet I will be confident.

⁴One thing have I asked of the Lord,
    that will I seek after;
that I may dwell in the house of the Lord
    all the days of my life,
to behold the beauty of the Lord,
    and to inquire in his temple.

⁵For he will hide me in his shelter
    in the day of trouble;
he will conceal me under the cover of his tent,
    he will set me high upon a rock.

⁶And now my head shall be lifted up
    above my enemies round about me;
and I will offer in his tent
    sacrifices with shouts of joy;
I will sing and make melody to the Lord.

⁷Hear, O Lord, when I cry aloud,
    be gracious to me and answer me!
⁸Thou hast said, "Seek ye my face."
    My heart says to thee,
"Thy face, Lord, do I seek."
⁹   Hide not thy face from me.

Turn not thy servant away in anger,
    thou who hast been my help.
Cast me not off, forsake me not,
    O God of my salvation!
¹⁰For my father and my mother have forsaken me,
    but the Lord will take me up.

¹¹Teach me thy way, O Lord;
    and lead me on a level path
    because of my enemies.
¹²Give me not up to the will of my adversaries;
    for false witnesses have risen against me,
    and they breathe out violence.

¹³I believe that I shall see the goodness of the LORD
   in the land of the living!
¹⁴Wait for the LORD;
   be strong, and let your heart take courage;
   yea, wait for the LORD!

Hidden in God

Human language cannot express the depth of religious experience and divine trust of the author of this great Psalm. All Psalms are a record of trust, but especially this one. Faith teaches trust and brings joyful light into our lives, even in the darkest hours. The same faith and trust make Christian life possible. Confidence depends on God and Christ, no matter what dangers face us. The first five verses tell us what this means in practice for a mature believer.

Clinging to God is nothing abstract or intangible, but is as real as the house of the Lord and its Altar. Trust is in fact anchored in the visible signs of God, the Rock. Now as then, faith flourishes on God's light in His holy Temple, there to experience the loveliness of the Lord and hide in the shelter of His "tent." Safe in His tent, the man of trusting faith can lift up his head and look unafraid on his enemies. To dwell in God's house is to have union with Him and conquer one's fears, a whole army of them. Life with and for God has its reward in His praises, and even if that entails sacrifice, all our troubles will be small, insignificant.

To desire God is to love Him. The author knows that his earthly dwelling with the Lord insures his heavenly one, the blessed vision of the face of God. He constantly begs God not to forsake him, not to hide His face. His confidence knows no bounds: even if his parents would forsake him, God would not. This strong reliance is evident in the last two verses (as well as in other Psalms and Old Testament texts). Following the Lord's level path leads to the "land of the living."

Trusting faith is a gift of God. It helps us to be at home in His world. As we cling to the Lord, we are conscious of our effort, but it is even more God's action that sustains us, lifts us up, wins us victory "high upon a rock." Cult is an encounter with God, who will not let us go empty, but gives the graces we need, be it personal experience of His tenderness, be it gentle peace of sensing the charm of our religion.

Nearness to God in authentic worship is for the man of faith a source of love and courage. The cult celebration does not end in ritual, but blossoms forth in communion with the Godhead, who is the main actor, also away from His sacred Altar.

Faith and trust are an ever-flowing fountain that leads to eternal life. If we seek His face in the celebrations around the Altar, Christ can fill our whole lives. Generally Christians do not know all that the Altar means. It is God's special place, the crossroads of two worlds, the rock of ages, where trust grows out of the Sacrifice-Banquet. There we live anew the Mysteries of Christ in our midst, share His sentiments of trust, become identified with His life-giving vitality. We lose our fears and false self and become truly free of real and phantom enemies. We must take seriously that He is the Light of the world (Jn. 8:12), that no one goes to the Father except through Him (Jn. 14:6), which includes His incarnation and sacramental system. He was consumed with passion for God's house, which He fulfilled in Himself. The Church prays the Psalm on Holy Saturday (noon) and I Wednesdays (vespers).

Psalm 28 (27)

> To thee, O Lord, I call;
>> my rock, be not deaf to me,
> lest, if thou be silent to me,
>> I become like those who go down to the Pit.
> ²Hear the voice of my supplication,
>> as I cry to thee for help,
> as I lift up my hands
>> toward thy most holy sanctuary.

³Take me not off with the wicked,
  with those who are workers of evil,
  who speak peace with their neighbors,
  while mischief is in their hearts.
⁴Requite them according to their work,
  and according to the evil of their deeds;
 requite them according to the work of their hands;
  render them their due reward.
⁵Because they do not regard the works of the LORD,
  or the work of his hands,
 he will break them down and build them up no more.

⁶Blessed be the LORD!
  for he has heard the voice of my supplications.
⁷The LORD is my strength and my shield;
  in him my heart trusts;
 so I am helped, and my heart exults,
  and with my song I give thanks to him.

⁸The LORD is the strength of his people,
  he is the saving refuge of his anointed.
⁹O save thy people, and bless thy heritage;
  be thou their shepherd, and carry them for ever.

The Reward of Trust

Here we have another piece of inspired prayer, and faith discerns its true value. God hears and rewards all prayer, even if we go "down to the pit," the realm of death and defeat. Delivery from sickness or any sort of misfortune and evil is not the final test of God "answering" our prayer. The ultimate proof of His mercy and favor is glory and happiness after death. In the Old Testament the belief in immortal glory was less clear than now with Christ's new revelation. Perhaps in the Old Testament God answered the immediate plea more frequently in order to build up people's faith and reliance on Him. But the essence of prayer remains the same, then and now. God alone is the rewarder of the just and punisher of the wicked. He looks for the sincere heart.

We turn to the holy places, where God dwells, in token of our submission to Him and His special presence. That token is an answer to His will, who wants us to be on His side and declare ourselves against

evil and deceitful men. If we lift up our hands toward His holy sanctuary, that already indicates allegiance to the Rock of our lives. That
already is a sign of His favor, so we do not pray mechanically, but
with our spirit.

Similarly, we do not pray against our personal enemies (if indeed
we must classify some that way). God is a merciful judge, and if we
ourselves have obtained mercy, we must extend it to others. It is not
our task to decide who is worthy of forgiveness and who deserves
punishment. Only the sin against the Spirit deserves eternal retribution
(see Jn. 14:10-31 and Mt. 12:32), and we are by no means the judge
of that. We must learn to distinguish between the sinner and sin, to
pray for the sinner and renounce sin. That is the law of Christ, who
taught forgiveness.

In the present Psalm, as in all others with similar words of retribution, we leave the final judgment to God and pray against the evil
spirit, the devil confirmed in sin, who is beyond hope. Turning our
hands to the sanctuary and raising our hearts to God can only mean that
"the work of our hands" is the repression of evil in the world.

Christ on the Cross showed us the way. His prayer was heard,
even as He "died the death." He won salvation for sinners, while He
hated sin more than any just man ever did. Verses 6-9 contain His
prayer, as the Father was silent. He suffered the fate of sinners (Heb.
2:14-18). The victim of deceit and hypocrisy, "He made him to be sin,
who knew no sin" (2 Cor. 5:21). The same sentiments we find in Jn. 17.
God has the final word. The fate of the Master is the fate of the disciple
(Jn. 15:18—16:4). This includes us, the members of His Body (Eph.
1:16-23).

The Church makes this prayer her own on Easter Wednesday
(noon) and I Fridays (noon).

Psalm 29 (28)

> Ascribe to the LORD, O heavenly beings,
>   ascribe to the LORD glory and strength.
> ²Ascribe to the LORD the glory of his name;
>   worship the LORD in holy array.

³The voice of the LORD is upon the waters;
   the God of glory thunders,
   the LORD, upon many waters.

⁴The voice of the LORD is powerful,
   the voice of the LORD is full of majesty.

⁵The voice of the LORD breaks the cedars,
   the LORD breaks the cedars of Lebanon.
⁶He makes Lebanon to skip like a calf,
   and Sirion like a young wild ox.

⁷The voice of the LORD flashes forth flames of fire.
⁸The voice of the LORD shakes the wilderness,
   the LORD shakes the wilderness of Kadesh.

⁹The voice of the LORD makes the oaks to whirl,
   and strips the forests bare;
   and in his temple all cry, "Glory!"

¹⁰The LORD sits enthroned over the flood;
   the LORD sits enthroned as king for ever.
¹¹May the LORD give strength to his people!
   May the LORD bless his people with peace!

The Voice of the Lord

Many people when they experience a violent storm think of the anger of God, just as the Psalmist does. That is a figure of speech, for God has neither voice nor anger like men do. It is a picture of His power and justice. But God loves mankind as much in a storm as during peaceful, sunny weather. To show that Israel's God is the Lord of creation, the author uses these phrases in one of the oldest Psalms, perhaps an ancient Canaanite hymn to a pagan storm-god adapted for sacred use. God has many "voices" and speaks in many ways through the things His creative power has fashioned.

The voice of the Lord comes over the waters with not only lightning and thunder but also in the weak whimper of an infant. His powerful wisdom is active in the hurricane and the things it destroys just as in the gentle, welcome whisper of a mother to her child. Whether He makes the earth quake and men fear, whether He causes the Lebanon Mountain Range leap like a calf, or the mighty Hermon (Sirion) like a young ox, it is man's inspired imagination that follows a storm into the steppeland (of Kadesh) beyond. The cedars of Lebanon were the choice trees that Solomon used in building the great Temple. It is the Temple where all cried "Glory!" Again a picture of the heavenly one, where the glory of God resounds forever among the "heavenly beings" (or "sons of God").

All created things heed the summons to give glory to the Name of the Lord because He is seated enthroned in eternal majesty above the storm as Lord of both pagans and Christians. The angels and saints obey His voice and fill the heavens with the triple *Sanctus*. The heavenly reward and fruit of this prayer is that "the Lord blesses his people with peace." We encounter the God of peace even in a storm. It strengthens our faith to know that amid the storms of life we are deep down at peace with our God of love.

Once God did appear amid storms, clouds, thunder and lightning (Ex. 19:16), at the early hour of the chosen people, to wean them away from pagan influences on Sinai. But that is not the whole story. At Bethlehem at the virgin birth of His Son, the heavens opened and the heavenly beings sang "Glory in heaven and peace on earth." When Jesus was baptized, the voice of the Father resounded, and again at the transfiguration on Mount Tabor. The voice of Christ over the raging storm brought sudden quiet (Mk. 4:39). He is the Word, begotten from all eternity, spoken in time, proclaimed loudly over all the earth.

In His Church we hear the living Voice of the Spirit, speaking loudly and clearly to the world in turmoil, calling for glory and promising peace. As the Father spoke our language at the incarnation of His Son, so now He continues to speak in His Mystical Body. In God's Temple all shout "Glory!" We the members of Christ join our voices to His in the symphony of glory. On the feast of Christ's Baptism (at the office of readings), we do so with the Church, also on I Tuesdays (lauds).

Psalm 30 (29)

I will extol thee, O LORD, for thou hast drawn me up,
    and hast not let my foes rejoice over me.
²O LORD my God, I cried to thee for help,
    and thou hast healed me.
³O LORD, thou hast brought up my soul from Sheol,
    restored me to life from among those gone down to the Pit.

⁴Sing praises to the LORD, O you his saints,
    and give thanks to his holy name.

⁵For his anger is but for a moment,
    and his favor is for a lifetime.
Weeping may tarry for the night,
    but joy comes with the morning.

⁶As for me, I said in my prosperity,
    "I shall never be moved."
⁷By thy favor, O LORD,
    thou hadst established me as a strong mountain;
thou didst hide thy face,
    I was dismayed.

⁸To thee, O LORD, I cried;
    and to the LORD I made supplication:
⁹"What profit is there in my death, if I go down to the Pit?
Will the dust praise thee?
    Will it tell of thy faithfulness?
¹⁰Hear, O LORD, and be gracious to me!
    O LORD, be thou my helper!"

¹¹Thou hast turned for me my mourning into dancing;
    thou hast loosed my sackcloth
    and girded me with gladness,
¹²that my soul may praise thee and not be silent.
    O LORD my God, I will give thanks to thee for ever.

Humility in Sickness

God is the Master of life and death. Gratitude for the gift of health
runs through this Psalm. The author had become presumptuous in
his good days, saying, "I shall never be moved." When his health suf-

fered, he came to his senses and saw the danger of his past life. The Lord saves in sickness if health serves salvation. Death and the grave (the pit, Sheol, netherworld) bring silence and the absence of praise. This is a common plea in the Psalms, a prayer pattern that Moses used, namely, that God's glory may prevail. Time and health are borrowed gifts of God, which we should use for His Name's sake.

History, like the individual's life, has its ups and downs. Our Psalm records these changes, as God's displeasure follows closely on human defections, just as on the other hand morning joy succeeds the tears of night. People never attain the golden middle way of constantly adhering to God's will. Conversion to God is genuine when we invite others to join us in thanking God. One can understand how this prayer became a public piece of worship by making known that God's cause is at stake. God did "not let my foes rejoice over me." (This phrase made it apt for the feast of the Immaculate Conception of Mary.)

Humility in sickness promotes humility in good health. A humble attitude is a healthy one. The Psalm teaches us this lesson. Better health is given us for better prayer, for breaking away from selfishness, for promoting the welfare of our community. The ultimate remedy is not always health, but salvation. This we read plainly in the life of our Savior, who prayed for release from suffering. He was heard in a way most frustrating to His enemies, by His resurrection, which made Him immune from hostility, suffering, and death. As He praises the Father forever, He invites us to learn His way of joy.

We can sing this Psalm, like other Psalms, because of our basic victory over sickness and death in the future life of immortality which the Lord promises us. ". . . giving thanks to the Father, who has qualified us to share in the inheritance of the saints in light. He has delivered us from the dominion of darkness and transferred us to the kingdom of his beloved Son, in whom we have redemption . . ." (Col. 1:12f.). This Psalm describes symbolically how He snatches us from the powers of darkness and sets us into the victory of His Son. On the Thursday after Easter (noon) and Holy Saturday (noon) we sing it with Christ in the Church, likewise on I Thursdays (vespers).

Psalm 31 (30)

In thee, O Lord, do I seek refuge;
let me never be put to shame;
in thy righteousness deliver me!
²Incline thy ear to me,
rescue me speedily!
Be thou a rock of refuge for me,
a strong fortress to save me!

³Yea, thou art my rock and my fortress;
for thy name's sake lead me and guide me,
⁴take me out of the net which is hidden for me,
for thou art my refuge.
⁵Into thy hand I commit my spirit;
thou hast redeemed me, O Lord, faithful God.

⁶Thou hatest those who pay regard to vain idols;
but I trust in the Lord.
⁷I will rejoice and be glad for thy steadfast love,
because thou hast seen my affliction,
thou hast taken heed of my adversities,
⁸and hast not delivered me into the hand of the enemy;
thou hast set my feet in a broad place.

⁹Be gracious to me, O Lord, for I am in distress;
my eye is wasted from grief,
my soul and my body also.
¹⁰For my life is spent with sorrow,
and my years with sighing;
my strength fails because of my misery,
and my bones waste away.

¹¹I am the scorn of all my adversaries,
a horror to my neighbors,
an object of dread to my acquaintances;
those who see me in the street flee from me.
¹²I have passed out of mind like one who is dead;
I have become like a broken vessel.
¹³Yea, I hear the whispering of many—
terror on every side!—
as they scheme together against me,
as they plot to take my life.

¹⁴But I trust in thee, O Lord,
    I say, "Thou art my God."
¹⁵My times are in thy hand;
    deliver me from the hand of my enemies and persecutors!
¹⁶Let thy face shine on thy servant;
    save me in thy steadfast love!

¹⁷Let me not be put to shame, O Lord,
    for I call on thee;
let the wicked be put to shame,
    let them go dumbfounded to Sheol.
¹⁸Let the lying lips be dumb,
    which speak insolently against the righteous
    in pride and contempt.

¹⁹O how abundant is thy goodness,
    which thou hast laid up for those who fear thee,
and wrought for those who take refuge in thee,
    in the sight of the sons of men!
²⁰In the covert of thy presence thou hidest them
    from the plots of men;
thou holdest them safe under thy shelter
    from the strife of tongues.

²¹Blessed be the Lord,
    for he has wondrously shown his steadfast love to me
    when I was beset as in a besieged city.
²²I had said in my alarm,
    "I am driven far from thy sight."
But thou didst hear my supplications,
    when I cried to thee for help.

²³Love the Lord, all you his saints!
    The Lord preserves the faithful,
    but abundantly requites him who acts haughtily.
²⁴Be strong, and let your heart take courage,
    all you who wait for the Lord!

Into Your Hands, Lord

"Love the Lord!" might serve as the title of this Psalm just as well since the Psalm culminates in the call to love (v. 23). It alternates between descriptions of the author's miseries and his trust in the Lord. Great adversity has struck him and he depicts his loneliness. He has lost contact with men, but found God. Through suffering he goes to God, the God of tender mercy. Although trials of pain resemble a crazy quilt of many colors and no design, yet the living God of love holds a definite pattern for each afflicted person. The account reminds us of the prophet Jeremiah's extreme anguish of soul and excruciating bodily distress. Added to that is the urgent cry for justice and protection against the intrigues and deceit of idolatrous enemies who seek his end.

The author unburdens his heart before God and finds the way and words of praise. His lament to God brings him divine comfort. He is faithful to God, and God is never closer than in the hour of suffering. "Into thy hand I commit my spirit. Thou hast redeemed me." God is his rock and mountain of refuge, his fortress and shelter, his tent of safety. Trust reaches for God despite all obstacles, and that is love. The author even urges others to love and praise God. Delivered from personal fears, he breaks forth into a hymn of blessing and thanks (vv. 21-24). Trusting the Lord and celebrating His goodness in such hard moments takes boldness and courage. Trust grows by trusting.

The full meaning of this Psalm shines forth in Christ, who used it when dying on the Cross, "a death He freely accepted" (see Jn. 10:18). He spoke the great final offering of redemption, "Father, into thy hands I commit my spirit" (Lk. 23:46). It was the hour when darkness and malice apparently triumphed (Lk. 22:53), when His enemies shouted, "He trusts in God. Let God deliver him now" (Mt. 27:43). Abandoned by man, the Father heard Him (Jn. 16:32).

Christ relives this Psalm in His mystical members, in us. We only experience facets, parts of His suffering, as when a man's whole life-work seems lost or his friends vanish from sight. Then to reach out in faith and trust for the love of God is a great sign of God's favor. Then suffering has the power to unite us to Him. A theophany (appearance, presence) of God has already taken place. Let us pray for the many of whom the Psalmist is an example and type. Coming into His worship-presence with the Lord's offering on our lips gives strength to ourselves and the grace to others to suffer with Him because His love is abundant in our hearts (Rom. 5:5; 8:17; Phil. 3:10f.).

On II Mondays (office of readings) and Wednesdays (compline), we pray this Psalm with Christ in His Church.

Psalm 32 (31)

Blessed is he whose transgression is forgiven,
    whose sin is covered.
²Blessed is the man to whom the LORD imputes no iniquity,
    and in whose spirit there is no deceit.

³When I declared not my sin, my body wasted away
    through my groaning all day long.
⁴For day and night thy hand was heavy upon me;
    my strength was dried up as by the heat of summer.

⁵I acknowledged my sin to thee,
    and I did not hide my iniquity;
I said, "I will confess my transgressions to the LORD";
    then thou didst forgive the guilt of my sin.

⁶Therefore let every one who is godly
    offer prayer to thee;
at a time of distress, in the rush of great waters,
    they shall not reach him.
⁷Thou art a hiding place for me,
    thou preservest me from trouble;
    thou dost encompass me with deliverance.

⁸I will instruct you and teach you
    the way you should go;
    I will counsel you with my eye upon you.
⁹Be not like a horse or a mule, without understanding,
    which must be curbed with bit and bridle,
    else it will not keep with you.

¹⁰Many are the pangs of the wicked;
    but steadfast love surrounds him who trusts in the LORD.
¹¹Be glad in the LORD, and rejoice, O righteous,
    and shout for joy, all you upright in heart!

Blessed Forgiveness

The farther the sinner goes away from God, the greater his self-inflicted suffering. The shortcut back to God and to sanity is sorrow for sin. This sorrow is also pain, healing pain according to God. At the outset, the author kept his guilt to himself, not admitting it to God. This increased his suffering. He tortured himself by doing so. His "body wasted away." Here we have God's revelation of His way of forgiveness: to confess one's sin and guilt to the Lord. That is the absolute condition for peace of conscience, for comfort and renewal. Humility is the way out of sin, humiliation "under the almighty hand of God" (1 Pet. 5:6). God has determined this way of rebirth.

So great is the blessedness of inner forgiveness of guilt that the author must share his joy with others. Every faithful man must pray this way till glad shouts of freedom ring all about him. In sinless purity his troubles are small. Only God can forgive sins. Man cannot forgive himself, or imagine his sins forgiven, if God has not spoken the word. As long as the sinner does not confess the guilt of wrongdoing, the inner gnawing of guilt only grows worse. Hiding one's guilt is a kind of deceit, self-deception. When God forgives, He enters into the human spirit and make-up.

This is wisdom for the sinner. God is the recourse and shelter for him. God follows up, in verses 8-9, to counsel the repentant one to follow the voice of right reason. Just as sin is irrational, senseless, and stubborn behavior, acting like a horse or a mule, so confession means liberation, the wisdom that builds up hope. The consequent joys of the just lead to the praise of God, who is near (Phil. 4:4ff.).

Our Psalm is one of the penitential Psalms in the Church. It would be wise to pray it after Confession, the sacrament of healing in the Church. Thereby we would realize how the sacramental way is a return to the rebirth of Baptism, according to the will of Christ. The holiness of God tolerates nothing impure (Is. 6:5). God grants pardon on His terms, not ours. Though this Psalm does not exhaust the process of forgiveness (see Psalms 51 and 38; also Jn. 14:6 and Lk. 15:11ff.), for Christ has added to our knowledge of expiation, it remains true that the confession of one's sins is basic (see also 1 Jn. 1:9). Rom. 4:7f. quotes part of our Psalm. Forgiveness was the mission of the Savior and in the Church continues in the Mystery-sign of mercy. The evident joy of the penitent, who emerges from the sacramental sign, is of the Holy Spirit (see also Rom. 7:15-25). We pray this Psalm with the Church every I Thursday (vespers).

Psalm 33 (32)

Rejoice in the LORD, O you righteous!
Praise befits the upright.
2Praise the LORD with the lyre,
make melody to him with the harp of ten strings!
3Sing to him a new song,
play skilfully on the strings, with loud shouts.

4For the word of the LORD is upright;
and all his work is done in faithfulness.
5He loves righteousness and justice;
the earth is full of the steadfast love of the LORD.

6By the word of the LORD the heavens were made,
and all their host by the breath of his mouth.
7He gathered the waters of the sea as in a bottle;
he put the deeps in storehouses.

8Let all the earth fear the LORD,
let all the inhabitants of the world stand in awe of him!
9For he spoke, and it came to be;
he commanded, and it stood forth.

10The LORD brings the counsel of the nations to nought;
he frustrates the plans of the peoples.
11The counsel of the LORD stands for ever,
the thoughts of his heart to all generations.
12Blessed is the nation whose God is the LORD,
the people whom he has chosen as his heritage!

13The LORD looks down from heaven,
he sees all the sons of men;
14from where he sits enthroned he looks forth
on all the inhabitants of the earth,
15he who fashions the hearts of them all,
and observes all their deeds.

16A king is not saved by his great army;
a warrior is not delivered by his great strength.
17The war horse is a vain hope for victory,
and by its great might it cannot save.

[18]Behold, the eye of the LORD is on those who fear him,
   on those who hope in his steadfast love,
[19]that he may deliver their soul from death,
   and keep them alive in famine.

[20]Our soul waits for the LORD;
   he is our help and shield.
[21]Yea, our heart is glad in him,
   because we trust in his holy name.
[22]Let thy steadfast love, O LORD, be upon us,
   even as we hope in thee.

Praise of Divine Providence

The opening verses of this Psalm summon us to great jubilation, with new song and the best of music, because of the Lord's goodness and greatness, His care of the world and mankind, especially for His chosen ones. The people of God are assembled in public worship, whence they draw their entire religious inspiration and dedication to the Lord. Among His glories is His creative power, for by the mere breath of His word all came into being. According to ancient imagery, He can contain the oceans in a small flask. And He watches over the doings of mankind, which gives meaning to the history of all the nations.

With verse 12 we come to His special revelation: "Blessed is the nation whose God is the Lord, the people whom he has chosen as his heritage." He who fashioned all men, knows His product, their inmost thinking and works. He will frustrate whatever is not according to His eternal plan, while He blesses those who in love carry out His holy will. The souls of those who fear Him wait for His coming in gladness. This points to the future and the hopes He holds out to them.

Rulers of nations might well ponder this Psalm since the arms race will come to nothing but grief and famine. No king is saved by his armies and weapons, be they horses or nuclear bombs. God can save from hunger and the sword, and He will prevail because not only did He make them out of nothing, but governs all by eternal decrees. We who live in affluence and devour or destroy the bread of the poor, ought to pray this Psalm with fear and trembling, for God is with the poor. The sinful abuse of the goods of this world He will mightily punish. The Word of God is sharper than a two-edged sword (Heb. 4:12). His faithful ones, on the other hand, can pray verses 20-22 with joyful trust.

The future in the Psalm is now, the new age and era of Christ. He is the Word of God made flesh, the Son of God and the Son of Mary. All things were created through Him (Jn. 1:1-3). He holds the governance of nations and individuals. In Him we have total confidence, "For in him all the fulness of God was pleased to dwell" (Col. 1:19; see also the previous verses). He is the fulness of this Psalm. Nothing can separate us from Him and His love (Rom. 8:31-39). With Him our dwelling is in heaven (Phil. 3:20; see also Eph. 1:17-23). He is the King of history and the King of our hearts. The Son of Mary will rule recalcitrant nations with a rod of iron (Rev. 12:5), while He will lead His faithful with a shepherd's staff.

If our faith in Him is living, we will sing the new song loudly, "To Him be dominion forever!" His Bride, the Church, sings it with the certitude of present salvation and the promise of final victory (Mt. 16:18). This Psalm occurs on Trinity Sunday (office of readings), the feasts of martyrs (office of readings), I Tuesdays (lauds), and verse 19 on the feast of the Sacred Heart.

Psalm 34 (33)

> I will bless the LORD at all times;
>   his praise shall continually be in my mouth.
> ²My soul makes its boast in the LORD;
>   let the afflicted hear and be glad.
> ³O magnify the LORD with me,
>   and let us exalt his name together!
>
> ⁴I sought the LORD, and he answered me,
>   and delivered me from all my fears.
> ⁵Look to him, and be radiant;
>   so your faces shall never be ashamed.
> ⁶This poor man cried, and the LORD heard him,
>   and saved him out of all his troubles.

⁷The angel of the LORD encamps
    around those who fear him, and delivers them.
⁸O taste and see that the LORD is good!
    Happy is the man who takes refuge in him!
⁹O fear the LORD, you his saints,
    for those who fear him have no want!
¹⁰The young lions suffer want and hunger;
    but those who seek the LORD lack no good thing.

¹¹Come, O sons, listen to me,
    I will teach you the fear of the LORD.
¹²What man is there who desires life,
    and covets many days, that he may enjoy good?
¹³Keep your tongue from evil,
    and your lips from speaking deceit,
¹⁴Depart from evil, and do good;
    seek peace, and pursue it.

¹⁵The eyes of the LORD are toward the righteous,
    and his ears toward their cry.
¹⁶The face of the LORD is against evildoers,
    to cut off the remembrance of them from the earth.
¹⁷When the righteous cry for help, the LORD hears,
    and delivers them out of all their troubles.
¹⁸The LORD is near to the brokenhearted,
    and saves the crushed in spirit.

¹⁹Many are the afflictions of the righteous;
    but the LORD delivers him out of them all.
²⁰He keeps all his bones;
    not one of them is broken.
²¹Evil shall slay the wicked;
    and those who hate the righteous will be condemned.

²²The LORD redeems the life of his servants;
    none of those who take refuge in him will be condemned.

Bless the Lord

    This song of praise contains a summary of Jewish Old Testament piety. Living in continual praise comprises fear of the Lord, seeking Him, turning away from evil and doing good, trusting Him in all troubles, making known His bounty, and more. It is the happy life. Being an alphabetic Psalm (a new letter heads each verse in Hebrew), it is somewhat repetitious and loosely knit, but it is easy to pray, delightful, and worth remembering. Many of its sentences have become common wisdom: "The Lord is near to the brokenhearted," "Taste and see that the Lord is good," and "Depart from evil and do good."

It is a Psalm for the poor man: the humble, rejected, the nobodies, the friends of God. The author is one of them; his experience of affliction is first-handed. A real servant of the Lord, his life is not easy, but happy, because the angel of the Lord is encamped all around him (as in the former Sinai days). He never feels that he is alone, as together with the holy community of God he tastes and sees the goodness of God.

The poor man knows happiness. Happiness is holiness. Nothing is wanting to him who loves (fears) the Lord. As for Job and for Christ, suffering brings him closer to God and happiness. St. Benedict in his *Rule* urges his monks to live by this Psalm: keep your tongue from evil and see good days, "Come, I will teach you the fear of the Lord," and he formed a community of men under God to live according to this Psalm. One point of rule was to learn the Psalms by heart, and he capitalized on this one. A greater example is the Mother of God who took it to heart and "magnified the Lord" as the chosen one among the poor.

If St. Augustine is right in saying that the New Testament lies concealed in the Old and the Old stands revealed in the New, then our Psalm becomes even more important. St. John gives a surprising fulfillment to our verse 20 in the passion of Christ: "Not a bone of him shall be broken" (Jn. 19:36). Peter the apostle quoted verses 12-16, and again, "You have tasted the kindness of the Lord" (in 1 Pet. 3:10-12 and 2:3). All Christians regard our Psalm the more precious as this phrase applies to receiving Christ in holy Communion (coming from the similarity between the Greek words for "Christ" and "goodness").

One could multiply the Lord's praise of the poor and little ones (e.g. Mt. 11:25) and how He built the membership of His Kingdom from among "rejects" and "fools." Doing that would merely prove that St. Augustine was right. The Church praises the Lord with this Psalm on the feast of the Guardian Angels (October 2, vespers) as well as on I and III Saturdays (noon prayer).

Psalm 35 (34)

Contend, O LORD, with those who contend with me;
fight against those who fight against me!
²Take hold of shield and buckler,
and rise for my help!
³Draw the spear and javelin
against my pursuers!
Say to my soul,
"I am your deliverance!"

⁴Let them be put to shame and dishonor
who seek after my life!
Let them be turned back and confounded
who devise evil against me!
⁵Let them be like chaff before the wind,
with the angel of the LORD driving them on!
⁶Let their way be dark and slippery,
with the angel of the LORD pursuing them!

⁷For without cause they hid their net for me;
without cause they dug a pit for my life.
⁸Let ruin come upon them unawares!
And let the net which they hid ensnare them;
let them fall therein to ruin!

⁹Then my soul shall rejoice in the LORD,
exulting in his deliverance.
¹⁰All my bones shall say,
"O LORD, who is like thee,
thou who deliverest the weak
from him who is too strong for him,
the weak and needy from him who despoils him?"

¹¹Malicious witnesses rise up;
>   they ask me of things that I know not.
¹²They requite me evil for good;
>   my soul is forlorn.
¹³But I, when they were sick—
>   I wore sackcloth,
>   I afflicted myself with fasting.
I prayed with head bowed on my bosom,
¹⁴   as though I grieved for my friend or my brother;
I went about as one who laments his mother,
>   bowed down and in mourning.

¹⁵But at my stumbling they gathered in glee,
>   they gathered together against me;
cripples whom I knew not
>   slandered me without ceasing;
¹⁶they impiously mocked more and more,
>   gnashing at me with their teeth.

¹⁷How long, O Lord, wilt thou look on?
>   Rescue me from their ravages,
>   my life from the lions!
¹⁸Then I will thank thee in the great congregation;
>   in the mighty throng I will praise thee.

¹⁹Let not those rejoice over me
>   who are wrongfully my foes,
and let not those wink the eye
>   who hate me without cause.
²⁰For they do not speak peace,
>   but against those who are quiet in the land
>   they conceive words of deceit.
²¹They open wide their mouths against me;
>   they say, "Aha, Aha!
>   our eyes have seen it!"

22Thou hast seen, O LORD; be not silent!
  O Lord, be not far from me!
23Bestir thyself, and awake for my right,
  for my cause, my God and my Lord!
24Vindicate me, O LORD, my God, according to thy righteousness;
  and let them not rejoice over me!
25Let them not say to themselves,
  "Aha, we have our heart's desire!"
 Let them not say, "We have swallowed him up."

26Let them be put to shame and confusion altogether
  who rejoice at my calamity!
 Let them be clothed with shame and dishonor
  who magnify themselves against me!

27Let those who desire my vindication
  shout for joy and be glad,
  and say evermore,
 "Great is the LORD,
  who delights in the welfare of his servant!"
28Then my tongue shall tell of thy righteousness
  and of thy praise all the day long.

Blessed Are They Who Suffer Injustice

Typical of many Psalms that complain to God and beg for justice is this Psalm where an innocent person faces his enemies by facing God. It seems that he, falsely accused at court, follows the customary procedure. Instruments of Satan, those who make lying charges against the good man, slander him, or plot evil snares against him, imitate the devil in every way. Formerly they gnashed their teeth at his good fortune; now they rejoice at his misfortune. When they were in trouble, he fasted for them and wore sackcloth as if mourning for a mother. He prayed for them and rendered good, but all to no avail. He wasted his kindness on them. They return evil for good and seek his death. They strike and tear at him like a pack of animals, holding him up to ridicule, even claiming they saw him do evil. It is a lengthy account of malice that knows no limits.

The world is full of such men who set snares for others. Think of the mercy killers and the abortionists. This Psalm fits perfectly their evil devices. God is still alive and in the picture! And His angels are around to do His work. We should pray this Psalm against the evil one that he may fall into the pit he has dug for others. We need unshaken trust in the Lord in whom there is salvation. He will come to the rescue as He is always near His faithful poor ones. Sometimes the prayer may rise to our lips, "How long, Lord, will you look on?" We wait for Him who has the strong weapons, symbolized by the arms of warfare. God knows when is the time for retribution.

The Psalm contains the story of Christ and Christians. It gives a preview of the Savior's tragedy and enshrines forever the complaints, trust, and victory of the poor man. On every page of the Gospel, Christ's enemies are out to catch Him. They carefully planned their sinful strategy. They accused Him of blasphemy, of stirring revolt, even of possession by the devil. The leaders from Galilee to Jerusalem tried to make Him an enemy of the people and a sinner. At His trial they set up false witnesses. Former mutual enemies, like Pilate and Herod, became friends to secure His defeat. Behind all this hid the prince of this world. Never was an accused man more innocent than Jesus, who sees this Psalm fulfilled in His own regard: "They hated me without cause" (v. 19 and Jn. 15:25).

The final victory of God and the Poor Man was the resurrection. He who reaped evil for good now triumphs and gives praise in the assembly of His just disciples. Now we realize how "Your sorrow will turn into joy" (Jn. 16:20). We learn patience by suffering, and evil with God's grace will never overcome us, no matter what transpires (Acts 9:5). Also with the help of many brethren, we endure, keeping our eyes on Jesus. We cling to Him and persevere in running the race (Heb. 12: 1-6). The whole of God's world is on our side, including the angels, as we give glory and finish the work that Christ left us. The Church prays our Psalm on Fridays of the I week (office of readings). This means that Christ lives and prays in His members (see Acts 9:5).

Psalm 36 (35)

Transgression speaks to the wicked
 deep in his heart;
there is no fear of God before his eyes.
²For he flatters himself in his own eyes
 that his iniquity cannot be found out and hated.
³The words of his mouth are mischief and deceit;
 he has ceased to act wisely and do good.

⁴He plots mischief while on his bed;
 he sets himself in a way that is not good;
 he spurns not evil.

⁵Thy steadfast love, O LORD, extends to the heavens,
 thy faithfulness to the clouds.
⁶Thy righteousness is like the mountains of God,
 thy judgments are like the great deep;
 man and beast thou savest, O LORD.

⁷How precious is thy steadfast love, O God!
 The children of men take refuge in the shadow of thy wings.
⁸They feast on the abundance of thy house,
 and thou givest them drink from the river of thy delights.
⁹For with thee is the fountain of life;
 in thy light do we see light.

¹⁰O continue thy steadfast love to those who know thee,
 and thy salvation to the upright of heart!
¹¹Let not the foot of arrogance come upon me,
 nor the hand of the wicked drive me away.
¹²There the evildoers lie prostrate,
 they are thrust down, unable to rise.

Godlessness and Godliness

The sinner is godless. The absence of God chills his whole being, just as waters freeze over and harden when the warm sun recedes. Sin speaks with a satanic voice to the frozen heart and robs him of the fear of God. Then with a false heart he also speaks with a foul mouth, saying to himself that God does not hear or see. Even at night, when the thought of God's presence should be uppermost, he devises new evil. Sin seems to have independent existence and therefore speaks with a voice, none other than the prince of this world of darkness. We can say then that the person of Satan is behind every sin, speaking to the sinner. History shows that the power of evil is great. Today Satan's way resembles a tornado path of crime. God's creatures become His enemies.

Verse 5 by a sudden turn makes godliness the central theme. It wants to crystallize our attitude against sin. God's kindness, faithfulness, just judgments, and steadfast love are like the mountains, immovable like His Providence. His plans are deep and inscrutable (see also Rom. 11:33). In His house His friends, "who take refuge in the shadow of Thy wings," enjoy the rich delights of every gift and grace, fountains and streams of life and light. In the light of faith we already perceive that ultimate godly existence in His land, where the divine light and festivity lasts forever. A final warning, wherein the night of the sinners shrouds them in darkness and prostration and contrasts with the land of blessed light and full communion with God, is a prayer for perseverance.

The perfections of God reside fully in Christ (Tit. 3:4f.; Rom. 3: 21-26; 5:8). In Him we possess the fountain of eternal life and banqueting at the messianic table of delights. He told us that He is the Truth and Light (Jn. 1:4f.; 3:18; 8:12), and He wants us to take His Word seriously. He wants us to abound in the merciful kindness of our God (1 Jn. 4:15f.). The more of godliness is in us, the farther removed are we from godlessness. Rom. 3:18 quotes our verse 1: "There is no fear of God before his [the sinner's] eyes." In the Church we pray this Psalm on the feast of the Sacred Heart (office of readings) and on I Wednesdays (lauds).

Psalm 37 (36)

Fret not yourself because of the wicked,
    be not envious of wrongdoers!
²For they will soon fade like the grass,
    and wither like the green herb.

³Trust in the LORD, and do good;
    so you will dwell in the land, and enjoy security.
⁴Take delight in the LORD,
    and he will give you the desires of your heart.

⁵Commit your way to the Lord;
    trust in him, and he will act.
⁶He will bring forth your vindication as the light,
    and your right as the noonday.

⁷Be still before the Lord, and wait patiently for him;
    fret not yourself over him who prospers in his way,
    over the man who carries out evil devices!

⁸Refrain from anger, and forsake wrath!
    Fret not yourself; it tends only to evil.
⁹For the wicked shall be cut off;
    but those who wait for the Lord shall possess the land.

¹⁰Yet a little while, and the wicked will be no more;
    though you look well at his place, he will not be there.
¹¹But the meek shall possess the land,
    and delight themselves in abundant prosperity.

¹²The wicked plots against the righteous,
    and gnashes his teeth at him;
¹³but the Lord laughs at the wicked,
    for he sees that his day is coming.

¹⁴The wicked draw the sword and bend their bows,
    to bring down the poor and needy,
    to slay those who walk uprightly;
¹⁵their sword shall enter their own heart,
    and their bows shall be broken.

¹⁶Better is a little that the righteous has
    than the abundance of many wicked.
¹⁷For the arms of the wicked shall be broken;
    but the Lord upholds the righteous.

¹⁸The Lord knows the days of the blameless,
    and their heritage will abide for ever;
¹⁹they are not put to shame in evil times,
    in the days of famine they have abundance.

20But the wicked perish;
    the enemies of the LORD are like the glory of the pastures,
    they vanish—like smoke they vanish away.

21The wicked borrows, and cannot pay back,
    but the righteous is generous and gives;
22for those blessed by the LORD shall possess the land,
    but those cursed by him shall be cut off.

23The steps of a man are from the LORD,
    and he establishes him in whose way he delights;
24though he fall, he shall not be cast headlong,
    for the LORD is the stay of his hand.

25I have been young, and now am old;
    yet I have not seen the righteous forsaken
    or his children begging bread.
26He is ever giving liberally and lending,
    and his children become a blessing.

27Depart from evil, and do good;
    so shall you abide for ever.
28For the LORD loves justice;
    he will not forsake his saints.

The righteous shall be preserved for ever,
    but the children of the wicked shall be cut off.
29The righteous shall possess the land,
    and dwell upon it for ever.

30The mouth of the righteous utters wisdom,
    and his tongue speaks justice.
31The law of his God is in his heart;
    his steps do not slip.

32The wicked watches the righteous,
    and seeks to slay him.
33The LORD will not abandon him to his power,
    or let him be condemned when he is brought to trial.

34Wait for the LORD, and keep to his way,
   and he will exalt you to possess the land;
   you will look on the destruction of the wicked.

35I have seen a wicked man overbearing,
   and towering like a cedar of Lebanon.
36Again I passed by, and lo, he was no more;
   though I sought him, he could not be found.

37Mark the blameless man, and behold the upright,
   for there is posterity for the man of peace.
38But transgressors shall be altogether destroyed;
   the posterity of the wicked shall be cut off.

39The salvation of the righteous is from the LORD;
   he is their refuge in the time of trouble.
40The LORD helps them and delivers them;
   he delivers them from the wicked, and saves them,
   because they take refuge in him.

Contentment in God

Contentment with God's dispositions for the just and unjust is poverty of spirit. Patience with the Lord and waiting for His good time to reward and punish will calm our anger and jealousy over the prosperity of the sinner. Before we can qualify for life in God, we must learn the transitoriness of wealth and the purpose of suffering. The author offers encouragement to the wavering and suggests moderation in ownership of the land, always serene trust in God's decisions. This Psalm of blessedness on earth reads like proverbs of wisdom by which to guide our life. It is an acrostic, alphabetic Psalm (where each stanza opens with a new letter), which explains the somewhat loose order of ideas.

The theme of the Psalm is consistent: "Be not envious of wrongdoers. . . . Trust in the Lord and do good, and enjoy security." Keeping this in mind, we become forward-looking when answering the disturbing questions of the just: Why do the wicked prosper? Why the suffering of good people? Why does God let the sinful rich get away with dishonesty and exploiting the poor? God in His Providence takes care of the present and future for the poor. "In the days of famine they have abundance." In the end "there is posterity [a future] for the man of peace" (v. 37).

Surely in those far-off days immediate and material answers to prayer were needed to sustain the faith of people (and today God answers our prayer sufficiently to engender strong trust). But the future time of God is decisive. No less than twelve times does the author point to the future, to the Lord's coming day, to possession that lasts forever, to future blessings of offspring, etc. Our Psalm awaits the New Testament revelation of Christ.

The world has not changed. There are the rich and poor. And the poor want to be rich because the temptation to wealth and power overcomes them. This Psalm directs our ambitions and trust in Providence gives us a right balance. We are pilgrims and like Abraham we live in tents "as in a foreign land" (Heb. 11:9). God knows what we need. Present goods are a stepping stone to heaven. "Cast your burden on the Lord and he will sustain you" (Ps. 55:22). The Psalm does not suggest neglect and destitution, but neither does it advocate unlimited wealth. Practical faith and reason look to the Lord for the golden way.

"Blessed are the meek, for they shall inherit the land" (Mt. 5:5). The Savior here quotes our verse 11. Without worrying about the way the Lord did His part in the Old Law, we live by the clear light of Christ. His answer remains the same: God's is the future. Jesus taught us how to pray this Psalm. He perfected the Law. He uttered woes for the rich (Lk. 6:24), warned against the security of abundance (Lk. 12:14ff., 21), praised self-denial (Mk. 8:34) and praised abandoning the best (Mk. 10:29f.), but all for His sake ("Take delight in the Lord," [4]). Then "you shall abide forever" (v. 27). Our verse 6 resembles Lk. 1:78: Christ is our Light from on high. We pray this Psalm on III Tuesdays at lauds.

Psalm 38 (37)

> O LORD, rebuke me not in thy anger,
>   nor chasten me in thy wrath!
> [2]For thy arrows have sunk into me,
>   and thy hand has come down on me.

³There is no soundness in my flesh
    because of thy indignation;
there is no health in my bones
    because of my sin.
⁴For my iniquities have gone over my head;
    they weigh like a burden too heavy for me.

⁵My wounds grow foul and fester
    because of my foolishness,
⁶I am utterly bowed down and prostrate;
    all the day I go about mourning.
⁷For my loins are filled with burning,
    and there is no soundness in my flesh.
⁸I am utterly spent and crushed;
    I groan because of the tumult of my heart.

⁹Lord, all my longing is known to thee,
    my sighing is not hidden from thee.
¹⁰My heart throbs, my strength fails me;
    and the light of my eyes—it also has gone from me.
¹¹My friends and companions stand aloof from my plague,
    and my kinsmen stand afar off.

¹²Those who seek my life lay their snares,
    those who seek my hurt speak of ruin,
    and meditate treachery all the day long.

¹³But I am like a deaf man, I do not hear,
    like a dumb man who does not open his mouth.
¹⁴Yea, I am like a man who does not hear,
    and in whose mouth are no rebukes.

¹⁵But for thee, O Lord, do I wait;
    it is thou, O Lord my God, who wilt answer.
¹⁶For I pray, "Only let them not rejoice over me,
    who boast against me when my foot slips!"

[17]For I am ready to fall,
 and my pain is ever with me.
[18]I confess my iniquity,
 I am sorry for my sin.
[19]Those who are my foes without cause are mighty,
 and mighty are those who hate me wrongfully.
[20]Those who render me evil for good
 are my adversaries because I follow after good.

[21]Do not forsake me, O LORD!
 O my God, be not far from me!
[22]Make haste to help me,
 O Lord, my salvation!

Mercy, Lord

As one of the penitential Psalms (see Psalm 6), this Psalm depicts the moral suffering of guilt as the ultimate pain and all other suffering as a picture of sin. The author describes in detail intense physical disease, besides grieving over lost friends and neighbors. He fears the future and believes that God inflicted all this because of his sins and folly, which he openly confesses.

Admission of sin before God is part of contrition. Whether the author deserved suffering for sin is for God to judge. He repents and in candid humility opens his heart to God. All his longing is for God's forgiveness. Although he is not without enemies who gloat over him, he does not rebuke them and in silence awaits the Lord. Let the foes' slander and gossip take its course. Speaking of God's "wrath" is a human way of regarding His attitude to sin, but His "anger" is just. In every way the sinner is at the mercy of God.

The enemies go beyond justice and charity in their rash zeal, interpreting the sickness of the poor victim. The same happens today. Even if a drunken driver smashes his car and his health, he should receive forgiveness and a helping hand of mercy. We pray this Psalm first for ourselves, then for the countless persons who are wasting away in their hopeless and helpless condition. A friend with a word of sympathy and affection can help a patient in sanctifying himself or herself in suffering. We are all sinners before God. Whether we offer ourselves in sickness for our own guilt or the sins of others, we can truthfully say with the praying Church, "Lord, we are justly afflicted for our sins." God does us no injustice (Rom. 7:14-20 and 1 Jn. 1:8f.).

A right conscience makes satisfaction for sin. Without that we could well be in love with our sins.

Christ Jesus revealed to us the redemptive value of suffering for others. His suffering was all vicarious. Instead of being finger-pointing enemies, we are called to be friends of sinners and the sick, like Christ the great victim soul, who turned silent in the face of lying accusations, who prayed for those who killed Him. The atonement lesson is part of the Word of God: "For our sake he made him to be sin, who knew no sin, so that in him we might become the righteousness of God" (2 Cor. 5:21). Again: "He committed no sin, no guile was found on his lips. When he was reviled, he did not revile in turn; when he suffered, he did not threaten; but he trusted to him who judges justly. . . . By his wounds you have been healed" (1 Pet. 2:22-24).

On Good Friday and every II Friday we use this Psalm (office of readings), as the dying Savior reenacts in our midst His love in suffering. We can also use it on other occasions, such as penitential services.

Psalm 39 (38)

> I said, "I will guard my ways,
> that I may not sin with my tongue;
> I will bridle my mouth,
> so long as the wicked are in my presence."
> ²I was dumb and silent,
> I held my peace to no avail;
> my distress drew worse,
>
> ³   my heart became hot within me.
> As I mused, the fire burned;
> then I spoke with my tongue:
>
> ⁴"Lord, let me know my end,
> and what is the measure of my days;
> let me know how fleeting my life is!
> ⁵Behold, thou hast made my days a few handbreadths,
> and my lifetime is as nothing in thy sight.
> Surely every man stands as a mere breath!
> ⁶   Surely man goes about as a shadow!
> Surely for nought are they in turmoil;
> man heaps up, and knows not who will gather!

7"And now, Lord, for what do I wait?
  My hope is in thee.
8Deliver me from all my transgressions.
  Make me not the scorn of the fool!
9I am dumb, I do not open my mouth;
  for it is thou who hast done it.
10Remove thy stroke from me;
  I am spent by the blows of thy hand.
11When thou dost chasten man
  with rebukes for sin,
 thou dost consume like a moth what is dear to him;
  surely every man is a mere breath!

12"Hear my prayer, O Lord,
  and give ear to my cry;
  hold not thy peace at my tears!
 For I am thy passing guest,
  a sojourner, like all my fathers.
13Look away from me, that I may know gladness,
  before I depart and be no more!"

Life's Pilgrimage

In dialogue with God, the author admits his flare-up of speech and then turns silent, apparently suffering an affliction sent by the Lord. While he reflects on the brevity and illusions of life, he asks God to deliver him from the scourge of the enemy's taunt. Sinning with the tongue is a prominent theme of the whole Psalter, and the author asks pardon for all his transgressions. He admits that God's chastening hand lies heavy upon him and begs Him to turn away His angry face. The whole Psalm is somewhat unusual in contents, but the author does not lose faith and trust in God.

Twice he speaks about the short span of life, which passes like a breath or phantom. He sees himself as a pilgrim, a wayfarer. It is the path of accepting God's will and man's dependency on Him for the gift of life. The things that man works for and clings to are like cobwebs that one sweeps away. Man saves and hoards the goods of this world, not knowing who will get them when he dies. If a man lives for his bank account and looks forward to a life of ease, God can call a halt suddenly, as the Lord tells us in Lk. 12:20: "Fool! This night your soul is required of you; and the things you have prepared, whose will they be?" Security in God alone avails and makes happy. "My hope is in thee" (v. 7). With this he recovers his sense of values. (These sentiments remind us of Ecclesiastes, or Qoheleth.)

By contrast, Christ directs our knowledge beyond death. God is the author of life, and Christ loved life, but He loved the will of the Father more. Jesus came that we might have the more abundant life (Jn. 10:10). There is more to life than we can see. The present life (and goods) exist for the sake of the future. "He who loves his life loses it" (Jn. 12:25), "And he who loses his life for my sake will find it" (Mt. 10: 39). This present life has great value for the next life. Our Lord proved it by giving us a sacrament of His special presence to those who are sick and in danger of life (see Jas. 5:14f.), all in the interest of salvation-life.

We pray this Psalm for ourselves and the world that holds life cheap. The divine thinking in it ennobles all human life with a spiritual, Christian culture. As we treasure the Psalm and live fruitfully as passing guests on God's earth till life's pilgrimage is over, we make this world a better place to live in and prepare for the higher life in His blessed Kingdom. On the II Wednesdays we pray it with the Church at her office of readings.

Psalm 40 (39)

I waited patiently for the Lord;
> he inclined to me and heard my cry.
²He drew me up from the desolate pit,
> out of the miry bog,
and set my feet upon a rock,
> making my steps secure.
³He put a new song in my mouth,
> a song of praise to our God.
Many will see and fear,
> and put their trust in the Lord.

⁴Blessed is the man who makes
     the LORD his trust,
  who does not turn to the proud,
     to those who go astray after false gods!
⁵Thou hast multiplied, O LORD my God,
     thy wondrous deeds and thy thoughts toward us;
     none can compare with thee!
  Were I to proclaim and tell of them,
     they would be more than can be numbered.

⁶Sacrifice and offering thou dost not desire;
     but thou hast given me an open ear.
  Burnt offering and sin offering
     thou hast not required.
⁷Then I said, "Lo, I come;
     in the roll of the book it is written of me;
⁸I delight to do thy will, O my God;
     thy law is within my heart."

⁹I have told the glad news of deliverance
     in the great congregation;
  lo, I have not restrained my lips,
     as thou knowest, O LORD.
¹⁰I have not hid thy saving help within my heart,
     I have spoken of thy faithfulness and thy salvation;
  I have not concealed thy steadfast love and thy faithfulness
     from the great congregation.

¹¹Do not thou, O LORD, withhold
     thy mercy from me,
  let thy steadfast love and thy faithfulness
     ever preserve me!
¹²For evils have encompassed me
     without number;
  my iniquities have overtaken me,
     till I cannot see;
  they are more than the hairs of my head;
     my heart fails me.

¹³Be pleased, O Lord, to deliver me!
   O Lord, make haste to help me!
¹⁴Let them be put to shame and confusion altogether
   who seek to snatch away my life;
  let them be turned back and brought to dishonor
   who desire my hurt!
¹⁵Let them be appalled because of their shame
   who say to me, "Aha, Aha!"

¹⁶But may all who seek thee
   rejoice and be glad in thee;
  may those who love thy salvation
   say continually, "Great is the Lord!"
¹⁷As for me, I am poor and needy;
   but the Lord takes thought for me.
Thou art my help and my deliverer;
   do not tarry, O my God!

I Come to Do Your Will, O God

Prayer frequently does not proceed on logical lines, and this Psalm is an example of abrupt changes. It contains great wisdom for our conversion to God, chiefly that of inner obedience to Him. Beginning with thanks and praise (vv. 1-5) for God's countless wonderful deeds, with his feet firmly set on the rock of God's security, the author proclaims to others (to the assembly) what God has done for him. That means a community of faith where many share in the praises of the Lord.

Although God ordered sacrifices in the Old Law (Lev. 6-7), He rejected empty ritual when it was mechanical and divorced from right moral conduct (see Is. 1:11ff.; Jer. 7:21-23 "obey my voice"; Dt. 6:24f.). Verses 6-8 remind us of the rejection of Saul as king for preferring sacrifice to God's more evident will (see 1 Sam. 15:22f.). The purpose of cult is love and obedience. The heart of all religion is loving God out of faith. Faith tells us what God wants and says; love then gives free obedience.

The author reiterates his call for help (vv. 11-12), for God's mercy, because of guilt, overwhelming sinfulness, as he is aware of having refused love and obedience. Then follows Psalm 70 in its entirety, another cry in affliction coming against enemies about to triumph. In the final verse, and in "Great is the Lord," he returns to the opening of the Psalm. So we can pray it as one Psalm. "Do not tarry, O my God" fits almost any Psalm.

Our Psalm has a strong messianic passage (vv. 6-8) which the author of Hebrews (10:5-10) applies to the Son of God coming into the world at His incarnation. That means God intended it for Christ. He had reached the end of Old Testament sacrificial ritual, and now inaugurated the new. By taking on human nature, a body, the Son of God became Mediator. He became High Priest, Altar, and sacrificial Gift and spoke the offering prayer: "Lo, I come; in the roll of the book it is written of me: I delight to do thy will, O my God; thy law is within my heart." "And by that will we have been sanctified through the offering of the body of Jesus Christ once for all" (Heb. 10:10). This sacrificial will of Jesus runs through His whole life, from the cradle to the Cross, like the thread that gives pattern to a tapestry, the great revelation of His purpose, the fulfillment of Psalm 40.

We pray this Psalm with Christ when we make the will of the Father our basic praise. That will was His very bread and food (Jn. 14:31 and 10:17f., especially 4:34), His triumph on the Cross to which all else was subordinate. It gives us fellowship in the Church and a new song of responsible witness in the assembly of the People of God. Not to proclaim God's wonders and trust would be sinful silence. Concealing the truth from the peoples of the earth is against God's will. In this process of praise our full powers must come to expression, for the lesson of this Man's suffering reveals the thoughts of God and becomes our salvation. Our prayer is most powerful, when we pray with the Church, as she uses this Psalm on Good Friday (noon), on II Mondays (noon) and for the dead (office of readings).

Psalm 41 (40)

Blessed is he who considers the poor!
The LORD delivers him in the day of trouble;
²the LORD protects him and keeps him alive;
he is called blessed in the land;
thou dost not give him up to the will of his enemies.
³The LORD sustains him on his sickbed;
in his illness thou healest all his infirmities.

⁴As for me, I said, "O LORD, be gracious to me;
  heal me, for I have sinned against thee!"
⁵My enemies say of me in malice:
  "When will he die, and his name perish?"
⁶And when one comes to see me, he utters empty words,
  while his heart gathers mischief;
  when he goes out, he tells it abroad.
⁷All who hate me whisper together about me;
  they imagine the worst for me.

⁸They say, "A deadly thing has fastened upon him;
  he will not rise again from where he lies."
⁹Even my bosom friend in whom I trusted,
  who ate of my bread, has lifted his heel against me.
¹⁰But do thou, O LORD, be gracious to me,
  and raise me up, that I may requite them!

¹¹By this I know that thou art pleased with me,
  in that my enemy has not triumphed over me.
¹²But thou hast upheld me because of my integrity,
  and set me in thy presence for ever.

¹³Blessed be the LORD, the God of Israel,
  from everlasting to everlasting!
  Amen and Amen.

Friend of the Poor

The lessons that God teaches us through inspired prayer are hard but happy, serious and blessed ones. Just as the Lord God beatifies the poor by His prior action, He now extends the same blessedness to all who take care of them. Even in this life, they are blessed who espouse the cause of the lowly. The cry to God in one's own sin and misery includes equal concern for all of God's favorites. One can establish the norms of true friendship from this Psalm.

On the wrong side are the "friends" (think of Job's "friends"), who utter "empty words," but out of sight and behind their backs betray the poor with their insincere speech and whispering slander. False phrases cut deeper than sharp knives. Many a "close" friend, who eats at our table, goes his way and does what this Psalm says—lets his evil imagination confuse sickness with sin. The author prays that his enemy may not triumph over him and hand him over. Let it suffice that God watches all that transpires and can take care of the common enemy.

The Savior was betrayed by His own follower and friend, who ate at His table and promptly went out and collected cheap money for His Master's death. Like Judas, all who are obstinate in sin reap the malediction that Christ spoke over the unfaithful Jerusalem (Lk. 19:41-44), or the unfruitful fig tree (Mt. 21:19-21), or the murderous traitors at the wedding table (Mt. 22:2-7), or against the pharisees who exploited the poor in the name of religion (see Mt. 23). But Christ went the way of the Cross because He came to heal and forgive. So He continues to go through our times and places hearing the cries of the poor, especially penitent sinners, and refusing to revenge Himself.

Jesus tried to convert Judas by calling him "Friend!" But there was no response. At the Last Supper, He quotes our Psalm, verse 9: "Even my bosom friend in whom I trusted, who ate of my bread, has lifted his heel against me" (Jn. 13:18; see also 6:71). Our mission and whole apostolate is to revolutionize the world with Christ's mercy. Instead of judging and condemning those "who kick their heel" against the God-given life of the unborn, we must pray and work for their conversion. While God will deal ultimately with sinners, as the Psalm says to induce faith, Christ gave us new light with His words: "Blessed are the poor in spirit . . ." (Mt. 5:3), which includes our extending mercy to others, "Blessed are the merciful" (v. 7).

The final verse 13 is a doxology of praise which ends Book I of the Psalms and is like a "Glory be. . . ." This should not obscure the great verse preceding it: "Thou hast set me in thy presence for ever." After teaching us many things, this Psalm directs our final joy to Christ's presence, where our modicum of suffering undergoes a great transfer to glory. Then we will see "that my enemy has not triumphed over me" (a verse that we pray on the Immaculate Conception feast at II vespers). Verse 2 is a traditional prayer for the Pope, and the whole Psalm occurs on Fridays of the I week (vespers).

Psalms 42 and 43 (41 and 42)

As a hart longs
    for flowing streams,
so longs my soul
    for thee, O God.
²My soul thirsts for God,
    for the living God.
When shall I come and behold
    the face of God?
³My tears have been my food
    day and night,
while men say to me continually,
    "Where is your God?"

⁴These things I remember,
    as I pour out my soul:
how I went with the throng,
    and led them in procession to the house of God,
with glad shouts and songs of thanksgiving,
    a multitude keeping festival.
⁵Why are you cast down, O my soul,
    and why are you disquieted within me?
Hope in God; for I shall again praise him,
    my help ⁶and my God.

My soul is cast down within me,
    therefore I remember thee
from the land of Jordan and of Hermon,
    from Mount Mizar,
⁷Deep calls to deep
    at the thunder of thy cataracts;
all thy waves and thy billows
    have gone over me.
⁸By day the LORD commands his steadfast love;
    and at night his song is with me,
    a prayer to the God of my life.

[9]I say to God, my rock:
"Why hast thou forgotten me?
Why go I mourning
because of the oppression of the enemy?"
[10]As with a deadly wound in my body,
my adversaries taunt me,
while they say to me continually,
"Where is your God?"

[11]Why are you cast down, O my soul,
and why are you disquieted within me?
Hope in God; for I shall again praise him,
my help and my God.

* * *

Vindicate me, O God, and defend my cause
against all ungodly people;
from deceitful and unjust men deliver me!
[2]For thou art the God in whom I take refuge;
why hast thou cast me off?
Why go I mourning
because of the oppression of the enemy?

[3]Oh send out thy light and thy truth;
let them lead me,
let them bring me to thy holy hill
and to thy dwelling!
[4]Then I will go to the altar of God,
to God my exceeding joy;
and I will praise thee with the lyre,
O God, my God.

[5]Why are you cast down, O my soul,
and why are you disquieted within me?
Hope in God; for I shall again praise him,
my help and my God.

Longing for God

These two Psalms were originally one, as the refrain shows. Together they express the same desire for God's face. And together they

deserve comment. Hounded by enemies, the author is fleeing in exile. Trouble overwhelms him. Even the powerful wonders of nature (cataracts, deep chasms, billows, mighty Hermon, etc.) echo the threats and dangers. All their beauty hardens into personal suffering. Tears are his food. He is athirst for God and for the signs of His presence.

The author's greatest pain is absence from Jerusalem, its Temple, the Altar, from God Himself. His desire for the holy places, "the face of God," grows with distance. Homesickness for the Altar is the cry of this man, who compares the yearning thirst of a deer for running water to his own longing for God's Altar. Here we have not merely lyricism of high quality, but profound Hebrew piety touching the realm of mysticism. Even the taunts of enemies, "Where is your God?" sharpens his pain. But his trust grows stronger. "Hope in God!" Hope means he will again take his place leading the throng in worship, in songs of praise and thanks. God commands steadfast love.

This Psalm is decisive not only for the Old Testament pious Jew but also for Christian piety in the New Testament. As no believing Jew could bypass the symbols of God's self-revealing presence (Sion, Jerusalem, Temple, Altar), so no disciple of Christ can bypass the fulfilment of them in the sacred liturgy. The liturgy is the new world of Christ's Signs. He is actively present in our midst, truly present. We must love and yearn for these Signs as firmly as we love and long for Christ. He who called Himself the Temple ("Destroy this temple. . . .") is also the Victim of sacrifice. The Church calls His Body the Altar (dedication of Holy Savior basilica, lessons, "Christ is the Altar"). Absence from Christ means absence from God. "No one comes to the Father but by me" (Jn. 14:6).

Where is our devotion to the Altar, "our exceeding joy" in the God of the Altar? Formerly every Mass opened at the foot of the Altar with Psalm 43. Now the Church uses it to accompany Christ's ascent to Calvary during Passiontide. The true maker of the Altar is not the architect or artist, but the consecrating bishop who makes it come alive with the fire of the Holy Spirit of Christ. That is the divine flame which consumes our gifts. Unbelievers still taunt us with "Where is your God?" as they did Jesus on the Cross. "He trusts in God; let God deliver him now. . . ." (Mt. 27:43) In fulfillment of Psalm 42, Jesus thirsted on the Cross as a wounded deer (see also Lk. 22:15), and He now leads the throng "in procession to the house of God." He is the living Center of the whole liturgical Mystery (Vatican II).

He is present, and our longing for Him grows keener, since our senses cannot see Him. "We walk by faith, not by sight" (see 2 Cor. 5:6ff.). All our longing is for the Lord, now at the earthly Rock-Altar, symbolic of the heavenly one (Heb. 10:19-22; Rev. 9:13, etc.). Absence from Christ is all sorrow and darkness. At His Altar we live in His light and victory. Gloriously present, He purifies the members of His Temple, as in His historical lifetime.

Until His resurrection He lived in exile. Now He is at home and leads us pilgrims and "exiles in this vale of tears" to the Father. Our faith is vital. Let our hope, too, be vital. With Christ the Lord we go to the Father. As a token of our total desire for heaven, we repeat the refrain with our last strength: "Why are you cast down, O my soul, and why are you disquieted within me? Hope in God; for I shall again praise him, my help and my God."

This Psalm can become our springboard into higher prayer, a Christ-mysticism. We have to do our best at giving an echo in our hearts to its phrases: "God, the living God," "I shall again praise him," "O God, my God," "Send out thy light and thy truth," "My help and my God," "My soul longs for thee, O God." The Church uses this Psalm also on Corpus Christi, on Easter, on Monday and Tuesday lauds and for her departed. The newly baptized once sang it on the way to the Altar of the Eucharist.

Psalm 44 (43)

We have heard with our ears, O God,
    our fathers have told us,
what deeds thou didst perform in their days,
    in the days of old:
²thou with thy own hand didst drive out the nations,
    but them thou didst plant;
thou didst afflict the peoples,
    but them thou didst set free;
³for not by their own sword did they win the land,
    nor did their own arm give them victory;
but thy right hand, and thy arm,
    and the light of thy countenance;
    for thou didst delight in them.

⁴Thou art my King and my God,
  who ordainest victories for Jacob.
⁵Through thee we push down our foes;
  through thy name we tread down our assailants.
⁶For not in my bow do I trust,
  nor can my sword save me.
⁷But thou hast saved us from our foes,
  and hast put to confusion those who hate us.
⁸In God we have boasted continually,
  and we will give thanks to thy name for ever.

⁹Yet thou hast cast us off and abased us,
  and hast not gone out with our armies.
¹⁰Thou hast made us turn back from the foe;
  and our enemies have gotten spoil.
¹¹Thou hast made us like sheep for slaughter,
  and hast scattered us among the nations.
¹²Thou hast sold thy people for a trifle,
  demanding no high price for them.

¹³Thou hast made us the taunt of our neighbors,
  the derision and scorn of those about us.
¹⁴Thou hast made us a byword among the nations,
  a laughingstock among the peoples.
¹⁵All day long my disgrace is before me,
  and shame has covered my face,
¹⁶at the words of the taunters and revilers,
  at the sight of the enemy and the avenger.

¹⁷All this has come upon us,
  though we have not forgotten thee,
  or been false to thy covenant.
¹⁸Our heart has not turned back,
  nor have our steps departed from thy way,
¹⁹that thou shouldst have broken us in the place of jackals,
  and covered us with deep darkness.

²⁰If we had forgotten the name of our God,
  or spread forth our hands to a strange god,
²¹would not God discover this?
  For he knows the secrets of the heart.
²²Nay, for thy sake we are slain all the day long,
  and accounted as sheep for the slaughter.

23Rouse thyself! Why sleepest thou, O Lord?
  Awake! Do not cast us off for ever!
24Why dost thou hide thy face?
  Why dost thou forget our affliction and oppression?
25For our soul is bowed down to the dust;
  our body cleaves to the ground.
26Rise up, come to our help!
  Deliver us for the sake of thy steadfast love!

A Faithful Remnant

The author of this nationwide lament writes in a desperate situation of military defeat and dispersion among the Gentiles, who ridicule the people of God. All their greatness of the past was God's doing. The first eight verses sound like a song of trust and praise for the great days of old, the glories and favors that He worked especially in time of war. What is usually credited to human skill, namely victory in battle, here is attributed to the Lord's right arm. This shows how lively the author's faith was.

Suddenly all is reversed. Their status is entirely different. The nation suffered a decisive defeat, and the enemy plundered them, sold them into captivity, and heaped disgrace upon them. Like helpless sheep they are herded and disposed of. This causes great spiritual danger to faith in God because the outside nations care nothing for their religion. To turn in defeat now to the God of past victories takes new faith. But their God is no ordinary god, not like other gods. Even in defeat and disgrace, He hears the faithful remnant. God is trying them as silver is tried in fire.

Where one expects admission of guilt, there is a cry of innocence (vv. 17-22). Perhaps they had forgotten their sin, as people easily do. God is testing them as never before, for their chastisement seemed prolonged despite their loyalty to the covenant and to God's Name. "For thy sake we are slain all the day long" is the reason the author gives, but God does not owe it to man to give reasons. Then prayer becomes genuine, in "blind" trust. Perhaps we see here a step forward in the life of prayer, both individual and community, a step which leads us to the suffering of Christ "without cause."

With great boldness he exclaims, "Rouse thyself! Why sleepest thou, O Lord?" God does not sleep, ever. Rather man is asleep and needs to wake up. God is at work here, awakening His dormant people.

The facile changes of voice, from "I" to "we," add to this conviction. God lets man think that he is awake, when faith needs new impetus.

We can think here of the "faithful remnant" of Israel spoken of by the prophet Isaiah (53:4-9). "Like a lamb that is led to the slaughter." St. Paul quotes our verse 22 in Rom. 8:36 to exemplify the true love of Christ: "For thy sake we are being killed all the day long; we are regarded as sheep to be slaughtered." Christ Jesus is the Suffering Servant of Isaiah, and we are the flock imitating the Shepherd.

Strong hope is born in suffering with and in Christ. In His Church, which is His Body, He renews the Mystery of His life and death. We share this with Him, as we are His members. Nothing can separate us from the love of Christ (Rom. 8:35), even though our "soul is bowed down to the dust; our body cleaves to the ground." We need to wake up and raise our heads "because [our] redemption is drawing near" (Lk. 21:28). We must even "rejoice in so far as you share Christ's sufferings" (1 Pet. 4:13). Jesus is in the same boat with us. He will quiet the storms in His good time. As the apostles woke Him up, He awakened them to His power and glory. The Church prays this Psalm on II and IV Thursdays (office of readings).

Psalm 45 (44)

My heart overflows with a goodly theme;
I address my verses to the king;
my tongue is like the pen of a ready scribe.

2You are the fairest of the sons of men;
grace is poured upon your lips;
therefore God has blessed you for ever.
3Gird your sword upon your thigh, O mighty one,
in your glory and majesty!

4In your majesty ride forth victoriously
for the cause of truth and to defend the right;
let your right hand teach you dread deeds!
5Your arrows are sharp
in the heart of the king's enemies;
the peoples fall under you.

⁶Your divine throne endures for ever and ever.
Your royal scepter is a scepter of equity;
⁷   you love righteousness and hate wickedness.
Therefore God, your God, has anointed you
with the oil of gladness above your fellows;
⁸   your robes are all fragrant with myrrh and aloes and cassia.
From ivory palaces stringed instruments make you glad;
⁹   daughters of kings are among your ladies of honor;
at your right hand stands the queen in gold of Ophir.

¹⁰Hear, O daughter, consider, and incline your ear;
forget your people and your father's house;
¹¹   and the king will desire your beauty.
Since he is your lord, bow to him;
¹²   the people of Tyre will sue your favor with gifts,
the richest of the people ¹³with all kinds of wealth.

The princess is decked in her chamber with gold-woven robes;
¹⁴   in many-colored robes she is led to the king,
with her virgin companions, her escort, in her train.
¹⁵With joy and gladness they are led along
as they enter the palace of the king.

¹⁶Instead of your fathers shall be your sons;
you will make them princes in all the earth.
¹⁷I will cause your name to be celebrated in all generations;
therefore the peoples will praise you for ever and ever.

A Royal Wedding Song

The poet and singer, a member of the royal court, at once strikes a note of joy for the occasion, probably a foreign princess' wedding to King Solomon. Tongue and pen go to work eagerly and heap lovely imagery and youthful genius doing honor to a royal couple: first to the king (vv. 2-9), then to his spouse (vv. 10-17). Written in the perspective of God, the whole song envisions a final, greater King, and so it is forward-looking, messianic.

God has endowed the bridegroom-king with grace and beauty, strength and skill, and above all, with justice and zeal for the poor. The "oil of gladness" that anoints him king flows from the hand of God. The riches, attested by precious perfume and ivory palaces and daughters of kings doing homage, befit him who takes the hand of a queen decked in the gold of Ophir (the finest). The king's person is sacred for his throne and anointing come from God.

The counterpart of noble praise is for the spouse, who clings to him and forgets her father's house. As was the oriental custom for brides, she does homage to her lord, who greatly desires her beauty. Now the rich will cater to her in seeking favors (she may come from Tyre whence guests brought gifts). There is far more to the literal picture, for her procession to the throne is uniquely glorious, her attire shimmers with gold brocade and embroidery, and a long train of virgins is in her splendid entourage.

Traditionally Eastern and Western Churches read in this Psalm and espousals of Christ and His Church, with Mary as the original type of the Church. We take this seriously since it is no afterthought, but part of the original meaning of the divine and human authors. The literal sense includes the Messiah and His Bride. In line with this, the author of Hebrews (1:8f.) refers verses 6 and 7 to the Son of God made man. Christ is King, equipped with all spiritual splendor. The Church is His Spouse (Eph. 5:23ff.) and loved one in life and death. This lovely, frequent image extends even into heaven, to the nuptials of the Lamb (Rev. 19:9). "Come, I will show you the Bride, the wife of the Lamb" (Rev. 21:2 and 9ff.), and John saw the new, holy Jerusalem adorned as a bride with divine glory.

A beautiful, true human wedlock describes Christ and His Church. It has inspired the highest mysticism in the Church. The prophets spoke of wedlock between God and humanity (Ez. 16:8ff. and Is. 62). The Canticle describes the love of Christ for His Church in great figures of speech. No wonder that Christ calls Himself the Bridegroom (Jn. 3:29 and Lk. 5:34f.). He, Spouse and Prince of peace, clothed in glory, gives us the weapons of the Spirit (Eph. 6:10-18). With Him we "ride forth victoriously" in battle.

This Psalm in its final sense has deeper thoughts than words can express. The Old Testament Psalms prepare us for the sacramental way of Christ. Following St. Paul, we call it "Mysterion," in which Mary His Mother takes the role of Bride. She is first in and of the Church, perfect without blemish, leading all to her King-Spouse. Her beauty, being spiritual, dwarfs the beauty of any human bride. She has left her father's house and knows only the will of the Father in her Son and Spouse. The Church fittingly uses this Psalm on Christmas (office of readings), on February 2, on II Mondays (vespers), IV Saturdays (noon), likewise for virgins and holy women (office of readings), those who uniquely are icons (images) of Mary and spouses of Christ.

Psalm 46 (45)

God is our refuge and strength,
  a very present help in trouble.
[2]Therefore we will not fear though the earth should change,
  though the mountains shake in the heart of the sea;
[3]though its waters roar and foam,
  though the mountains tremble with its tumult.

[4]There is a river whose streams make glad the city of God,
  the holy habitation of the Most High.
[5]God is in the midst of her, she shall not be moved;
  God will help her right early.
[6]The nations rage, the kingdoms totter;
  he utters his voice, the earth melts.
[7]The LORD of hosts is with us;
  the God of Jacob is our refuge.

[8]Come, behold the works of the LORD,
  how he has wrought desolations in the earth.
[9]He makes wars cease to the end of the earth;
  he breaks the bow, and shatters the spear,
  he burns the chariots with fire!
[10]"Be still, and know that I am God.
  I am exalted among the nations,
  I am exalted in the earth!"
[11]The LORD of hosts is with us;
  the God of Jacob is our refuge.

God With Us

This Psalm inspired the great song "A mighty fortress is our God." As an exceptional triumph of unbounded trust, the literal encounter with God which inspired it must have been one of the most astounding of sacred history. Many regard the original event as that of 2 Kg. 18-19, when the mighty Sennacherib attacked Jerusalem in King Hezekiah's days. He trusted in the Lord like nobody before or after (18:5). He prayed with his people. While the enemy stood outside and in mockery blasphemed God and His holy city, Isaiah the prophet came forward and spoke for the Lord. That night an angel of the Lord slew 185,000 Assyrians "at the break of dawn."

Many phrases in that long history account remind us of this Psalm, especially of the refrain, "The Lord of hosts is with us; the God of Jacob is our refuge." Faith, if it is divine, conquers human doubt. All doubts against faith are human or diabolical. When we see God working like that, faith becomes stronger than the ground we stand on. Upheavals, earthquakes, tidal waves, and falling mountains cannot shake divine faith. The Savior said, "Heaven and earth will pass away, but my words will not pass away" (Mt. 24:35).

This happy, triumphant faith speaks throughout the Psalm. "The nations rage, the kingdoms totter; he utters his voice, the earth melts." The enemy dies of fear. God invites us to look at "the works of the Lord," how He stops war without war since He is the God of peace. And the reason? "God is in the midst of her." "Be still and know that I am God," exalted above all nations. His presence is in Zion, the old and new. At times He led Israel's armies; this time He broke the bows and spears and shields since faith was pure and strong. All hostility faded before that presence.

The stream that delights the city is a figure of God's favors. From the earthly paradise to the heavenly, rivers of water delight both God and man. Christ uses water as a carrier of divine life in Baptism. In Him the image has far greater meaning than the ancient flow of tunneled spring water (dug by the same King Hezehiah around 700 B.C. See 2 Kg. 20:20). Is verse 4 a reference to this stream of Siloah? At any rate, the mention of fresh water here means life and protection, clearly blessings of God on high.

"God with us" is the Name of Christ (Mt. 1:23). His final Kingdom is a Kingdom of peace. Without Christ the history of man is a history of wars. "I have overcome the world" (Jn. 16:33), the evil and unbelieving world. Born of God in the Baptism of faith, our victory is the same because He is with us. That is our faith in the Son of God and Son of Mary. He is with us in His Church and her sacramental system, where flow the many rivulets of His life-giving Spirit. As we grow in the Spirit (Eph. 2:21f.), rivers of living water will flow, as Jesus promised (Jn. 7:38f.), and our victory is secure.

Praying this Psalm with the Church is a way of calling on the Name of the Lord who pours on us His Spirit (Acts 2:17-21). The Church prays it on December 29 and on the feasts of the Blessed Virgin Mary (office of readings), then on I Fridays and feasts of a church dedication (at vespers).

Psalm 47 (46)

Clap your hands, all peoples!
Shout to God with loud songs of joy!
²For the LORD, the Most High, is terrible,
a great king over all the earth.
³He subdued peoples under us,
and nations under our feet.
⁴He chose our heritage for us,
the pride of Jacob whom he loves.

⁵God has gone up with a shout,
the LORD with the sound of a trumpet.
⁶Sing praises to God, sing praises!
Sing praises to our King, sing praises!
⁷For God is the king of all the earth;
sing praises with a psalm!

⁸God reigns over the nations;
God sits on his holy throne.
⁹The princes of the peoples gather
as the people of the God of Abraham.
For the shields of the earth belong to God;
he is highly exalted!

God's Kingship

This short, powerful Psalm extols God as King, supreme over all kings, nations, and gods of heaven and earth. All peoples must celebrate His Kingship with shouts and clapping of gladness and reverence. In our day we treat kings shabbily, but the terms king and kingship still denote supremacy. When Israel demanded a king of Samuel, the Lord answered that He was their King (1 Sam. 8:7), but He then gave in. We must consider this Psalm a festive processional hymn at the installation of God's Ark in its place of primacy amid a great conclave of people (1 Kg. 8:6). The throng responds with great shouts and trumpet blasts, for this is the triumph of their God over all that claims greatness.

But the Psalm is also forward-looking and universal, as it invites all peoples to bend their knee. This prophetic intent finds fulfillment only in Christ, and that determines the way we pray it. We celebrate His universal sovereignty over the chosen people of the God of Abraham. The King of the universe is also the King of history. All generations must acclaim Him. Our turn has come to fulfill the oracles of prophecy and to join the universal chorus of praise.

His universal supremacy lies specifically in His glorified humanity. Jesus of Nazareth, Son of Mary, we proclaim King of history. Literally, our humanity in Christ's is at the Father's right hand. Very rightly the Church uses our Psalm at His Ascension, the visible moment of ascending His throne on high, the moment that all nations must celebrate. The God-man goes up as King with shouts of joy and clapping of hands as a sign to all the world. We are grateful that the "King of kings and Lord of lords" calls for and accepts our best efforts at solemnity, which is music, as our earthly accompaniment to His heavenly enthronement.

Instituting the feast of Christ the King was a stroke of genius. Our celebration of it gives witness to all of His supremacy. To all the Old Testament joy, we add the New Testament fact that in Christ our humanity has the most real King. We are with Him at the heavenly throne. There we await the consummation of His Kingship at the end of time. And so we pray the Psalm as a present guarantee of His future Coming in glory and our sharing with Him.

God is always present, yet He is always coming. The Psalm holds everything together in one vision of faith: past history, present Mystery, future glory. That is God's work. And the divine joy must seize us to lift up our hearts, and bodies too. When Christ said to Pilate, "My kingship is not of this world" (Jn. 18:36), He opened up a world vision for us to share and strive for. We must work for the day when there will be one flock and one Shepherd-King. We, great and small, are God's courtiers and kinglets (1 Cor. 3:23 and Rev. 21:24), who echo on earth the heavenly homage: "To him who sits upon the throne and to the Lamb be blessing and honor and glory and might for ever and ever" (Rev. 5:13). Besides Ascension Day (vespers), this Psalm resounds in the Church on Christmas and Epiphany (noon) and on I Wednesdays (lauds). It deserves frequent private practice. "Sing praise with a Psalm."

Psalm 48 (47)

Great is the LORD and greatly to be praised
    in the city of our God!
His holy mountain, 2beautiful in elevation,
    is the joy of all the earth,
Mount Zion, in the far north,
    the city of the great King.
3Within her citadels God
    has shown himself a sure defense.

4For lo, the kings assembled,
    and came on together.
5As soon as they saw it, they were astounded,
    they were in panic, they took to flight;
6trembling took hold of them there,
    anguish as of a woman in travail.
7By the east wind thou didst shatter
    the ships of Tarshish.
8As we have heard, so have we seen
    in the city of the LORD of hosts,
  in the city of our God,
    which God establishes for ever.

9We have thought on thy steadfast love, O God,
    in the midst of thy temple.
10As thy name, O God,
    so thy praise reaches to the ends of the earth.
  Thy right hand is filled with victory;
11   let Mount Zion be glad!
  Let the daughters of Judah rejoice
    because of thy judgments!

12Walk about Zion, go round about her,
    number her towers,
13consider well her ramparts,
    go through her citadels;
  that you may tell the next generation
14   that this is God,
  our God for ever and ever.
    He will be our guide for ever.

The City of Our God

The holy hill called Zion, a low mountain in Jerusalem, is yet the highest in the world as God's special dwelling place. The Psalm extols it and is the counterpiece of prayer to Psalm 47, which celebrates God's Kingship. Israel stood in proud awe and sacred joy at the sight of Zion and Jerusalem. We call it the Holy City even today. The divine favors given it will continue to make it one of the wonders of the world. God built it and He fortified it. He chose it in preference to any place on earth. "Within her citadels God has shown himself . . . ," so that hostile kings fled in fright at the very sight, as the east wind sweeps away and shatters the ships of Tharsis (a distant, mighty seaport).

God is invisible, transcendent, yet He uses visible symbols to describe His omnipotent presence and beauty. What pagans dreamt about in their myths of the highest dwellings of the gods "in the far north" (probably Olympus), here is fulfilled reality. The glory of God touches earth, mountain, city, and Temple, and so brings to pass the aspirations of humanity. Since God has chosen Jerusalem as His home, no other place can compete with her. Pilgrims from afar sought the Temple, and as they viewed its invincible towers and walls and castles, they went back to tell the next generation, "That this is our God," the God of power and security, of attractive beauty and joy, of justice and kindness. They had seen as they had heard the visible proof of their faith.

Today the physical appearance of Jerusalem with her walls no longer evokes the same faith. But that is no longer the purpose of Zion in its faded glory. We have a new faith in Zion, the Temple and City of Christ and His Holy Spirit. Of this we are living members. We mean the Church, His Body. Jesus called Himself the Temple, and He promised the Church indefectibility (Mt. 16:18). "Destroy this temple, and in three days I will raise it up" (Jn. 2:19f.). He fulfilled this prophecy, and made His Church indestructible. From the ancient Zion we step up to the New One, which is His Home; from the temporary we rise to the eternal, still in visible signs of faith, still forward-looking to consummation.

Our boast is the Lord Jesus. Look about you: His glorious presence is not in a far-away city on a hill, but in our midst in the Signs of His salvation and love. The humble parish church with its Font and Altar and Tabernacle is Christ's home of family union. There and in the diocese we have all the sacraments and signs of His new dwelling with men. Through the hands of bishop and priests, the Holy Spirit is the Architect. Paul proclaims it (Eph. 1:18-23 and 4:12-16) with absolute security (Rom. 8:32-39). Do we tell the next generation this? How do we pray this Psalm?

Each person has his or her story to tell of God's presence and goodness, of this highest and most beautiful Mountain of the world. Sit, ponder a beautifully mighty mountain range, then go, meditate on the Altar, and pray your faith, "Great is the Lord in Zion!" Your pride comes alive since you are no tourist in Old Jerusalem, but a reborn citizen of God come home. There is nothing beyond it, this side of heaven. "You have come to Mount Zion" (Heb. 12:22ff. and Rev. 19). Such is our God!

This Psalm serves the Church for prayer with Christ on I Thursdays (noon), but especially on Christmas (noon), when we see in His human Mother the fulfillment of the symbols of home and love and care.

Psalm 49 (48)

> Hear this, all peoples!
>> Give ear, all inhabitants of the world,
> 2both low and high,
>> rich and poor together!
> 3My mouth shall speak wisdom;
>> the meditation of my heart shall be understanding.
> 4I will incline my ear to a proverb;
>> I will solve my riddle to the music of the lyre.
>
> 5Why should I fear in times of trouble,
>> when the iniquity of my persecutors surrounds me,
> 6men who trust in their wealth
>> and boast of the abundance of their riches?
> 7Truly no man can ransom himself,
>> or give to God the price of his life,
> 8for the ransom of his life is costly,
>> and can never suffice,
> 9that he should continue to live on for ever,
>> and never see the Pit.

[10]Yea, he shall see that even the wise die,
   the fool and the stupid alike must perish
   and leave their wealth to others.
[11]Their graves are their homes for ever,
   their dwelling places to all generations,
   though they named lands their own.
[12]Man cannot abide in his pomp,
   he is like the beasts that perish.

[13]This is the fate of those who have foolish confidence,
   the end of those who are pleased with their portion.
[14]Like sheep they are appointed for Sheol;
   Death shall be their shepherd;
 straight to the grave they descend,
   and their form shall waste away;
   Sheol shall be their home.
[15]But God will ransom my soul from the power of Sheol,
   for he will receive me.

[16]Be not afraid when one becomes rich,
   when the glory of his house increases.
[17]For when he dies he will carry nothing away;
   his glory will not go down after him.
[18]Though, while he lives, he counts himself happy,
   and though a man gets praise when he does well for himself,
[19]he will go to the generation of his fathers,
   who will never more see the light.
[20]Man cannot abide in his pomp,
   he is like the beasts that perish.

Woe to the Rich

Calling on all peoples to heed his wisdom, the Psalmist sets out to solve a universal problem "with the music of the lyre" or harp. The wisdom comes from God and therefore deserves to be set to music. His proverb is not only for the pride of the rich but also for the envy of the poor. That makes it as modern today as the day he wrote it. (See the comments on Psalm 37.) Wealth brings power and independence, temptations and false hopes. Death is the end of wealth. "You cannot take it with you" (vv. 11-13). No man can buy an extension to his life or redeem himself; the price is too high.

The wealthy are stupid. They resemble the beasts that die and disappear. Poor and rich alike end in the grave. Death is their shepherd. Attachment to riches is godlessness. The nether world (Sheol, the pit) claims those who without hope die rich, while the just man dies with hope. Here (v. 15) lies a decisive difference: "But God will ransom my soul from the power of Sheol, for he will receive me" (15). This is the solution of the problem or riddle that there is hope beyond the grave. Though vaguely stated, God will redeem the just person from the nether world. This Psalm therefore contains the belief in the afterlife. The fate of the just differs from that of the sinner. He who has prudence will differ from the beasts that perish (v. 20). The moral: do not envy the wealthy!

We pray this Psalm in the context of Christ and His Church and derive our attitudes toward the goods of this world from Him. He brought us more light on the fate after the just man's death in the parable of poor Lazarus (Lk. 16:19ff.). And He speaks about hoarding and complacency in the language of our Psalm: "Fool! This night your soul is required of you; and the things you have prepared [hoarded], whose will they be?" (Lk. 12:16-21). On the one hand, "Woe to you that are rich, for you have received your consolation" (Lk. 6:24); on the other, "Blessed are the poor in spirit . . ." (Mt. 5:3). The best way is to make friends in heaven with "the unrighteous mammon" (Lk. 16:9), by giving "to the poor, and you will have treasure in heaven" (Mk. 10:21).

Hoarding, while the poor keep on starving, is hostility to one's own soul. Man is more soul than body. The rich man is more body than soul. The social and economic problem of the wealthy and poor will always be with us, that is, as long as we do not heed the message of Christ and of this Psalm. While St. James paraphrases the warning of our Psalm (5:1-6), St. Paul sums it up: "The love of money is the root of all evils" (1 Tim. 6:6-10). We do well to join the Church on II Tuesdays (vespers) in singing this Psalm in order that we may "solve our problem with the harp" (see also 2 Kg. 3:15).

Psalm 50 (49)

The Mighty One, God the LORD,
    speaks and summons the earth
    from the rising of the sun to its setting.
²Out of Zion, the perfection of beauty,
    God shines forth.
³Our God comes, he does not keep silence,
    before him is a devouring fire,
    round about him a mighty tempest.
⁴He calls to the heavens above
    and to the earth, that he may judge his people:
⁵"Gather to me my faithful ones,
    who made a covenant with me by sacrifice!"
⁶The heavens declare his righteousness,
    for God himself is judge!

⁷"Hear, O my people, and I will speak,
    O Israel, I will testify against you.
    I am God, your God.
⁸I do not reprove you for your sacrifices;
    your burnt offerings are continually before me.
⁹I will accept no bull from your house,
    nor he-goat from your folds.
¹⁰For every beast of the forest is mine,
    the cattle on a thousand hills.
¹¹I know all the birds of the air,
    and all that moves in the field is mine.

¹²"If I were hungry, I would not tell you;
    for the world and all that is in it is mine.
¹³Do I eat the flesh of bulls,
    or drink the blood of goats?
¹⁴Offer to God a sacrifice of thanksgiving,
    and pay your vows to the Most High;
¹⁵and call upon me in the day of trouble;
    I will deliver you, and you shall glorify me."

¹⁶But to the wicked God says:
    "What right have you to recite my statutes,
        or take my covenant on your lips?
¹⁷For you hate discipline,
        and you cast my words behind you.
¹⁸If you see a thief, you are a friend of his;
        and you keep company with adulterers.

¹⁹"You give your mouth free rein for evil,
        and your tongue frames deceit.
²⁰You sit and speak against your brother;
        you slander your own mother's son.
²¹These things you have done and I have been silent;
        you thought that I was one like yourself.
    But now I rebuke you, and lay the charge before you.

²²"Mark this, then, you who forget God,
        lest I rend, and there be none to deliver!
²³He who brings thanksgiving as his sacrifice honors me;
        to him who orders his way aright
        I will show the salvation of God!"

The Sacrifice of Praise

With Zion as His glorious center of judgment, God summons
heaven and earth to the trial of His covenant people, amid a devouring
fire and raging storm that remind us of His appearance on Sinai (Ex.
19:16). On that day in the desert His "faithful ones" had sealed the
covenant with sacrifice that God had commanded. Now in His oracle
He recalls for them the meaning of sacrifice and praise and morality
and that the whole world is His, including the animals of sacrifice. He
rebukes the pagan belief which held that deities (idols) need food and
drink. The Lord of all suffers no hunger or thirst.

True sacrifice is praise together with the fulfilling of one's vows
(obligations and promises). Ritual offerings are good and necessary,
but always in conjunction with moral integrity. Only if religion is not
divorced from morality will God accept the people's sacrifices and
ritual prayers. God is invisible and unseen, yet present and seeing. He
will hear their prayers only if they do not defy His will and laws by
a mechanical, rote ritual. In a further oracle to the wicked, He makes
this clear: "reciting my statutes" and taking "my covenant on your lips"

is empty ritual and hypocrisy. Also the prophets castigate the absence of discipline and virtue while mouthing prayers and going through the motions of sacrifice. The author of the Psalm specifies thievery, adultery, deceit, and slander, spreading rumors against one's brother. One could easily extend the list of modern evils which people connive at or commit while professing religion.

Christ goes even further in requiring purity of sacrifice "in spirit and in truth" (Jn. 4:24; see also Rom. 12:1). What we offer is already His. God wants our free service, and our gift offerings are tokens of that. There is much "shell Christianity" or sacrifice without "fulfilling of vows," without honoring God by honest lives. Purity of heart, moral innocence, brotherly love are always radically necessary. Christ the Judge exposed the hypocrisy of Pharisees and scribes, who enforced religion and reaped its benefits while they cursed the crowds (Jn. 7:49 and Lk. 20:47; see also Mt. 23:13ff.). The Savior went all the way in reducing this Psalm to action.

Christ, God and man, is the center of our cult and sacrifice. With Him as Judge, our moral motive must be pure. He repeats the words of our Psalm: "I am God, your God." God is a "devouring fire" (Heb. 12:29). Only sincerity and justice count before His judgment. No one can buy salvation with empty sacrifices. Faith and morality go together (Jas. 1:22; 2:18ff.), just as do virtue and ritual. "Not everyone who says to me, 'Lord, Lord,' shall enter the Kingdom of heaven, but he who does the will of my Father" (Mt. 7:21 and Jn. 14:21).

The last Word of God is a promise of salvation and feasting with God to all who offer "thanksgiving as his sacrifice." The equivalent Word of Christ is blessedness for those who "hear the word of God and keep it" (Lk. 11:28). With love and reverence we await the glorious Coming of the Shepherd-Judge, who knows our works (Rev. 2-3), who awaits our conversion. Meanwhile we pray this Psalm with Him on III Mondays and IV Saturdays (office of readings) to qualify for His promises.

Psalm 51 (50)

Have mercy on me, O God, according to thy steadfast love;
according to thy abundant mercy blot out my transgressions.
²Wash me thoroughly from my iniquity,
and cleanse me from my sin!

³For I know my transgressions,
     and my sin is ever before me.
⁴Against thee, thee only, have I sinned,
     and done that which is evil in thy sight,
 so that thou art justified in thy sentence
     and blameless in thy judgment.
⁵Behold, I was brought forth in iniquity,
     and in sin did my mother conceive me.

⁶Behold, thou desirest truth in the inward being;
     therefore teach me wisdom in my secret heart.
⁷Purge me with hyssop, and I shall be clean;
     wash me, and I shall be whiter than snow.
⁸Fill me with joy and gladness;
     let the bones which thou hast broken rejoice.
⁹Hide thy face from my sins,
     and blot out all my iniquities.

¹⁰Create in me a clean heart, O God,
     and put a new and right spirit within me.
¹¹Cast me not away from thy presence,
     and take not thy holy Spirit from me.
¹²Restore to me the joy of thy salvation,
     and uphold me with a willing spirit.

¹³Then I will teach transgressors thy ways,
     and sinners will return to thee.
¹⁴Deliver me from bloodguiltiness, O God,
     thou God of my salvation,
     and my tongue will sing aloud of thy deliverance.

¹⁵O Lord, open thou my lips,
     and my mouth shall show forth thy praise.
¹⁶For thou hast no delight in sacrifice;
     were I to give a burnt offering,
     thou wouldst not be pleased.
¹⁷The sacrifice acceptable to God is a broken spirit;
     a broken and contrite heart,
     O God, thou wilt not despise.

¹⁸Do good to Zion in thy good pleasure;
    rebuild the walls of Jerusalem,
¹⁹then wilt thou delight in right sacrifices,
    in burnt offerings and whole burnt offerings;
    then bulls will be offered on thy altar.

The *Miserere*

This great and beautiful penitential Psalm comes as a transplant from David's heart to ours. It is one of the best known and most used prayers of the entire Psalter. King David prayed it for his misdeeds (2 Sam. 11-12). Justice and mercy met in his heart-rending conversion. They met in the heart-rending death of Christ the Savior. The Church's spirituality of repentance grew from the anguish of his deeds and from this divinely inspired act of contrition. It is the most decisive of all the Psalms on repentance.

There is self-accusation, admission of guilt. There is interior, heartfelt sorrow for sin. There is readiness for atonement, even for social restitution. There is in this cry for mercy, above all else, a return to God. As sinners all, we need this lesson on forgiveness. Sin is no different today than the first fall of man and woman. Sin is an inner lie, the abuse of freedom, striking at God with His gifts to us. It is presumption of a puny, selfish creature of God.

We must look to God for the terms of mercy. We are forgiven, not when we imagine it, but when He says so. "Only God can forgive sins." As in David's day, He sent a messenger to denounce sin and then declare forgiveness, so in Christ's day and now. Penance is the only way. That includes admission of sin, sorrow for it, before God and His people and to oneself. Penance is painful. The way back to the heart of God is the way of the Cross. No one can fool God. That means absolute sincerity and truthfulness. Such humility is hard, but the only and easiest way out. The "ritual way" (liturgy) demands this inner conversion of heart. Then penance becomes renewal, the new beginning of praise.

Conscience trouble lies deep in man. From his mother's womb he inclines to sin. Further, all during his life he must follow up the cleansing. Restraint of impulses is in order. The memory of past sins can harass, unless God removes it. New involvements come up constantly. This Psalm accords with the experience of original and personal sin. In true affliction of soul, we seek a new spirit of living, the Holy

Spirit of Christ. Sprinkling with hyssop branches (Ex. 12:22) symbolizes the total blotting out and washing clean.

God looks to the heart. He regards the pleasing sacrifice of a contrite spirit, which also the Church presupposes before admitting people to the Sacrifice. "Let a man examine himself . . ." (1 Cor. 11:27f.). Unworthy reception of Communion is a sacrilege. Every Eucharistic celebration opens with contrition for sin. Christ's will for mercy is forever crystallized, since the resurrection, in the sacraments. Here, in the world of sacred Signs, He remits sin, creates a new heart and makes us Temples of His Holy Spirit (1 Cor. 6:19), providing we have the sentiments of this Psalm. The power of the Holy Spirit is called "the remission of sins" in the Pentecostal liturgy (see Heb. 9:13f.; Lk. 4:18; Rom. 5:5) because of Jesus' prayer, "Father, forgive them."

Did Jesus, who was without sin or guilt, ever pray this Psalm? Not for Himself, but for us. We call that vicarious. He took upon Himself the burden of sin. "He was wounded for our transgressions, and he was bruised for our iniquities . . . and the Lord has laid on him the iniquity of us all" (Is. 53:5f.). "He makes himself an offering for sin . . . and he shall bear their iniquities" (Is. 53:10f.). He died that we might live.

Revelation tells us that man cannot undo his sin by himself. To forgive is divine. Every sin, further, has social implications. Man is responsible for his brother. "Then I will teach transgressors Thy ways and sinners will return to thee" (v. 13). We lead others into sin; we must lead them also to God's mercy. Penance requires a great common effort. Gratitude over our forgiveness urges us to extend the gift to other erring sheep. Then we "rebuild the walls of Jerusalem" with a moral reconstruction and make the city of God secure. Then all can rejoice. If there is "joy in heaven," then also on earth. The *Miserere* becomes a resurrection song. The Church uses Psalm 51 on Good Friday, on I, II, III, and IV Fridays, and for the deceased, always at lauds.

Psalm 52 (51)

Why do you boast, O mighty man,
  of mischief done against the godly?
  All the day ²you are plotting destruction.
Your tongue is like a sharp razor,
  you worker of treachery.
³You love evil more than good,
  and lying more than speaking the truth.
⁴You love all words that devour,
  O deceitful tongue.

⁵But God will break you down for ever;
  he will snatch and tear you from your tent;
  he will uproot you from the land of the living.
⁶The righteous shall see, and fear,
  and shall laugh at him, saying,
⁷"See the man who would not make God his refuge,
  but trusted in the abundance of his riches,
  and sought refuge in his wealth!"

⁸But I am like a green olive tree
  in the house of God.
I trust in the steadfast love of God
  for ever and ever.
⁹I will thank thee for ever,
  because thou hast done it.
I will proclaim thy name, for it is good,
  in the presence of the godly.

Organized Evil

This Psalm is not likely to attract us to prayer unless we are really concerned about promoting God's Kingdom and salvation. To ignore or neglect it might mean that we have a narrow notion of the "spiritual life." It rouses curiosity to hear someone called champion of evil, and we can think of modern competitors for the title. But it is not as simple as that; we are involved. Professional liars, all who cultivate that razor-sharp art, are attacking us, so that we need God's help desperately. We are not neutral on the sidelines or reading a sensational account about "enemy number one," but we are in the act and have to take sides.

Sins of the tongue, lying, slander, bearing false witness, trusting in ill-gotten wealth, etc., still merit the invectives that the Psalmist hurls at the guilty one, be it Doeg in David's day or some modern godless pervert who thrives on evil. When a man receives such reprimands and is ejected from the sacred assembly, it is a sign that all have high moral standards and responsibility to God. But when a whole society tolerates and connives at evil on a vast scale, it is corrupt thinking and loss of the moral sense and no fear of God's retribution. The greater the evil, the more is God out of sight, and the greater the danger to all men.

By Old Testament standards, God and man reacted swiftly against evil. After all, God had ordered, "You shall purge the evil from the midst of you" (Dt. 24:7). Men had to prove they were on God's side. God meted out visible punishment in order to educate His people to the gravity of sin and to foster faith in His Word and power. The faithful considered it their duty to call down divine retribution on God's and their own enemies. Idolators received the severest judgment (Dt. 13: 1-5; 17:2-7). We find hard words in verse 5 (as elsewhere in the Psalms, e.g. 109).

This is imperfect in the light of the New Testament ("Love your enemies!"), but so is divorce, which God permitted because of "your hardness of heart" (Mk. 10:2-9). Coming out of a pagan past and environment, the people of God gradually gave up revenge, divorce, etc. God did not work sudden miracles of morality, but saw a purpose in step-by-step improvement. That purpose may have been to teach us to spiritualize the harsh literal judgments.

God is the God of love and mercy, and Jesus taught us the final step of this. He does not want us to pray this or any Psalm against personal enemies for revenge, but in the way He prayed it. He prayed with and for the good world, but against the evil world, which He saw more clearly than we do. That evil world is manipulated by the prince of evil, the fallen spirits, "the mighty man of evil" (v. 1; Jn. 17:9 and 8:44). The devil is beyond redemption, fixed in evil, and all out to rob us of salvation. So we do not pray it "with mental reservations," but outright against Satan, who goes about like a lion seeking our eternal death (1 Pet. 5:8f.). If we trust steadfastly in God, we are "a green olive tree in the house of God," grafted on the Tree which is Christ (see Rom. 11:17-24). With song and joy we pray this Psalm victoriously with the Church (II Wednesdays, lauds and office of readings). Other action is always in order, but Psalm prayer overcomes our lack of courage.

Psalm 53 (52)

The fool says in his heart,
"There is no God."
They are corrupt, doing abominable iniquity;
there is none that does good.

[2]God looks down from heaven
upon the sons of men
to see if there are any that are wise,
that seek after God.

[3]They have all fallen away;
they are all alike depraved;
there is none that does good,
no, not one.

[4]Have those who work evil no understanding,
who eat up my people as they eat bread,
and do not call upon God?

[5]There they are, in great terror,
in terror such as has not been!
For God will scatter the bones of the ungodly;
they will be put to shame, for God has rejected them.

[6]O that deliverance for Israel would come from Zion!
When God restores the fortunes of his people,
Jacob will rejoice and Israel be glad.

The Spectacle of Fools

This Psalm is the same, almost word for word, as Psalm 14 (except v. 6). Scholars, following the sacred text, keep the two separate. It does not seem necessary to add comments, other than pointing out that the folly of sin is its own punishment and causes fear where there is no reason to fear.

Seen from the gallery of heaven, earth must present a unique spectacle of fools who keep on sinning only to reap the results of their blindness and godlessness. Closing their eyes to the divine light and ready guidance, men go about like blind mice in a maze. They begin to fear each other. Mutual distrust is born of fear and sin. They will inevitably run into and collide with the almighty hand of their Maker and Savior. One of the Savior's warnings was that all fears are vain, except that of the all-knowing Judge and Master. The Church uses this prayer on II Tuesdays at noon.

Psalm 54 (53)

Save me, O God, by thy name,
and vindicate me by thy might.
²Hear my prayer, O God;
give ear to the words of my mouth.

³For insolent men have risen against me,
ruthless men seek my life;
they do not set God before them.

⁴Behold, God is my helper;
the Lord is the upholder of my life.
⁵He will requite my enemies with evil;
in thy faithfulness put an end to them.

⁶With a freewill offering I will sacrifice to thee;
I will give thanks to thy name, O LORD, for it is good.
⁷For thou hast delivered me from every trouble,
and my eye has looked in triumph on my enemies.

Victory in His Name

Prayer is personal contact with God at the highest level of our being. When prayer is inspired by God, like the Psalms, it also reflects His thoughts and will. Related to Psalm 20, this one begs God for help in the same way that Moses prayed: for His Name's sake. God hears all sorts of prayer providing it is sincere and comes from a humble heart. The author prays with unswerving faith, and he received prompt relief.

The place where David's prayer was heard is called the Rock of Rescue, a name familiar to the Old Testament man of prayer. When the enemy was closing in on David, perhaps among strangers in the land of Ziph (see 2 Sam. 23:15-29), there was no human hope. Being heard by God in that desperate moment must have left a deep impression on him. It greatly increased his trust in God. David kept God before his eyes and did not forget to thank Him for delivery from the enemy. He passed on his faith and trust to the community of God's chosen people and strengthened them in turn. David was not revengeful when he had Saul at his mercy, as the story proves. He could have destroyed Saul, but spared him as God's anointed, thus leaving judgment to God to "put an end to them."

Instead, he promises a votive sacrifice to the Lord for his rescue. All this is very Christlike, who let His enemies go free that He might redeem them and us. When they hated Him without cause (Jn. 15:25), He trusted the more in His heavenly Father. Because He was forgiving, we are redeemed. God will always requite the enemy who masterminds evil both against Christ and His members.

The Lord taught us to pray in His Name (Jn. 16:24-26). Practice teaches us the power of Christ's Name, which is prayer in God's Name. When we pray with the Church, then especially do we pray in His Name, as when we use this Psalm on II Tuesdays (noon) and parts of it on Good Friday (also noon).

Psalm 55 (54)

Give ear to my prayer, O God;
    and hide not thyself from my supplication!
2Attend to me, and answer me;
    I am overcome by my trouble.
I am distraught 3by the noise of the enemy,
    because of the oppression of the wicked.
For they bring trouble upon me,
    and in anger they cherish enmity against me.

4My heart is in anguish within me,
    the terrors of death have fallen upon me.
5Fear and trembling come upon me,
    and horror overwhelms me.
6And I say, "O that I had wings like a dove!
    I would fly away and be at rest;
7yea, I would wander afar,
    I would lodge in the wilderness,
8I would haste to find me a shelter
    from the raging wind and tempest."

⁹Destroy their plans, O Lord, confuse their tongues;
    for I see violence and strife in the city.
¹⁰Day and night they go around it on its walls;
    and mischief and trouble are within it,
¹¹   ruin is in its midst;
  oppression and fraud
    do not depart from its market place.

¹²It is not an enemy who taunts me—
    then I could bear it;
  it is not an adversary who deals insolently with me—
    then I could hide from him.
¹³But it is you, my equal,
    my companion, my familiar friend.
¹⁴We used to hold sweet converse together;
    within God's house we walked in fellowship.
¹⁵Let death come upon them;
    let them go down to Sheol alive;
    let them go away in terror into their graves.

¹⁶But I call upon God;
    and the Lord will save me.
¹⁷Evening and morning and at noon
    I utter my complaint and moan,
    and he will hear my voice.
¹⁸He will deliver my soul in safety
    from the battle that I wage,
    for many are arrayed against me.
¹⁹God will give ear, and humble them,
    he who is enthroned from of old;
  because they keep no law,
    and do not fear God.

²⁰My companion stretched out his hand against his friends,
    he violated his covenant.
²¹His speech was smoother than butter,
    yet war was in his heart;
  his words were softer than oil,
    yet they were drawn swords.

²²Cast your burden on the LORD,
 and he will sustain you;
he will never permit
 the righteous to be moved.

²³But thou, O God, wilt cast them down
 into the lowest pit;
men of blood and treachery
 shall not live out half their days.
But I will trust in thee.

Cast Your Cares on the Lord

A man of faith, deeply troubled by the wicked, ruthless, godless men about him, takes refuge in the Lord. He lives in a city where evil is overwhelming, with every sort of strife and violence, injustice, deception and murder. Evil stalks boldly on the walls, in the streets, in the marketplace. Smooth lying coming from false hearts threatens his life, so that he would fly away from it all like an innocent dove to find peace and security somewhere in the desert. The author is a gentle and sensitive person who sees no way of saving himself from the widespread social evil.

His worst suffering came from the betrayal by an intimate, trusted friend, a comrade in life and at the Temple worship. His pain over this was greater than all the rest. Lawless enemies he could stand, but this treachery struck the deepest wound. The whole reminds us of Jer. 9:1-9. The author asks for retribution for the men saturated with unrepented sin (19). While this call for divine vengeance was a kind of formula in the Old Testament lest the just be contaminated by evil (see Num. 26:10f.), yet the author leaves the dispensing of final justice to God. Christ, who taught the law of mercy, did so too.

Enlightening for us is the custom of praying three times daily (v. 17) at the chief hours of morning, noon, and evening (see also Dan. 6:10), which the Church took over along with the Psalmody. "He will hear my voice." And in verse 22 he has the beautiful, memorable words, "Cast your burden on the Lord and he will sustain you," a kind of prayer axiom in Israel, which St. Peter quotes (1 Pet. 5:7). Refining this prayer then, as Christ did, we have Christian prayer.

Our Lord saw evil more clearly than ever a just man did. The universality and depth of it, the malice of a whole city and society and the human race, the treachery of a close friend who was an apostle (Jn. 6:70f.), was constantly before His eyes. He knew all suffering. Barabbas the criminal was preferred to Christ. Jesus died that he and we might go free. Freely He submitted to hatred and violence, to treachery and every kind of malice. If He had retaliated, we would not be redeemed. In His preaching He threatened sinners with eternal punishment if they did not repent. But His last words on the Cross were of mercy and forgiveness: "Truly, I say to you, today you will be with me in paradise" (Lk. 23:43).

We can make our own the constant prayer, "But I will trust in thee, O Lord" and "O that I had wings like a dove!" and fly to the heart of God. The Church uses our Psalm on II Wednesdays (noon) and parts of it on IV Fridays (office of readings).

Psalm 56 (55)

Be gracious to me, O God,
　　for men trample upon me;
　　all day long foemen oppress me;
²my enemies trample upon me all day long,
　　for many fight against me proudly.
³When I am afraid,
　　I put my trust in thee.
⁴In God, whose word I praise,
　　in God I trust without a fear.
　　What can flesh do to me?

⁵All day long they seek to injure my cause;
　　all their thoughts are against me for evil.
⁶They band themselves together, they lurk,
　　they watch my steps.
As they have waited for my life,
⁷　　so recompense them for their crime,
　　in wrath cast down the peoples, O God!

⁸Thou hast kept count of my tossings;
    put thou my tears in thy bottle!
    Are they not in thy book?
⁹Then my enemies will be turned back
    in the day when I call.
    This I know, that God is for me.
¹⁰In God, whose word I praise,
    in the LORD, whose word I praise,
¹¹in God I trust without a fear.
    What can man do to me?

¹²My vows to thee I must perform, O God;
    I will render thank offerings to thee.
¹³For thou hast delivered my soul from death,
    yea, my feet from falling,
that I may walk before God
    in the light of life.

In God I Trust

This Psalm is a prayer for divine pity. Surrounded by enemies, who are watching him with evil eyes, the author (probably David playing the madman in 1 Sam. 21:10-15) has serious reason to fear for his life. For him the protection of God is more real than the menacing threats of all his foes. That is living faith. He repeats the words, "What can men do to me?" This is the refrain, as constant as the harassment of his intriguing enemies. Continued trust brings him comfort and trains him to abide in God's shelter. God tries His faithful servant until he boasts in the Lord.

Amid tears and the tossings of sleepless nights, the author knows that God watches and remembers all. In the homely figures of book and bottle, he describes how God gathers up the tears and keeps a record of his sufferings. Few men can stand defamation without fighting back, but our author complains to the Lord-with-him and so gives glory to God in his dark hours. Upon delivery from death, he vows offerings to the Lord for rescue and freedom. He again "walks before God in the light of life." This visible rescue is symbolic for us in our spiritual and material crises because God's help is real in Christ.

God keeps "count" of our actions performed freely and courageously in trust of Him. His recording angel is at work in the divine "bookkeeping" (see also Ps. 69:28; 87:6; 139:16). Of such acts of trust in suffering, it says, "Are they not in thy book?" It is a very human, yet comforting way of depicting the divine omniscience (see also Ex. 32:32). Following Rev. 20:12, Christian piety clings to this fact.

St. Jerome considers this Psalm as one showing forth Christ in His passion. Jesus, who cried out to the Father, feared God more than man and with unshakable trust overcame the fear of death in the Garden of Gethsemane. Christian hope is "the light of life" in moments and hours of darkness; it "has a great reward" (Heb. 10:35). Because of Jesus' prayer, and this Psalm is also His prayer, we live in strong hope of delivery from the evil one (Jn. 17:15). This is one of the "promises of Christ," who tells us to fear only Him who can cast into hell (Lk. 12:4f.). A sign of perseverance is the refrain "What can man do to me?" This Psalm serves the Church on II Thursdays (noon office).

Psalm 57 (56)

Be merciful to me, O God, be merciful to me,
    for in thee my soul takes refuge;
in the shadow of thy wings I will take refuge,
    till the storms of destruction pass by.
²I cry to God Most High,
    to God who fulfils his purpose for me.

³He will send from heaven and save me,
    he will put to shame those who trample upon me.
God will send forth his steadfast love and his faithfulness!

⁴I lie in the midst of lions
    that greedily devour the sons of men;
their teeth are spears and arrows,
    their tongues sharp swords.

⁵Be exalted, O God, above the heavens!
    Let thy glory be over all the earth!

⁶They set a net for my steps;
    my soul was bowed down.
They dug a pit in my way,
    but they have fallen into it themselves.

⁷My heart is steadfast, O God,
  my heart is steadfast!
I will sing and make melody!
⁸   Awake, my soul!
Awake, O harp and lyre!
  I will awake the dawn!
⁹I will give thanks to thee, O Lord, among the peoples;
  I will sing praises to thee among the nations.
¹⁰For thy steadfast love is great to the heavens,
  thy faithfulness to the clouds,

¹¹Be exalted, O God, above the heavens!
  Let thy glory be over all the earth!

Awake, My Soul

Every Psalm in its own way refreshes our spirits each time we pray it with new faith and expectation. The Holy Spirit fills our spirits with a richness we can never exhaust and transfers us from the kingdom of darkness to the light of a new day. We live in the day of Christ (Col. 1:12f. and Eph. 3:18f.). Love out of faith is the key to all the Psalmody.

Our Psalm has two parts (vv. 1-6 and 7-11), each with the refrain that exalts God's glory. Composed by one in a storm of trouble, very likely King David (see 1 Sam. 24), it shows how his faith in time of enmity and danger of death prevailed over the most adverse human conditions. While the experience of foes hounding him went on, his trust experience grew beyond measure. We find this in all the Psalms. "The shadow of thy wings" is the favored expression (also Psalm 91) that makes devouring lions and armed men look harmless. God's help is more vivid and real to the author than nets or traps set for his undoing. His heart is ever ready and steadfast, singing praise in time of trouble.

Then follows a surprising passage replete with joy and the hope of a new day: "Awake, my soul!" With voice and instrument he hails the dawn. The rising of this man of faith reverses the order of nature: himself awakening, he wakes up the day. This describes union with God after the dark night of suffering. The Spirit of God seizes him and lifts him to an ineffable dawn. The author rises above himself to sing thanks and praise to all nations, leaving dangers and threats far below.

We adopt this great spiritual document as our way. Leaving justice to God's wise disposition, we look forward with God's eyes and thoughts. As He watches over us and spreads the wings of His care over us, we realize that the light of the dawn comes from the sun. The light of the Old Testament revelation (also in the Psalms) is the light of Christ coming. There is no lack of enemies, spiritual enemies who surround us. If we are not aware of them, the worse for us. (See Eph. 6:10ff. and 1 Pet. 5:8f.) They are still devouring lions, but the power of Satan is nothing compared to God's.

This is a morning prayer of Christians, who sing it so loudly that they awaken others to the day of Christ. On the one hand this Psalm is a response to His coming; on the other it is the voice of Christ in us at the hour of worship. He awakens our souls to faith and fills us with His life-giving Spirit. Verses 7-11 can serve as a beautiful realization of His glory that is over all the earth, as we "address one another in Psalms and hymns and spiritual songs" (Eph. 5:18f.) and give thanks, celebrating the Eucharist. The Church sings this song on I Thursdays (lauds) and II Thursdays (noon).

Psalm 58 (57)

Do you indeed decree what is right, you gods?
Do you judge the sons of men uprightly?

²Nay, in your hearts you devise wrongs;
your hands deal out violence on earth.

³The wicked go astray from the womb,
they err from their birth, speaking lies.
⁴They have venom like the venom of a serpent,
like the deaf adder that stops its ear,
⁵so that it does not hear the voice of charmers
or of the cunning enchanter.

⁶O God, break the teeth in their mouths;
tear out the fangs of the young lions, O Lord!
⁷Let them vanish like water that runs away;
like grass let them be trodden down and wither.
⁸Let them be like the snail which dissolves into slime,
like the untimely birth that never sees the sun.
⁹Sooner than your pots can feel the heat of thorns,
whether green or ablaze, may he sweep them away!

> [10]The righteous will rejoice when he sees the vengeance;
>   he will bathe his feet in the blood of the wicked.
> [11]Men will say, "Surely there is a reward for the righteous;
>   surely there is a God who judges on earth."

God Judges Human Judges

Full of passionate castigations against corrupt judges, this divinely inspired Psalm in derision calls them "you gods," rulers of all kinds, men in authority who share God's power but pervert justice, the courts, and morality. Instead of subjecting themselves to God, they "work evil" and "devise wrongs" for the downfall of the just. A severe Psalm for its strong poetic imagery, it has fallen into disuse because of its retribution language; yet it carries an important message for us from God.

What the Psalm describes is "poisoning of the wells," the very sources when evil becomes inborn so to say, a second nature. Like the poisonous serpents that resist every appeal of clemency, these judges reap a terrible fate as they finally pay for their sins. The author appeals to a higher court, to God Himself, to execute judgment.

In a time and culture when crudeness prevailed, the frequent visible intervention of God worked as a powerful deterrent to injustice in high places. The Old Testament practice of drastic retribution stands in high relief in this very ancient Psalm; yet what we now regard as imperfect and superseded was then effective and necessary in God's estimation. God was leading His people out of rank paganism, so the literal intolerance of injustice here became a moral lesson for basic renewal.

For us who live at the other extreme of "liberty" and tolerance of evil, God is still speaking in this Psalm. The passion for justice, so vehement in the Lord's life, speaks to us in this piece. God speaks variously in different times (Heb. 1:1f.). Now He speaks through Christ, who clearly explained that it was the "hardness of heart" of the ancients (Mk. 10:5f.) that was God's reason for allowing abuses. There would seem to be less purpose reciting this Psalm were it not for the Savior's praying it and were it not that the perversion of justice in our day has reached an all-time high and established the greatest blemish on our history.

God is still living (v. 10) and watching the world for the sake of the poor, the helpless, the believer. The mighty will be mightily punished (Wis. 6:6), even though in our era justice is mellowed by mercy.

Injustice is as sinful as ever. Our Lord uses the language of this Psalm when He exposes the Pharisees as a "brood of vipers" (Mt. 3:7), yet He died on the Cross for all. In both Testaments God cursed evil (Dt. 20:17f.; 27:14-26; Mt. 23; Lk. 19:42ff.; Jn. 8:44; 12:31; 15:22 etc.). Though Christ died for sinners, His mercy cannot reach the impenitent (Jn. 8:24). He deemed it necessary to submit to false judges and witnesses so that they might have the grace of repentance.

Grateful for the warning of the literal sense, we pray this Psalm in hope of converting all who abuse their authority, judges included. This Psalm has an important function in our society, namely, to put the whole moral order back on its right hinges. Out of deference for the uneducated primitive, who might apply this Psalm for personal vengeance, the Church refrains from the public use of it in her liturgy.

Psalm 59 (58)

Deliver me from my enemies, O my God,
    protect me from those who rise up against me,
²deliver me from those who work evil,
    and save me from bloodthirsty men.

³For, lo, they lie in wait for my life;
    fierce men band themselves against me.
For no transgression or sin of mine, O LORD,
⁴   for no fault of mine, they run and make ready.

Rouse thyself, come to my help, and see!
⁵   Thou, LORD God of hosts, art God of Israel.
Awake to punish all the nations;
    spare none of those who treacherously plot evil.

⁶Each evening they come back,
    howling like dogs
    and prowling about the city.
⁷There they are, bellowing with their mouths,
    and snarling with their lips—
    for "Who," they think, "will hear us?"

8But thou, O Lord, dost laugh at them;
  thou dost hold all the nations in derision.
9O my Strength, I will sing praises to thee;
  for thou, O God, art my fortress.
10My God in his steadfast love will meet me;
  my God will let me look in triumph on my enemies.

11Slay them not, lest my people forget;
  make them totter by thy power, and bring them down,
  O Lord, our shield!
12For the sin of their mouths, the words of their lips,
  let them be trapped in their pride.
  For the cursing and lies which they utter,
13   consume them in wrath,
  consume them till they are no more,
  that men may know that God rules over Jacob
  to the ends of the earth.

14Each evening they come back,
  howling like dogs
  and prowling about the city.
15They roam about for food,
  and growl if they do not get their fill.

16But I will sing of thy might;
  I will sing aloud of thy steadfast love in the morning.
  For thou hast been to me a fortress
  and a refuge in the day of my distress.
17O my Strength, I will sing praises to thee,
  for thou, O God, art my fortress,
  the God who shows me steadfast love.

God Is My Strength

Nearly all the Psalms have undergone change, additions, and adaptations for worship during the centuries before Christ, which makes it harder to interpret them now or discern the situation and author of their origin. The author of this Psalm may have been a king who is fighting two enemies, a foreign nation and internal foes that were revolting. It is against the latter that he prays especially, for they are far more dangerous: bloodthirsty, traitorous, prowling guerrillas whom he compares to packs of nightly howling dogs. They defy God as they say, "Who will hear us?" But they are guilty of many more sins, pride, lying, and cursing.

The Psalmist takes refuge in God, who protects the just. May He deal with the enemy, lest they beguile His people. For God it is a small matter to dispose of them; for the king it is a great delivery from disaster and a help to instill faith and right order everywhere. To us the punishment sounds severe and extreme since we are unaware of the facts, but this way of prayer is common in the Old Testament poetic, passionate Psalms. People will come to recognize God as the sole ruler of Jacob, and even "to the ends of the earth" His power will be felt. (See also the comments on the preceding Psalm.)

We would stand to benefit by making our own the repeated refrain, "O my Strength! I will sing praise to thee, for thou, O God, art my fortress." To do so, as we become conscious of our spiritual foes, would be Christlike. Jesus, the Savior, entered into the spirit of this Psalm when He was surrounded by deadly enemies. He was innocent and could have summoned legions of angels to His defense, but He only appealed to His Father in prayer. He foretold a great catastrophe (Lk. 21:20ff.), but this was the Father's concern. And He died forgiving His torturers; otherwise there would have been only justice and no merciful redemption.

In His present glory, He is with us in a special manner, as we pray this Psalm in His way, which is the way of charity (Rom. 8:35ff.). Nothing can separate us from His love as we join the Church in praying it (parts on II Fridays at noon).

Psalm 60 (59)

O God, thou hast rejected us, broken our defenses;
    thou hast been angry; oh, restore us.
2Thou hast made the land to quake,
    thou hast rent it open;
    repair its breaches, for it totters.
3Thou hast made thy people suffer hard things;
    thou hast given us wine to drink that made us reel.

4Thou hast set up a banner for those who fear thee,
    to rally to it from the bow.

⁵That thy beloved may be delivered,
  give victory by thy right hand and answer us!

⁶God has spoken in his sanctuary:
  "With exultation I will divide up Shechem
  and portion out the Vale of Succoth.
⁷Gilead is mine; Manasseh is mine;
  Ephraim is my helmet;
  Judah is my scepter.
⁸Moab is my washbasin;
  upon Edom I cast my shoe;
  over Philistia I shout in triumph."

⁹Who will bring me to the fortified city?
  Who will lead me to Edom?
¹⁰Hast thou not rejected us, O God?
  Thou dost not go forth, O God, with our armies.
¹¹O grant us help against the foe,
  for vain is the help of man!
¹²With God we shall do valiantly;
  it is he who will tread down our foes.

Rally Around God's Banner

What mistakes led to the military disaster we do not know, but the losses were heavy as God did not go forth with Israel's armies. The first verses tell of the reverses and national demoralization which was part of the cup of defeat. The author compares the cup to doped wine of wrath, which the people had to drink. After this the Psalm changes to a hopeful tone as he quotes God's oracle and promises from the sanctuary. The whole world belongs to God, but verses 6-8 describe how He apportioned out certain parts.

There is Shechem of Canaan which God gave to Abraham; then Succoth of the Jaboc Valley where Jacob got the name Israel; next Gilead and Manasseh northeast across the Jordan; Ephraim, a chief northern tribe, and Judah that had the capital Jerusalem. There were the subjected peoples of Moab across the Dead Sea, and Edom lower south, a traditional enemy of God's people, like the Philistines. All these comprised the united kingdom under David and Solomon. It brought comfort and courage to hear this oracle again (found also in Ps. 108:7-13; see Gen. 33:17-19) and be under God's plan and banner.

God had worked wonders for them, but with their best effort and faithful cooperation.

"Who will bring me to the fortified city?" This was probably the famous Petra of the desert, a fabulous fortress of natural mountains and the last holdout. The simple answer is: "With God we shall do valiantly," and with a prayer for God's help the Psalm ends. The people of old are symbolic of the New. God metes out to nations and individuals their gifts and spheres of action, also their boundaries and limitations. He widens the borders and cuts them back. Fidelity is the price.

We stand before Him with heads bowed in shame and grief as we contemplate losses and defections, the shrinkage of His visible Kingdom of which we are stewards. It is the spiritual counterpart of the military disaster described in this Psalm. We are paying the penalty for the moral breakup. We have not kept His covenant. We have been unfaithful in keeping the unity of the Church as Christianity is "split wide open." So-called Christian nations have not provided justice for the poor, and they are rocked to the foundations by the terrorism of majorities and minorities seeking their rights. Individuals do not keep their appetites in check and as a result vast numbers lack the food and energy they need. Some grow fat, others lean. A war economy and the arms race show that God is not marching with our armies. We must again rally around Christ and His banner.

This is an ecumenical prayer. God wants to reapportion the world and rejuvenate His people. He has not rejected us; we have rejected Him. We overcome our doubts by adopting His promises and certainties. He holds out mercy (Rom. 11:12-24), but on His terms. There will be one flock and one Shepherd (Jn. 10:16). The Lord prayed for our unity (Jn. 17:23). He is the Rock of decision (Jn. 12:47ff.). "For he is our peace, who has made us both one, and has broken down the dividing wall of hostility . . ." (Eph. 2:14ff.). He prays this Psalm in the Church on II Fridays (noon) according to this intention.

Psalm 61 (60)

Hear my cry, O God,
     listen to my prayer;
²from the end of the earth I call to thee,
     when my heart is faint.

Lead thou me
> to the rock that is higher than I;
³for thou art my refuge,
> a strong tower against the enemy.

⁴Let me dwell in thy tent for ever!
> Oh to be safe under the shelter of thy wings!
⁵For thou, O God, hast heard my vows,
> thou hast given me the heritage of those who fear thy name.

⁶Prolong the life of the king;
> may his years endure to all generations!
⁷May he be enthroned for ever before God;
> bid steadfast love and faithfulness watch over him!

⁸So will I ever sing praises to thy name,
> as I pay my vows day after day.

God's Heart Forever

Away from God's sanctuary, at "the end of the earth," far removed from safety and hope, the author's heart grows faint and weak. Whether it was the king or another person who prays for him, he begs for the things that bring him security and refuge "under the shelter of thy wings." God has accepted his vows (promises), but continues to try His faithful servant. The Psalmist perseveres in his praise and godly expectations. Here the picture is one of exile from God (like Psalms 42 and 43), who alone sustains hope. The cry of the heart is for God's home and presence.

"Let me dwell in thy tent forever." God's tent was on Zion, His tabernacle, where the wings of the protecting Cherubim sheltered the whole nation. This belief and hope was so firm that it was the heart of Israel's piety. There stood the Rock higher than human strength could reach, the peak of rest. It stands for the ultimate aspiration for union with God, the home of immortality. Because it was given as a promise by God Himself through the prophet Nathan (v. 8), all hearts aspired to the divine home, hearts that feel themselves away from God, "at the end of the earth."

At the incarnation God set up His tent among humankind. The ancient goat's-hair tent was a simple, temporary promise of His new dwelling with men. The "tent forever," where God is enthroned, is none other than the humanity of Jesus Christ, where all find their safe home. The final and greatest descendant of David is Christ, who gathers our vows, our hopes and fears, our praise, while we are in exile, and safely places us on the Rock of refuge, too high for unaided human strength to reach. That is the Sacred Heart of the Savior in which kindness and faithfulness assist humanity to attain rest and safety.

Here we see again the harmony of public and personal piety. Visible worship and cult leads us to the high mountain, to God's home, to the rest of immortality. Such is the humanity and heart of Christ, so tangible and near that it includes the heart of His Mother, who wove the cloth for His tent. The Heart of God takes the shape of our hearts and lives. Christ has that all-embracing Heart to shelter His flock (Mt. 23:37), a place of refuge for all. His Shepherd-Heart still beats for His flock at the right hand of the Father, where our real home is. As Shepherd, He still spreads the table where we eat in the sight of our foes (Psalm 23) and repeats the desert experience of old in an exalted, fulfilled manner (Jn. 6:43ff.). His hand is the Father's hand that feeds, protects, and leads to eternal safety (Jn. 10:28f.).

Let this Psalm weld us together and with Christ, as we pray it on the feast of the Sacred Heart (office of readings) and on II Saturdays (noon).

Psalm 62 (61)

> For God alone my soul waits in silence;
>> from him comes my salvation.
> ²He only is my rock and my salvation,
>> my fortress; I shall not be greatly moved.
>
> ³How long will you set upon a man
>> to shatter him, all of you,
>> like a leaning wall, a tottering fence?
> ⁴They only plan to thrust him down from his eminence.
>> They take pleasure in falsehood.
> They bless with their mouths,
>> but inwardly they curse.

⁵For God alone my soul waits in silence,
for my hope is from him.
⁶He only is my rock and my salvation,
my fortress; I shall not be shaken.
⁷On God rests my deliverance and my honor;
my mighty rock, my refuge is God.

⁸Trust in him at all times, O people;
pour out your heart before him;
God is a refuge for us.
⁹Men of low estate are but a breath,
men of high estate are a delusion;
in the balance they go up;
they are together lighter than a breath.
¹⁰Put no confidence in extortion,
set no vain hopes on robbery;
if riches increase, set not your heart on them.

¹¹Once God has spoken;
twice have I heard this:
that power belongs to God;
¹²   and that to thee, O Lord, belongs steadfast love.
For thou dost requite a man
according to his work.

Abandonment to God

The lesson of this Psalm appears in the very first verse: "For God alone my soul waits in silence," and "God is a refuge for us" (v. 8). A moral Psalm teaching divine wisdom, this prayer comes out of bitter human experiences. The author records his feelings when attacked by enemies. These enemies are hypocrites, who bless and curse at the same time. Helpless and greatly tormented, he turns to God where alone he finds comfort and peace. He does not cease to extol God as his Rock and stronghold and salvation. He repeats the simple formula of inner calm: God only, my Rock and hope!

On God's scale, mortal man weighs less than a breath. With a borrowed existence and nothing to call his own, all props other than God vanish, wealth especially. In the light of faith there is no human greatness or prestige, no power or esteem. Everything comes from God. Man achieves his right balance only when he realizes that God is his origin and end. This thought also banishes fear and distress, quiets the emotions, gives peace of heart. All men need to come to this basic religious truth of their dependence on God. This wisdom he passes on to other people, to trust God at all times. He urges them to "pour out your heart before him" and thereby sets himself up as a teacher of wisdom.

"Once God has spoken," and two things the author heard (v. 11f.). This phrase is a Hebrew poetic way of uttering a proverb, namely, "Power belongs to God, and to thee, O Lord, belongs steadfast love." God's word is infinitely rich, and contains many meanings. He also repays all our good deeds, thus crowning His own gifts and graces with new rewards.

We have no fortresses as in bygone days; we have much more: God in whom we trust! Living faith in Him as our life's foundation gives strength and peace and quiet. Our soul is quiet in God alone. This Psalm has the power to give our entire lives a serene happiness, the kind our Savior promised in the Sermon on the Mount. While the whole world builds false fortresses, stockpiles wealth and arms, here we learn detachment: "If riches increase, set not your heart on them." We follow Jesus, who put no trust in man, not even His own disciples (Lk. 22:44f.), who taught us supernatural trust. It is His gift, not the neat product of psychological know-how.

Through His resurrection and sharing His life with us, He has raised us up on "a mighty rock." Daily He lifts us to new heights in the house of God, His Church, through His Word and Work. It is His Spirit that shrinks our feelings of doubt, anguish, and affliction, then expands our being with a shared divine sonship. Ever since Jesus said, "I have overcome the world" (Jn. 16:33), martyrs are at peace and we have absolute confidence in Him. As we turn our hearts to God, we learn abandonment to God, the message of this Psalm, a prayer for all occasions. The Church makes this prayer of Christ her Spouse more effective on II Wednesdays, at vespers, and calls for trust in Him (Jn. 14:27).

Psalm 63 (62)

O God, thou art my God, I seek thee,
    my soul thirsts for thee;
my flesh faints for thee,
    as in a dry and weary land where no water is.
[2]So I have looked upon thee in the sanctuary,
    beholding thy power and glory.
[3]Because thy steadfast love is better than life,
    my lips will praise thee.
[4]So I will bless thee as long as I live;
    I will lift up my hands and call on thy name.

[5]My soul is feasted as with marrow and fat,
    and my mouth praises thee with joyful lips,
[6]when I think of thee upon my bed,
    and meditate on thee in the watches of the night;
[7]for thou hast been my help,
    and in the shadow of thy wings I sing for joy.
[8]My soul clings to thee;
    thy right hand upholds me.

[9]But those who seek to destroy my life
    shall go down into the depths of the earth;
[10]they shall be given over to the power of the sword,
    they shall be prey for jackals.
[11]But the king shall rejoice in God;
    all who swear by him shall glory;
    for the mouths of liars will be stopped.

Clinging to God

What rain is for arid land, union with God is for the Psalmist and for us. Without life-giving moisture, we have wasteland devoid of growth and life. Dry land is a picture of thirst and longing for God. Thirst in the body can be most intense pain. The author seeks God in the authentic way and place, in His Temple, where He has revealed His power, glory, and kindness, where He also receives the praise of His greatness. God's presence is a rich banquet of food and drink that satiates the soul. Calling on His Name day and night, meditating on God in his solitary hours, resting in the shadow of God's wings, and clinging to His holy place, that is the author's inmost desire.

In the background linger threatening enemies who seek his life, but they will reap God's judgment in due time. Enmity matters little, so strong is the constant longing for God, so keen is the nostalgia for Him. Hunger and thirst are true images for the soul's deepest desire because God is the total source and goal of man's being. Longing is love and love is longing. "O God, my God, my soul thirsts for thee; my flesh faints for thee." If a king is speaking this Psalm, we have royalty seeking Royalty. Separation from God is death.

No one ever prayed this Psalm with the same longing that Christ had for the Father. It contains the ultimate yearning of His Heart. With His humanity He kept constant vigil for the Father, also during the watches of the night. His humanity is also the hand that grips us tightly and leads us to the Father. True God and man, He came to pick up humankind and bring us home. Therefore His heavenly longing was for our benefit. He manifested it in the Temple worship and teaching, where His parents found Him (Lk. 2:44f.). He spent nights in prayer (Lk. 6:12). He taught the crowds to long for the food He was giving (Jn. 6), the Eucharist, and His drink, the Holy Spirit (Jn. 4:10ff.). After teaching us so clearly, He gave us His Body and Blood, food and drink, that we might satiate our hunger and thirst for Him, for God. His love knew no bounds: He Himself longed greatly for this Banquet (Lk. 22:15f.).

There were His enemies, first those who became friends and received Him, then other enemies who did not receive Him, who do not "call on His Name," but even curse it. For all He laid down His life. The impenitent ones shall meet eternal frustration, while the faithful ones will share His glory as King (Jn. 17:24 and Rev. 3:24). They will satiate their thirst with the beatific vision forever, the "face to face" experience in heaven (1 Cor. 13:12).

Our life now should abound with this Psalm, with the desire for heaven. If heaven is our home, where is our homesickness? our night watches with Christ? our gravitating to God? We should not only seek God "with all spiritual longing" (St. Benedict), but pray for those in exile away from God, in sin. We have Communion now with God through Christ's Body and Blood. Without it we languish and die like a wasteland deprived of life and growth. The greater our destiny, the greater our frustration in missing eternal beatitude. We pray this Psalm with the Church on I Sundays (lauds), when Christ is "always making intercession" for us (Heb. 7:25).

Psalm 64 (63)

Hear my voice, O God, in my complaint;
    preserve my life from dread of the enemy,
²hide me from the secret plots of the wicked,
    from the scheming of evildoers,
³who whet their tongues like swords,
    who aim bitter words like arrows,
⁴shooting from ambush at the blameless,
    shooting at him suddenly and without fear.
⁵They hold fast to their evil purpose;
    they talk of laying snares secretly,
thinking, "Who can see us?
⁶   Who can search out our crimes?
We have thought out a cunningly conceived plot."
    For the inward mind and heart of a man are deep!

⁷But God will shoot his arrow at them;
    they will be wounded suddenly.
⁸Because of their tongue he will bring them to ruin;
    all who see them will wag their heads.
⁹Then all men will fear;
    they will tell what God has wrought,
    and ponder what he has done.

¹⁰Let the righteous rejoice in the LORD,
    and take refuge in him!
Let all the upright in heart glory!

God Protects the Just

Couched in ancient images, this Psalm describes a modern situation: the ruthless intrigues of the wicked and God's answer to the complaints of the righteous. In Old Testament times, the pattern of prayer includes cries for help, then details of the foes' evil-doing, the self-defense of the sinner, God's intervention for justice, and the joyful proclamation of the just man and assembly. It seems that here the innocent man has to defend himself against planned evil, and in desperation he calls on God for protection. Personal enemies attack him, not with real weapons, but with poisonous tongues that are worse than arrows and swords, with hidden malice more dangerous than open warfare.

God repays in kind. He defeats the subtle plans and lays bare the stupidity of all evil plots for all men to see. God's work is so sudden that men must fear. Divine wisdom is never at a loss against the deep thoughts of man. "Who can see us?" This short-sighted question is for God to answer. He tears away the mask of human cunning and deceit and makes an example of evil intent. When "all men will fear," His triumph puts to rest the concerns of the just.

Human malice and intrigue never reached lower depths than in the life and death of the Savior. One calumny followed the other. Never was innocence more pure and holy; never was human folly more blind and mistaken. His enemies called Him a blasphemer (Mk. 14:63f.) and treated Him with contempt (Lk. 23:11). They accused Him of leading men astray (Jn. 7:47ff.) and said He was possessed by a demon (Jn. 8:48). In their perversity they called Him a sinner (Jn. 9: 24; 18:30) and brought false witnesses against Him (Mk. 14:57f.). They shot accusations at Him like arrows, but the arrows of God were sharper in the resurrection, which was His sudden, unexpected triumph. Never was the joy of the just vindicated so quickly and proclaimed to all men.

In this Psalm we "ponder what he has done" and "tell what he has done": God's way of justice and mercy. Fear gives way to love, or rather they embrace in Christ. As we bring our sorrows before Him in humility, He directs us to His Body the Church for the answer and solution. There we experience the blessed mercy and justice of the Lord in quick answer. With Christ and His members in the Church, this Psalm restores us, on Holy Saturday (lauds), feast of the apostle John (December 27, office of readings), II Saturdays (noon), and common of the apostles (office of readings). We pray it not with secret thoughts of revenge, but with genuine, sincere purpose, in a transferred spiritual sense.

Psalm 65 (64)

Praise is due to thee, O God, in Zion;
and to thee shall vows be performed,
2   O thou who hearest prayer!
To thee shall all flesh come
3   on account of sins.
When our transgressions prevail over us,
thou dost forgive them.
4Blessed is he whom thou dost choose and bring near,
to dwell in thy courts!
We shall be satisfied with the goodness of thy house,
thy holy temple!

5By dread deeds thou dost answer us with deliverance,
O God of our salvation,
who art the hope of all the ends of the earth,
and of the farthest seas;
6who by thy strength hast established the mountains,
being girded with might;
7who dost still the roaring of the seas,
the roaring of their waves,
the tumult of the peoples;
8so that those who dwell at earth's farthest bounds
are afraid at thy signs;
thou makest the outgoings of the morning and the evening
to shout for joy.

9Thou visitest the earth and waterest it,
thou greatly enrichest it;
the river of God is full of water;
thou providest their grain,
for so thou hast prepared it.
10Thou waterest its furrows abundantly,
settling its ridges,
softening it with showers,
and blessing its growth.
11Thou crownest the year with thy bounty;
the tracks of thy chariot drip with fatness.
12The pastures of the wilderness drip,
the hills gird themselves with joy,
13the meadows clothe themselves with flocks,
the valleys deck themselves with grain,
they shout and sing together for joy.

God's Blessings

In Zion praise is due for God's mercy and bounty. The holy Temple is the center and setting to which "all flesh" tends, from which all blessings flow. There the sinner finds solace and the goodness of the Lord. God will tolerate nothing unholy in His presence, and He chooses those who dwell in His courts. There the God of salvation forgives sins, which is a revelation of peace and a prerequisite for His praises. Here as nowhere else He hears the petitions of His people gathered in communal worship. Happiness and hope of salvation are gifts of the God of Zion.

Blessed are the servants of the Lord on whom His choice rests. They will experience His favors in His house and beyond. They will shout for joy in His presence, while those afar off stand in dread fear of His signs of power. The God of power is "girded with might," who controls the powers of nature and quiets the "tumult of the peoples." If we see that this mighty God is benign, then He is for us the God of joy.

In this beautiful song all nature rejoices, not only the distant east and west but also the nearby fields, rivers, hills, and meadows. The "river of God" provides moisture and crops, so that the harvest "drips" with plenty. The flocks in the pastures resemble a wide cloak of white. Valleys are decked with grain in fulness that rejoices the eye. All "shout and sing together" because their Maker has blessed the land and crowned the year.

People should pray this Psalm not only in thanksgiving for a good harvest but also in anticipation of weather and rain that make hearts rejoice. Spring and summer alike are festival times of happy song. God's goodness here pictures His bountiful salvation. Things that give joy to the human heart are, after all, but feeble imitations of the glorious blessings God has in store for us. Our Psalm has special power to help realize the spiritual realities and harvest. We hold a stewardship of this earth, and God's staggering abundance in it is dwarfed by the invisible richness that flows from His Temple. If all nature sings and shouts, then we should too! We lack the language and words to describe the Lord's Coming, as we receive water and oil, bread and wine as the blessed carriers of that Coming.

Singing is an exalted form of praise. The ultimate reason for singing is Christ's glorious presence and Coming. If we could break through the veil of faith, we would break forth in song. "All flesh" must come to Him singing because supernature demands it more even than nature. The springtime and harvest of humanity in God is here. The Cross of Christ brought joy into the whole world. The incarnation and resurrection have filled the Temple of His Body with uncounted gifts of the Spirit, fountains and showers of grace. The Psalms prepare us to live in the world of Christ and God. If only we could read the Signs. Nothing has changed. Christ still multiplies Bread. God has kept His promise.

The Church is the place of song and joy, of sunrise and sunset, of rich banqueting and divine Providence, even to the farthest bounds of the earth. She sings this guarantee of final fruition on II Tuesdays at lauds.

Psalm 66 (65)

Make a joyful noise to God, all the earth;
2   sing the glory of his name;
        give to him glorious praise!
3Say to God, "How terrible are thy deeds!
        So great is thy power that thy enemies cringe before thee.
4All the earth worships thee;
        they sing praises to thee,
        sing praises to thy name."

5Come and see what God has done:
        he is terrible in his deeds among men.
6He turned the sea into dry land;
        men passed through the river on foot.
    There did we rejoice in him,
7   who rules by his might for ever,
    whose eyes keep watch on the nations—
        let not the rebellious exalt themselves.

8Bless our God, O peoples,
        let the sound of his praise be heard,
9who has kept us among the living,
        and has not let our feet slip.
10For thou, O God, hast tested us;
        thou hast tried us as silver is tried.

11Thou didst bring us into the net;
    thou didst lay affliction on our loins;
12thou didst let men ride over our heads;
    we went through fire and through water;
  yet thou hast brought us forth to a spacious place.

13I will come into thy house with burnt offerings;
    I will pay thee my vows,
14that which my lips uttered
    and my mouth promised when I was in trouble.
15I will offer to thee burnt offerings of fatlings,
    with the smoke of the sacrifice of rams;
  I will make an offering of bulls and goats.

16Come and hear, all you who fear God,
    and I will tell what he has done for me.
17I cried aloud to him,
    and he was extolled with my tongue.
18If I had cherished iniquity in my heart,
    the Lord would not have listened;
19But truly God has listened;
    he has given heed to the voice of my prayer.

20Blessed be God,
    because he has not rejected my prayer
    or removed his steadfast love from me!

Public and Private Praise

We praise God by praising His works. Each individual (vv. 13-20), no less than the community (vv. 1-12), can duplicate this Psalm by raising their voices of praise to God. The official worship in the Temple, plus the personal witness of "what he has done for me," combine in the revealed order of prayer. All must cry out, shout loudly and sing, for He has set our feet in open "spacious places," the wide freedom of God's world. God's glory radiates to all peoples and countries. It unites many voices, as His works have no end.

The author recalls the great love of God for Israel in the Exodus and His guidance of the people through the desert, watching over them against their enemies. He gave life to them: comfort, food, light, and, surprisingly, suffering of trials to refine them, as with a tempering fire. God tests and tries those He has chosen as His own, so it is necessary to thank Him also for the hard things, not just for the agreeable side of life. The snares on the way, the burdens on our backs, the authority of men sometimes riding roughshod over our heads: these are the "fire and water" that purify and strengthen us. We should carry no trace of evil within us and be pure in His sight.

Christ the Savior repeats the call to praise that we find in this Psalm. It reflects His action and prayer as Head of the Church. He sublimates the Psalm by giving it a higher sense. In Him we discover the great unity of communal and personal work of salvation. Always oriented to the Father's house, He brings praise, suffering, and glory together into one. Suffering and the way of the Cross was His trial by fire and water. Not with fatlings of flocks nor with burnt offerings of holocausts did He "pay his vows" to God, but with His precious Blood and doing the will of His Father. Also His blessed Mother proclaimed the great things God had done for her.

All the enemies must capitulate and come in humble homage to find grace and mercy and learn to repeat this Psalm after Him. Greater than the events of the Red Sea and Exodus is the victory of His resurrection. He promises us the same victory and glory. The fall of Jerusalem and of persecuting empires are now historic ruins along the path of history, but Christ continues to reign in His Church and heavenly Kingdom. We go forward to welcome His Second Coming in glory. Obedience to God comes first; all else is secondary as we go to meet Him.

Sharing with Him means baptism of suffering (Mk. 10:38f.), even laying down our lives for God that we may receive them back (2 Cor. 4:14f.) and singing praise while we are tested as silver in the fire (1 Pet. 1:6f.) that we may fill the final measure of praise (Rev. 19:1-8). Now we join the earthly symphony by praying this Psalm with the Church on the feast of the Baptism of Christ, on IV Sundays, and Easter Sunday (office of readings).

Psalm 67 (66)

May God be gracious to us and bless us
and make his face to shine upon us,
²that thy way may be known upon earth,
thy saving power among all nations.
³Let the peoples praise thee, O God;
let all the peoples praise thee!

⁴Let the nations be glad and sing for joy,
for thou dost judge the peoples with equity
and guide the nations upon earth.
⁵Let the peoples praise thee, O God;
let all the peoples praise thee!

⁶The earth has yielded its increase;
God, our God, has blessed us.
⁷God has blessed us;
let all the ends of the earth fear him!

Praise for God's Blessings

A spirit of thankful joy fills this Psalm. A priestly blessing (close variant of Moses' command in Num. 6:22-27 and of what we find in other Psalms), this prayer tells us that all blessings come from God and lead to Him. His way of praise is lively, dramatic, and communal (responses). All nations of the world must come to know Him as the only source of saving blessings. They must worship Him and love Him entirely for His own sake.

If His face shines on us, there is joy. God is the source of joy. All people have a right to this joy, as to His salvation. His justice rules humanity; hence the refrain, "Let all the peoples praise thee." Revelation makes known God's will; faith is the acceptance of it. The knowledge of God revealing Himself is His first gift. He comes first and last. Even after enjoying His favors, we remain in fear and awe of Him who is our great God and Creator. The beginning and end of the Psalm teach us reverent love.

He knows our needs before we ask anything. The fruits of a good harvest come from His open hand. "God, our God, has blessed us." His care is constant control. We cannot manipulate Him by our narrow intentions. He wants us to ask for things we need, even for what we think "we have coming," always turning to Him with truly free service, childlike trust and joyful thanks. Then the Psalm takes on a spiritual meaning.

If the earth yields fruit according to God's plan, we must yield the fruit of pure praise for His sake. Do we use His gifts for our sake and forget about the poor? The Psalm is a test of unselfishness. Food, like God's salvation, is for all. The nations can truly praise Him when the hungry poor come to their rights. Only then, when justice has been done, can the ends of the earth rejoice and sing.

On the lips of Christ and in the Church, the Psalm has wonderful relevance. The "earth has yielded its increase" in Christ's birth of the Virgin Mary. The fruit of her immaculate Womb, Christ is God's greatest blessing (Rom. 8:32), and He uses this Psalm for a constant spiritual harvest of blessings. The Our Father contains it: "Give us this day our daily bread!" And with Christ "dwelling in our hearts through faith" (Eph. 3:17-19), "let all the peoples praise thee."

This expanded view of the Psalm gives the Christian another approach to the eternal, spiritual gifts that God distributes to the world through the Spirit of Christ. We pray it that way. The harvest is great and ready (Mt. 9:37), and we learn to pass on what we have received. How else than letting the light of His face shine on others (Mt. 5:16 and 1 Pet. 2:12) can the whole world join in this universal praise? We pray, "Come, Lord Jesus!" because we have the vocation to share gifts and truth with "the peoples." The Church continues this blessing in her prayer on III Tuesdays (noon) and II Wednesdays (vespers). Let us not tie Christ's hands or muffle His voice!

Psalm 68 (67)

> Let God arise, let his enemies be scattered;
>   let those who hate him flee before him!
> ²As smoke is driven away, so drive them away;
>   as wax melts before fire,
>   let the wicked perish before God!
> ³But let the righteous be joyful;
>   let them exult before God;
>   let them be jubilant with joy!

⁴Sing to God, sing praises to his name;
      lift up a song to him who rides upon the clouds;
      his name is the Lord, exult before him!

⁵Father of the fatherless and protector of widows
      is God in his holy habitation.
⁶God gives the desolate a home to dwell in;
      he leads out the prisoners to prosperity;
      but the rebellious dwell in a parched land.

⁷O God, when thou didst go forth before thy people,
      when thou didst march through the wilderness,
⁸the earth quaked, the heavens poured down rain,
      at the presence of God;
    yon Sinai quaked at the presence of God,
      the God of Israel.
⁹Rain in abundance, O God, thou didst shed abroad;
      thou didst restore thy heritage as it languished;
¹⁰thy flock found a dwelling in it;
      in thy goodness, O God, thou didst provide for the needy.

¹¹The Lord gives the command;
      great is the host of those who bore the tidings:
¹²   "The kings of the armies, they flee, they flee!"
  The women at home divide the spoil,
¹³   though they stay among the sheepfolds—
  the wings of a dove covered with silver,
      its pinions with green gold.
¹⁴When the Almighty scattered kings there,
      snow fell on Zalmon.

¹⁵O mighty mountain, mountain of Bashan;
      O many-peaked mountain, mountain of Bashan!
¹⁶Why look you with envy, O many-peaked mountain,
      at the mount which God desired for his abode,
      yea, for the Lord will dwell for ever?

¹⁷With mighty chariotry, twice ten thousand,
    thousands upon thousands,
    the Lord came from Sinai into the holy place.
¹⁸Thou didst ascend the high mount,
    leading captives in thy train,
    and receiving gifts among men,
  even among the rebellious, that the Lord God may
    dwell there.

¹⁹Blessed be the Lord,
    who daily bears us up;
    God is our salvation.
²⁰Our God is a God of salvation;
    and to God, the Lord, belongs escape from death.

²¹But God will shatter the heads of his enemies,
    the hairy crown of him who walks in his guilty ways.
²²The Lord said,
    "I will bring them back from Bashan,
    I will bring them back from the depths of the sea,
²³that you may bathe your feet in blood,
    that the tongues of your dogs may have their portion from
      the foe."

²⁴Thy solemn processions are seen, O God,
    the processions of my God, my King, into the sanctuary—
²⁵the singers in front, the minstrels last,
    between them maidens playing timbrels:
²⁶"Bless God in the great congregation,
    the Lord, O you who are of Israel's fountain!"
²⁷There is Benjamin, the least of them, in the lead,
    the princes of Judah in their throng,
    the princes of Zebulun, the princes of Naphtali.

²⁸Summon thy might, O God;
>show thy strength, O God, thou who hast wrought for us.
²⁹Because of thy temple at Jerusalem
>kings bear gifts to thee.
³⁰Rebuke the beasts that dwell among the reeds,
>the herd of bulls with the calves of the peoples.
>Trample under foot those who lust after tribute;
>scatter the peoples who delight in war.
³¹Let bronze be brought from Egypt;
>let Ethiopia hasten to stretch out her hands to God.

³²Sing to God, O kingdoms of the earth;
>sing praises to the Lord,
³³to him who rides in the heavens, the ancient heavens;
>lo, he sends forth his voice, his mighty voice.
³⁴Ascribe power to God,
>whose majesty is over Israel,
>and his power is in the skies.
³⁵Terrible is God in his sanctuary,
>the God of Israel,
>he gives power and strength to his people.

Blessed be God!

God's Solemn Procession

This picturesque and highly figurative Psalm has many obscurities. These comments refer to what seems more certain. When God arises in heaven to take possession of His people, there is great turmoil. Enemies vanish like smoke; the wicked melt away like wax. One triumph after the other delights His followers, who "exult before him" (v. 4). It strikes us that first comes the joyous welcome of the poor: orphans, widows, prisoners hail God in Zion. The panorama of God riding on the clouds of the ancient heavens in a chariot moves in quick succession from one victory to another. Rebels alone (enemies like Edom, Moab, and Ammon) flee in fear, while the women divide the spoils.

The procession starts from Egypt (called "beasts that dwell in the reeds," verse 30) and takes His people through the desert, as the earth quakes and rain falls in abundance. God shepherds them like a flock and gives them a home. We call it the Exodus. The conquest goes on, as God chooses women for military conquest (Deborah).

That became a song in Israel: while men rest among the sheepfolds, the Almighty scatters the foe through the hand of a woman. Then mountains come alive: Salmon and Bashan to the north dominate by their majestic height, yet God does not choose them for His dwelling, as in the pagan myths. The lowly Zion He makes His highest sanctuary on earth. As other mountains look on in jealousy, God enters "his place of rest." From Sinai to Zion is His procession.

There follow the local "daily" victories of Israel's God (vv. 21-23), including carnage we little understand in our late day. Next, the procession of God to His holy place, amid singers, maidens, choirs, and princes, is a display of pomp and might. Subjected kings bring tribute instead of demanding it, the enemies lie prostrate or join in singing praise (v. 30), all in homage to the God of Israel as they cry "Blessed be God."

All this finds its ultimate realization only in Christ, as we learn from Eph. 4:3, which quotes our verse 18. Ascending on high, Jesus Christ took a large entourage of captives, redeemed humanity, "even among the rebellious." From heaven He distributes gifts. History has become Mystery. The Old Testament literal events have given way to the New Testament reality. God uses the things of time and space to lift us into His world of worship, which is the liturgical reality. The Church too is in procession, with Christ leading us to heavenly mansions (Jn. 14:2). He took us the enemy captive, but there are other enemies wailing outside (Rev. 6:15-17). His great intervention continues: His conquests, His protection of the flock, His promises of salvation, till the second Coming in glory. Mary, the great Woman of His Kingdom, personifies the greatest triumph.

"Blessed be the Lord who daily bears us up; God is our salvation" (v. 19). Pilgrims in the great Exodus, let us keep our eyes on Christ, join in the contest, swell the procession with "captives," nobles from Egypt and Ethiopia, prodigals and sinners, as we rehearse the Mystery by praying the Psalm on Ascension day and on III Tuesdays (office of readings).

Psalm 69 (68)

Save me, O God!
For the waters have come up to my neck.
²I sink in deep mire,
     where there is no foothold;
I have come into deep waters,
     and the flood sweeps over me.
³I am weary with my crying;
     my throat is parched.
My eyes grow dim
     with waiting for my God.

⁴More in number than the hairs of my head
     are those who hate me without cause;
mighty are those who would destroy me,
     those who attack me with lies.
What I did not steal
     must I now restore?
⁵O God, thou knowest my folly;
     the wrongs I have done are not hidden from thee.

⁶Let not those who hope in thee be put to shame through me,
     O Lord God of hosts;
let not those who seek thee be brought to dishonor
     through me,
     O God of Israel.
⁷For it is for thy sake that I have borne reproach,
     that shame has covered my face.
⁸I have become a stranger to my brethren,
     an alien to my mother's sons.

⁹For zeal for thy house has consumed me,
     and the insults of those who insult thee have fallen on me.
¹⁰When I humbled my soul with fasting,
     it became my reproach.
¹¹When I made sackcloth my clothing,
     I became a byword to them.
¹²I am the talk of those who sit in the gate,
     and the drunkards make songs about me.

¹³But as for me, my prayer is to thee, O Lord.
  At an acceptable time, O God,
    in the abundance of thy steadfast love answer me.
  With thy faithful help ¹⁴rescue me
    from sinking in the mire;
  let me be delivered from my enemies
    and from the deep waters.
¹⁵Let not the flood sweep over me,
    or the deep swallow me up,
    or the pit close its mouth over me.

¹⁶Answer me, O Lord, for thy steadfast love is good;
    according to thy abundant mercy, turn to me.
¹⁷Hide not thy face from thy servant;
    for I am in distress, make haste to answer me.
¹⁸Draw near to me, redeem me,
    set me free because of my enemies!

¹⁹Thou knowest my reproach,
    and my shame and my dishonor;
    my foes are all known to thee.
²⁰Insults have broken my heart,
    so that I am in despair.
  I looked for pity, but there was none;
    and for comforters, but I found none.
²¹They gave me poison for food,
    and for my thirst they gave me vinegar to drink.

²²Let their own table before them become a snare;
    let their sacrificial feasts be a trap.
²³Let their eyes be darkened, so that they cannot see;
    and make their loins tremble continually.
²⁴Pour out thy indignation upon them,
    and let thy burning anger overtake them.
²⁵May their camp be a desolation,
    let no one dwell in their tents.
²⁶For they persecute him whom thou hast smitten,
    and him whom thou hast wounded, they afflict still more.
²⁷Add to them punishment upon punishment;
    may they have no acquittal from thee.
²⁸Let them be blotted out of the book of the living;
    let them not be enrolled among the righteous.

²⁹But I am afflicted and in pain;
   let thy salvation, O God, set me on high!

³⁰I will praise the name of God with a song;
   I will magnify him with thanksgiving.
³¹This will please the Lord more than an ox
   or a bull with horns and hoofs.
³²Let the oppressed see it and be glad;
   you who seek God, let your hearts revive.
³³For the Lord hears the needy,
   and does not despise his own that are in bonds.

³⁴Let heaven and earth praise him,
   the seas and everything that moves therein.
³⁵For God will save Zion
   and rebuild the cities of Judah;
 and his servants shall dwell there and possess it;
³⁶   the children of his servants shall inherit it,
   and those who love his name shall dwell in it.

The Broken Heart

Afflicted with suffering in body and soul, the author is near death and cries in desperation to God for relief from pain and his enemies. Vivid figures describe his plight: the deep mire, a watery grave, parched throat, dim eyesight, shame and insults, hostile gossip, scandal taken by his brothers, drunken songs, and public disgrace. Even those dear to him suffer. Others blaspheme his zeal for God's house, and wags speculate about his guilt. Before God he admits his folly and faults, but rejects unjust accusations. For instance, they ask him to restore what he did not steal.

For God's sake he bears insults and injuries. That suffering for God's cause is no doubt the characteristic of this Psalm, a kind of vicarious suffering. His fasting, sackcloth, zeal for God, all are misinterpreted. The more intensely does he cry to God for justice and vengeance. God cannot hide His face from such injury: the foes are God's. No one takes his part; on the contrary, they add to his grief by giving him gall and vinegar.

In accord with the Old Law, the lowly will end rejoicing while the enemy will end in affliction. The retribution (vv. 22-28) is such that the author would not inflict, but leaves to God. Harsh as it sounds to our ears, it is a serious reminder of God's justice in punishing sinners. We do not pray it against people, but against impenitent spiritual powers that threaten salvation. That means our prayer is not for vengeance against sin, but compassion for sinners, following the example of Christ the Savior.

Verses 29ff. return to praise in the midst of affliction. "I will praise the name of God with a song," the song of a suffering heart. Confidence again takes over, and the Lord will rebuild the cities of Judah. Those who love His Name He will recall to dwell in their land. Similar to Psalm 22, which echoes Christ's abandonment, our Psalm is strikingly messianic. The author, like Jeremiah the prophet, is a type of the suffering Savior. While the Lord never had any sin to admit (as in v. 5), He made this Psalm His own.

Christ became an outcast to His own brethren, and without cause they hated Him (Jn. 15:25). He stooped down to our abject condition and took upon Himself the sins of the world (Jn. 8:46 and 2 Cor. 5:21). Insults of blasphemy fell on Him. His purging of God's Temple out of zeal brought Him new enmity (Jn. 2:14-20). Hatred for Him was hatred against the Father (Jn. 15:23). Dying on the Cross, Jesus thirsted and they gave Him vinegar, again to fulfill this Psalm (Jn. 19:29f.), a last act of His life. Rom. 15:3 refers to our Psalm: "The reproaches of those who reproached thee fell on me" [Christ]. Even the treason of Judas recalls our Psalm in Acts 1:20. Jesus had the power to retaliate, but He did not. Therefore all the poor rejoice and the cities of Judah are rebuilt. He died as a criminal that criminals might rejoice. The Church of martyrs and all who suffer trials of faith have new hope because of His broken Heart. We pray the Psalm, parts of it on III Fridays (office of readings).

Psalm 70 (69)

> Be pleased, O God, to deliver me!
> O LORD, make haste to help me!
> ²Let them be put to shame and confusion
> who seek my life!
> Let them be turned back and brought to dishonor
> who desire my hurt!
> ³Let them be appalled because of their shame
> who say, "Aha, Aha!"

⁴May all who seek thee
    rejoice and be glad in thee!
May those who love thy salvation
    say evermore, "God is great!"
⁵But I am poor and needy;
    hasten to me, O God!
Thou art my help and my deliverer;
    O LORD, do not tarry!

Lord, Have Mercy

Besides serving as part of Psalm 40 (39) (vv. 13-17, see comments there), this is also an independent Psalm. As a universal cry for God's assistance, the first verse has become the best known of the whole Psalter because the ancient Christians (see John Cassian, *Conference* 10) popularized it by using it at every occasion, in hard times and good, so that it became the opening prayer of every hour of the Church's office, and still answers the needs of all the sinners on the way. We use the whole of it on III Wednesdays (vespers) and in the office for the deceased.

Psalm 71 (70)

In thee, O LORD, do I take refuge;
    let me never be put to shame!
²In thy righteousness deliver me and rescue me;
    incline thy ear to me, and save me!
³Be thou to me a rock of refuge,
    a strong fortress to save me,
    for thou art my rock and my fortress.

⁴Rescue me, O my God, from the hand of the wicked,
    from the grasp of the unjust and cruel man.
⁵For thou, O Lord, art my hope,
    my trust, O LORD, from my youth.
⁶Upon thee I have leaned from my birth;
    thou art he who took me from my mother's womb.
My praise is continually of thee.

⁷I have been as a portent to many;
    but thou art my strong refuge.
⁸My mouth is filled with thy praise,
    and with thy glory all the day.
⁹Do not cast me off in the time of old age;
    forsake me not when my strength is spent.
¹⁰For my enemies speak concerning me,
    those who watch for my life consult together,
¹¹and say, "God has forsaken him;
    pursue and seize him,
    for there is none to deliver him."

¹²O God, be not far from me;
    O my God, make haste to help me!
¹³May my accusers be put to shame and consumed;
    with scorn and disgrace may they be covered
    who seek my hurt.
¹⁴But I will hope continually,
    and will praise thee yet more and more.
¹⁵My mouth will tell of thy righteous acts,
    of thy deeds of salvation all the day,
    for their number is past my knowledge.
¹⁶With the mighty deeds of the Lord God I will come,
    I will praise thy righteousness, thine alone.

¹⁷O God, from my youth thou hast taught me,
    and I still proclaim thy wondrous deeds.
¹⁸So even to old age and gray hairs,
    O God, do not forsake me,
  till I proclaim thy might
    to all the generations to come.
Thy power ¹⁹and thy righteousness, O God,
    reach the high heavens.

Thou who hast done great things,
    O God, who is like thee?
²⁰Thou who hast made me see many sore troubles
    wilt revive me again;
  from the depths of the earth
    thou wilt bring me up again.
²¹Thou wilt increase my honor,
    and comfort me again.

²²I will also praise thee with the harp
    for thy faithfulness, O my God;
  I will sing praises to thee with the lyre,
    O Holy One of Israel.
²³My lips will shout for joy,
    when I sing praises to thee;
    my soul also, which thou hast rescued.
²⁴And my tongue will talk of thy righteous help
    all the day long,
  for they have been put to shame and disgraced
    who sought to do me hurt.

Rock of the Aged

Many a phrase in this Psalm is known to us from other Psalms. That is as we expect from an elderly author who lived all his life in fidelity to the Lord. Sheer, unbounded praise alternates with acts of trust, even as the Psalmist repeatedly begs for divine help more insistently with the advancing years. God is his Rock of refuge and strong fortress from the womb to the tomb. His venerable gray hair, however, is also the occasion for new trials, recriminations of accusers, and there is no lack of enemies, those who watch to take advantage of him. Old age is not serene and quiet, respected for wisdom of experience, but its spent strength changes over to new anxieties.

There are those who pounce on the aged and take advantage of their weakness. The shadows lengthen with the years, as "many sore troubles" crop up, not least of all from oppressors of the elderly, even the criminally violent. We think here of the "mercy killers" for whom life is cheap, "cruel men" without humane feelings. While the life span of men and women is growing, so are the enemies who consider advanced age useless. This is the meaning of verse 7: "I have been as a portent to many," a sign of evil and an easy target. Failing health is a sign of age, but the author's faith grows the stronger.

Hope and trust are the music of the years. Total dependence on God is the childlikeness of the Gospel. Trust and confidence is the greatest heritage that old people can pass on to the young. To proclaim God's deeds, His might and victories to the young is the glory and dignity and sanctity of declining years. The simple fact that God takes good care of those who live by faith is enough. This is music to the young generation. The Psalmist speaks of the harp and the lyre, with which the elderly count their blessings "without number" (v. 15). God is always near and brings new comfort.

We are grateful for this inspired hymn of praise in Israel's repertoire of prayer, as it rejuvenates old age. Just as the coming of the infant Jesus fulfilled all the hopes of Simeon and Anna (Lk. 2:22ff., 36ff.), so He does in the Holy Anointing not only of the sick but also of the aged. He takes over their suffering, their whole lives. Older people could spend much more time singing the praises of the Lord, cultivating the memory of God in devout recollection. They could be renewed in their comeback from the depths (v. 20) and rise above their enemies; they could experience a blessedness that exceeds their wildest dreams of health and strength and security. Such is the foretaste of the resurrection, for "all generations to come."

The Church renews herself constantly at the font of Baptism, as well as in the other sacraments and in liturgical prayer. Let our dear old folks "renew their youth like the eagle's" (Ps. 103:5), as they join the Church praying this Psalm on III Mondays (noon). Instead of living in the past, they become forward-looking.

Psalm 72 (71)

> Give the king thy justice, O God,
>> and thy righteousness to the royal son!
> ²May he judge thy people with righteousness,
>> and thy poor with justice!
> ³Let the mountains bear prosperity for the people,
>> and the hills, in righteousness!
> ⁴May he defend the cause of the poor of the people,
>> give deliverance to the needy,
>> and crush the oppressor!
>
> ⁵May he live while the sun endures,
>> and as long as the moon, throughout all generations!
> ⁶May he be like rain that falls on the mown grass,
>> like showers that water the earth!
> ⁷In his days may righteousness flourish,
>> and peace abound, till the moon be no more!

⁸May he have dominion from sea to sea,
    and from the River to the ends of the earth!
⁹May his foes bow down before him,
    and his enemies lick the dust!
¹⁰May the kings of Tarshish and of the isles
    render him tribute,
  may the kings of Sheba and Seba
    bring gifts!
¹¹May all kings fall down before him,
    all nations serve him!

¹²For he delivers the needy when he calls,
    the poor and him who has no helper.
¹³He has pity on the weak and the needy,
    and saves the lives of the needy.
¹⁴From oppression and violence he redeems their life;
    and precious is their blood in his sight.

¹⁵Long may he live,
    may gold of Sheba be given to him!
May prayer be made for him continually,
    and blessings invoked for him all the day!
¹⁶May there be abundance of grain in the land;
    on the tops of the mountains may it wave;
    may its fruit be like Lebanon;
  and may men blossom forth from the cities
    like the grass of the field!
¹⁷May his name endure for ever,
    his fame continue as long as the sun!
May men bless themselves by him,
    all nations call him blessed!

¹⁸Blessed be the Lord, the God of Israel,
    who alone does wondrous things.
¹⁹Blessed be his glorious name for ever;
    may his glory fill the whole earth! Amen and Amen!

²⁰The prayers of David, the son of Jesse, are ended.

The King of Kings

In human form God's words celebrate the crowning of perhaps
King Solomon, wishing him great power, wealth, wisdom, and peace.

This interests us, as historically God made a covenant with David through the prophet Nathan (2 Sam. 7:1-17) to the effect that David was God's choice and God was with him, that He would deal with his enemies and his name was to endure forever. All this and more becomes the prayer for the new king of Israel: protection of the poor, material blessings of field and flock, long life, the expansion of his realm from the Euphrates River to far lands of the West, to distant places in the South, then homage and tribute of foreign kings and nations, abundance of every kind.

This was historically true. What interests us more is the symbolic worth of this, its spiritual application to Christ. Basic is the belief that God is King. The brilliant earthly reign is symbolic of greater things to come. The extravagant wishes and rich oriental imagery are greatly magnified in Christ. This royal Psalm is prophetic of Him the King of kings. The superlative blessings came truly only in a spiritual sense in His Kingdom. First comes the welfare of the poor and lowly (again in v. 12), then the universal homage to Christ in the Christian world. And always abundant salvation for all.

This Psalm becomes important, not because we rehearse Solomon's past splendor, but for his reference to the Lord Christ, who reigns in everlasting glory. Wise men from the East brought Him gold of Arabia. His power is universal, to the ends of the earth. His mission is to the afflicted of all classes. His Kingdom will outlast the sun and moon. Kings and peoples will bow to Him and find their happiness in His reign of plenty. "May men bless themselves by him" and "all nations call him blessed" (v. 17). While the last royalty is disappearing in the world, the Church celebrates Christ's coronation.

God is the origin of this transcending meaning of kingship. Christ has conquered all enemies (Satan, death, sin) and paid the price of His Lordship by His precious Blood. The inhabitants of the whole world must realize that. Wars will cease in His realm of peace. The poorest of the poor are the sinners, and they rejoice in the plenty of salvation and holiness. The King's concern for the social order passes over to His Body, the Church (Rom. 14:17-19). In the final triumph all His members share in His royalty. Now we join in worship with the King of kings in His Kingdom, the Church: "Blessed is He who comes in the Name of the Lord."

Christ is with us in His total royal glory, and it is a short step to the heavenly reality. While the final verses (18f.) are a doxology closing the second book of the Psalter, they fit the Psalm perfectly. Through

Christ the whole world is filled with glory (Rev. 19:11-16). The Church prays our Psalm on Christ the King, Epiphany, and December 29 (office of readings), also on II Thursdays (vespers).

Psalm 73 (72)

Truly God is good to the upright,
    to those who are pure in heart.
2But as for me, my feet had almost stumbled,
    my steps had well nigh slipped.
3For I was envious of the arrogant,
    when I saw the prosperity of the wicked.

4For they have no pangs;
    their bodies are sound and sleek.
5They are not in trouble as other men are;
    they are not stricken like other men.
6Therefore pride is their necklace;
    violence covers them as a garment.
7Their eyes swell out with fatness,
    their hearts overflow with follies.
8They scoff and speak with malice;
    loftily they threaten oppression.
9They set their mouths against the heavens,
    and their tongue struts through the earth.

10Therefore the people turn and praise them;
    and find no fault in them.
11And they say, "How can God know?
    Is there knowledge in the Most High?"
12Behold, these are the wicked;
    always at ease, they increase in riches.
13All in vain have I kept my heart clean
    and washed my hands in innocence.
14For all the day long I have been stricken,
    and chastened every morning.

¹⁵If I had said, "I will speak thus,"
   I would have been untrue to the generation of thy children.
¹⁶But when I thought how to understand this,
   it seemed to me a wearisome task,
¹⁷until I went into the sanctuary of God;
   then I perceived their end.
¹⁸Truly thou dost set them in slippery places;
   thou dost make them fall to ruin.
¹⁹How they are destroyed in a moment,
   swept away utterly by terrors!
²⁰They are like a dream when one awakes,
   on awaking you despise their phantoms.

²¹When my soul was embittered,
   when I was pricked in heart,
²²I was stupid and ignorant,
   I was like a beast toward thee.
²³Nevertheless I am continually with thee;
   thou dost hold my right hand.
²⁴Thou dost guide me with thy counsel,
   and afterward thou wilt receive me to glory.
²⁵Whom have I in heaven but thee?
   And there is nothing upon earth that I desire besides thee.
²⁶My flesh and my heart may fail,
   but God is the strength of my heart and my portion
      for ever.

²⁷For lo, those who are far from thee shall perish;
   thou dost put an end to those who are false to thee.
²⁸But for me it is good to be near God;
   I have made the Lord God my refuge,
   that I may tell of all thy works.

The Temptation of Riches

As long as the just man keeps God in sight, he will not succumb to the false appeals around him, such as envy of the godless rich. With simple candor the Psalmist speaks to the assembly of Israel to warn them, with divine wisdom, against seductions of affluence and arrogance. He humbly admits that he was about to follow the scandalous examples and nearly slipped into mouthing blasphemies against God. The prosperous seem so secure, without suffering, well fed, free from all burdens of other men. Openly proud and violent, they boldly pervert society with ungodly humanism. They rationalize God out of their lives.

Faith in God coming from the sanctuary (v. 17) corrects such vicious thinking. God is in charge. He cares and gives right counsel amid the Psalmist's temptations and doubts. Morality oriented to God is not in vain. He deals with worldliness, vindicates virtue, purity, and patient trust in Himself. Sin may look more attractive till we see that right conduct is God's will and wisdom for man.

True learning includes right morals, personal humility. The Psalm is very modern and reflects our conflicts. Sinful ways are slippery roads and deceptive paths. Without moral wisdom man becomes a brute beast, traitor to God and humanity. We are surrounded with easygoing fellow men and women who trust in riches and pleasure. Life is becoming more brutal by the hour, as vicious commercials pursue men into their homes with the network of false values and philosophies. People defend follies, "find no fault in them" (v. 10), become less than human in the end. That is, until they heed God's chastening voice (v. 14).

From the sanctuary we hear it. Victory over temptation means overcoming a dream. Fascination with material prosperity is enmity with God. Fellowship with God is grace and light. It means knowing the right way. Communion with God overcomes our shortsightedness and supplies even natural wants. It brings justice and happiness. "To be near God" is happiness (v. 28). God's invisible world holds our real prosperity.

This is a great Psalm. It tells us that reason without faith will bring ruin. Appearances deceive. The temptation to envy is an illusion. Our existence calls for battle, resistance to impulses. The final eight verses are gems of God for our necklace. Every phrase is loaded with God's message for us. St. Augustine's favorite Psalm verse was 28. We can hear the Lord's voice promising to "receive me to glory" (v. 24), He "holds my right hand" (v. 23) on a tortuous path. He lends His voice to this New Testament wisdom, the wisdom of the beatitudes, the warnings against material riches (Lk. 12:20). He is the Hand by which the Father guides us (Jn. 14:23). In Him God's glory is present (Jn. 17: 1ff.).

Today the educated, "cultured" classes mislead the masses away from faith in God. The bait is affluence, the lure prosperity. Education, instead of forming leaders of the poor, teaches competition and reading the commercials. We cling to God in hope (Heb. 10:32ff.), as we learn to pray this Psalm with the Church (on IV Mondays, office of readings).

Psalm 74 (73)

O God, why dost thou cast us off for ever?
Why does thy anger smoke
against the sheep of thy pasture?
[2]Remember thy congregation, which thou hast gotten of old,
which thou hast redeemed to be the tribe of thy heritage!
Remember Mount Zion, where thou hast dwelt.
[3]Direct thy steps to the perpetual ruins;
the enemy has destroyed everything in the sanctuary!

[4]Thy foes have roared in the midst of thy holy place;
they set up their own signs for signs.
[5]At the upper entrance they hacked
the wooden trellis with axes.
[6]And then all its carved wood
they broke down with hatchets and hammers.
[7]They set thy sanctuary on fire;
to the ground they desecrated the dwelling place of
thy name.
[8]They said to themselves, "We will utterly subdue them";
they burned all the meeting places of God in the land.

[9]We do not see our signs;
there is no longer any prophet,
and there is none among us who knows how long.
[10]How long, O God, is the foe to scoff?
Is the enemy to revile thy name for ever?
[11]Why dost thou hold back thy hand,
why dost thou keep thy right hand in thy bosom?

¹²Yet God my King is from of old,
 working salvation in the midst of the earth.
¹³Thou didst divide the sea by thy might;
 thou didst break the heads of the dragons on the waters.
¹⁴Thou didst crush the heads of Leviathan,
 thou didst give him as food for the creatures of
  the wilderness.
¹⁵Thou didst cleave open springs and brooks;
 thou didst dry up ever-flowing streams.
¹⁶Thine is the day, thine also the night;
 thou hast established the luminaries and the sun.
¹⁷Thou hast fixed all the bounds of the earth;
 thou hast made summer and winter.

¹⁸Remember this, O Lord, how the enemy scoffs,
 and an impious people reviles thy name.
¹⁹Do not deliver the soul of thy dove to the wild beasts;
 do not forget the life of thy poor for ever.

²⁰Have regard for thy covenant;
 for the dark places of the land are full of the habitations
  of violence.
²¹Let not the downtrodden be put to shame;
 let the poor and needy praise thy name.

²²Arise, O God, plead thy cause;
 remember how the impious scoff at thee all the day!
²³Do not forget the clamor of thy foes,
 the uproar of thy adversaries which goes up continually!

God's City in Ruins

Out of the ruins and ashes of Jerusalem, but from the faithful remnant of suffering Jews, rises this Psalm and appeal. The stunned nation of Israel stands in bitter sorrow over the profaned holy places of God, over the impious enemy who scoffs and blasphemes. The story of devastation stands in 2 Kg. 25:8ff. (probably 587 B.C.), and the Psalmist writes long after the event. "How long, O Lord, is the foe to scoff?" Trusting hope comes from God's original covenant. The Temple was its symbol and guarantee. Even though the kings and nation sinned by infidelity, hope goes back to the original promises.

After his portrayal of destruction, the author appeals to God's power (vv. 9-17). If God created the sun and moon, the days and nights and seasons, after He smashed dragons and made water gush from rocks, then why should He delay action against His honor and Name? Why should He forget the poor and let His dove Israel become the prey of the hawk? Too long has He been silent and sent no prophet to speak in His Name. Has the Shepherd abandoned His flock? The Psalmist records all this suffering of faith. He looks to God as King after the earthly king has gone into captivity. The eventual restoration of Israel and the return from captivity is the answer to this prayer.

How do we carry on in the face of defeat and ruin? Does our faith become stronger or weaker? When whole Christian nations fail in faith, when the Church suffers persecution, when the voice of Peter goes unheard, does our faith cry out, "Arise, Lord!" Pagan emblems fill our homes and lives, and there are false prophets and shepherds around us (Mt. 7:22; 24:11; 2 Cor. 11:12-15). We need God's Voice to summon us to Zion; we need Him to restore the ruins. While we admit our guilt and promise to return to His covenant, Christ must come to the rescue.

He had warned His people and the City of its final destruction. This Psalm echoes His cry to the New City and in the Church of the centuries and world today (see 1 Pet. 2:9f. and 1 Cor. 3:16f.). We, the flock of faith and Baptism, are the New Temple, and the powers of hell are out to destroy us. The world of culture and religions are a shambles, and while no evil power can destroy the Rock-Church (Mt. 16:18), yet the ruins of ancient Jerusalem are a prophecy we must take seriously. In this Psalm we hear the Spirit speaking loudly.

We need to animate our faith the more in the face of devastation of divine and human values and life. "When the Son of man comes, will he find faith on earth?" (Lk. 18:8). We cannot excuse ourselves with "We do not see our signs" (v. 9), for we have the living Voice in Peter and the light in Christ's Kingdom (Col. 1:13). "Let us hold fast the confession of our hope without wavering, for he who promised is faithful" (Heb. 10:23). According to the Book of Revelation, the showdown is coming and the final combat is shaping up, but those in Christ already celebrate the victory of faith (v. 19). Our faith rises above all the ruins of the past as we pray this Psalm on III Tuesdays (vespers).

Psalm 75 (74)

We give thanks to thee, O God; we give thanks;
we call on thy name and recount thy wondrous deeds.

²At the set time which I appoint
I will judge with equity.
³When the earth totters, and all its inhabitants,
it is I who keep steady its pillars.
⁴I say to the boastful, "Do not boast,"
and to the wicked, "Do not lift up your horn;
⁵do not lift up your horn on high,
or speak with insolent neck."

⁶For not from the east or from the west
and not from the wilderness comes lifting up;
⁷but it is God who executes judgment,
putting down one and lifting up another.
⁸For in the hand of the LORD there is a cup,
with foaming wine, well mixed;
and he will pour a draught from it,
and all the wicked of the earth
shall drain it down to the dregs.

⁹But I will rejoice for ever,
I will sing praises to the God of Jacob.
¹⁰All the horns of the wicked he will cut off,
but the horns of the righteous shall be exalted.

God the Judge

Opening with thanks to God for His wondrous deeds, the author at once lets God Himself speak (vv. 2-5). In His good time He will summon all to judgment and single out especially the boastful and wicked. All sin is proud boasting; all sin is lifting up one's horns to match strength with God. He who set the world on its pillars and sustains it will break the arrogant horns of sinners and bend their stubborn necks. It is He who lowers the proud and lifts up the humble (v. 10). With this oracle God assures the just that he can afford to be patient and the wicked will tremble in anticipation.

The author continues to explain (vv. 6-8) what this means. Neither from east or west must people expect relief ("lifting up"), but justice will come from the God of Jacob. The Master of the universe, who lowers and raises men according to their deeds, will pour out wrath against sinners. In the familiar image of the "cup of God's wrath," spiced for intoxication, He deals out punishment. All who have done evil will drink this cup to the dregs. Repeatedly we read (in Rev.) how the defeated enemy is drunk with the wine of God's wrath. History confirms this divine wisdom; there is no escape from His justice.

No Psalm is more relevant in the New Testament and in our era. Christians believe in Christ coming and they stand on tiptoe awaiting His imminent judgment. "He will come to judge the living and the dead." On the final day He will separate the sheep from the goats (Jn. 5:22-24). He will vindicate His elect (Lk. 18:7) and exalt the lowly (Lk. 14:11). Matthew describes His Coming in power and glory (24:30). Christ is supreme (Col. 1:15-18). No one can take this judgment lightly. Even if we are now one in solidarity with the Body of Christ, we as individuals pray this Psalm as did persons in the Old Testament since the judgment of the nations will also strike us as individuals.

The Lord founded the earth from the beginning (Heb. 1:10) and will forever silence those who are haughty against the Rock or in any way raise their horns against Christ. Mighty Rome fell (Rev. 14:8) and Jerusalem fell. Christ the Lord "will tread the winepress of the fury of the wrath of God the Almighty" (Rev. 19:15). He "raised a horn of salvation" (Lk. 1:69) in gloriously rising from the dead. Because of that we "will rejoice for ever" (v. 9). Now we assemble in humble faith with the Church (on III Wednesdays, at noon) to sing this Psalm, awaiting the blessedness of God's judgment.

Psalm 76 (75)

In Judah God is known,
  his name is great in Israel.
²His abode has been established in Salem,
  his dwelling place in Zion.
³There he broke the flashing arrows,
  the shield, the sword, and the weapons of war.

⁴Glorious art thou, more majestic
    than the everlasting mountains.
⁵The stouthearted were stripped of their spoil;
    they sank into sleep;
 all the men of war
    were unable to use their hands.
⁶At thy rebuke, O God of Jacob,
    both rider and horse lay stunned.

⁷But thou, terrible art thou!
    Who can stand before thee
    when once thy anger is roused?
⁸From the heavens thou didst utter judgment;
    the earth feared and was still,
⁹when God arose to establish judgment
    to save all the oppressed of the earth.

¹⁰Surely the wrath of men shall praise thee;
    the residue of wrath thou wilt gird upon thee.
¹¹Make your vows to the Lord your God, and perform them;
    let all around him bring gifts
    to him who is to be feared,
¹²who cuts off the spirit of princes,
    who is terrible to the kings of the earth.

The Lion of Judah

All hostile kings and princes facing the power of God will fall into a state of shock and paralysis. The presence of Him on Zion will reduce them, their heroes and horses, and stun them to helplessness. Their power will fade before the wrath of the Almighty, while God's praises rise from His chosen nation in His City of Peace (Salem, shalom), and even former foes bring Him gifts of homage. Great is His Name over all the earth. If the events of history in 2 Kg. 18-19 are the source of this Psalm, it shows literally how God's enemies stop dead in their tracks when they witness God rising to help Jacob. While the people slept, God's angel put the foe to sleep and left Judah with the spoils.

When God acts, He shows the primacy of His intervention. The believer experiences this and it strengthens his faith, so that he offers vows and sacrifices to God in recognition of His greatness. Even pagan nations subject themselves to "the residue of wrath" that converts to the Lord, and God "girds himself" with these conquered subjects as with a garment (see Rev. 1:13). There is universalism here, both in the new subjects and in the oppressed of the earth (v. 9). And so His greatness grows.

If persons and events of Israel's history are images of the future, then this Psalm is prophetic of the God-man's victorious power and peace in the new order. The New Testament teaches the same lesson as this Psalm. Christ is Savior and Victor in glory, most of all in His final Coming in judgment we call the Parousia. He is the Lion of Judah. He left the guards of His tomb immobile as He rose gloriously from the dead. While His face appeared like lightning, their faces were like dead men (Mt. 28:2-4). He brought the Kingdom of peace, and He rules victorious. His Name is above every name (Phil. 2:9). His rule is over His flock (Jn. 10:1-18) and over the ruler of this world (Jn. 12:31).

His Coming in judgment will be like lightning (Mt. 24:27), while all His enemies will suffer power failure and paralysis. The just will rejoice for their delivery is at hand (Lk. 21:28). "In Judah God is known." Christ is known by His own. "The Lord will judge his people. It is a fearful thing to fall into the hands of the living God" (Heb. 10:31f.). We anticipate peace through His victory, as we celebrate this Psalm in the Church on Holy Saturday, the Friday of Easter, on II and IV Sundays, always at noonday prayer.

Psalm 77 (76)

> I cry aloud to God,
>> aloud to God, that he may hear me.
> ²In the day of my trouble I seek the Lord;
>> in the night my hand is stretched out without wearying;
>> my soul refuses to be comforted.

³I think of God, and I moan;
     I meditate, and my spirit faints.
⁴Thou dost hold my eyelids from closing;
     I am so troubled that I cannot speak.
⁵I consider the days of old,
     I remember the years long ago.
⁶I commune with my heart in the night;
     I meditate and search my spirit:
⁷"Will the Lord spurn for ever,
     and never again be favorable?
⁸Has his steadfast love for ever ceased?
     Are his promises at an end for all time?
⁹Has God forgotten to be gracious?
     Has he in anger shut up his compassion?"
¹⁰And I say, "It is my grief
     that the right hand of the Most High has changed."

¹¹I will call to mind the deeds of the LORD;
     yea, I will remember thy wonders of old.
¹²I will meditate on all thy work,
     and muse on thy mighty deeds.
¹³Thy way, O God, is holy.
     What god is great like our God?
¹⁴Thou art the God who workest wonders,
     who hast manifested thy might among the peoples.
¹⁵Thou didst with thy arm redeem thy people,
     the sons of Jacob and Joseph.

¹⁶When the waters saw thee, O God,
     when the waters saw thee, they were afraid,
     yea, the deep trembled.
¹⁷The clouds poured out water;
     the skies gave forth thunder;
     thy arrows flashed on every side.
¹⁸The crash of thy thunder was in the whirlwind;
     thy lightnings lighted up the world;
     the earth trembled and shook.
¹⁹Thy way was through the sea,
     thy path through the great waters;
     yet thy footprints were unseen.
²⁰Thou didst lead thy people like a flock
     by the hand of Moses and Aaron.

The Saving Memory of God

Keeping alive the memory of God is prayer, constant prayer, "prayer without ceasing." The noblest human activity and reflection of God's glory, prayer makes God the center of our lives. This Psalm is the fruit of long, hard trials of the author. God seems to have forgotten about him. Day and night he struggles for God. His spirit is faint and troubled. Nothing can console or comfort him. Nothing can compensate for His "absence." It is the lament of an individual speaking for his people from whom God has apparently withdrawn His merciful hand.

The cause of this prolonged darkness may be a sin of Israel, or it may be a trial, God's love trying the faith of His people. Actually God's thought has not ceased nor has He ended His wonders. The people have forgotten Him and need to rouse themselves to the memory of God's merciful deeds of the past. The memory of sin is short-lived, and God is stirring their hearts to awaken them to new reliance on Him. He wants them to rehearse the past, the path He made through the water and desert under the guidance of Moses and Aaron. He is still their Shepherd.

The relief of suffering and complaint is praise (vv. 11-20). The author buries his worries in the remembrance of nature giving way to God, to the strong arm of Moses parting the Re(e)d Sea amid crashes of thunder and downpours of rain—"God's arrows" that told His people of His presence, "though thy footprints were unseen." "Thy way, O God,.is holy." The mercy of God is absolute, but so is His justice. He manifests His love by mercy and justice, comfort and punishment. Pain and crisis is a warning.

The lesson of the Psalm illuminates our crisis more than lightning illumines the world. God is always speaking and revealing Himself, even when He tests His faithful ones. To keep alive the memory of God and tell the story of the Cross (Heb. 5:7f.) is the lesson for us. Christ met the Father on Calvary in suffering as well as on Tabor in glory. For us too "thy way was through the sea," the waters of Baptism that are the path of Christ's salvation. The Father willed His passion and death, vicariously, for us. We hear His voice of complaint in Psalms 22 and 88. The Church utters these cries of abandonment with the Lord. She relives that past in the present age, in her Mystery-worship. That is cultivating memory where it is most powerful.

We learn but slowly. We are spoon-fed in learning the memory of God. The Holy Spirit does not abandon us, but in darkness and crises gives us the light we need. We can revolve Psalm 77 in our hearts day and night and pray it with the Church on II Wednesdays (at lauds). This means clinging to God, "holding fast the confession of our hope" (Heb. 10:23), for God in Christ is faithful.

Psalm 78 (77)

Give ear, O my people, to my teaching;
    incline your ears to the words of my mouth!
²I will open my mouth in a parable;
    I will utter dark sayings from of old,
³things that we have heard and known,
    that our fathers have told us.
⁴We will not hide them from their children,
    but tell to the coming generation
the glorious deeds of the Lᴏʀᴅ, and his might,
    and the wonders which he has wrought.

⁵He established a testimony in Jacob,
    and appointed a law in Israel,
which he commanded our fathers
    to teach to their children;
⁶that the next generation might know them,
    the children yet unborn,
and arise and tell them to their children,
⁷   so that they should set their hope in God,
and not forget the works of God,
    but keep his commandments;
⁸and that they should not be like their fathers,
    a stubborn and rebellious generation,
a generation whose heart was not steadfast,
    whose spirit was not faithful to God.

⁹The Ephraimites, armed with the bow,
     turned back on the day of battle.
¹⁰They did not keep God's covenant,
     but refused to walk according to his law.
¹¹They forgot what he had done,
     and the miracles that he had shown them.
¹²In the sight of their fathers he wrought marvels
     in the land of Egypt, in the fields of Zoan.
¹³He divided the sea and let them pass through it,
     and made the waters stand like a heap.
¹⁴In the daytime he led them with a cloud,
     and all the night with a fiery light.
¹⁵He cleft rocks in the wilderness,
     and gave them drink abundantly as from the deep.
¹⁶He made streams come out of the rock,
     and caused waters to flow down like rivers.

¹⁷Yet they sinned still more against him,
     rebelling against the Most High in the desert.
¹⁸They tested God in their heart
     by demanding the food they craved.
¹⁹They spoke against God, saying,
     "Can God spread a table in the wilderness?
²⁰He smote the rock so that water gushed out
     and streams overflowed.
   Can he also give bread,
     or provide meat for his people?"

²¹Therefore, when the Lord heard, he was full of wrath;
     a fire was kindled against Jacob,
     his anger mounted against Israel;
²²because they had no faith in God,
     and did not trust his saving power.
²³Yet he commanded the skies above,
     and opened the doors of heaven;
²⁴and he rained down upon them manna to eat,
     and gave them the grain of heaven.

²⁵Man ate of the bread of the angels;
    he sent them food in abundance.
²⁶He caused the east wind to blow in the heavens,
    and by his power he led out the south wind;
²⁷he rained flesh upon them like dust,
    winged birds like the sand of the seas;
²⁸he let them fall in the midst of their camp,
    all around their habitations.
²⁹And they ate and were well filled,
    for he gave them what they craved.
³⁰But before they had sated their craving,
    while the food was still in their mouths,
³¹the anger of God rose against them
    and he slew the strongest of them,
    and laid low the picked men of Israel.

³²In spite of all this they still sinned;
    despite his wonders they did not believe.
³³So he made their days vanish like a breath,
    and their years in terror.
³⁴When he slew them, they sought for him;
    they repented and sought God earnestly.
³⁵They remembered that God was their rock,
    the Most High God their redeemer.
³⁶But they flattered him with their mouths;
    they lied to him with their tongues.
³⁷Their heart was not steadfast toward him;
    they were not true to his covenant.
³⁸Yet he, being compassionate,
    forgave their iniquity,
    and did not destroy them;
he restrained his anger often,
    and did not stir up all his wrath.
³⁹He remembered that they were but flesh,
    a wind that passes and comes not again.

⁴⁰How often they rebelled against him in the wilderness
and grieved him in the desert!
⁴¹They tested him again and again,
and provoked the Holy One of Israel.
⁴²They did not keep in mind his power,
or the day when he redeemed them from the foe;
⁴³when he wrought his signs in Egypt,
and his miracles in the fields of Zoan.
⁴⁴He turned their rivers to blood,
so that they could not drink of their streams.
⁴⁵He sent among them swarms of flies, which devoured them,
and frogs, which destroyed them.
⁴⁶He gave their crops to the caterpillar,
and the fruit of their labor to the locust.
⁴⁷He destroyed their vines with hail,
and their sycamores with frost.
⁴⁸He gave over their cattle to the hail.
and their flocks to thunderbolts.
⁴⁹He let loose on them his fierce anger,
wrath, indignation, and distress,
a company of destroying angels.
⁵⁰He made a path for his anger;
he did not spare them from death,
but gave their lives over to the plague.
⁵¹He smote all the first-born of Egypt,
the first issue of their strength in the tents of Ham.
⁵²Then he led forth his people like sheep,
and guided them in the wilderness like a flock.
⁵³He led them in safety, so that they were not afraid;
but the sea overwhelmed their enemies.
⁵⁴And he brought them to his holy land,
to the mountain which his right hand had won.
⁵⁵He drove out nations before them;
he apportioned them for a possession
and settled the tribes of Israel in their tents.

56Yet they tested and rebelled against the Most High God,
　　and did not observe his testimonies,
57but turned away and acted treacherously like their fathers;
　　they twisted like a deceitful bow.
58For they provoked him to anger with their high places;
　　they moved him to jealousy with their graven images.
59When God heard, he was full of wrath,
　　and he utterly rejected Israel.
60He forsook his dwelling at Shiloh,
　　the tent where he dwelt among men,
61and delivered his power to captivity,
　　his glory to the hand of the foe.
62He gave his people over to the sword,
　　and vented his wrath on his heritage.
63Fire devoured their young men,
　　and their maidens had no marriage song.
64Their priests fell by the sword,
　　and their widows made no lamentation.
65Then the Lord awoke as from sleep,
　　like a strong man shouting because of wine.
66And he put his adversaries to rout;
　　he put them to everlasting shame.

67He rejected the tent of Joseph,
　　he did not choose the tribe of Ephraim;
68but he chose the tribe of Judah,
　　Mount Zion, which he loves.
69He built his sanctuary like the high heavens,
　　like the earth, which he has founded for ever.
70He chose David his servant,
　　and took him from the sheepfolds;
71from tending the ewes that had young he brought him
　　to be the shepherd of Jacob his people,
　　of Israel his inheritance.
72With upright heart he tended them,
　　and guided them with a skilful hand.

Living Tradition Under God

How the leading tribe of Ephraim was rejected, how the small tribe of David's Judah was chosen, plus the contrasting account of Israel's infidelity and God's fidelity, here becomes inspired, poetic meditation, history in prayer form. It is salutary for us of the New Law to learn how we arrived where we are now. Defections of God's people are as frequent and modern as they were past and ancient. Man's record of sinning is bettered only by divine forgiveness, most of all in Christ in whom God's nature and mercy came to us. The last word is mercy (vv. 65ff.), and this Psalm tells the wonderful story.

God always thinks of us and loves us first. His election of us and covenant with us depends on His first love, not on our merits. This keynote comes in the first eight verses, where we see the pattern of the divine parable and Mystery of Christ. The Savior too spoke in parables (Mt. 13:35) so that we could understand. With literary freedom that does not keep to the order of history, the author weaves the pattern of human backsliding and divine mercy. Beginning with northern Ephraim, he returns to Egypt (v. 12); he tells of the desert doubts, then reverses to the plagues of Egypt (v. 43). Cowardice, rebellion, stubborn distrust, and doubts in the face of miracles, lying, tempting God, apostasy, and more are the sins that provoked His anger and then always elicited mercy. He even heeded their apparent conversions, as when men pray for help only when they are in trouble.

Tanis is the old capital of Egypt. Silo was the place of the Ark to the north in the promised land. It fell to the Philistines but was regained by David and Judah and became God's dwelling in Sion, Jerusalem. The "high places" (v. 58) are the hilltops of pagan idol worship, which signify falling away from the true God. Our Psalm ends when God "awoke as from sleep," making a new beginning with the choice of the shepherd David and thereby suggests the whole future. Like Psalms 105 and 106, it points to a future Shepherd and New Zion and New Israel.

Here we feel the heartbeat of tradition, with the living Voice addressing us and reminding us to pass on what we have received (vv. 1-8). This is important for the Church as it was for the people of God in those distant days. Faith and trust are wisdom that parents must hand on to their offspring. Here we touch the spiritual message of God, the parable of our times. Christ is the great Teacher of spiritual history. His signs dwarf the old ones. He puts us on probation of faith, the total faith. Not only do we accept His Shepherd care (Jn. 21:15-17) and "the bread of angels" (v. 25; see Jn. 6:31) and His merciful forgiveness (Acts 5:31), but we accept our mission to the world for generations to come. God's clear writing is on the wall for us.

All comparisons and parables are for our instruction (1 Cor. 10: 1-11) to elucidate God's reality and way for us. We must not harden our hearts against the divine Voice (Heb. 3:7-9), but answer with faith (Jn. 12:37) so we may stand fast now and live forever (Heb. 10:28f.). In the City of the living God (Heb. 12:22), we raise our voices with the living Voice in the recitation of this Psalm on IV Fridays (vv. 1-39) and IV Saturdays (vv. 40-72, office of readings).

Psalm 79 (78)

O God, the heathen have
    come into thy inheritance;
    they have defiled thy holy temple;
    they have laid Jerusalem in ruins.
²They have given the bodies of thy servants
    to the birds of the air for food,
    the flesh of thy saints to the beasts of the earth.
³They have poured out their blood like water
    round about Jerusalem,
    and there was none to bury them.
⁴We have become a taunt to our neighbors,
    mocked and derided by those round about us.

⁵How long, O LORD? Wilt thou be angry for ever?
    Will thy jealous wrath burn like fire?
⁶Pour out thy anger on the nations
    that do not know thee,
 and on the kingdoms
    that do not call on thy name!
⁷For they have devoured Jacob,
    and laid waste his habitation.

⁸Do not remember against us the iniquities of our forefathers;
    let thy compassion come speedily to meet us,
    for we are brought very low.
⁹Help us, O God of our salvation,
    for the glory of thy name;
 deliver us, and forgive our sins,
    for thy name's sake!
¹⁰Why should the nations say,
    "Where is their God?"
 Let the avenging of the outpoured blood of thy servants
    be known among the nations before our eyes!

[11]Let the groans of the prisoners come before thee;
    according to thy great power preserve those doomed
    to die!
[12]Return sevenfold into the bosom of our neighbors
    the taunts with which they have taunted thee, O Lord!
[13]Then we thy people, the flock of thy pasture,
    will give thanks to thee for ever;
    from generation to generation we will recount thy praise.

God Amid National Tragedy

The people of God never suffered a greater disaster than the one here described (probably the destruction of Jerusalem and the Temple in 587 B.C. See also Psalms 44 and 74). The prospect of another such tragedy made Christ weep over Jerusalem (Lk. 19:41-44). It happened in 70 A.D. under Roman rule. Pagans desecrated everything holy, left corpses unburied, took prisoners, condemned others to death. Jeremiah foretold it as the judgment of God against His unfaithful nation (26:4-6, 7:32). In both cases it was divine punishment. The neighbor nations laughed (v. 4), and the author makes this the motive for help: "For the glory of thy Name . . . for thy Name's sake" (v. 9).

The Psalmist knows himself as one with God and His people. His faith makes him pray as he does. Moses had prayed that way: for Your Name's sake deliver Your people! God Himself inspires this way of appeal. As the author admits national guilt, great iniquities of the past (vv. 5-9), this Psalm includes repentance for sin. Finally, he promises praise and thanks "from generation to generation." His faith in God is resilient, for he knows that the divine mercy never ends.

So long as there is sin and evil in the world, God wants us to pray with these sentiments, for the glory of His Name is always at stake. Temporal retribution will follow if He deems it timely to defend His honor, when the godless taunt, "Where is their God?" First and always, God wants us to return to Him in time of distress and cling to Him in faith and hope. Sometimes God's plan includes the salvation of others through the death of His faithful ones, as in time of persecution when the blood of martyrs became the seed of Christianity.

God inspires the right way of prayer. In every situation He broadens our vision and hearts to take in His wise plan of salvation. Often, when we are straightened on every side, God "pours out" mercy on the nations and sinners, as was the Father's will in regard to His Son,

who died that others might live. That was "retribution" in the form
of mercy, seven times over (v. 12). Or do we suppose that the world
will be converted to Christ by affluence and indulgence and security?
That would be the philosophy of so-called Christians, not the thinking
of faith. Is there enough sacrifice to raise the ruins behind the Iron
Curtain or to convert China and India?

Christ prayed this Psalm and He wants us to pray it. He promised
suffering and persecution to His followers, Jews and Gentiles alike.
After their suffering the Jews will be saved (Rom. 11:11-16). The Book
of Revelation reveals many thoughts from our Psalm (e.g. 6:10; 11:7-9;
12:17; 13:7, 15 and 19:1-8). Christ prays the Psalm in and with the Church
on III Thursdays (at noon, in parts).

Psalm 80 (79)

Give ear, O Shepherd of Israel,
> thou who leadest Joseph like a flock!
Thou who art enthroned upon the cherubim, shine forth
²   before Ephraim and Benjamin and Manasseh!
Stir up thy might,
> and come to save us!

³Restore us, O God;
> let thy face shine, that we may be saved!

⁴O Lᴏʀᴅ God of hosts,
> how long wilt thou be angry with thy people's prayers?
⁵Thou hast fed them with the bread of tears,
> and given them tears to drink in full measure.
⁶Thou dost make us the scorn of our neighbors;
> and our enemies laugh among themselves.

⁷Restore us, O God of hosts;
> let thy face shine, that we may be saved!

⁸Thou didst bring a vine out of Egypt;
    thou didst drive out the nations and plant it.
⁹Thou didst clear the ground for it;
    it took deep root and filled the land.
¹⁰The mountains were covered with its shade,
    the mighty cedars with its branches;
¹¹it sent out its branches to the sea,
    and its shoots to the River.
¹²Why then hast thou broken down its walls,
    so that all who pass along the way pluck its fruit?
¹³The boar from the forest ravages it,
    and all that move in the field feed on it.

¹⁴Turn again, O God of hosts!
    Look down from heaven, and see;
  have regard for this vine,
¹⁵   the stock which thy right hand planted.
¹⁶They have burned it with fire, they have cut it down;
    may they perish at the rebuke of thy countenance!
¹⁷But let thy hand be upon the man of thy right hand,
    the son of man whom thou hast made strong for thyself!
¹⁸Then we will never turn back from thee;
    give us life, and we will call on thy name!

¹⁹Restore us, O Lord God of hosts!
    let thy face shine, that we may be saved!

Prayer for Unity

The author is carried away by the sight of his suffering people. He pleads with God, the Shepherd of the flock and Master of the vineyard. With great urgency he uses the figures of flock and vineyard to remind the Lord God of His past blessings. It is a prayer for restoration, as the refrain indicates. He prays for the brother-tribes, the separated ones to the north (mainly Ephraim, Benjamin, and Manasseh), at a moment when they suffered catastrophe (perhaps led into captivity, 721 B.C.). He appeals to the God of the Ark and Zion, when fire and sword threatened His heritage, when His people ate the bread of tears because they had abandoned the Lord (v. 18).

The enemy has prevailed and the vineyard is exposed to every passerby and foreign ruler (boar of the forest). From the ocean to the Euphrates River and into the forests of Lebanon, God's vine had spread under His care. A transplant from Egypt to the Holy Land, the vine clearly stands for the people of God, the object of His love. Even though God was "angry," He does not let this prayer go unheard. He gives His people new leadership ("let thy hand be upon the man of thy right hand, the son of man whom thou hast made strong for thyself"). He will shine His face on them by visiting them with new favors. New life and faith will bring new praise and dedication. The unity already existing between north and south is common faith. "Restore us, O God!"

Tearing the people of God apart is rending the seamless garment of Christ (St. Augustine). Christianity is torn apart for centuries. The Lord still speaks of "other sheep" who must enter His fold (Jn. 10:16). Our prayer is:

Shepherd of the New Israel, restore us to unity. From Your presence on Zion, shine on us, Christ of glory. You who are clothed in light, shine on our darkness, on all the segments of humanity for more abundant life. The walls are down for every invasion of false opinion and ravaging enemy. May Your right hand be with Your leaders, the men of Your choice, pope and bishops. In Your Church many are sick and some are dead (1 Cor. 11:30). You are the Son of man, come lead us to the Father, the Vintager.

If Moses craves to see Your face and You answered him, then show Your face in our time. We are in the darkness of error and sin. Restore us, let Your face shine anew upon us. Lord, You gave the parable of the vineyard (Mt. 21:33ff.); give it Your care more than ever. Deliver us not into the hands of the enemy of our salvation. Unite all to Yourself in this fulness of time (Eph. 1:9f.). Let the walls of division crumble (Eph. 2:14-16), as we plead for unity and peace. Be with us, as we pray this Psalm in Your Church (on II Thursdays, at lauds, and III Thursdays, at noon).

Psalm 81 (80)

Sing aloud to God our strength;
    shout for joy to the God of Jacob!
²Raise a song, sound the timbrel,
    the sweet lyre with the harp.
³Blow the trumpet at the new moon,
    at the full moon, on our feast day.
⁴For it is a statute for Israel,
    an ordinance of the God of Jacob.
⁵He made it a decree in Joseph,
    when he went out over the land of Egypt.

I hear a voice I had not known:
⁶"I relieved your shoulder of the burden;
    your hands were freed from the basket.
⁷In distress you called, and I delivered you;
    I answered you in the secret place of thunder;
    I tested you at the waters of Meribah.
⁸Hear, O my people, while I admonish you!
    O Israel, if you would but listen to me!
⁹There shall be no strange god among you;
    you shall not bow down to a foreign god.
¹⁰I am the Lord your God,
    who brought you up out of the land of Egypt.
    Open your mouth wide, and I will fill it.

¹¹"But my people did not listen to my voice;
    Israel would have none of me.
¹²So I gave them over to their stubborn hearts,
    to follow their own counsels.
¹³O that my people would listen to me,
    that Israel would walk in my ways!
¹⁴I would soon subdue their enemies,
    and turn my hand against their foes.
¹⁵Those who hate the Lord would cringe toward him,
    and their fate would last for ever.
¹⁶I would feed you with the finest of the wheat,
    and with honey from the rock I would satisfy you."

God's Call to Worship

Ever since Israel came out of Egypt by divine guidance, there was great reason for rejoicing, song, and instrumental music. The inner reason was not the decree of law, but that of delivery from slavery and the presence of God. Their victorious faith called for the festive trumpet, or "shofar," to remind them of God's call. This Psalm marks the new moon and Feast of Tabernacles, the opening of the new year (our September), new nationhood. We also call it the covenant on Sinai. The basket of slavery God took from their shoulders.

Then the author lets God speak His oracle (vv. 6-16). God's Voice had become unfamiliar because the people ignored the basic first commandment: "I am the Lord your God!" He reviews sacred history, how He performed deeds of love for them, feeding them and protecting them from enemies. They had only to open their mouths and God filled them with choice foods. Then they sinned and sank into sad silence. They hardened their hearts and went devious ways, earning for themselves God's wrath. With that comes the new call.

Mercy prevails over punishment. That is God's way, but it entails repentance. That too is the way His love chose for them. It was new love, greater than the former. God is willing to do even greater things for His people, providing they are faithful. All this pictures Baptism and the new covenant, the new journey to our heavenly home. It is new moon and a new year of salvation, new protection from enemies, new joyous praise in cult, new faith. God's promises are fulfilled in the "finest of the wheat and with honey from the rock" (v. 16). He invites us to festive singing and music like never before.

God speaks to us in Christ, and we hear our language and accent. The incarnation through Mary begins the new era of salvation, a Mystery plan of greater love than before. The call is to new fervor and fidelity, not as the stagnant waters of Meribah witnessed the people's rebellion. Our vocation is to the new revelation. Being receptive means to open our mouths for the divine food and favors. This is a striking new year's Psalm when prayed in the Church with Christ. We not only meditate it in our hearts but also "Sing aloud to God our strength."

The only obstacle to celebration is sin and sadness. The sinner cannot afford to sing, except in repentance. Heaven is all joy and solemnity. The former urgency to music has not ceased, but increased. Singing this Psalm keeps the memory of Christ fresh, alive, and present. Especially in the holy Eucharist all is fulfilled: Christ is our Word and

Bread, the finest Wheat from heaven (Jn. 6:32), containing all sweet-
ness and delights. Accordingly the Church uses the Psalm on Corpus
Christi (office of readings) and on II Thursdays (noon). Whoever
hungers and thirsts, let him come to Christ. We not only sanctify time
("the new moon"), but re-live and reenact His total salvation as we
associate with Him. With the Bread of immortality our feast will last
forever (v. 15).

Psalm 82 (81)

God has taken his place in the divine council;
in the midst of the gods he holds judgment:
²"How long will you judge unjustly
and show partiality to the wicked?
³Give justice to the weak and the fatherless;
maintain the right of the afflicted and the destitute.
⁴Rescue the weak and the needy;
deliver them from the hand of the wicked."

⁵They have neither knowledge nor understanding,
they walk about in darkness;
all the foundations of the earth are shaken.

⁶I say, "You are gods,
sons of the Most High, all of you;
⁷nevertheless, you shall die like men,
and fall like any prince."

⁸Arise, O God, judge the earth;
for to thee belong all the nations!

Godliness of Justice

In this prayer we beg God for just judges. All who mete out justice
on earth represent God and share His royal power. Like kings of the
earth, "You are gods, sons of the Most High, all of you" (v. 6). The
laws of justice, which they must enforce, are expressions of the divine
will. Justice is truth, and God is all truth. The divine Voice speaking
here calls to task those who pervert justice and truth. Partiality to the

wicked and to the rich and powerful seems to have been prevalent, while they neglected the poor and weak and needy. Favoritism is a constant temptation to those who share in God's high prerogative.

Because judges are godlike in power and prestige, God keeps special watch over them and their decisions. He laid down norms for judges already in Ex. 23:6-9, and the prophets of God watched jealously over them (e.g. Is. 3:14f.). Psalm 58 is also meant for them (see comments). And God's final act will be a universal judgment.

The divine oracle (vv. 2-7) contains much that is applicable to judges today. In the courts the virtues of justice and truth must prevail. The poor and helpless and destitute usually are the first victims of the miscarriage of justice, as when millions of unborn, living babies suffer violent death at the hands of science and pleasure and when these murders are protected by judges of the country. This breakdown of justice shakes the last pillar of the civil order. It throws society into the darkness of brutality and incurs God's angry castigation. The more enlightened the society, the more heinous the crime against helpless persons. The unborn are the most helpless of the poor. God will arise against all false mediators of justice, "and you shall die like men" (v. 7).

Christ Jesus, who is Judge of the living and the dead, brings the divine council and assembly directly into our midst. He used our verse 6 (in Jn. 10:34f.) when He proclaimed Himself Son of God. Because He is God and man, the Father has given Him all power of judgment (Jn. 5:22). He is our last court of appeal and through the Church teaches justice and truth. The administration of justice in civil courts is a service of God (Rom. 13:3-6 and 1 Pet. 2:13-15). Obeying this justice, when it is not perverted ungodliness, is also service of God. To God belongs all civil society.

The Church prays our Psalm on IV Mondays at noon.

Psalm 83 (82)

O God, do not keep silence;
　　do not hold thy peace or be still, O God!
²For lo, thy enemies are in tumult;
　　those who hate thee have raised their heads.
³They lay crafty plans against thy people;
　　they consult together against thy protected ones.
⁴They say, "Come, let us wipe them out as a nation;
　　let the name of Israel be remembered no more!"
⁵Yea, they conspire with one accord;
　　against thee they make a covenant—
⁶the tents of Edom and the Ishmaelites,
　　Moab and the Hagrites,
⁷Gebal and Ammon and Amalek,
　　Philistia with the inhabitants of Tyre;
⁸Assyria also has joined them;
　　they are the strong arm of the children of Lot.

⁹Do to them as thou didst to Midian,
　　as to Sisera and Jabin at the river Kishon,
¹⁰who were destroyed at Endor,
　　who became dung for the ground.
¹¹Make their nobles like Oreb and Zeeb,
　　all their princes like Zebah and Zalmunna,
¹²who said, "Let us take possession for ourselves
　　for the pastures of God."

¹³O my God, make them like whirling dust,
　　like chaff before the wind.
¹⁴As fire consumes the forest,
　　as the flame sets the mountains ablaze,
¹⁵so do thou pursue them with thy tempest
　　and terrify them with thy hurricane!
¹⁶Fill their faces with shame,
　　that they may seek thy name, O Lord.
¹⁷Let them be put to shame and dismayed for ever;
　　let them perish in disgrace.
¹⁸Let them know that thou alone,
　　whose name is the Lord,
　　art the Most High over all the earth.

Military Enemies Face Defeat

God's enemies are in review here to remind the Israelites of God's consistent help and to build up their faith for new dangers that threaten. The old foes are in verses 9-12, the new in 4-8. New coalitions will end like the old because they are God's enemies. Traditional foes and new ones on all sides are determined to destroy the very name Israel, but no, one can conspire with impunity against God. He will ruin them if they do not convert and seek His face.

We need to recall that this is prayer and not military history in review. One could spend much time studying to identify all the tribes and leaders mentioned, who are forgotten now in defeat at the powerful hand of God. Divine vengeance awaited them and the divine anger compares with a raging forest fire, a tornado, and all the destructive forces of nature the author could think of. The faithful are to rouse themselves and realize that God is in charge and that He will not remain silent and passive amid new dangers that face them.

We must learn that we are powerless to cope with our opposition unless God is on our side. He alone can help. But we also pray for the conversion of our enemy that the Name of the Lord may be praised the more. As we were once enemies of God and received mercy, so may the new enemies learn to praise Him for His justice, kindness, and forgiveness. As we received mercy, we want to extend it to others. This is God-inspired prayer, and in praying it we join the intentions of Christ with our own. We can hardly pray it solely in the literal, historical sense, but in Christ's fuller meaning. He prayed for Peter and His Church against the powers of hell. He wept over Jerusalem as He prayed (Lk. 19:41-44), and He continues to pray for the Church, His Bride (Mt. 10:16-20 and Jn. 16:1-11), as He is always with His persecuted members (Acts 8:2; 9:5).

All that matters is that His Name be exalted above all names in heaven and on earth and that we bestir ourselves to contribute to the glory of His Name so that also His enemy may come to praise Him, "that they may seek thy Name, O Lord." This Psalm is not used in the new office, no doubt because of the preponderance of obscure historical names.

Psalm 84 (83)

How lovely is thy dwelling place,
   O LORD of hosts!
²My soul longs, yea, faints
      for the courts of the LORD;
   my heart and flesh sing for joy
      to the living God.

³Even the sparrow finds a home,
      and the swallow a nest for herself,
      where she may lay her young,
   at thy altars, O LORD of hosts,
      my King and my God.
⁴Blessed are those who dwell in thy house,
      ever singing thy praise!

⁵Blessed are the men whose strength is in thee,
      in whose heart are the highways to Zion.
⁶As they go through the valley of Baca
      they make it a place of springs;
      the early rain also covers it with pools.
⁷They go from strength to strength;
      the God of gods will be seen in Zion.

⁸O LORD God of hosts, hear my prayer;
      give ear, O God of Jacob!
⁹Behold our shield, O God;
      look upon the face of thine anointed!

¹⁰For a day in thy courts is better
      than a thousand elsewhere.
   I would rather be a doorkeeper in the house of my God
      than dwell in the tents of wickedness.
¹¹For the LORD God is a sun and shield;
      he bestows favor and honor.
   No good thing does the LORD withhold
      from those who walk uprightly.
¹²O LORD of hosts,
      blessed is the man who trusts in thee!

Pilgrim Song of Zion

After learning that "I am a sojourner on earth" (Ps. 119:18; see also Psalm 122), the pilgrim approaches Psalm 84 with understanding of the heart, for it is a pilgrimage song, a song of Zion that he wants to learn by heart. And it comes from a heart filled with zeal and longing for the courts of the Lord. "My heart and my flesh sing for joy to the living God," the Lord of hosts. He has arrived at his pilgrim goal: Zion, the Temple and the Altar. No Psalm says it more poignantly (see also Psalms 42-43 and 87, which are touching, each in its own way).

The Altar of the Temple is the true home of God on earth. "My King and my God," is an outburst of faith, much like Thomas' "My Lord and my God" when he touched the glorified Savior's wound. Other phrases of this Psalm sound mystical, as "crying out for the living God," or "they go from strength to strength," rising to new heights till they see "the God of gods in Zion" and receive His "favor and honor." While "the face of thine anointed," refers to the king or high priest, we apply it to Christ, the Anointed *par excellence*, who is the Heart of the New Zion and Goal of our pilgrimage of longing and praise. We have arrived to be His guests.

Living in the house of the Lord is an unending blessing, as the pilgrims praise the Lord unceasingly. God is their strength. In their hearts are the highways to Zion, and in Christ they rise to new strength, going from glory to glory. They enrich the valleys, the world they pass through. "They make it a place of springs." Their pilgrim journey is a blessing for all they meet. Surely life in the sanctuary is preferable to "dwelling in the tents of wickedness." "A day in thy courts is better than a thousand elsewhere." Christ is our daily companion in His house.

Just as the Lord was consumed with zeal for His Father's house (Jn. 2:13-17), we are inflamed with the divine instincts for the place where His glory dwells and works. Reverence for His and our home is a normal family reaction. If we have the roads to Zion in our hearts, then we are sensitive to His presence. Christ called Himself the Temple and made us living members of His Temple. He wants us to give evidence of having arrived, of being at home, having enthusiasm for His visible house and undying attraction for our heavenly home. While the Kingdom of God is present in us, we await its final revelation in the Fountainhead of delight and praise and grace. If we become strong centers of "constancy in prayer" (Rom. 12:12) and ever-flowing streams of devotion for the place where His glory dwells, we will attract also those who live in the tents of wickedness. Prayed with the Church at her morning prayer, at the consecration of an Altar, or on Holy Thursday, or on the Transfiguration, this Psalm becomes a springboard to higher prayer and a foretaste of God's eternal glory.

Psalm 85 (84)

LORD, thou wast favorable to thy land;
    thou didst restore the fortunes of Jacob.
²Thou didst forgive the iniquity of thy people;
    thou didst pardon all their sin.

³Thou didst withdraw all thy wrath;
    thou didst turn from thy hot anger.

⁴Restore us again, O God of our salvation,
    and put away thy indignation toward us!
⁵Wilt thou be angry with us for ever?
    Wilt thou prolong thy anger to all generations?
⁶Wilt thou not revive us again,
    that thy people may rejoice in thee?
⁷Show us thy steadfast love, O LORD,
    and grant us thy salvation.

⁸Let me hear what God the LORD will speak,
    for he will speak peace to his people,
    to his saints, to those who turn to him in their hearts.
⁹Surely his salvation is at hand for those who fear him,
    that glory may dwell in our land.

¹⁰Steadfast love and faithfulness will meet;
    righteousness and peace will kiss each other.
¹¹Faithfulness will spring up from the ground,
    and righteousness will look down from the sky.
¹²Yea, the LORD will give what is good,
    and our land will yield its increase.
¹³Righteousness will go before him,
    and make his footsteps a way.

The Promised Harmony

Heaven and earth are God's creation. Man in his sinfulness is always tearing them apart. God in His wisdom and mercy will restore them in His healing vision. While differing studies throw new light on the Psalm text and bring out new meanings, this one deserves comment in its traditional form until the Church of tomorrow adopts the fruits of research into her readings. The present text has great faith value and much personal comfort. Restoration by God of His plan and order is the theme of this prayer.

The first thing in restoring all things is the pardon of sins, conversion to salvation. To remit the guilt of sin is one thing, to repair its damage is another. While the author thanks God for the mercy of having abolished sin, he earnestly begs for further help in undoing the damages, restoring the social order, and in conditioning the earth for a new increase, a new harvest. Awaiting God's Word, the dry earth and desolate humanity lie helplessly in need. The people need revival. Until righteousness and peace embrace and kiss, the divine assistance will have to come to the rescue. Never will the human order be completed or perfect till God and His glory hold the primacy both in heaven and on earth. That is the perspective of faith.

God's blessings are peace, the fruit of justice, and truth, the source of justice, and kindness. Unassisted by God's Spirit, man never seems to achieve the right balance of these virtues. When man counts on the divine assistance, hope becomes optimism. Progress is slow. Meanwhile the human spirit is afflicted until man seeks first the glory of His Kingdom. The Psalm also teaches a lesson in patiently waiting for God; giving precedence to the spiritual over the temporal order is the hard lesson of faith. When "faithfulness springs up from the ground . . . , the Lord will give what is good and our land will yield its increase."

The new order in Christ Jesus is the wonderful realization of this Psalm, for truth has sprung up from the earth at the incarnation, when God's glory dwelt in our midst (Jn. 1:14), when "grace and truth came through Jesus Christ" (Jn. 1:17). In Him the grace of God appeared visibly, justice and peace kissed. "Bedew us, heavens, from above," we sing in Advent, and Christ's Coming at Christmas is the response from above. In the holy Virgin's birthgiving, the earth has yielded its increase (v. 12). This Coming seems to transfer all to the spiritual order, but Christ is also concerned about the temporal order of justice and peaceful happiness. Even if the Church is a pilgrim Church on earth (2 Cor. 5:6f. and Rom. 8:23), she stands for a better human order, justice, peace, and love. In the process this Psalm teaches endurance, patience until the redemption is complete. As we await the final stage, "when tears will be no more" because the promised harmony has come, the Church herself undergoes purification and suffering. She prays our Psalm on III Tuesdays (noon) and on December 30 (office of readings).

Psalm 86 (85)

Incline thy ear, O LORD, and answer me,
   for I am poor and needy.
²Preserve my life, for I am godly;
   save thy servant who trusts in thee.
Thou art my God; ³be gracious to me, O Lord,
   for to thee do I cry all the day.
⁴Gladden the soul of thy servant,
   for to thee, O Lord, do I lift up my soul.
⁵For thou, O Lord, art good and forgiving,
   abounding in steadfast love to all who call on thee.
⁶Give ear, O LORD, to my prayer;
   hearken to my cry of supplication.
⁷In the day of my trouble I call on thee,
   for thou dost answer me.

⁸There is none like thee among the gods, O Lord,
   nor are there any works like thine.
⁹All the nations thou hast made shall come
   and bow down before thee, O Lord,
   and shall glorify thy name.
¹⁰For thou art great and doest wondrous things,
   thou alone art God.
¹¹Teach me thy way, O LORD,
   that I may walk in thy truth;
   unite my heart to fear thy name.
¹²I give thanks to thee, O Lord my God, with my whole heart,
   and I will glorify thy name for ever.
¹³For great is thy steadfast love toward me;
   thou hast delivered my soul from the depths of Sheol.

¹⁴O God, insolent men have risen up against me;
   a band of ruthless men seek my life,
   and they do not set thee before them.
¹⁵But thou, O Lord, art a God merciful and gracious,
   slow to anger and abounding in steadfast love and
      faithfulness.
¹⁶Turn to me and take pity on me;
   give thy strength to thy servant,
   and save the son of thy handmaid.
¹⁷Show me a sign of thy favor,
   that those who hate me may see and be put to shame
   because thou, Lord, hast helped me and comforted me.

Lord, Direct My Heart!

First this Psalm brings us insistent prayer (vv. 1-7), then the praises of God's greatness lead to a personal lament and call for help. A poor, yet important person, perhaps a king, gathers praise, thanks, and petition into one prayer. If the Psalm seems to lack originality and rings with familiar themes of other Psalms, the author's filial faith is unique and his moral tone touching.

In profound humility of heart, the petitioner presents his requests to the only true God, who alone can relieve his distress. While haughty, fierce men seek his life, he effectively trusts in the Lord God. Without Him there can be no true joy in life. Other gods are no gods (vv. 8 and 10), and their comfort is an illusion. There is a minimum of retribution spirit (v. 14), perhaps because the author stood in need of forgiveness (v. 5). "Teach me thy way, O Lord, that I may walk in thy truth; unite my heart to fear thy name" (v. 11).

In its universal spirit (v. 9), this Psalm is prophetic of the era of Christ, when all nations have come to adore Him. Deep devotion shines forth in this Psalm, and the author appears as a man of constant prayer (apart from his sinful lapses). Having been rescued from the depths of danger, he clings to God asking for some sign of divine favor (v. 17) because his position was public and representative.

The Savior's mission to the poor is reflected in this Psalm. Though Christ was without guilt and sin, He identified His lot with sinners, and we can see it as a prayer of Christ for His sentiments are here. At the height of persecution, at the Last Supper, Jesus thanked the Father for the glory to come. He alone knows the Father (Mt. 11:27 and Jn. 7:28f.). As a result, He speaks for the Father and brings us hope and

provident mercy. The Psalm also rings like an echo to Jesus in Gethsemane (Mt. 26:36ff.), bringing hope to the sick and dying.

Psalm 86 serves the Church at important prayer moments: the
Epiphany (noon, in part), III Wednesdays (lauds), Mondays (compline), and for the deceased (noon).

Psalm 87 (86)

On the holy mount stands the city he founded;
2   the LORD loves the gates of Zion
      more than all the dwelling places of Jacob.
3Glorious things are spoken of you,
      O city of God.

4Among those who know me I mention Rahab and Babylon;
      behold, Philistia and Tyre, with Ethiopia—
      "This one was born there," they say.
5And of Zion it shall be said,
      "This one and that one were born in her";
      for the Most High himself will establish her.
6The LORD records as he registers the peoples,
      "This one was born there."

7Singers and dancers alike say,
      "All my springs are in you."

Holy Mother Church

Despite its difficulties, this Psalm brings an important, decisive,
and glorious message for prayer, namely, that Zion will be the universal
Mother of many children and nations. The Lord God loved Jerusalem
and its gates above all other places on earth. He chose Zion and made
Jerusalem secure and perfect. In it were many castles and palaces,
"many mansions." The glorious expectations expressed in this Psalm
about Zion were never fulfilled in an earthly way. God's Word points
to the New Jerusalem and Zion, the Church on earth, where nations
would find their home. This is divine logic and high joy.

The gates of ancient cities were important. Those of Jerusalem
were also strong and beautiful. God Himself calls Jerusalem His City,
His footstool and dwelling. Faithful Jews found Him here, as they

pilgrimaged annually and oftener to this center. The Psalm records the origin of the phrase "City of God." We also find here that the capital of the kingdom becomes the capital of all nations, of the world. God speaks here and goes through the register of Zion's members. He reads the names of former strangers, neighbors, and enemies, nations that became faithful offspring. Egypt (called Rahab, a sea monster) has come to serve the Lord. There are Philistia and Tyre and Ethiopia, peoples nearby and far away, registered as natives born there. Also Babylon, the great former enemy, is among them. Like the citizens of Zion, all "are born there."

That many can say, "My home is in Zion," is the work of the Almighty. This is the new universality, the glory of the messianic era. The Church, which is the New Zion, is the Mother of numerous children. St. Paul says it clearly (Gal. 4:26f.): "The Jerusalem above is free, and she is our mother. That is why Scripture says: 'Rejoice, O barren one that dost not bear; break forth and shout, thou who art not in travail; for the desolate hath more children than she who hath a husband.'"

Home is where one's mother is. Every man and woman in the New City of God can make the boast: "I have come home." Newcomers are no longer strangers, but members of God's family. It is their greatest glory. This Psalm foretells the Church as the home of all peoples. They are born there through Baptism. They have found the wellsprings of joy and song.

Small wonder that the Church uses Psalm 87 at the dedication of churches (office of readings), also on feasts of the Virgin-Mother Mary, especially January 1 (office of readings). Ever since Christmas, when Christ became visible, we speak of the origin of the Church (with St. Leo). The Mother of nations is foretold by Isaiah (2:2). "Glorious things" are already spoken of her; more glorious will be her heavenly existence as the Bride and Spouse of the Lamb.

Psalm 88 (87)

> O LORD, my God, I call for help by day;
>   I cry out in the night before thee.
> ²Let my prayer come before thee,
>   incline thy ear to my cry!

³For my soul is full of troubles,
  and my life draws near to Sheol.
⁴I am reckoned among those who go down to the Pit;
  I am a man who has no strength,
⁵like one forsaken among the dead,
  like the slain that lie in the grave,
 like those whom thou dost remember no more,
  for they are cut off from thy hand.
⁶Thou hast put me in the depths of the Pit,
  in the regions dark and deep.
⁷Thy wrath lies heavy upon me,
  and thou dost overwhelm me with all thy waves.
⁸Thou hast caused my companions to shun me;
  thou hast made me a thing of horror to them.
 I am shut in so that I cannot escape;
⁹   my eye grows dim through sorrow.
 Every day I call upon thee, O Lord;
  I spread out my hands to thee.
¹⁰Dost thou work wonders for the dead?
  Do the shades rise up to praise thee?
¹¹Is thy steadfast love declared in the grave,
  or thy faithfulness in Abaddon?
¹²Are thy wonders known in the darkness,
  or thy saving help in the land of forgetfulness?

¹³But I, O Lord, cry to thee;
  in the morning my prayer comes before thee.
¹⁴O Lord, why dost thou cast me off?
  Why dost thou hide thy face from me?
¹⁵Afflicted and close to death from my youth up,
  I suffer thy terrors; I am helpless.
¹⁶Thy wrath has swept over me;
  thy dread assaults destroy me.
¹⁷They surround me like a flood all day long;
  they close in upon me together.
¹⁸Thou hast caused lover and friend to shun me;
  my companions are in darkness.

Hour of Darkness

The sacred writer calls for God's help in his extreme sickness and
desolation of spirit and state of abandonment. The whole Psalm reflects
his helplessness. Whichever way he turns, he sees affliction with no

sign of God's merciful love. They are the lamentations of a dying man without ray of light or sign of God answering his plea for health and comfort. God is silent, as he prays daily for life and relief. The poor sick man regards this as a sign of divine wrath, and that increases his anguish.

There are many names for Sheol, the realm of death (e.g. the grave, the pit, abyss, the nether world, mire). Old Testament Jews knew little about the afterlife; therefore he asks the questions, "Dost thou work wonders for the dead? Do the shades rise up to praise thee? Are thy wonders known in the darkness?" (vv. 10f.). These questions were inevitable because a veil lay over the next life. Occasionally we find a ray of hope, as in Ps. 16:10. But the ancients measured prayers for help by present tangible results.

The afflicted man prays till the end and does not lose his firm trust in seeking God. In this he is serene. Though friends and neighbors are gone, God is near. Maybe he was an outcast, perhaps his sickness was leprosy. That would make his laments the more agonizing, but his faith in God the more remarkable.

Christ gave the answer to the question, "Are thy wonders known in the darkness?" The answer is yes. The answer is the resurrection, the final hope of all believers in Christ. All men must die and must pray this Psalm at some time without hope of recovery, as the Savior did ("My God, my God, why hast thou forsaken me?" Ps. 22:1). In His prayer in the Garden, He taught us. That and Calvary was His hour of darkness in prayer, abandoned by friends. "Thy will be done, not Mine," and the Father heard His cry (Heb. 5:7). With that He freed "those who through fear of death were subject to lifelong bondage" (Heb. 2:15). The last word is "Glory!" (see Lk. 24:26), the great new revelation of Jesus, death with great hope.

We attach special importance to this Psalm. It seems to bring no answer, yet its apparent hopelessness is full of hope. We pray it after Christ, and it is the hardest and happiest prayer. That prayer will never be mechanical. We tell God our troubles, even the temptation to despair, and accept the trials He permits (Heb. 12:7). He answers after death. We do well to say this Psalm for the dying and terminal patients, for all types of hopeless "cases," the faraway despairing ones who have no one to help. This is the hard lesson of the Cross, but the happy one. God hears all prayer.

The Church uses our Psalm on Good Friday (noon), at Friday compline, and on IV Tuesdays (noon prayer).

Psalm 89 (88)

I will sing of thy steadfast love, O Lord, for ever;
 with my mouth I will proclaim thy faithfulness to all
  generations.
²For thy steadfast love was established for ever,
 thy faithfulness is firm as the heavens.
³Thou hast said, "I have made a covenant with my chosen one,
 I have sworn to David my servant:
⁴'I will establish your descendants for ever,
 and build your throne for all generations.' "

⁵Let the heavens praise thy wonders, O Lord,
 thy faithfulness in the assembly of the holy ones!
⁶For who in the skies can be compared to the Lord?
 Who among the heavenly beings is like the Lord,
⁷a God feared in the council of the holy ones,
 great and terrible above all that are round about him?
⁸O Lord God of hosts,
 who is mighty as thou art, O Lord,
 with thy faithfulness round about thee?
⁹Thou dost rule the raging of the sea;
 when its waves rise, thou stillest them.
¹⁰Thou didst crush Rahab like a carcass,
 thou didst scatter thy enemies with thy mighty arm.
¹¹The heavens are thine, the earth also is thine;
 the world and all that is in it, thou hast founded them.
¹²The north and the south, thou hast created them;
 Tabor and Hermon joyously praise thy name.
¹³Thou hast a mighty arm;
 strong is thy hand, high thy right hand.
¹⁴Righteousness and justice are the foundation of thy throne;
 steadfast love and faithfulness go before thee.
¹⁵Blessed are the people who know the festal shout,
 who walk, O Lord, in the light of thy countenance,
¹⁶who exult in thy name all the day,
 and extol thy righteousness.
¹⁷For thou art the glory of their strength;
 by thy favor our horn is exalted.
¹⁸For our shield belongs to the Lord,
 our king to the Holy One of Israel.

[19]Of old thou didst speak in a vision
    to thy faithful one, and say:
  "I have set the crown upon one who is mighty,
    I have exalted one chosen from the people.
[20]I have found David, my servant;
    with my holy oil I have anointed him;
[21]so that my hand shall ever abide with him,
    my arm also shall strengthen him.
[22]The enemy shall not outwit him,
    the wicked shall not humble him.
[23]I will crush his foes before him
    and strike down those who hate him.
[24]My faithfulness and my steadfast love shall be with him,
    and in my name shall his horn be exalted.
[25]I will set his hand on the sea
    and his right hand on the rivers.
[26]He shall cry to me, 'Thou art my Father,
    my God, and the Rock of my salvation.'
[27]And I will make him the first-born,
    the highest of the kings of the earth.
[28]My steadfast love I will keep for him for ever,
    and my covenant will stand firm for him.
[29]I will establish his line for ever
    and his throne as the days of the heavens.
[30]If his children forsake my law
    and do not walk according to my ordinances,
[31]if they violate my statutes
    and do not keep my commandments,
[32]then I will punish their transgression with the rod
    and their iniquity with scourges;
[33]but I will not remove from him my steadfast love,
    or be false to my faithfulness.
[34]I will not violate my covenant,
    or alter the word that went forth from my lips.
[35]Once for all I have sworn by my holiness;
    I will not lie to David.
[36]His line shall endure for ever,
    his throne as long as the sun before me.
[37]Like the moon it shall be established for ever;
    it shall stand firm while the skies endure."

³⁸But now thou hast cast off and rejected,
  thou art full of wrath against thy anointed.
³⁹Thou hast renounced the covenant with thy servant;
  thou hast defiled his crown in the dust.
⁴⁰Thou hast breached all his walls;
  thou hast laid his strongholds in ruins.
⁴¹All that pass by despoil him;
  he has become the scorn of his neighbors.
⁴²Thou hast exalted the right hand of his foes;
  thou hast made all his enemies rejoice.
⁴³Yea, thou hast turned back the edge of his sword,
  and thou hast not made him stand in battle.
⁴⁴Thou hast removed the scepter from his hand,
  and cast his throne to the ground.
⁴⁵Thou hast cut short the days of his youth;
  thou hast covered him with shame.

⁴⁶How long, O LORD? Wilt thou hide thyself for ever?
  How long will thy wrath burn like fire?
⁴⁷Remember, O Lord, what the measure of life is,
  for what vanity thou hast created all the sons of men!
⁴⁸What man can live and never see death?
  Who can deliver his soul from the power of Sheol?

⁴⁹Lord, where is thy steadfast love of old,
  which by thy faithfulness thou didst swear to David?
⁵⁰Remember, O Lord, how thy servant is scorned;
  how I bear in my bosom the insults of the peoples,
⁵¹with which thy enemies taunt, O LORD,
  with which they mock the footsteps of thy anointed.

⁵²   Blessed be the LORD for ever! Amen and Amen.

Jesus, King of the Jews

To the faithful Jew this Psalm represented a crisis in faith. On the one hand the author recounts the divine promises and favors to David's line; on the other he depicts how God deserted the same royalty and its influence on the people. The fidelity of God is at stake. Hence the question, "How long, O Lord?" (v. 46). The author's faith in God remains unshaken.

The whole range of royal history comes to mind, from David's anointing and the promises given by God (1 Sam. 16:1ff.) till the captivity in 587 B.C., when the nation lamented the downfall of throne, crown, sword, city walls, the royal line. The conquest of Israel was a national catastrophe. Where is the covenant and the promises given to the Davidic dynasty forever (vv. 3-4 and 19-37), that divine oracle to Nathan the prophet (2 Sam. 7:8-17; the end is recorded in 2 Kg. 25:6-22)?

All this happened despite the power, glory, and fidelity of God, who is King and Lord of hosts, whose supremacy the author praises (vv. 5-18). He is transcendentally supreme in heaven and on earth, from the sea (crushing the monster Rahab that stood for chaos) to the mountains that proclaim His majesty. He created the north and the south, and hitherto the people of God celebrated His "mighty arm." By His will their victory (horn) was firm. In worship and out they shouted for joy to God. Nothing escaped His Kingship. Now He has abandoned His covenant with them and deserted them, while the enemy triumphed. Is this the end of royal messianism?

The answer lies in the future, in Christ, the Son of God and Son of David. "The Lord God will give to him the throne of his father David" (Lk. 1:32f.). The sons of David failed to keep the covenant, while God remained faithful (vv. 34-37; although it is a long Psalm, it is short on human self-accusation!). God's loving kindness vastly exceeds the original words to David. The long-range plan of God is beyond human imagination.

We believe that Christ's Kingship and Kingdom are real and spiritual. The Church is the present Kingdom of Christ, founded by His suffering, death, and glory. This is the fulfillment of the Psalmist's hopes. His Church will last forever (Mt. 16:18). Times of catastrophe must not shake our faith in God. Even when history repeats itself and the Church has suffered losses through the centuries, the Church goes on singing the Psalms. God's message comes through clearly. Faith today requires the same adherence to Christ, even when enemies of the Church trample on Christ's Royalty.

The situation is new. It calls for faith in Christ's second Coming, which will be the triumph of divine fidelity. His promises will come true, gloriously. The Father loves the Son (Jn. 3:35) and awaits the defeat of His foes (Heb. 2:8 and 10:12f.). Praying this Psalm strengthens and challenges our faith. We declare our loyalty now by praying it and entering the Mystery of Christ at Christmas (December 30, office of readings, vv. 2-29), then on Tuesdays, Wednesdays, and Thursdays

of Week III (office of readings). The final verse 52 marks the end of
Book III of the Psalter.

Psalm 90 (89)

Lord, thou hast been our dwelling place
in all generations.
²Before the mountains were brought forth,
or ever thou hadst formed the earth and the world,
from everlasting to everlasting thou art God.

³Thou turnest man back to the dust,
and sayest, "Turn back, O children of men!"
⁴For a thousand years in thy sight
are but as yesterday when it is past,
or as a watch in the night.

⁵Thou dost sweep men away; they are like a dream,
like grass which is renewed in the morning;
⁶in the morning it flourishes and is renewed;
in the evening it fades and withers.

⁷For we are consumed by thy anger;
by thy wrath we are overwhelmed.
⁸Thou hast set our iniquities before thee,
our secret sins in the light of thy countenance.

⁹For all our days pass away under thy wrath,
our years come to an end like a sigh.
¹⁰The years of our life are threescore and ten,
or even by reason of strength fourscore;
yet their span is but toil and trouble;
they are soon gone, and we fly away.

¹¹Who considers the power of thy anger,
and thy wrath according to the fear of thee?
¹²So teach us to number our days
that we may get a heart of wisdom.

¹³Return, O Lord! How long?
    Have pity on thy servants!
¹⁴Satisfy us in the morning with thy steadfast love,
    that we may rejoice and be glad all our days.
¹⁵Make us glad as many days as thou hast afflicted us,
    and as many years as we have seen evil.
¹⁶Let thy work be manifest to thy servants,
    and thy glorious power to their children.
¹⁷Let the favor of the Lord our God be upon us,
    and establish thou the work of our hands upon us,
    yea, the work of our hands establish thou it.

Divine Wisdom on Aging

God's ageless youthfulness stands in the eternal present in contrast to man's short-lived span of life. God lived before all time, He lives through all time, and He will be when time is no more. Time, like man's whole being, is a borrowed gift. A thousand years are but a passing shadow, a bubble dream, like grass that withers in the sun. Timelessness befits the nature of God. At His nod man returns to dust, which is a matter of experience and of faith. (See Psalms 8 and 144, "What is man?")

Faith tells us the why of man's abbreviated days, when God's original will was to have him live immortally, without dying. The cause of death is sin, and God's consequent judgment (vv. 9 and 11). "We are consumed by thy anger." The first sin drove man and woman out of paradise and back to dust. In God's sight our secret sins are open (v. 8).

Since our days and years are numbered by God, we must "rejoice and be glad all our days" (v. 14), make them fruitful and successful. The wonder of it is that we can work with wisdom and merit all our years. Fruitless toil is frustrating when our work is not "wrought in God" (Jn. 3:21). Toil in time has meaning and value when performed in God's wisdom. "Teach us to number our days, that we may get a heart of wisdom" (v. 12). If the favor of God is upon the labor of the years, they are established in heavenly success (v. 17). Christ's revelation and redemption gives "success to our hands."

We cry with the Psalmist, "Have pity on thy servants" (v. 13). Even feeble old age becomes valuable in the vineyard of the Lord because a call at the eleventh hour is paid in full by the Lord. Faith corrects all human impressions on aging and dying. To an unbelieving world, this Christian dynamism makes little sense perhaps, but the Savior did His most valuable work when motionless on the Cross. And when He sent His Spirit, it became true "that your old men shall dream dreams" (Acts 2:17), because of the wonders that happened.

Our Savior is the center of this Psalm. He must have meditated on it long and deeply. Because He gave time and space a redemptive value, He answers those who cry to Him, "Stay with us, for it is toward evening and the day is now far spent" (Lk. 24:29). And though He did not live out half His life span, our mortal years are filled to the last with His life-giving power. We see this Psalm also in the light of His resurrection, and that makes all the difference. A new wisdom and motivation takes over the world's worn-out attitudes (Mt. 16:25f.; see also Jn. 12:24f.), and tired old men and women come to life. We pray this wholesome Psalm with Christ in a special way on III Thursdays (office of readings) and IV Mondays (lauds). He "satisfies us in the morning" of His rising with holiness and sinlessness that becomes the aged.

Psalm 91 (90)

He who dwells in the shelter of the Most High,
   who abides in the shadow of the Almighty,
²will say to the LORD, "My refuge and my fortress;
   my God, in whom I trust."
³For he will deliver you from the snare of the fowler
   and from the deadly pestilence;
⁴he will cover you with his pinions,
   and under his wings you will find refuge;
   his faithfulness is a shield and buckler.
⁵You will not fear the terror of the night,
   nor the arrow that flies by day,
⁶nor the pestilence that stalks in darkness,
   nor the destruction that wastes at noonday.

⁷A thousand may fall at your side,
   ten thousand at your right hand;
   but it will not come near you.
⁸You will only look with your eyes
   and see the recompense of the wicked.

⁹Because you have made the LORD your refuge,
   the Most High your habitation,
¹⁰no evil shall befall you,
   no scourge come near your tent.

¹¹For he will give his angels charge of you
   to guard you in all your ways.
¹²On their hands they will bear you up,
   lest you dash your foot against a stone.
¹³You will tread on the lion and the adder,
   the young lion and the serpent
      you will trample under foot.

¹⁴Because he cleaves to me in love, I will deliver him;
   I will protect him, because he knows my name.
¹⁵When he calls to me, I will answer him;
   I will be with him in trouble,
   I will rescue him and honor him.
¹⁶With long life I will satisfy him,
   and show him my salvation.

The Battle Psalm of Christ

Originally spoken by the king who says to the Lord, "My refuge and my fortress, my God, in whom I trust," this Psalm refers to Christ and constantly comes true in His followers who cling to Him. We learn what it means to dwell in the protecting shadow of the Almighty, when danger and terror surround us continually. All the evils mentioned in Psalm 91—snares, pestilence, darkness, rocks on our path, poisonous serpents, and wild animals—picture the spiritual dangers. These are even more real than material perils.

Applied to our spiritual milieu, the Psalm gives a clear image of temptation and the ongoing warfare. We do not see the enemy as Christ did. All the works of the devil are disguised deceptions, and we are naively unaware of them. The night is symbolic of that ignorance of danger. St. Peter warns us: "Be sober, be watchful. Your adversary, the devil, prowls around like a roaring lion seeking some one to devour" (1 Pet. 5:8). Amid all the attacks of Satan, we have God's watchful protection, as Christ did. This divine Word engenders trust in God and sets us up in His own "habitation."

What could be more inspiring than God holding His arms over and around us like a mother bird spreading her wings over her young? We rest in the "shadow of the Almighty." He is a buckler and a shield in the battle. Whether the warfare is open or concealed, He is protecting us. Darkness holds no fears if we cling to Him. His mighty, guarding angels are a sign of His presence. "For he will give his angels charge of you" (v. 11). The entire Bible testifies to them and their concern for us. They see through Satan's lying tactics in the bright vision of God. They accompany us, as they did Christ's humanity.

Satan used this Psalm to tempt Christ in His weakness after forty days of fasting. He did not distort the text, but used it for a rash purpose not willed by God, suggesting that Christ throw Himself into danger in a sensational way to see if the angels would carry Him to safety (see Mt. 4:6). This gives us a striking example of what the Savior did not mean, when He said, "Everything written about me in the . . . Psalms must be fulfilled" (Lk. 24:44). Jesus uncovered the demon's deception. The Church used the whole Psalm 91 with the Gospel of temptation on the I Sunday of Lent formerly, so we would learn the law of battle during Lent and in time of temptation. Our victory is as sure as Christ's, if we cling to Him. We will see "the recompense of the wicked."

God speaks in the Psalm: "Because he cleaves to me in love, I will deliver him" (v. 14 to the end). We must call on Him. "The Lord is my refuge." Living and dying, we can fill our lives with this Psalm. The Church uses it especially as a night prayer (compline), a happy choice because of our incorporation into Christ. Jesus calls on His Father and glorifies Him (Jn. 8:54). In turn the Father glorifies His Son. As a bird wants to protect her young, so He gathers His people (Mt. 23:37). He shares His power over serpents and scorpions (Lk. 10:19), and the victory He won in battle (Rom. 8:28-30), with many brethren gives "long life" (v. 16) in final glory. Cling to God; the angels are here; love prevails; His victory is ours!

Psalm 92

It is good to give thanks to the Lord,
    to sing praises to thy name, O Most High;
²to declare thy steadfast love in the morning,
    and thy faithfulness by night,
³to the music of the lute and the harp,
    to the melody of the lyre.
⁴For thou, O Lord, hast made me glad by thy work;
    at the works of thy hands I sing for joy.

⁵How great are thy works, O Lord!
    Thy thoughts are very deep!
⁶The dull man cannot know,
    the stupid cannot understand this:
⁷that, though the wicked sprout like grass
    and all evildoers flourish,
they are doomed to destruction for ever,
⁸   but thou, O Lord, art on high for ever.
⁹For lo, thy enemies, O Lord,
    for lo, thy enemies shall perish;
    all evildoers shall be scattered.

¹⁰But thou hast exalted my horn like that of the wild ox;
    thou hast poured over me fresh oil.
¹¹My eyes have seen the downfall of my enemies,
    my ears have heard the doom of my evil assailants.

¹²The righteous flourish like the palm tree,
    and grow like a cedar in Lebanon.
¹³They are planted in the house of the Lord,
    they flourish in the courts of our God.
¹⁴They still bring forth fruit in old age,
    they are ever full of sap and green,
¹⁵to show that the Lord is upright;
    he is my rock, and there is no unrighteousness in him.

The Gift of Understanding

Endowed with faith, our knowing spirit understands the thoughts
and works of God. As in the preface of the Mass we sing, "It is good to
give thanks to the Lord," so we praise Him day and night for His wonders. The greater our insight into His Mysteries, the more we celebrate

with voice and music His salvation. This calm yet animated Psalm gives royal recognition to His wisdom in dealing with man. The gift of understanding His ways is a joy-giving experience. God's point of view transcends our short-sightedness and corrects our shortcomings. The wicked and evildoers are too dull to fathom the ways of God. Their only yardsticks are opulence and prosperity, false standards that lead to ruin and eternal destruction. They live like animals and run off the right track. On the other hand, the just and faithful man, living in wisdom, never loses his freshness and vitality, even in advancing years. God gives joy with insight and facility with fortitude, another gift of the Holy Spirit. The "horn" expresses this. Anointing with fresh, rich oil tells of the fulness of the Spirit (see also Psalm 23).

As in Psalm 1, the symbol of the god-like man is the flourishing tree planted along running waters, so again the just man will grow like the palm tree and the cedars of Lebanon. The latter, which furnished the material for the Temple of God's dwelling, is a beloved image. This cedar wood stands for indefectibility, like the faithful man who trusts God and is "full of sap and green" even in old age. The Holy Spirit is known by all the figures of attractiveness and beauty, strength and ease (facility), joy and music, the aroma of perfumed oil, festivity and abundance, and the best of human art. On the other hand, the lot and doom of the wicked are without hope.

This Psalm becomes an all-out, joyous religious experience in the Body of Christ, the Church. Here we join Christ's intonation and carry on with joyful gratitude, most of all in the Eucharist. There is no greater fruitfulness than that coming from union with the Lord, being "planted in the house of the Lord" (v. 13). In His courts we are grafted onto the tree which is Christ. There we flourish with increasing understanding and wisdom even into eternal life. In Christ's vineyard old age is never useless because life in God has no retirement. God blesses the growth He initiates, and this fruitfulness is beyond human knowing (Jn. 15:5; 2 Cor. 4:16 speaks of renewal of the inner man). Wisdom comes with life in the Spirit, who is the "Oil of gladness."

"We do not lose heart," no matter how decrepit we get, for we pass "from glory to glory." This Psalm serves the Church on II and IV Saturdays (lauds), and at the office of readings for pastors and holy women, those who exemplify evergreen life and fruitfulness.

Psalm 93 (92)

The LORD reigns; he is robed in majesty;
the LORD is robed, he is girded with strength.
Yea, the world is established; it shall never be moved;
2   thy throne is established from of old;
thou art from everlasting.

3The floods have lifted up, O LORD,
the floods have lifted up their voice,
the floods lift up their roaring.
4Mightier than the thunders of many waters,
mightier than the waves of the sea,
the LORD on high is mighty!

5Thy decrees are very sure;
holiness befits thy house,
O LORD, for evermore.

God Forever

While this Psalm unmasks all human substitutes for God, it strengthens faith both in community and individuals to commit themselves to Him for all time, for His own sake. He the transcendent God, the *Deus solus*, is enthroned eternally in heaven, almighty, firm, and trustworthy. All His perfections are infinite, so that praise of His holiness befits His heavenly as well as His earthly abode. Robed in splendid light beyond all visible royal glory, He commands reverence from every creature.

All the symbols of power and impressive phenomena known to man, the thunder of mighty tides, the deafening crash of ocean waves beating the rocks, are nothing compared to His power on high, His majesty as King. Man can trust and love this God and His will. His decrees of old (and this is an ancient piece of Psalmody), frequently given and received in fear, have ceded to the law of love which is in Christ Jesus.

Of the love of Christ, we can affirm what the *Song of Solomon* says, "Many waters cannot quench love, neither can floods drown it" (8:7). The waters of human malice and hatred, the tyranny of passion and violence, the floods of ingratitude, weakness and sin, all the noisy tumult of hell and Satan, are powerless against the love and charity of Christ. Such is the power of His mercy and loving kindness, which reigned supreme on the Cross. Such is the love of the God-man begotten in and born of the Virgin Mary.

As firmly as God the King stood in Jewish faith, so firmly does the love of Christ the King stand in the faith of the People of God. We pray this Psalm with enthusiasm and submission to Christ the Lord, the King clothed in light and strength. We give Him all the honor we give to God the Father. Jesus said, "No one comes to the Father, but by me" (Jn. 14:6). Since He is God-with-us and His dwelling is in the New Zion, holiness becomes His house and His members.

His enthronement is also in our hearts and homes, in the whole world of faith. It takes many voices to praise Him and express our love, so this is a great common prayer. His Kingship is now, but of another world (Jn. 18:36). Rejoice, then, all who welcome His Coming. The enthusiasm and dynamism of this Psalm must seize and carry us aloft. The "praise of his glory" is our divine vocation (Eph. 1:12). Let us do now what we will do for all eternity (Rev. 21:1ff.; 11:15; 1:15). Join the voice that sounds like many waters, be grateful for picking up His intonation in the Church now (every III Sunday at lauds) and in the halls of heaven forever.

Psalm 94 (93)

O LORD, thou God of vengeance,
   thou God of vengeance, shine forth!
²Rise up, O judge of the earth;
   render to the proud their deserts!
³O LORD, how long shall the wicked,
   how long shall the wicked exult?

⁴They pour out their arrogant words,
   they boast, all the evildoers.
⁵They crush thy people, O LORD,
   and afflict thy heritage.
⁶They slay the widow and the sojourner,
   and murder the fatherless;
⁷and they say, "The LORD does not see;
   the God of Jacob does not perceive."

⁸Understand, O dullest of the people!
    Fools, when will you be wise?
⁹He who planted the ear, does he not hear?
  He who formed the eye, does he not see?
¹⁰He who chastens the nations, does he not chastise?
  He who teaches men knowledge,
¹¹   the LORD, knows the thoughts of man,
        that they are but a breath.

¹²Blessed is the man whom thou dost chasten, O LORD,
        and whom thou dost teach out of thy law
¹³to give him respite from days of trouble,
        until a pit is dug for the wicked.
¹⁴For the LORD will not forsake his people;
        he will not abandon his heritage;
¹⁵for justice will return to the righteous,
        and all the upright in heart will follow it.

¹⁶Who rises up for me against the wicked?
        Who stands up for me against evildoers?
¹⁷If the LORD had not been my help,
        my soul would soon have dwelt in the land of silence.
¹⁸When I thought, "My foot slips,"
        thy steadfast love, O LORD, held me up.
¹⁹When the cares of my heart are many,
        thy consolations cheer my soul.
²⁰Can wicked rulers be allied with thee,
        who frame mischief by statute?
²¹They band together against the life of the righteous,
        and condemn the innocent to death.
²²But the LORD has become my stronghold,
        and my God the rock of my refuge.
²³He will bring back on them their iniquity
        and wipe them out for their wickedness;
        the LORD our God will wipe them out.

Love of God's Justice

If we are concerned about God's glory, then we are concerned also about justice to the poor. God's people must have special love for the widow, the stranger, and the orphan. God watches over the order of law and justice in this world. He instructs the nations in ways of righteousness. At the opening of this Psalm, the author twice invokes the vengeance of the Lord to take action against the evildoers who are in power, who defend their murderous presumption by pretending that God does not see them. God, who created the eye and ear, sees and hears the cries of the afflicted. He knows their every thought.

The pit which the fools dig is hell, the "pit for the wicked" (v. 13). Blessed is the man who abides by God's law. He will be at rest in time of trouble because God will be the advocate for all the poor, defenceless ones. There will be no "land of silence" (v. 17), no silent grave for those who trusted in the Lord. "O Lord, how long?" is only a short cry, as in the end the wicked are confounded. This is a lesson in the Lord's school: to wait patiently and place our complaints before Him.

"My foot slips," reminds us of Peter walking on water. "Help me, Lord, I am sinking." Jesus rescued him. He sustains us when our faith begins to sink. He comforts us—"When the cares of my heart are many." His kindness and justice are the same as those of the God of the Psalmist. He will take action against those "who frame mischief by statute" (v. 20), who pervert justice. True, the innocent suffer, but only the innocent triumph. The Psalm reminds us of the legalism of the Pharisees, the legalism from which Jesus suffered most. As in Psalms 51 and 58, we thank God for the chastening effect of justice (v. 12), that "the Lord has become my stronghold and my God the rock of my refuge" (v. 22).

Our Lord and Savior shared the Psalmist's righteous anger and at the same time taught by Word and example the way for us. Although He taught as "one having power," He did not use the whip to purge the courts that falsely condemned Him, to save Himself from injustice in high places. He who condemned the Pharisees (Mt. 23) was the same as blessed those who suffer injustice (Mt. 5:10f.). No one was more concerned for the widow and orphan and stranger than He. No one prayed this Psalm more sincerely than He, when Pilate washed his hands "in innocence." The thoughts of God guide us, who want to be His disciples and like Paul echo verse 11: "The Lord knows the thoughts of man, that they are but a breath" (see 1 Cor. 3:20).

We cling to Christ our Rock, as we cling to God in praying this Psalm with the Church on IV Wednesdays (noon).

Psalm 95 (94)

O come, let us sing to the LORD;
    let us make a joyful noise to the rock of our salvation!
[2]Let us come into his presence with thanksgiving;
    let us make a joyful noise to him with songs of praise!
[3]For the LORD is a great God,
    and a great King above all gods.
[4]In his hand are the depths of the earth;
    the heights of the mountains are his also.
[5]The sea is his, for he made it;
    for his hands formed the dry land.

[6]O come, let us worship and bow down,
    let us kneel before the LORD, our Maker!
[7]For he is our God,
    and we are the people of his pasture,
    and the sheep of his hand.

O that today you would hearken to his voice!
[8]   Harden not your hearts, as at Meribah,
    as on the day at Massah in the wilderness,
[9]when your fathers tested me,
    and put me to the proof, though they had seen my work.
[10]For forty years I loathed that generation
    and said, "They are a people who err in heart,
    and they do not regard my ways."
[11]Therefore I swore in my anger
    that they should not enter my rest.

Today You Hear His Voice

A double invitation comes in this Psalm, namely, to worship the God of creation and revelation, to kneel before our Maker and Savior. The God who is Lord of all the earth is also the Shepherd of His chosen flock. The God of gods is the Rock of refuge. The Creator who made the depths of water and heights of land revealed Himself as the Guide of His people. He has a twofold claim on man as the God of nature and supernature, the God of reason and revelation.

Come, let us bow in adoration to this Lord of justice and love! Worship is our twofold answer of love, the wisdom of man as man and the wisdom of man as the adopted son of God. To do less would be imitating our fathers at Meribah and Massah in the desert (Ex. 17:1-7), where they doubted the Lord and tempted (tested) Him by their rebellion to Moses. We kneel in humility to qualify for worship. We sin if we doubt after seeing water flow from a rock, after seeing God's work.

The Jews who doubted and rebelled never entered the promised land ("My rest") as a punishment. The figure of God "loathing" the erring generation is a terrible threat, and who dares to risk his eternal salvation? Instead of being filled with grateful praise for this tremendous divine favor, they "hardened their hearts" and forfeited God's rest. We find this "rest" explained at length in Heb. 4, which quotes our Psalm. Christians who reject the invitation will never enter eternal rest.

"O that today you would hearken to his voice!"

There is no escaping the Voice. "He who hears you hears me" (Lk. 10:16). Jesus is the Rock (1 Cor. 10:4; 9-11: "The Rock was Christ"), the Rock whence flow the baptismal waters and the Voice that still speaks. Closing our ears means hardening our hearts. Surely, this Psalm is prophetic of the perennial praises in the Church today. His invitation is always to His new presence.

As Christ guides us through the Exodus, we the sheep of His flock recognize His Voice in the Church and celebrate His great redemption with joyful thanksgiving. His Holy Spirit fills the Church, as we "sing to the Lord" and praise Him "in Psalms and hymns and spiritual songs" (Eph. 5:19; see Col. 3:16). The themes of Psalms 8 and 95 are similar. Heaven resounds with praise and adoration (Rev. 14:7, especially 19: 1-8). This is the great invitatory Psalm of the Church. We are accustomed to Christ's daily summons to His prayer in the office of readings.

Psalm 96 (95)

> O sing to the LORD a new song;
>   sing to the LORD, all the earth!
> [2]Sing to the LORD, bless his name;
>   tell of his salvation from day to day.
> [3]Declare his glory among the nations,
>   his marvelous works among all the peoples!

⁴For great is the LORD, and greatly to be praised;
    he is to be feared above all gods.
⁵For all the gods of the peoples are idols;
    but the LORD made the heavens.
⁶Honor and majesty are before him;
    strength and beauty are in his sanctuary.

⁷Ascribe to the LORD, O families of the peoples,
    ascribe to the LORD glory and strength!
⁸Ascribe to the LORD the glory due his name;
    bring an offering, and come into his courts!
⁹Worship the LORD in holy array;
    tremble before him, all the earth!

¹⁰Say among the nations, "The LORD reigns!
    Yea, the world is established, it shall never be moved;
    he will judge the peoples with equity."

¹¹Let the heavens be glad, and let the earth rejoice;
    let the sea roar, and all that fills it;
¹²   let the field exult, and everything in it!
  Then shall all the trees of the wood sing for joy
¹³   before the LORD, for he comes,
    for he comes to judge the earth.
  He will judge the world with righteousness,
    and the peoples with his truth.

Glory to God in the Highest

With the same theme as Psalms 47, 93, 97, 98, and 99, and almost identical with 1 Chr. 16:23-33 (where David regulated the worship before the Ark), our Psalm breaks forth in pure joy at the Coming of God. Man is at his best when giving high praise in sacrifice to God, when with perfect love (fear of God) he enlists the whole world in a symphony of glorifying the Lord of heaven and earth. God is the center of festive joy in the whole universe. Just as heaven is a continuous celebration of His greatness, so man speaks for His visible universe, besides reflecting a still greater glory in Christ Jesus and His Body.

In heaven praise is perfect, as there is no competition from false gods, but on earth a variety of deities and idols of people distract the true believer in his worship. Human freedom is a special reflection of God when it is untarnished by false worship of man himself and of earthly goods. Authentic worship is given when the earth stands "in holy array" (v. 9). Entering God's courts requires right decisions in faith, so that God can truly reign.

The "families of nations" recall the Lord's "one flock and one Shepherd." When that unity transpires, the common language will be glory and praise. The heavens broke open at Bethlehem, when Christ was born, and could not contain the new song of glory at the incarnation of the Son of God. We call it Christ's first Coming. God is always coming in the messianic era, and praise erupts when men are aware of it. The reason for glory is the same as in this Psalm. Rejoicing and high festival are the only response to His Coming. Ever new song, total rejoicing, beautiful melody in community is the only welcome.

The Psalms speak of Christ. "We have beheld his glory" (Jn. 1:14). His glory is inexhaustible (Heb. 1:8), since it is the majesty of the High Priest exalted forever (Heb. 8:1f.; 9:24-26; see also Rev. 1:12-16 and 19:11-16). "All the trees of the woods sing for joy" (v. 12); all nature longs for the redemption, to be taken into the sacramental system as a carrier of His Coming in Sign. Glory is becoming to man as the "fruit of lips" and voice and heart (Heb. 13:15), the echo of heaven's glory. The New Testament sings to Christ, the Son of David's line (Acts 2: 29-36). Glory to Christ on earth is our refrain to the heavenly voices.

Unceasing witness to this glory occurs on the Church's festivals, on Easter Saturday (noon), Epiphany, and December 31 (office of readings), September 14 (office of readings) and III Mondays (lauds). All comment falls short of this Psalm's greatness.

Psalm 97 (96)

> The LORD reigns; let the earth rejoice;
>   let the many coastlands be glad!
> ²Clouds and thick darkness are round about him;
>   righteousness and justice are the foundation of his throne.
> ³Fire goes before him,
>   and burns up his adversaries round about.
> ⁴His lightnings lighten the world;
>   the earth sees and trembles.
> ⁵The mountains melt like wax before the LORD,
>   before the Lord of all the earth.

⁶The heavens proclaim his righteousness;
　　and all the peoples behold his glory.
⁷All worshipers of images are put to shame,
　　who make their boast in worthless idols;
　　all gods bow down before him.
⁸Zion hears and is glad,
　　and the daughters of Judah rejoice,
　　because of thy judgments, O God.
⁹For thou, O LORD, art most high over all the earth;
　　thou art exalted far above all gods.

¹⁰The LORD loves those who hate evil;
　　he preserves the lives of his saints;
　　he delivers them from the hand of the wicked.
¹¹Light dawns for the righteous,
　　and joy for the upright in heart.
¹²Rejoice in the LORD, O you righteous,
　　and give thanks to his holy name!

God Is King

God's glory is concealed and inaccessible; still it is near and revealed. The Psalm is like a continuation of the preceding one (see also Psalm 47). Heaven and earth manifest the Lord, yet He is utterly transcendent. All the nations of the earth must bow down before this King to the shamed confusion of idol worshippers. Those who see His signs or self-revelation, in Zion or abroad, rejoice in His glory. As light dawns, so gladness prevails in Jerusalem and villages and towns (the daughters of Zion). This Psalm reflects the ancient battle of nations: whosoever won imposed their idol gods on the defeated. All these false gods, imposters, bow to the one and only God.

The remembrance of the God of Mount Sinai gives us the images of clouds, darkness, and storm lightning (Ex. 19:16-19). Fire and earth-shaking thunder overawed the people. Even the mountains melted like wax at the Lord's presence. Moses entered the dark cloud and there saw God "face to face." As a result the divine glory shone on his face, and the people could not stand to look at that brilliance, so he veiled his face.

The Kingship of God includes ownership of the world, but it is essentially a spiritual Kingdom of truth, justice, and holiness. God hates evil and loves justice, which He will vindicate in final judgment to the joy of the upright. The light and joy which are dawning will grow like the day into full glory for all the saints. There is no "hobnobbin" with the divinity as with those who "boast in worthless idols" (v. 7).

The glory of Christ is the glory of God. Filled with the Holy Spirit, His glory shone through. This is true especially in St. John's Gospel where His miracles are signs of glory. The sacraments too are Signs worked by the exalted, ascended Christ (e.g. Jn. 6:62). This wonderful Psalm has many points of contact with the life and work of the Savior. Christ the King has purchased the Kingdom with His Blood and will turn it over to the Father. Heb. 1:6-8 reminds us of Psalm 97. Christ's second Coming will bring all the blessings of light and joy and preserve us from the wicked. To Him, "To the King of ages, immortal, invisible, the only God, be honor and glory for ever and ever. Amen" (1 Tim. 1:17).

We use it as responsory for the Mass of the Transfiguration (August 6). It also fits the Epiphany, Easter, the Ascension, Pentecost, Christ the King, and His Coming to judge the world. We use it for the arch-angels, on the last day of the civil year, and the feasts of apostles (office of readings), and on Wednesdays (lauds).

Psalm 98 (97)

O sing to the LORD a new song,
for he has done marvelous things!
His right hand and his holy arm
have gotten him victory.
²The LORD has made known his victory,
he has revealed his vindication in the sight of the nations.
³He has remembered his steadfast love and faithfulness
to the house of Israel.
All the ends of the earth have seen
the victory of our God.

⁴Make a joyful noise to the LORD, all the earth;
break forth into joyous song and sing praises!
⁵Sing praises to the LORD with the lyre,
with the lyre and the sound of melody!
⁶With trumpets and the sound of the horn
make a joyful noise before the King, the LORD!

⁷Let the sea roar, and all that fills it;
> the world and those who dwell in it!
⁸Let the floods clap their hands;
> let the hills sing for joy together
⁹before the LORD, for he comes to judge the earth.
 He will judge the world with righteousness,
> and the peoples with equity.

All the Earth Praise the Lord!

Much like Psalm 96 in spirit and content, this Psalm enlists all men and nations in the praise of Israel's God. Those who have seen His victory and experienced His salvation break forth in song over His wonderful deeds. His revelation and kindness to the house of Israel gives all the ends of the earth cause for rejoicing. If the land and sea and the rivers and mountains clap their hands and sing, can man do less? The inanimate, forced movement of sea and floods is awe-inspiring, but man has to devise talented melody with the lyre, trumpet, and horn in the free service of his Lord and King, who has come and is coming.

The song of music is man's welcome. Music, like the Psalms, comes from the heart. While the sticks and stones have a fixed, mute melody to their Maker, not so man. He sees God's glory in all the universe and His salvation is achieved progressively. God's Coming in the Old Testament was, so to say, a cradle-measure and the faith response a cradle-faith compared to the New Testament. Now we have reason to rejoice and sing more perfectly.

The new revelation of God and His Coming is in the sacred humanity of Jesus Christ. In Him, God reaches out His hand for our reconciliation. Let us reach out with humility to grasp this powerful Hand of God in our midst, one like ours, to which we can cling. Faith sees this. Faith grows as God comes closer. We see more clearly the unfolding of salvation through the mediating humanity of Jesus Christ. And so this Psalm means even more to us than to the people for whom it was first written.

The unseen world of God is as real as our visible world. Spiritual facts and truths are ultimate realities. The ever-coming Godhead, surrounded by signs of kindness, faithfulness, and power, is now most fully in our possession, until the final revelation in heaven, when faith dissolves in the divine vision. The Psalm is prophetic of the last consummated glory and Kingship, when all the ends of the earth will see what they now believe. The unconverted and obstinate world does not live in this hope, as it rejects the evidence, the revelation, and signs of the Kingdom.

In the perspective of Christ, we celebrate the anticipation of His glorious second Coming. All creation rejoices in waiting for this moment (Rom. 8:18-25) called the Parousia. Our enlightened faith sees the Coming of the resurrected Christ as always imminent (Eph. 1:15-23 and Acts 17:30f.). This faith of the early Church (1 Thess. 1:6-10), which saw the fullness of the Word of God, is in the Psalms in particular (Col. 3:16f.). No wonder the Church sings this Psalm on a feast celebrating the humanity of Christ, the Sacred Heart, and December 31 (office of readings), on Epiphany (noon), and on III Wednesdays (lauds).

Psalm 99 (98)

The LORD reigns; let the peoples tremble!
 He sits enthroned upon the
  cherubim; let the earth quake!
²The LORD is great in Zion;
 he is exalted over all the peoples.
³Let them praise thy great and terrible name!
 Holy is he!
⁴Mighty King, lover of justice,
 thou hast established equity;
thou hast executed justice
 and righteousness in Jacob.
⁵Extol the LORD our God;
 worship at his footstool!
 Holy is he!

⁶Moses and Aaron were among his priests,
 Samuel also was among those who called on his name.
 They cried to the LORD, and he answered them.
⁷He spoke to them in the pillar of cloud;
 they kept his testimonies,
 and the statutes that he gave them.

⁸O LORD our God, thou didst answer them;
   thou wast a forgiving God to them,
   but an avenger of their wrongdoings.
⁹Extol the LORD our God,
   and worship at his holy mountain;
   for the LORD our God is holy!

Holy Is His Name

The awesome, transcendent, all-powerful, and just God made
Zion in Jerusalem His footstool. He who is high above earth and heaven
chose to dwell in the Ark of the covenant among Jacob, or Israel, His
people. The King of heaven deigned to have an earthly throne, the
cherubim of the Ark. There He received the homage due Him and
taught His people amid awe and trembling the basics of righteousness
and love. Even then He chose mediators from among His people,
Moses and Aaron and Samuel, to call on His Name and to watch over
His statutes. He did not tolerate the injustices of men and he punished
them, but He was also a forgiving God. His people were surrounded
by other peoples steeped in primitive sinning, and God used them
to lift up His chosen nation. His demand for adoration from His own
people always has this one reason: "The Lord our God is holy!"

Might and mildness, which seem so incompatible to men in power,
God blends in His very nature, which He reveals here in teaching them
true religion. Power, equity, and mercy by no means exhaust His nature
because all His qualities are infinite. An eternity enables only the blessed
to begin exploring His perfections. The surprise and grateful joy is
that He wants men to pray to Him, that He wants to answer those
prayers and use mediators in the process (see Heb. 5:4).

The sinner can neither manipulate nor bribe God. Being a forgiving God, he extends His holiness to all who turn to Him. His holiness
makes mankind holy. Looking with desire at a rich man will leave a
poor man poor, but regarding God with desire and longing makes
the poor man holy. Praise and worship are special contacts with God
that sanctify men and women. Contact with God in the Old Testament
was a mere foretaste of union with Him in the New. "In these last days
he has spoken to us by a Son, whom he appointed heir of all things"
(Heb. 1:2).

In Christ Jesus, God and man, we have a unique new mediatorship (1 Tim. 2:5) from which all priesthood derives it mediatorial

character. He alone is King. In Him the whole Kingdom has arrived (Mt. 3:2 and 12:28). To Him every knee must bend in heaven, on earth, and under the earth (Phil. 2:10f.). "Holy is His Name." The earth trembled at His resurrection. A voice from heaven confirmed Christ's judgment (Jn. 12:29-31). In Him dwells the fulness of divinity (Col. 2:9-12). Our baptismal sharing in this God-man has a unique value, as we pray this Psalm with the Church on August 6, January 1, and December 27 (office of readings), also on every III Thursday (lauds). The humanity of Jesus, taken from the Virgin-Mother Mary, is the instrument of His Mediatorship, also in prayer.

Psalm 100 (99)

Make a joyful noise to the LORD, all the lands!
2   Serve the LORD with gladness!
Come into his presence with singing!

3Know that the LORD is God!
It is he that made us, and we are his;
we are his people, and the sheep of his pasture.

4Enter his gates with thanksgiving,
and his courts with praise!
Give thanks to him, bless his name!

5For the LORD is good;
his steadfast love endures for ever,
and his faithfulness to all generations.

Enter His Gates With Song

Joy in divine service is the mark of God's elect. Entry into God's house is always a privilege, and rejoicing comes from our faith that we are the sheep of His flock. That depends on His prior choice and because His special presence in our midst is His first decision. Those who appreciate the nearness of God in sign (Ark, Temple, Altar) will never cease giving thanks and praise. They will want to learn this Psalm by heart. Worship of God in His Temple is service, man's highest service. That is the meaning of the word "liturgy," public service in His special presence.

Entry requires high personal virtue: faith, humble sentiments, and forgetfulness of all else. This Psalm is a prelude to approaching God's sacred precincts. The sheep of His pasture have an instinct for sacred places, where divine love reaches the heights of goodness. Not to be happy on arriving at His courts would be a sign that something is wrong or deficient. Where is our joyous faith when we enter His Temple?

In the ancient Church all the assembly rose and chanted for joy at the summons, "He is entering" ("introit"). People sang because the entry of the priest or bishop meant the coming of Christ. Christ had called Himself the door and gateway for His flock (Jn. 10:7-9), and consequently the door or portals or sacred edifices received special art emphasis. This treatment still claims the admiration of artists and people of faith. Does our sobriety in this regard indicate a lessening of faith? The Church building is the visible sign of Christ and His fold. The Shepherd is concerned about entry.

He is the way to the Father. In Him we are new creatures (2 Cor. 5:17). Our Baptism means entry into God's Family and home. "No one comes to the Father but by me" (Jn. 14:6). The baptistery, which graces the entrance of churches, should be a constant reminder of this truth and fact. This New Testament faith, adding a new dimension to our Psalm, brings joy and love in God which nothing can suppress. God our Savior, as well as our Creator, is in this Psalm. The joy of the author is a weak anticipation of our happiness. "But you are a chosen race, a royal priesthood, a holy nation, God's own people" (1 Pet. 2:9). "See what love the Father has given us, that we should be called children of God, and so we are" (1 Jn. 3:1). Faithful to Him, the Church of Christ uses this Psalm on I and III Fridays (at lauds), reminding us to enter His gates singing.

Psalm 101 (100)

> I will sing of loyalty and of justice;
>   to thee, O LORD, I will sing.
> ²I will give heed to the way that is blameless.
>   Oh when wilt thou come to me?

I will walk with integrity of heart
 within my house;
³I will not set before my eyes
 anything that is base.

I hate the work of those who fall away;
 it shall not cleave to me.
⁴Perverseness of heart shall be far from me;
 I will know nothing of evil.

⁵Him who slanders his neighbor secretly
 I will destroy.
The man of haughty looks and arrogant heart
 I will not endure.

⁶I will look with favor on the faithful in the land,
 that they may dwell with me;
he who walks in the way that is blameless
 shall minister to me.

⁷No man who practices deceit
 shall dwell in my house;
no man who utters lies
 shall continue in my presence.

⁸Morning by morning I will destroy
 all the wicked in the land,
cutting off all the evildoers
 from the city of the Lord.

Charter for Men in Office

We can predict the state of the nation by the quality of its governing men, who like the author of this Psalm (probably King David himself) set up courts and administration according to principles of justice and mercy. The ruler himself coming first, a living example of integrity, lets it be known that there will be no men of deceit around him, no favorites in his house, no self-seekers in his service. This Psalm is a prayer for leaders and subjects alike, each with his or her own responsibility. The Lord God is in the picture. It serves as an examination of conscience for high and low, for those who seek favors and those who dispense them. Religion is the basis for every man's conscience.

"Morning by morning I will destroy all the wicked of the land" tells of his projected daily courts of justice in poetic figure. These courts will guarantee the rights of the poor downtrodden, and his mercy will temper justice, just as God's does. There is nothing arbitrary here, and the faithful of the land will dwell in peace. The known rule of God becomes law and custom in the land. While virtue and kindness are hard to legislate, every honest effort bears fruit. The results in practice may never be perfect, but salvation will blossom out in a society where men walk the way of integrity.

"O when wilt thou come to me?" is spoken to God and suggests many ways in which God will be present to men of goodwill. Since this is a royal Psalm, it calls for a more intimate union with God at His coming with the Ark into the king's city, or the Coming of Christ into his royal line. Everyone must ask himself that question, as the answer will break down evil and build up decisions for God and against dishonesty of intention. God will not come to those described as "perverse of heart," except to punish them.

Would that this Psalm could be given to all men in office who hold a public trust of God and man (Rom. 13:1-5). The world is ever in need of governors with such a program. "Thus you will know them by their fruits" (Mt. 7:20). God has come in Jesus Christ. He clearly points out the way (Jn. 4:25). Therefore we can sing again of kindness and judgment. He came to do the will of the Father (Heb. 10:7). His integrity is the way for all. Liars and perverse hearts have no place in His heavenly Kingdom. They are "outsiders" (Rev. 22:15; see also 2 Tim. 3:1-5). "God judges those outside: 'Drive out the wicked person from among you' " (1 Cor. 5:13), now for his conversion, hereafter forever.

The Church, like Christ, wills not the death of the sinner, but his conversion and life. This intention is in her public prayer of this Psalm on IV Wednesdays (lauds). Our personal praying of it expands the soul to take in Christ's intentions.

Psalm 102 (101)

Hear my prayer, O Lord;
   let my cry come to thee!
2Do not hide thy face from me
   in the day of my distress!
Incline thy ear to me;
   answer me speedily in the day when I call!

3For my days pass away like smoke,
   and my bones burn like a furnace.
4My heart is smitten like grass, and withered;
   I forget to eat my bread.
5Because of my loud groaning
   my bones cleave to my flesh.
6I am like a vulture of the wilderness,
   like an owl of the waste places;
7I lie awake,
   I am like a lonely bird on the housetop.
8All the day my enemies taunt me,
   those who deride me use my name for a curse.
9For I eat ashes like bread,
   and mingle tears with my drink,
10because of thy indignation and anger;
   for thou hast taken me up and thrown me away.
11My days are like an evening shadow;
   I wither away like grass.

12But thou, O Lord, art enthroned for ever;
   thy name endures to all generations.
13Thou wilt arise and have pity on Zion;
   it is the time to favor her;
   the appointed time has come.
14For thy servants hold her stones dear,
   and have pity on her dust.
15The nations will fear the name of the Lord,
   and all the kings of the earth thy glory.
16For the Lord will build up Zion,
   he will appear in his glory;
17he will regard the prayer of the destitute,
   and will not despise their supplication.

¹⁸Let this be recorded for a generation to come,
 so that a people yet unborn may praise the LORD:
¹⁹that he looked down from his holy height,
 from heaven the LORD looked at the earth,
²⁰to hear the groans of the prisoners,
 to set free those who were doomed to die;
²¹that men may declare in Zion the name of the LORD,
 and in Jerusalem his praise,
²²when peoples gather together,
 and kingdoms, to worship the LORD.

²³He has broken my strength in midcourse;
 he has shortened my days.
²⁴"O my God," I say, "take me not hence
 in the midst of my days,
thou whose years endure
 throughout all generations!"

²⁵Of old thou didst lay the foundation of the earth,
 and the heavens are the work of thy hands.
²⁶They will perish, but thou dost endure;
 they will all wear out like a garment.
Thou changest them like raiment, and they pass away;
²⁷ but thou art the same, and thy years have no end.
²⁸The children of thy servants shall dwell secure;
 their posterity shall be established before thee.

Man's Fragility, God's Stability

Human nature quickly reaches its end. Only God can lengthen man's days and restore him. All the suffering of a dying man and of broken humanity, here so vividly described, is a picture of loneliness without God. The urgent cry of the Psalmist is for God's help and mercy for himself and for Zion. The pain and distress is physical, but verses 9 and 10 tell us there is also sin and God's punishment (ashes, tears, and God's wrath suggest this). Together with Psalms 6, 32, 38, 51, 88, and 130, this forms a group called the penitential Psalms. In his desperate condition, the author's greatest need is God's redeeming pity, described in verses 12 to the end.

This personal appeal becomes a national prayer for the restoration of Zion and its praises. The petition of the abandoned one is for the rebuilding of Zion in all its glory, with the nations of the earth paying homage to God (v. 22). God's eternity and unchanging stability become the motive of prayer: human and earthly things perish and deteriorate like an old garment, but the Lord is immortal and never grows old. His everlasting sameness is at one and the same time man's comfort and desire. Because He abides forever, man can pray that it is time for mercy, time for present and future security.

The hope of the dying man centers not only in himself, but in God's chosen people. This hope comes true in the appearance of the God-man on our scene at the appointed time for universal pardon and mercy. The author of Hebrews (1:10-12) refers us to verses 25-27 on Christ in His humanity. The second Person of the Godhead put on the fragile garment of our human nature at the incarnation, and at the resurrection He strengthened it with His immortality and unchanging divine permanence.

Going back, we can see Jesus suffering and dying in verses 1-11, without any guilt of sin, however, and abiding forever in the rest of the Psalm. His opening prayer, "Hear my prayer, O Lord, let my cry come to thee!" serves the Church as a frequent versicle in her office and ritual. "The hour has come," of Jesus before His passion, recalls verse 13. Because He suffered loneliness, man has found togetherness, a growing unity of nations together praising His Name. Those doomed to die (v. 20), like Barabbas, go free because Jesus went to the Cross. All of us are saved from eternal death and go free because of His vicarious suffering. Indeed the writer's hope is more than fulfilled.

Let us join the Church praying for the ripe, rich harvest of those dying with and without the longing for redemption and in doing so build up the new Zion on earth, for heaven. This Psalm occurs on IV Tuesdays (office of readings).

Psalm 103 (102)

Bless the LORD, O my soul;
and all that is within me,
bless his holy name!
²Bless the LORD, O my soul,
and forget not all his benefits,
³who forgives all your iniquity,
who heals all your diseases,
⁴who redeems your life from the Pit,
who crowns you with steadfast love and mercy,
⁵who satisfies you with good as long as you live
so that your youth is renewed like the eagle's.

⁶The LORD works vindication
and justice for all who are oppressed.
⁷He made known his ways to Moses,
his acts to the people of Israel.
⁸The LORD is merciful and gracious,
slow to anger and abounding in steadfast love.
⁹He will not always chide,
nor will he keep his anger for ever.
¹⁰He does not deal with us according to our sins,
nor requite us according to our iniquities.
¹¹For as the heavens are high above the earth,
so great is his steadfast love toward those who fear him;
¹²as far as the east is from the west,
so far does he remove our transgressions from us.
¹³As a father pities his children,
so the LORD pities those who fear him.
¹⁴For he knows our frame;
he remembers that we are dust.

¹⁵As for man, his days are like grass;
he flourishes like a flower of the field;
¹⁶for the wind passes over it, and it is gone,
and its place knows it no more.
¹⁷But the steadfast love of the LORD
is from everlasting to everlasting
upon those who fear him,
and his righteousness to children's children,
¹⁸to those who keep his covenant
and remember to do his commandments.

¹⁹The Lord has established his throne in the heavens,
   and his kingdom rules over all.
²⁰Bless the Lord, O you his angels,
   you mighty ones who do his word,
   hearkening to the voice of his word!
²¹Bless the Lord, all his hosts,
   his ministers that do his will!
²²Bless the Lord, all his works,
   in all places of his dominion.
Bless the Lord, O my soul!

God So Loved the World

This exquisite Psalm of tender kindness and pure joy is a prayer to thank God for His mercies to individuals and people, for His works in heaven and on earth. The repeated phrase, "Bless the Lord, O my soul!" is like music in the hearing of God and man. Sharing God's love calls forth new love. His merciful love is greater in forgiveness than in the display of power and justice. Pardon for sin, healing of sickness, and the ongoing donation of the Lord's favors awaken the soul to praise and thanks, which are identical. "God is love" is in a special way the New Testament theme, yet here it stands out like a prophecy. The benefits of the past are prophetic of an even greater bounty.

Nothing under heaven rejuvenates people like the pardon of sin. God knows the thin, tenuous dust-nature of man, whom he destined to be the noble carrier of His divine life of grace. By nature man is passing, by grace he will live forever. Both grace and nature are divine gifts, the one to keep man humble, the other to make him eternally exalted and happy. Despite human sinning, God's wrath gives way to His kindness, which is boundless. As He dealt with Moses and His people during the long Exodus, so He deals with all that seek mercy. He is the origin of human fatherhood and motherhood; therefore He Himself is fatherly and ever generous with those who call themselves His sons.

We are especially grateful for the description of sin forgiven. As we would hope from a loving Father, His forgiveness means new and greater love. Sins repented of are forgotten, erased, entirely taken away and undone. Only God can achieve this: remove our evildoing as far as the East is from the West, as far as the heavens are from the earth. It is a miracle of love. The prophet Hosea depicts God's fatherly compassion in terms of "bands of love" (11:1-4). The sinner is afraid to offend a God of such love. The author enlists all the angels at God's heavenly throne to bless the Lord, and even the generations to come to pass on the "precept" of love. Past, present, and future must remember this law of Christ.

His Coming as man was the peak of divine love, for mankind found full redemption in Christ Jesus. No wisdom of human ingenuity could have invented such a phantasy of love. "For God so loved the world that he gave his only Son" (Jn. 3:16) that we might have life eternal. "Your youth is renewed like the eagle's" (v. 5). What is legendary about the eagle is literally true of us because of Christ's resurrection, His immortality, and eternal youthfulness. Jesus' dying on the Cross brought us total forgiveness and a new love; His resurrection gives us rebirth in Baptism. Godliness, new health and life, new victory, new light and joy are all fruits of a love that is greater than the hatred. of the sinner. *A felix culpa!* O happy fault of Adam!

We rise above sadness and servile fear, as we fall in line with Christ and His Church singing the Psalm on IV Wednesdays, on September 29 (feast of all the angels, office of readings). We invite the whole world to praise God with us, to awaken people to glorify and "Bless the Lord, O my soul!"

Psalm 104 (103)

Bless the LORD, O my soul!
O LORD my God, thou art very great!
Thou art clothed with honor and majesty,
2   who coverest thyself with light as with a garment,
who hast stretched out the heavens like a tent,
3   who hast laid the beams of thy chambers on the waters,
who makest the clouds thy chariot,
who ridest on the wings of the wind,
4who makest the winds thy messengers,
fire and flame thy ministers.

⁵Thou didst set the earth on its foundations,
    so that it should never be shaken.
⁶Thou didst cover it with the deep as with a garment;
    the waters stood above the mountains.
⁷At thy rebuke they fled;
    at the sound of thy thunder they took to flight.
⁸The mountains rose, the valleys sank down
    to the place which thou didst appoint for them.
⁹Thou didst set a bound which they should not pass,
    so that they might not again cover the earth.

¹⁰Thou makest springs gush forth in the valleys;
    they flow between the hills,
¹¹they give drink to every beast of the field;
    the wild asses quench their thirst.
¹²By them the birds of the air have their habitation;
    they sing among the branches.
¹³From thy lofty abode thou waterest the mountains;
    the earth is satisfied with the fruit of thy work.

¹⁴Thou dost cause the grass to grow for the cattle,
    and plants for man to cultivate,
  that he may bring forth food from the earth,
¹⁵   and wine to gladden the heart of man,
  oil to make his face shine,
    and bread to strengthen man's heart.
¹⁶The trees of the LORD are watered abundantly,
    the cedars of Lebanon which he planted.
¹⁷In them the birds build their nests;
    the stork has her home in the fir trees.
¹⁸The high mountains are for the wild goats;
    the rocks are a refuge for the badgers.
¹⁹Thou hast made the moon to mark the seasons;
    the sun knows its time for setting.
²⁰Thou makest darkness, and it is night,
    when all the beasts of the forest creep forth.
²¹The young lions roar for their prey,
    seeking their food from God.
²²When the sun rises, they get them away
    and lie down in their dens.
²³Man goes forth to his work
    and to his labor until the evening.

²⁴O Lord, how manifold are thy works!
    In wisdom hast thou made them all;
    the earth is full of thy creatures.
²⁵Yonder is the sea, great and wide,
    which teems with things innumerable,
    living things both small and great.
²⁶There go the ships,
    and Leviathan which thou didst form to sport in it.

²⁷These all look to thee,
    to give them their food in due season.
²⁸When thou givest to them, they gather it up;
    when thou openest thy hand,
       they are filled with good things.
²⁹When thou hidest thy face, they are dismayed;
    when thou takest away their breath, they die
    and return to their dust.
³⁰When thou sendest forth thy Spirit, they are created;
    and thou renewest the face of the ground.

³¹May the glory of the Lord endure for ever,
    may the Lord rejoice in his works,
³²who looks on the earth and it trembles,
    who touches the mountains and they smoke!
³³I will sing to the Lord as long as I live;
    I will sing praise to my God while I have being.
³⁴May my meditation be pleasing to him,
    for I rejoice in the Lord.
³⁵Let sinners be consumed from the earth,
    and let the wicked be no more!
  Bless the Lord, O my soul!
    Praise the Lord!

All Creation Praises the Lord

A review of Gen. 1, reminding us that all things come from the hand of God, this beautiful nature Psalm determines our piety as we look around the world we live in. The Lord is telling us how to appreciate all creatures with the gift of understanding. We do well to shout the *Alleluia* of praise, as we realize His wisdom in making and preserving the earth and all its creatures. All nature comes from His creative power and looks to His face and spirit for life. Sustaining the animate world is as great as creating it.

The picture here is the common man's viewpoint, a man with vivid imagination. God is robed in light as with a cloak (v. 2), the heavens are a huge tent, the clouds are His chariot, the wings of the wind His motive power, and the ocean a vast covering garment. We call it the cosmogony of that day, like the science of our day. Interesting as it is, the spiritual message behind it captures our attention. God is not being identified with His creation, but He is apart from it and totally different, transcendent we say. God is beyond and apart from time and space, other than His handiwork, and infinite. All things have their built-in ability to praise, but especially man with his voice of freedom.

A litany of praise: mountains and valleys, water springs and food for beasts and birds, homes for the stork and wild goat, day and night for lions, bread, wine and oil for man, the monsters of the sea as God's playthings, the ocean as a symbol of God's vastness. All things reflect God's wisdom and goodness in some way. So does man, most of all in praising God, as the author does at the beginning and end of the Psalm. Man alone can sing joyful praise, as he blesses the Lord for all His works.

This Psalm does not stand isolated in the Scriptures. Heb. 1:7 quotes verse 4: "Who makest the winds thy messengers, flames and fires thy ministers," referring these to the angels. The Church applies verse 30: "When thou sendest forth thy spirit, they are created, and thou renewest the face of the ground," to Pentecost, and aptly so, for the "spirit" means breath and life. The Spirit's coming at Pentecost was the great renewal of the face of the earth, including man, and was the birth of Christ's Church in her sacramental power. The fulness of the Psalm points to a greater fulness of the Holy Spirit with a superabundance of supernatural life.

Psalm 104 teaches us openness to the Holy Spirit, not in a cramped selfish lifestyle but in bold surrender of self to praise and love. At our meal prayers we use verses 27f., as we affirm the goodness of created things, such as the food that God made to be eaten with a blessing (see 1 Tim. 4:1-4). Christ is the firstborn of all creatures (Col. 1:16ff.) who ate and drank. This Psalm is a wholesome balancer for our day when science claims self-sufficiency and independence. We ask for the Spirit's gift of knowledge, as the Church enters deeply into this Psalm at Pentecost, on II Sundays, and Wednesday after Easter (office of readings).

Psalm 105 (104)

O give thanks to the LORD, call on his name,
    make known his deeds among the peoples!
2Sing to him, sing praises to him,
    tell of all his wonderful works!
3Glory in his holy name;
    let the hearts of those who seek the LORD rejoice!
4Seek the LORD and his strength,
    seek his presence continually!
5Remember the wonderful works that he has done,
    his miracles, and the judgments he uttered,
6O offspring of Abraham his servant,
    sons of Jacob, his chosen ones!

7He is the LORD our God;
    his judgments are in all the earth.
8He is mindful of his covenant for ever,
    of the word that he commanded,
      for a thousand generations,
9the covenant which he made with Abraham,
    his sworn promise to Isaac,
10which he confirmed to Jacob as a statute,
    to Israel as an everlasting covenant,
11saying, "To you I will give the land of Canaan
    as your portion for an inheritance."

12When they were few in number,
    of little account, and sojourners in it,
13wandering from nation to nation,
    from one kingdom to another people,
14he allowed no one to oppress them;
    he rebuked kings on their account,
15saying, "Touch not my anointed ones,
    do my prophets no harm!"

¹⁶When he summoned a famine on the land,
>   and broke every staff of bread,
¹⁷he had sent a man ahead of them,
>   Joseph, who was sold as a slave.
¹⁸His feet were hurt with fetters,
>   his neck was put in a collar of iron;
¹⁹until what he had said came to pass
>   the word of the Lord tested him.
²⁰The king sent and released him,
>   the ruler of the peoples set him free;
²¹he made him lord of his house,
>   and ruler of all his possessions,
²²to instruct his princes at his pleasure,
>   and to teach his elders wisdom.

²³Then Israel came to Egypt;
>   Jacob sojourned in the land of Ham.
²⁴And the Lord made his people very fruitful,
>   and made them stronger than their foes.
²⁵He turned their hearts to hate his people,
>   to deal craftily with his servants.

²⁶He sent Moses his servant,
>   and Aaron whom he had chosen.
²⁷They wrought his signs among them,
>   and miracles in the land of Ham.
²⁸He sent darkness, and made the land dark;
>   they rebelled against his words.
²⁹He turned their waters into blood,
>   and caused their fish to die.
³⁰Their land swarmed with frogs,
>   even in the chambers of their kings.
³¹He spoke, and there came swarms of flies,
>   and gnats throughout their country.
³²He gave them hail for rain,
>   and lightning that flashed through their land.
³³He smote their vines and fig trees,
>   and shattered the trees of their country.
³⁴He spoke, and the locusts came,
>   and young locusts without number;
³⁵which devoured all the vegetation in their land,
>   and ate up the fruit of their ground.
³⁶He smote all the first-born in their land,
>   the first issue of all their strength.

37Then he led forth Israel with silver and gold,
    and there was none among his tribes who stumbled.
38Egypt was glad when they departed,
    for dread of them had fallen upon it.
39He spread a cloud for a covering,
    and fire to give light by night.
40They asked, and he brought quails,
    and gave them bread from heaven in abundance.
41He opened the rock, and water gushed forth;
    it flowed through the desert like a river.
42For he remembered his holy promise,
    and Abraham his servant.

43So he led forth his people with joy,
    his chosen ones with singing.
44And he gave them the lands of the nations;
    and they took possession of the fruit of the peoples' toil,
45to the end that they should keep his statutes,
    and observe his laws.
    Praise the LORD!

God in Our Family History

Resembling Psalm 78, except for the negative defections, this Psalm relates God's promotion of His sacred people in a positive, straight line forward from Abraham to the promised land. It is a festive thanksgiving song (partially quoted in 1 Chr. 16:8ff.), and its Alleluia is a summons to celebration with song, praising God and recalling His great deeds and early revelation to God's family of faith. God's action is all positive here, a call and recall "forever" to His glorious interventions in the memory of the nation.

Sacred history begins with the covenant with Abraham, the father of faith. God chose him and his descendants and led them through hard and dark ways. God's presence was their light. He calls the early patriarchs "prophets" and "anointed ones," for they were His own in a special way. Egypt is the land of Ham, and it was there He multiplied his wonders to free His people from slavery. A "thousand generations" means "forever." Joseph in Egypt turned the tide, as God used his suffering for a greater good. "He made him lord of his house, and ruler of all his possessions" is later applied to another Joseph, the legal father of Jesus Christ. By suffering, Joseph became an early image of Christ, who saved His people by the great redemption.

Then follows Moses, the chief fashioner of the holy nation and instrument of God's miracles. He led the people out, and when they emerged from the Red Sea dry-shod, that became the birthday of sacred Psalmody, for the nation broke out in praise of God (see Ex. 15 and v. 43 of our Psalm). Miriam started the canticle that continues until today. Whenever the Jews encountered God, they burst forth in Psalms (the canticles too are Psalms). God accompanied them on the journey, in the cloud, with bread and water, through the words of Moses, in the worship, all forecasts of the sacraments, prefigurations of God's presence in the new covenant of Christ Jesus.

Our faith in this family history calls us to join the earthly chorus, which took centuries of preparation. This and other Psalms call for sung prayer. With its Alleluia, we, who have arrived in the family heritage of Christ, sing this Old Testament commentary and rejoice in its fulfillment forever. Forever? We await the final day of heavenly Easter triumph, as we children of Abraham rehearse this hymn of God's covenant. Our faith must go all the way. We revel in memory, not like paging through an old family album, but memory in Christ that is powerful: it reenacts and makes present Christ's Coming in the great Eucharist. There the Savior actualizes His promises of the past, makes present the Mysteries of His redemptive history, and anticipates His Coming in glory.

No, this Psalm when prayed in the Body of Christ is not mere history or memory of the past, but present salvation in Him who is always coming. The Church prays the Psalm with Christ present on Holy Saturday (office of readings) and on I Saturdays (also office of readings).

Psalm 106 (105)

Praise the Lord!
O give thanks to the Lord, for he is good;
for his steadfast love endures for ever!
²Who can utter the mighty doings of the Lord,
or show forth all his praise?
³Blessed are they who observe justice,
who do righteousness at all times!

⁴Remember me, O Lᴏʀᴅ, when thou showest favor to
    thy people;
    help me when thou deliverest them;
⁵that I may see the prosperity of thy chosen ones,
    that I may rejoice in the gladness of thy nation,
    that I may glory with thy heritage.

⁶Both we and our fathers have sinned;
    we have committed iniquity, we have done wickedly.
⁷Our fathers, when they were in Egypt,
    did not consider thy wonderful works;
 they did not remember the abundance of thy steadfast love,
    but rebelled against the Most High at the Red Sea.
⁸Yet he saved them for his name's sake,
    that he might make known his mighty power.
⁹He rebuked the Red Sea, and it became dry;
    and he led them through the deep as through a desert.
¹⁰So he saved them from the hand of the foe,
    and delivered them from the power of the enemy.
¹¹And the waters covered their adversaries;
    not one of them was left.
¹²Then they believed his words;
    they sang his praise.

¹³But they soon forgot his works;
    they did not wait for his counsel.
¹⁴But they had a wanton craving in the wilderness,
    and put Got to the test in the desert;
¹⁵he gave them what they asked,
    but sent a wasting disease among them.

¹⁶When men in the camp were jealous of Moses
    and Aaron, the holy one of the Lᴏʀᴅ,
¹⁷the earth opened and swallowed up Dathan,
    and covered the company of Abiram.
¹⁸Fire also broke out in their company;
    the flame burned up the wicked.

¹⁹They made a calf in Horeb
    and worshiped a molten image.
²⁰They exchanged the glory of God
    for the image of an ox that eats grass.
²¹They forgot God, their Savior,
    who had done great things in Egypt,
²²wondrous works in the land of Ham,
    and terrible things by the Red Sea.
²³Therefore he said he would destroy them—
    had not Moses, his chosen one,
stood in the breach before him,
    to turn away his wrath from destroying them.

²⁴Then they despised the pleasant land,
    having no faith in his promise.
²⁵They murmured in their tents,
    and did not obey the voice of the Lord.
²⁶Therefore he raised his hand and swore to them
    that he would make them fall in the wilderness,
²⁷and would disperse their descendants among the nations,
    scattering them over the lands.

²⁸Then they attached themselves to the Baal of Peor,
    and ate sacrifices offered to the dead;
²⁹they provoked the Lord to anger with their doings,
    and a plague broke out among them.
³⁰Then Phinehas stood up and interposed,
    and the plague was stayed.
³¹And that has been reckoned to him as righteousness
    from generation to generation for ever.

³²They angered him at the waters of Meribah,
    and it went ill with Moses on their account;
³³for they made his spirit bitter,
    and he spoke words that were rash.

³⁴They did not destroy the peoples,
>   as the Lord commanded them,
³⁵but they mingled with the nations
>   and learned to do as they did.
³⁶They served their idols,
>   which became a snare to them.
³⁷They sacrificed their sons
>   and their daughters to the demons;
³⁸they poured out innocent blood,
>   the blood of their sons and daughters,
> whom they sacrificed to the idols of Canaan;
>   and the land was polluted with blood.
³⁹Thus they became unclean by their acts,
>   and played the harlot in their doings.

⁴⁰Then the anger of the Lord was kindled against his people,
>   and he abhorred his heritage;
⁴¹he gave them into the hand of the nations,
>   so that those who hated them ruled over them.
⁴²Their enemies oppressed them,
>   and they were brought into subjection under their power.
⁴³Many times he delivered them,
>   but they were rebellious in their purposes,
>   and were brought low through their iniquity.
⁴⁴Nevertheless he regarded their distress,
>   when he heard their cry.
⁴⁵He remembered for their sake his covenant,
>   and relented according to the abundance of his
>   steadfast love.
⁴⁶He caused them to be pitied
>   by all those who held them captive.

⁴⁷Save us, O Lord our God,
>   and gather us from among the nations,
> that we may give thanks to thy holy name
>   and glory in thy praise.

⁴⁸Blessed be the Lord, the God of Israel,
>   from everlasting to everlasting!
> And let all the people say, "Amen!"
>   Praise the Lord!

Prayer in Dispersion

After the opening prayer, the Psalmist's theme alternates between "We have sinned" and "Many times he delivered them" (v. 43). Written in captivity, this Psalm repeats the instances of human sinning and divine forgiving that summarize the history of Israel. It resembles Psalm 78 and relates not just history, but sacred history in which God had a special part. The ups and downs, mostly downs, of the Exodus people pass before our eyes in quick succession. The best commentary to this pattern would be the Old Testament history itself, which lends detail and depth to many defections of the people.

The mercy of God is constant and unfailing. At the Red Sea it started when they complained about food in the desert. After that they rebelled against Moses and Aaron. Horeb stands for Sinai and Ham for Egypt. The worship of the golden calf is well known. But more repulsive sacrifices and rituals followed. Disobedience, stubbornness (see Dt. 9:6ff.), doubting, and constant murmuring against the leaders chosen by God were the common offenses. Moses stood in the breach and pleaded as mediator, and even he doubted at Meribah, so that God punished him by refusing him entrance into the promised land. The Psalm does not give an exhaustive list, nor does it enumerate the failures in the right historical order.

The Jews grew into a nation amid pagan neighbors. The Lord's command to avoid contact or even to exterminate them had divine reasons, which we do not always learn. As a result of the people's failure to obey God, they learned new evils and idolatrous ways. Sinning and then the cry for mercy went on till the captivity (587 B.C.), when the long punishment began. At this point verse 47 becomes clear, "Gather us from among the nations." Even is dispersion God's compassion was the last word.

All people, like the Jews, have a short memory for God's benefits. We repeat in our lives their story of rebelling and forgetting, of ingratitude and infidelity to God. The New Testament is the last episode in forgiveness for the ever fickle human spirit. We must guard against presumption, taking His mercy for granted. The New Law is, "Where sin increased, grace abounded all the more . . . through Jesus Christ our Lord" (Rom. 5:20f.). All because God so loved the world, that he gave His Son for our eternal life (Jn. 3:16). He will never deny help to those who ask sincerely because Christ repaid ingratitude and presumption with mercy.

We sing this praise of His mercy in the Church on II Saturdays (office of readings). The last verse of the Psalm is a doxology which closes Book IV of the Psalms, a later division.

Psalm 107 (106)

O give thanks to the Lord,
for he is good;
for his steadfast love endures for ever!
2Let the redeemed of the Lord say so,
whom he has redeemed from trouble
3and gathered in from the lands,
from the east and from the west,
from the north and from the south.

4Some wandered in desert wastes,
finding no way to a city to dwell in;
5hungry and thirsty,
their soul fainted within them.
6Then they cried to the Lord in their trouble,
and he delivered them from their distress;
7he led them by a straight way,
till they reached a city to dwell in.
8Let them thank the Lord for his steadfast love,
for his wonderful works to the sons of men!
9For he satisfies him who is thirsty,
and the hungry he fills with good things.

10Some sat in darkness and in gloom,
prisoners in affliction and in irons,
11for they had rebelled against the words of God,
and spurned the counsel of the Most High.
12Their hearts were bowed down with hard labor;
they fell down, with none to help.
13Then they cried to the Lord in their trouble,
and he delivered them from their distress;
14he brought them out of darkness and gloom,
and broke their bonds asunder.
15Let them thank the Lord for his steadfast love,
for his wonderful works to the sons of men!
16For he shatters the doors of bronze,
and cuts in two the bars of iron.

[17]Some were sick through their sinful ways,
    and because of their iniquities suffered affliction;
[18]they loathed any kind of food,
    and they drew near to the gates of death.
[19]Then they cried to the LORD in their trouble,
    and he delivered them from their distress;
[20]he sent forth his word, and healed them,
    and delivered them from destruction.
[21]Let them thank the LORD for his steadfast love,
    for his wonderful works to the sons of men!
[22]And let them offer sacrifices of thanksgiving,
    and tell of his deeds in songs of joy!

[23]Some went down to the sea in ships,
    doing business on the great waters;
[24]they saw the deeds of the LORD,
    his wondrous works in the deep.
[25]For he commanded, and raised the stormy wind,
    which lifted up the waves of the sea.
[26]They mounted up to heaven, they went down to the depths;
    their courage melted away in their evil plight;
[27]they reeled and staggered like drunken men,
    and were at their wits' end.
[28]Then they cried to the LORD in their trouble,
    and he delivered them from their distress;
[29]he made the storm be still,
    and the waves of the sea were hushed.
[30]Then they were glad because they had quiet,
    and he brought them to their desired haven.
[31]Let them thank the LORD for his steadfast love,
    for his wonderful works to the sons of men!
[32]Let them extol him in the congregation of the people,
    and praise him in the assembly of the elders.

³³He turns rivers into a desert,
   springs of water into thirsty ground,
³⁴a fruitful land into a salty waste,
   because of the wickedness of its inhabitants.
³⁵He turns a desert into pools of water,
   a parched land into springs of water.
³⁶And there he lets the hungry dwell,
   and they establish a city to live in;
³⁷they sow fields, and plant vineyards,
   and get a fruitful yield.
³⁸By his blessing they multiply greatly;
   and he does not let their cattle decrease.

³⁹When they are diminished and brought low
   through oppression, trouble, and sorrow,
⁴⁰he pours contempt upon princes
   and makes them wander in trackless wastes;
⁴¹but he raises up the needy out of affliction,
   and makes their families like flocks.
⁴²The upright see it and are glad;
   and all wickedness stops its mouth.
⁴³Whoever is wise, let him give heed to these things;
   let men consider the steadfast love of the Lord.

Song of the Redeemed

The great worship assembly gathered from the four directions hears the witness of four groups, each of which proclaims its predicament, its cry to the Lord and His answer, and then thanks Him for a wonderful rescue. In each case the mighty works of God strengthen the faith of the whole community. Four times the refrain for God's help echoes forth: "Let them thank the Lord for his steadfast love, for his wonderful works to the sons of men." Each group (beginning with "Some") has its story to tell. Some wasted away in the desert with hunger and thirst, others sat in dark prisons and chains for their rebellion, some were sick unto death, and some "went down to the sea in ships," went through a severe storm, and the Lord "made the storm be still."

After this follows a general hymn of praise in which each group finds its particular divine favor repeated in a general way (vv. 33-43). Plentiful water, rich harvests and vineyards, increasing flocks and family progeny, always relief for the poor are the favors that bring the people solidarity in faith and common joy. Material blessings and answers to prayer made them conscious of being God's people.

All this becomes the image and guarantee of spiritual blessings and redemption in the New Order of Christ. The old literal sense is necessary to grasp, as by a parable, the culmination of divine favors in the Church, the new Assembly of the Savior. The upright believe, while the unbeliever is silenced, as they behold Christ repeating these deeds and doing even greater wonders. He healed the sick to prove that He had power to forgive sins (Mt. 9:6f.). He quieted the storm at sea with a gesture to rescue His disciples and strengthen them in faith (Mk. 4:37-41). He fed the hungry crowd in the desert (Jn. 6) and prefigured feeding the hungry of the world with His redemptive Eucharist. In the Acts, His Spirit released prisoners miraculously, to substantiate His messianic work in the Church, the release of prisoners from the power of Satan.

Jesus still saves the world from dangers and eternal death. He proclaims to the assembly the blessedness of the believing poor (Lk. 6:20-26). During our lifetime and association with the Lord, we have every reason to echo the refrain, "Let them give thanks to the Lord," both in our "private" lives and in the public Assembly, as we pray this Psalm with the People of God every III Saturday (office of readings).

Psalm 108 (107)

> My heart is steadfast, O God,
> > my heart is steadfast!
> I will sing and make melody!
> > Awake, my soul!
> ²Awake, O harp and lyre!
> > I will awake the dawn!
> ³I will give thanks to thee, O Lord, among the peoples,
> > I will sing praises to thee among the nations.
> ⁴For thy steadfast love is great above the heavens,
> > thy faithfulness reaches to the clouds.
>
> ⁵Be exalted, O God, above the heavens!
> > Let thy glory be over all the earth!
> ⁶That thy beloved may be delivered,
> > give help by thy right hand, and answer me!

⁷God has promised in his sanctuary.
"With exultation I will divide up Shechem,
and portion out the Vale of Succoth.
⁸Gilead is mine; Manasseh is mine;
E'phraim is my helmet;
Judah my scepter.
⁹Moab is my washbasin;
upon Edom I cast my shoe;
over Philistia I shout in triumph."

¹⁰Who will bring me to the fortified city?
Who will lead me to Edom?
¹¹Hast thou not rejected us, O God?
Thou dost not go forth, O God, with our armies.
¹²O grant us help against the foe,
for vain is the help of man!
¹³With God we shall do valiantly;
it is he who will tread down our foes.

My Heart Is Ready

Two parts of this Psalm are found in two previous Psalms. Verses 1-5 are the same as 57:7-11, while verses 7-13 are identical with 60:6-12. The reader may refer to these Psalms for further comment.

With a steadfast, ready heart, the author sings praise to the accompaniment of lyre and harp. He awakens his whole being to the great spiritual action of praise, just as the dawn awakens him to a new day in God's world. He makes known his thanks and praise publicly before he petitions for graces. This is a norm of all prayer: praise always comes first. God knows what we need and want before we ask. And there is greater love in praise, outgoing love, centered on God and not on oneself.

The prayer of petition is also necessary as a next step. Here it heartens people and king to recall God's promises, solemn promises that came from His sanctuary. The whole world belongs to the Creator, but He portions it out to His people according to His will. In verses 9-11, we pass in review the neighboring and other lands, which the Lord intends for His chosen nation. All except Judah seem lost in battles, and so the Psalmist pleads again that God may lead their armies to the fortified city (Petra in the desert) and generally help against the enemy.

"With God we shall do valiantly" is a prayer for every situation, providing we act in faith. Prayer in defeat may be more perfect than prayer in victory, when things go well. The Church uses this Psalm on IV Wednesdays (lauds).

Psalm 109 (108)

Be not silent, O God of my praise!
²For wicked and deceitful mouths are opened against me,
    speaking against me with lying tongues.
³They beset me with words of hate,
    and attack me without cause.
⁴In return for my love they accuse me,
    even as I make prayer for them.
⁵So they reward me evil for good,
    and hatred for my love.

⁶Appoint a wicked man against him;
    let an accuser bring him to trial.
⁷When he is tried, let him come forth guilty;
    let his prayer be counted as sin!
⁸May his days be few;
    may another seize his goods!
⁹May his children be fatherless,
    and his wife a widow!
¹⁰May his children wander about and beg;
    may they be driven out of the ruins they inhabit!
¹¹May the creditor seize all that he has;
    may strangers plunder the fruits of his toil!
¹²Let there be none to extend kindness to him,
    nor any to pity his fatherless children!
¹³May his posterity be cut off;
    may his name be blotted out in the second generation!
¹⁴May the iniquity of his fathers be remembered before the Lord,
    and let not the sin of his mother be blotted out!
¹⁵Let them be before the Lord continually;
    and may his memory be cut off from the earth!
¹⁶For he did not remember to show kindness,
    but pursued the poor and needy
    and the brokenhearted to their death.
¹⁷He loved to curse; let curses come on him!
    He did not like blessing; may it be far from him!

¹⁸He clothed himself with cursing as his coat,
  may it soak into his body like water,
  like oil into his bones!
¹⁹May it be like a garment which he wraps round him,
  like a belt with which he daily girds himself!

²⁰May this be the reward of my accusers from the Lord,
  of those who speak evil against my life!
²¹But thou, O God my Lord,
  deal on my behalf for thy name's sake;
  because thy steadfast love is good, deliver me!
²²For I am poor and needy,
  and my heart is stricken within me.
²³I am gone, like a shadow at evening;
  I am shaken off like a locust.
²⁴My knees are weak through fasting;
  my body has become gaunt.
²⁵I am an object of scorn to my accusers;
  when they see me, they wag their heads.

²⁶Help me, O Lord my God!
  Save me according to thy steadfast love!
²⁷Let them know that this is thy hand;
  thou, O Lord, hast done it!
²⁸Let them curse, but do thou bless!
  Let my assailants be put to shame; may thy servant
   be glad!
²⁹May my accusers be clothed with dishonor;
  may they be wrapped in their own shame as in a mantle!

³⁰With my mouth I will give great thanks to the Lord;
  I will praise him in the midst of the throng.
³¹For he stands at the right hand of the needy,
  to save him from those who condemn him to death.

The Innocent Man on Trial

The ultimate court of appeal is the tribunal of God, where the helpless man has final recourse. An innocent victim of powerful, lying tongues, the just man is filled with the sentiments of Christ Himself, as he prays, "In return for my love they accuse me, even as I make prayer for them. So they reward me evil for good, and hatred for my love" (vv. 4-5), which could well be a prayer of Christ, the innocent Lamb led to the Cross. Furthermore, he refers his whole case to God (vv. 20-31), leaving it to Him to administer justice, adding (v. 28) "Let them curse, but do you bless!"

That this Psalm is a prayer at a court trial is clear from verses 6-7 and again from 20-31. Knowing this helps us to pray it right, as verses 6-19, called "the cursing section," very likely is a quotation of the accusing enemies, not the Psalmist's own words. Whether spoken by the enemies or hurled back by the innocent man, it should stand in quotation marks. We do not know the literal meaning of that section. It is unlikely that a man with a Christlike spirit, mentioned above, should in the next breath descend to such harsh language. In any case, the section stands as an extreme formulation of Old Testament retribution that nowhere finds stronger expression. As passionate anger it goes too far, beyond the "lex talionis" (rule of revenge), "Eye for eye, tooth for tooth . . ." (Ex. 21:23f.).

To hate evil is Godlike, to save the sinner Christlike. Our Lord always condemns evil, but spares the sinner. He suffered the most diabolical hatred that man had ever perpetrated. In His passion and death, He submitted out of freely chosen love to cruelty, thereby establishing the new law of forgiveness of enemies. "But I say to you that hear, Love your enemies, do good to those who hate you, bless those who curse you" (Lk. 6:27f.). Rom. 12:14-21 also embodies the law of love. St. Peter, who applies verse 8 to the traitor Judas (Acts 1:15-20), tells us that God wills all to turn to Him in penance (1 Pet. 3:9). The Lord, who perfected the Old Law, saw evil and diabolical influence more clearly than we, who are too quick in demanding retribution. Whatever designs God had in formerly allowing the "lex talionis," now it is different, reversed! Was He adapting to a more primitive cultural stage of development of those times?

We pray the retribution parts of the Psalms in the sense that Christ and His Church prays them, never against personal enemies, but against Satan and his reprobate world (Jn. 17:9ff.; also 12:31 and 16:11). We can pray the section (vv. 6-19) as a "Begone, Satan!" as an exorcism of the evil spirits who are "legion." Then the Old Testament imperfections will be perfected in the New. The literal, retribution anger will serve the spiritual victory of Christ, who will exorcize evil from our world and promote His Kingdom of love. And the sinner will live and convert to the Lord God. In this sense, may God have mercy on the poor abortionists and banish the evil spirit that instigates all these and other crimes, the devil: "He was a murderer from the beginning" (Jn. 8:44).

The Church refrains from using this Psalm in her official prayer, probably awaiting the day when people can grasp a more spiritual meaning of its harsh section.

Psalm 110 (109)

The LORD says to my lord:
"Sit at my right hand,
till I make your enemies your footstool."

²The LORD sends forth from Zion
your mighty scepter.
Rule in the midst of your foes!
³Your people will offer themselves freely
on the day you lead your host
upon the holy mountains.
From the womb of the morning
like dew your youth will come to you.
⁴The LORD has sworn
and will not change his mind,
"You are a priest for ever
after the order of Melchizedek."

⁵The Lord is at your right hand;
he will shatter kings on the day of his wrath.
⁶He will execute judgment among the nations,
filling them with corpses;
he will shatter chiefs over the wide earth.
⁷He will drink from the brook by the way;
therefore he will lift up his head.

King and Priest

The Church prays this Psalm in the messianic sense (also Psalm 2). The wording praises not only a king's enthronement but also Christ's glorious Kingship and Priesthood. It is richly beautiful and speaks of Christ. The princely power and victory of the earthly king is evident. God assures this in making his enemies his footstool. Passages like "With thee is the royal dignity . . . , from the womb before the dawn I begot thee" (Greek text), speak more clearly of Christ's divine origin than of a king's human birth.

The Messiah is greater than His father David, as we gather from the Lord's own use of this Psalm. It comes as a divine interpretation, when Christ declares: "How is it then that David, inspired by the Spirit, calls him Lord, saying, "The Lord said to my Lord, Sit at my right hand, till I put thy enemies under thy feet'? If David thus calls him Lord, how is he his son?" (Mt. 22:43-45) David, the author, speaks prophetically of Christ. Similarly, the priestly office was not that of a king; yet here we have the "order of Melchizedek," which differs from that of Aaron or Levi (Gen. 14:18-20). Melchizedek is king and priest, "resembling the Son of God he continues a priest for ever" (Heb. 7:1-10; also 5:5f. and 7:17). He is a type of Christ. Abraham paid tithes to him.

While we do not know the full import of the last three verses, they do imply victory over enemies. "He will drink from the brook," may indicate an ordeal of humiliation, after which He will triumph ("He will lift up his head"). It lets us think of His passion and resurrection. Faith sees His royal throne and priestly Altar as one. He was lifted up on the Cross-Altar as King-Priest.

He is Priest, first, because of the union of His human nature with the divine in the II Person of the Trinity; second, because of His salvific work, His suffering, death, and rising, in that humanity taken from a human Mother. He is King, first by His royal descent from the Davidic line, and second by His union with the Divinity and the redemptive conquest and glorification. "For there is one God and there is one mediator between God and men, the man Christ Jesus" (1 Tim. 2:5). He is Priest forever because the "man Christ Jesus" is forever linked to the Divinity of the second Person. At the right hand of the Father, He makes intercession for us because of His ascension into heaven (Heb. 8:1 and 10:12f. quotes our Psalm, as in 1:13 and 7:25; see also 1 Cor. 15:25f.; Eph. 1:20; 1 Pet. 3:21f.).

By our redemptive Baptism into Christ Jesus, we are "a chosen race, a royal priesthood, a holy nation, God's own people" (1 Pet. 2:9). In virtue of Baptism, we share uniquely in this Psalm and use it in His Body the Church very often—on Easter, Ascension, Pentecost, Christmas, Epiphany, the Annunciation, Corpus Christi, Christ the King, the Transfiguration, Exaltation of the Cross, All Saints, and every Sunday, always at vespers.

Psalm 111 (110)

Praise the LORD.
I will give thanks to the
LORD with my whole heart,
in the company of the upright, in the congregation.
²Great are the works of the LORD,
studied by all who have pleasure in them.
³Full of honor and majesty is his work,
and his righteousness endures for ever.
⁴He has caused his wonderful works to be remembered;
the LORD is gracious and merciful.
⁵He provides food for those who fear him;
he is ever mindful of his covenant.
⁶He has shown his people the power of his works,
in giving them the heritage of the nations.
⁷The works of his hands are faithful and just;
all his precepts are trustworthy,
⁸they are established for ever and ever,
to be performed with faithfulness and uprightness.
⁹He sent redemption to his people;
he has commanded his covenant for ever.
Holy and terrible is his name!
¹⁰The fear of the LORD is the beginning of wisdom;
a good understanding have all those who practice it.
His praise endures for ever!

Thanks Is Praise

Alleluia is the opening victorious cry. It means "praise the Lord," and it has come down to us in our worship in the original Hebrew. Like the *Amen* it never needed translation because it was so widely used and generally understood. The "company of the upright" is the sacred assembly, one in faith and worship in the Temple. This assembly is the carrier of revelation and therefore also of right faith and prayer. Individuals together thank God with all their heart because praise and sacrifice were the highest actions of their life. And in the midst of the faith assembly at worship, God performed His great salvation and revealed His perfections.

God's deeds speak of His wisdom, majesty, generosity, and power. Beginning with creation, His works are full of wonder and delight. Those who ponder them, find in them the mirror of His perfections and every reason for praise and thanks. Greatest among His ancient works are the guidance and mercy shown to His people in the desert, when He fed them with manna (Ex. 16:4ff.) and water from the rock. He delivered them from their enemies, made a covenant with them, and gave them a homeland. God was no abstract deity, but a personal God, near, alive, real, and generous—a Shepherd.

We must ponder deeply the works of God, both natural and supernatural. True wisdom lies in doing His will, in the fear of offending Him. "Holy and terrible is his name!" Serving Him is praise. (For a better understanding of the place of wisdom in Jewish piety, see the Book of Wisdom and Prov. 9:10.)

Our Psalm has great prayer value in Christ, who performed God's greatest deeds. In the holy Eucharist "He has caused his wonderful works to be remembered" (v. 4). When asked, "What work do you perform?" (Jn. 6:30), Jesus pointed to the new Bread from heaven, the fulfillment of the desert manna "for the life of the world." The Eucharist is all-powerful memory and means thanks. The works of the Exodus are a mere rehearsal of the Reality He enacted. "The Father who dwells in me does his works. . . . Believe me for the sake of the works themselves" (Jn. 14:10f.; see also 5:19ff.).

In the midst of the assembly, we praise His Name (Heb. 2:12) by celebrating the Eucharist of thanks. With the Virgin Mary we humbly pray, "Holy is his Name," who has done great things for us (Eph. 1: 18-20 and 2:5f.). For associating us with the wisdom of the Cross (1 Cor. 1:17ff.), we celebrate His praise by thanksgiving. This Psalm occurs on the Feasts of Corpus Christi and the Sacred Heart and on III Sundays (always at vespers).

Psalm 112 (111)

Praise the LORD.
>Blessed is the man who fears the LORD,
>who greatly delights in his commandments!
>²His descendants will be mighty in the land;
>the generation of the upright will be blessed.
>³Wealth and riches are in his house;
>and his righteousness endures for ever.
>⁴Light rises in the darkness for the upright;
>the LORD is gracious, merciful, and righteous.

⁵It is well with the man who deals generously and lends,
  who conducts his affairs with justice.
⁶For the righteous will never be moved;
  he will be remembered for ever.
⁷He is not afraid of evil tidings;
  his heart is firm, trusting in the LORD.
⁸His heart is steady, he will not be afraid,
  until he sees his desire on his adversaries.
⁹He has distributed freely, he has given to the poor;
  his righteousness endures for ever;
  his horn is exalted in honor.
¹⁰The wicked man sees it and is angry;
  he gnashes his teeth and melts away;
  the desire of the wicked man comes to nought.

Godliness of the Just Man

A companion piece to Psalm 111, which extols the overall greatness of God's works, this *Alleluia* Psalm praises the Lord's marvels in the man who fears the Lord. In God we have the qualities of justice and mercy in an infinite measure; in the just man we find them reflected in moral holiness or "perfection." It is a blessedness that is God-given. In that light we say that this prayer anticipates the Lord's saying, "You therefore must be perfect, as your heavenly Father is perfect" (Mt. 5:48).

One of his blessings was numerous posterity, like himself upright. Another was well-being and economic plenty, which he shared with the poor. "He has distributed freely, he has given to the poor," and his generosity lived after him. His conduct was a shining light for his community, for he was gracious, merciful, righteous, and courageous. For his trust in the Lord, he earned firm stability in the eyes of his fellows. His horn (prestige, power) was exalted, as a reward for his godly life in society. Those blessings spread to others, as his memory lived on forever.

God's solicitude for the poor always receives emphasis. Christ the Lord took over this divine care, for His whole mission was to the poor (Lk. 4:18, 21). The life of the just man stands in glaring contrast to that of the wicked, whose evil desires will "come to nought" (also Psalm 1). God's abundance scattered abroad through the generous person will benefit the poor. St. Paul quotes verse 9: "He scatters abroad, he gives to the poor; high righteousness endures for ever" (2 Cor. 9:9).

We see in this Psalm not only a picture of Christ who was perfect (Heb. 7:26f.) and loved the Father (Jn. 14:30f.) and who was the Light of the world (Jn. 8:12), but who by His resurrection is our contemporary and carries on now, distributing heavenly gifts to His saints. The fruitfulness of those who live on the vine of Christ (Jn. 15:1-10) will be an eternal memorial in His Kingdom. Spreading material blessings to the poor is symbolic of the greater spiritual ones, the graces that Christ puts into our hands for the "poor." The saints in heaven and on earth share the godliness of divine life (2 Pet. 1:4). As we are renewed in Christ (2 Cor. 4:16f.), we give freely to others and so radiate the graciousness of Christ.

Let us add to His praise in the world by living out this Psalm, not only praying it. Very appropriately it occurs on Epiphany, IV Sundays, and the commons of pastors and holy men (always at vespers).

Psalm 113 (112)

Praise the LORD!
　　Praise, O servants of the LORD,
　　praise the name of the LORD!

²Blessed be the name of the LORD
　　from this time forth and for evermore!
³From the rising of the sun to its setting
　　the name of the LORD is to be praised!
⁴The LORD is high above all nations,
　　and his glory above the heavens!

⁵Who is like the LORD our God,
　　who is seated on high,
⁶who looks far down
　　upon the heavens and the earth?

⁷He raises the poor from the dust,
  and lifts the needy from the ash heap,
⁸to make them sit with princes,
  with the princes of his people.
⁹He gives the barren woman a home,
  making her the joyous mother of children.
Praise the Lord!

Praise of God for Mothers

Framed between two *Alleluias,* the Psalm summons the "servants of the Lord" to new and enthusiastic praise of the glory of His Name. As in Psalms 111-118 and 146-150, the *Alleluia* is for the Lord alone, whose unconditional dominion and greatness requires our unending lauds in time and space. God's infinite lordship in heaven and on earth must be as constant as man's existence. We cannot picture or imagine God. We cannot even define Him, and our descriptions of Him fall short of His reality. He is always different, apart and beyond created things, uncreated and incomprehensible. We call it transcendency. There are traces of Him all around us, human analogies or comparisons, by which we seek to know Him. "Who is like the Lord our God, who is seated on high . . . ?" (v. 5) He expects no answer because there is none.

The wonder of God baffles us. Yet He stoops down to lift up the poor and lowly and endows them with nobility similar to His own (they become "partakers of the divine nature" 2 Pet. 1:4). The Son of God broke through our finite shell, so to say, and became one of us. Christ is the transcendent God and visible man. He is vested in the glory of God and the garment of human nature. The Heart of God shines forth in the Heart of the Savior. It happened when He chose the husbandless Virgin Mary to be His incomparable Mother. Thereby He who was "far away" became near, our Brother.

The Psalm climaxes in the final verse: "He gives the barren woman a home, making her the joyous mother of children." The childless wife was one of the poor. The barren woman was looked down upon. Many regarded her sterility as a divine disfavor. Think of Sarah (Gen. 16: 1ff.) or Hannah (1 Sam. 1:5ff.) or Elizabeth (Lk. 1:25). The miraculous Motherhood of Mary transcends all of God's gifts to mankind: it meant redemption. Her *Magnificat* reflects the glory of God in the voluntary .sterility of virginity.

God raised up the apostles as princes of His Kingdom and Mary as the Mother of the Church, the "joyous mother of children." We should exhaust ourselves in constant praise of this Mystery. Formerly the Jews used this Psalm on great feasts. Psalm 113 now occurs on all solemn feasts of the Church, almost always at vespers: Christmas, Ascension, Pentecost, Christ the King, Sacred Heart, Holy Trinity, Exaltation of the Cross (office of readings), Presentation (February 2), Annunciation, III Sundays, All Saints, common of the Blessed Virgin, commons of pastors, virgins, holy men and women. The Psalm helps us "declare the wonderful deeds of him who called you out of darkness into his marvellous light" (1 Pet. 2:9).

Psalm 114 (113A)

When Israel went forth from Egypt,
  the house of Jacob from a people of strange language,
²Judah became his sanctuary,
  Israel his dominion.

³The sea looked and fled,
  Jordan turned back.
⁴The mountains skipped like rams,
  the hills like lambs.

⁵What ails you, O sea, that you flee?
  O Jordan, that you turn back?
⁶O mountains, that you skip like rams?
  O hills, like lambs?

⁷Tremble, O earth, at the presence of the LORD,
  at the presence of the God of Jacob,
⁸who turns the rock into a pool of water,
  the flint into a spring of water.

God's Coming

At God's approach all nature trembles. When God led His people out of Egypt and into the promised land, nature stood in reverent awe. The waters yielded and the mountains "skipped like lambs." Nothing became an obstacle to His advance at the head of His flock. This is the *Alleluia* song of the crossing of the Jordan River (see Jos. 3:17), perhaps for the annual celebration of the Passover. Highly dramatic and imaginative, this short poem celebrates with poetic brilliance the last wonders of the Exodus. At the end it records the earlier miracle of flint turning into a spring of water.

Why all this joyous imagery? The author himself answers: because of "the presence of the God of Jacob." "Judah became his sanctuary, Israel his dominion." The self-revelation of God changed everything. The touch of God suggests the joy of the Holy Spirit at the birth of a nation, at the cradle of freedom. The Psalm describes the epiphany (appearance) of God.

As the Psalm skips centuries of sacred history, so we skip many hundreds of years in applying it to the present perspective of faith. The Old Testament is foretelling the future, the new age of Christ which is now. The hour and day and age of Christ's saving grace are now. His present and future Coming are even greater than the marvels of the past. The joy is present joy. We are His sanctuary where He dwells. We can afford to put our best faculties and inmost heart to work in reciting or singing this Psalm.

Why so? Because more important than the hills leaping like yearling sheep is the cure by Peter and John of the lame man (Acts 4:8) and his leaping about and praising God in the Temple. More important than the waters fleeing at the Jordan is the quieting of the storm by Jesus, which begot faith in the disciples and in us. When the disciples were frightened at the approach of Jesus, He quieted them: "Fear not. It is I." And He abides with us still (Mt. 28:20 and Jn. 14:23).

We are the pilgrim Church bringing joy and reverent fear into the whole world of individuals and nations. It is the approach of Christ Himself. If we do not shout for joy, the stones will cry out. On Easter, Pentecost, Trinity Sunday, and I Sundays, the Church relives the Coming of Christ through this Psalm (vespers) and proclaims the good news to all the world.

Psalm 115 (113B)

Not to us, O LORD, not to us,
    but to thy name give glory,
        for the sake of thy steadfast love and thy faithfulness!
²Why should the nations say,
    "Where is their God?"

³Our God is in the heavens;
    he does whatever he pleases.
⁴Their idols are silver and gold,
    the work of men's hands.
⁵They have mouths, but do not speak;
    eyes, but do not see.
⁶They have ears, but do not hear;
    noses, but do not smell.
⁷They have hands, but do not feel;
    feet, but do not walk;
    and they do not make a sound in their throat.
⁸Those who make them are like them;
    so are all who trust in them.

⁹O Israel, trust in the Lord!
    He is their help and their shield.
¹⁰O house of Aaron, put your trust in the Lord!
    He is their help and their shield.
¹¹You who fear the Lord, trust in the Lord!
    He is their help and their shield.

¹²The Lord has been mindful of us; he will bless us;
    he will bless the house of Israel;
    he will bless the house of Aaron;
¹³he will bless those who fear the Lord,
    both small and great.

¹⁴May the Lord give you increase,
    you and your children!
¹⁵May you be blessed by the Lord,
    who made heaven and earth!

¹⁶The heavens are the Lord's heavens,
  but the earth he has given to the sons of men.
¹⁷The dead do not praise the Lord,
    nor do any that go down into silence.
¹⁸But we will bless the Lord
    from this time forth and for evermore.
  Praise the Lord!

Trust in God, Not in Idols

If God were the figment of human hands, like the pagan idols, then glory would come to man; but the opposite is true: man is God's creature. Anyone who worships what his hands have made is a fool. The author mocks the helplessness of non-gods made to the image of man. Those who fashion idols out of silver and gold become like the idols, worthless. Antiquity swarmed with false deities, and God's people were generally on the alert against idol worship (Ps. 135:15-18). Pagan blasphemy harrassed them, "Where is their God?" Against such enemies the God of heaven and earth took care of Himself easily.

Trust in the Lord was the answer. It brought immediate, abundant blessings to the house of Israel, Aaron, and to those who feared the Lord (proselytes, converts). God is the supreme Lord of all who has portioned out the earth as man's domain under the provident care of its Creator. Human ownership cannot compete with God's dominion. The blessings of growth and increase still depend on Him and not on man.

It is easy to pray this Psalm until we reach the crucial issue of idolatry, which affects contemporary man. He practices idolatry in subtler forms and gives praise to his own works instead of praising God. "Not to us, Lord, not to us, but to thy name give glory." All the world idolizes wealth and money, pleasure and power, science and technology. Trust in God then suffers or vanishes entirely. Man acts as if he were self-sufficient and facetiously asks, "Where does God come in?" He lives for present things, life and opportunities and rewards.

This worldliness stands in contradiction to God and Christ, to the world of belief. God blesses those who believe (2 Cor. 9:8ff.). He wants us to work and use the good earth, not to surrender to it, not to make it our final home. We work for God's purposes while on earth for a short time. And we must make the most of our allotted time, "Because the days are evil" (Eph. 5:16). "Therefore do not be foolish, but understand what the will of the Lord is. And do not get drunk with wine, for that is debauchery; but be filled with the Spirit, addressing one another in psalms and hymns and spiritual songs, singing and making melody to the Lord with all your heart" (Eph. 5:17-19).

In that way we reap divine blessings, while we contribute whatever is humanly good and right, without becoming slaves and idolaters to the work of our hands. The Church uses this Psalm on II Sundays at vespers.

Psalm 116 (114 and 115)

I love the LORD, because he has heard
    my voice and my supplications.
²Because he inclined his ear to me,
    therefore I will call on him as long as I live.
³The snares of death encompassed me;
    the pangs of Sheol laid hold on me;
    I suffered distress and anguish.
⁴Then I called on the name of the LORD:
    "O LORD, I beseech thee, save my life!"

⁵Gracious is the LORD, and righteous;
    our God is merciful.
⁶The LORD preserves the simple;
    when I was brought low, he saved me.
⁷Return, O my soul, to your rest;
    for the LORD has dealt bountifully with you.

⁸For thou hast delivered my soul from death,
    my eyes from tears,
    my feet from stumbling;
⁹I walk before the LORD
    in the land of the living.

* * *

¹⁰I kept my faith, even when I said,
    "I am greatly afflicted";
¹¹I said in my consternation,
    "Men are all a vain hope."

¹²What shall I render to the LORD
    for all his bounty to me?
¹³I will lift up the cup of salvation
    and call on the name of the LORD,
¹⁴I will pay my vows to the LORD
    in the presence of all his people.
¹⁵Precious in the sight of the LORD
    is the death of his saints.
¹⁶O LORD, I am thy servant;
    I am thy servant, the son of thy handmaid.
    Thou hast loosed my bonds.

¹⁷I will offer to thee the sacrifice of thanksgiving
    and call on the name of the LORD.
¹⁸I will pay my vows to the LORD
    in the presence of all his people,
¹⁹in the courts of the house of the LORD,
    in your midst, O Jerusalem.
Praise the LORD!

I Love You, Lord

These two Psalms, which form one in the Hebrew (v. 10 starts Vulgate 115), are the rich piety of faith in suffering. Like so many other Psalms that came out of sickness and hopeless situations, this one abounds with prayer, gratitude, and witness before the whole community. Other precious spiritual lessons of the past emerge from it. As an *Alleluia* Psalm, it enjoyed a special place in Jewish festal worship.

Most prominent in the author's sentiments is thanksgiving. He extols God for His mercy and graciousness with the lowly. When he was near death and no man could help, God heard his cry. Now that health is restored, he is able to praise the Lord privately and publicly in the assembly. Faith begets faith. A new peace has taken over and calmness of soul replaces his former anguish. In gratitude he vowed a peace offering, and this was great in the eyes of fellow believers and worshippers. Taking "the cup of salvation" after God came to the rescue was the divine way of giving thanks. Although He used God's own gifts to thank Him, that was the only way because He loved us first (1 Jn. 4:19). That way we follow in the Mass offertory ("Blessed are You. . . . Through Your goodness we have this bread to offer, which earth has given . . .").

The Psalmist remembers his mother, also God-fearing, who made him to be a servant of God. Faithful to her, he stands in the courts of the Lord, in the presence of God's people, fulfilling his vowed offering. In total dedication to the Lord, he brings sacrifice and gives publicity to his gratitude. The verse "Precious in the sight of the Lord is the death of his saints" no longer is a problem here, since modern study (Ugaritic scholarship) clarified that immortality shines through in this verse and in many Psalm passages (also v. 9: "I walk before the Lord in the land of the living").

God is the God of the living. Jesus said this even more clearly (Mt. 22:32). Instituting the Sacrifice of His death and rising as a visible banquet, He sanctified forever the "Cup" of salvation (Mt. 26:27f. and

1 Cor. 10:16). He is the Son of another Handmaid of the Lord (Lk. 1:38), and coming into the world He offered Himself (Heb. 10:5ff.). We know that He gave thanks on the Cross because He did so at the Last Supper (Mk. 14:23), and so the name thanksgiving (Eucharist) clings forever to His central act.

At a time when many ask divine favors, but promptly forget to say thanks to God, we take the "cup of salvation" for others. In Hebrew, praise and thanks are the same. This popular Psalm of the Church's prayer occurs on Corpus Christi, Good Friday, Holy Saturday, III Sundays, II Fridays, September 14, All Saints, and commons of apostles and martyrs (always at vespers), on Wednesday after Easter at noon prayer. Especially verses 10-19 are used.

Psalm 117 (116)

> Praise the LORD, all nations!
> Extol him, all peoples!
> [2]For great is his steadfast love toward us;
> and the faithfulness of the LORD endures for ever.
> Praise the LORD!

All Nations Praise Him

This is the shortest of all the Psalms, but the one with the essential message! In two verses it summarizes the universal call to all the world to praise God. The reason is God Himself, His unfailing goodness to man, and fidelity to His promises of mercy. Bonded to God in divine fellowship and to each other in holy brotherhood, all the nations must answer the summons. Before God all human barriers disappear.

Christ repeated the invitation when He sent His disciples to evangelize all peoples, "Go into all the world" (Mk. 16:15). St. Paul, who is the great missioner of praise to the Gentile world, quotes our Psalm in Rom. 15:11 and writes more about his mission in Eph. 3:4-10. The attraction to praise must also come from Christians letting their light shine into the world (according to Mt. 5:16) so that mankind will gladly join this chorus.

The Church uses our Psalm on the Feasts of Christ the King, the Ascension, the Transfiguration, and the common of apostles (all vespers), and on I and III Saturdays at noon and lauds. Some texts open the Psalm with an *Alleluia*.

Psalm 118 (117)

O give thanks to the Lord, for he is good;
   his steadfast love endures for ever!

²Let Israel say,
   "His steadfast love endures for ever."
³Let the house of Aaron say,
   "His steadfast love endures for ever."
⁴Let those who fear the Lord say,
   "His steadfast love endures for ever."

⁵Out of my distress I called on the Lord;
   the Lord answered me and set me free.
⁶With the Lord on my side I do not fear.
   What can man do to me?
⁷The Lord is on my side to help me;
   I shall look in triumph on those who hate me.
⁸It is better to take refuge in the Lord
   than to put confidence in man.
⁹It is better to take refuge in the Lord
   than to put confidence in princes.

¹⁰All nations surrounded me;
   in the name of the Lord I cut them off!
¹¹They surrounded me, surrounded me on every side;
   in the name of the Lord I cut them off!
¹²They surrounded me like bees,
   * they blazed like a fire of thorns;
   in the name of the Lord I cut them off!
¹³I was pushed hard, so that I was falling,
   but the Lord helped me.
¹⁴The Lord is my strength and my song;
   he has become my salvation.

¹⁵Hark, glad songs of victory
   in the tents of the righteous:
 "The right hand of the Lord does valiantly,
¹⁶   the right hand of the Lord is exalted,
   the right hand of the Lord does valiantly!"
¹⁷I shall not die, but I shall live,
   and recount the deeds of the Lord.
¹⁸The Lord has chastened me sorely,
   but he has not given me over to death.

¹⁹Open to me the gates of righteousness,
that I may enter through them
and give thanks to the Lord.

²⁰This is the gate of the Lord;
the righteous shall enter through it.

²¹I thank thee that thou hast answered me
and hast become my salvation.
²²The stone which the builders rejected
has become the head of the corner.
²³This is the Lord's doing;
it is marvelous in our eyes.
²⁴This is the day which the Lord has made;
let us rejoice and be glad in it.
²⁵Save us, we beseech thee, O Lord!
O Lord, we beseech thee, give us success!

²⁶Blessed be he who enters in the name of the Lord!
We bless you from the house of the Lord.
²⁷The Lord is God,
and he has given us light.
Bind the festal procession with branches,
up to the horns of the altar!

²⁸Thou art my God, and I will give thanks to thee;
thou art my God, I will extol thee.

²⁹O give thanks to the Lord, for he is good;
for his steadfast love endures for ever!

Blessed Is He Who Comes

This *Alleluia* Psalm is highly dramatic and fruitful in reference
to Christ. As a great victory procession through portals to the Altar
amid *Hosannas* ("send salvation"), it abounds with thanks and religious enthusiasm. The first call to praise, because God's love is eternal,
is to the whole house of Israel; next the call is to the priestly tribe of
Aaron, and finally it is to all believers, pilgrims, and converts to join
the jubilant procession. Lively with refrain and response and fresh
with the king's astounding defeat of numerous enemies, all the assembly

surges to the Altar with song and dance and garland signs of participation.

The author's trust reaches great heights. When God's right arm prevails and human strength is low, confidence abounds. No prince or power can replace trust in the Lord. Verses like "It is better to take refuge in the Lord than to put confidence in man" (v. 5) contain wisdom for a lifetime. Such trust becomes a life force that is not only personal but social. If the enemies are countless as bees, the "right hand of the Lord does valiantly" (v. 15), providing we rely on Him.

The victory experience of God's intervention engendered hope forever in Israel's history and Christianity. Arriving at God's Temple, priests and people vie with each other in celebrating blessings with thanks. The victor shouts, "Open to me the gates of righteousness" (v. 19), and the answer comes, "This is the gate of the Lord" (v. 20). Only the just and holy may enter. God's choice is decisive: He chose the rejected stone and made it the cornerstone, and this is His day of salvation. God is always the Center of festivity. The Psalm ends, as it began, with a blessing of praise.

The throngs welcomed Christ into Jerusalem with palms and with this Psalm, "Blessed is he who comes in the name of the Lord." It was the anticipation of His royal Easter triumph (Mt. 21:9f.; Mk. 11:9). The King of Justice entered the gates of justice on the eve of His spiritual warfare, receiving the messianic *Hosannas*. He was the stone which the builders rejected (Jesus quotes our Psalm in Mt. 21:42-44; St. Peter preaches it in Acts 4:11f.; see also 1 Pet. 2:4-7; 1 Cor. 3:11; Rom. 9:33; Eph. 2:20-22).

We are pilgrims, gathered by Christ in Baptism, going in procession to His Altar. Using this Easter song, we join in holy fellowship to enrich the Altar and reap its glorious fruits of redemption. Short of heaven, this is our great goal and stopping place. There we arm for the great victorious battle, where Christ renews His Mystery, no matter if the enemy is "legion." Because of His resurrection, we celebrate Sunday as a day the Lord has made, another Easter. We enter this Mystery-presence and become living stones of the new Temple (Eph. 2:20), where we pray this Psalm with Christ's Bride the Church (on Easter and Pentecost noon, on the Wednesday of Easter at office of readings, on I and III Sundays at noon, on II and IV Sundays at lauds, finally at the common of martyr(s) at vespers). This "Solid food is for the mature" (Heb. 5:14).

Psalm 119 (118)

Blessed are those whose way is blameless,
who walk in the law of the Lord!
²Blessed are those who keep his testimonies,
who seek him with their whole heart,
³who also do no wrong,
but walk in his ways!
⁴Thou hast commanded thy precepts
to be kept diligently.
⁵O that my ways may be steadfast
in keeping thy statutes!
⁶Then I shall not be put to shame,
having my eyes fixed on all thy commandments.
⁷I will praise thee with an upright heart,
when I learn thy righteous ordinances.
⁸I will observe thy statutes;
O forsake me not utterly!

⁹How can a young man keep his way pure?
By guarding it according to thy word.
¹⁰With my whole heart I seek thee;
let me not wander from thy commandments!
¹¹I have laid up thy word in my heart,
that I might not sin against thee.
¹²Blessed be thou, O Lord;
teach me thy statutes!
¹³With my lips I declare
all the ordinances of thy mouth.
¹⁴In the way of thy testimonies I delight
as much as in all riches.
¹⁵I will meditate on thy precepts,
and fix my eyes on thy ways.
¹⁶I will delight in thy statutes;
I will not forget thy word.

¹⁷Deal bountifully with thy servant,
that I may live and observe thy word.
¹⁸Open my eyes, that I may behold
wondrous things out of thy law.
¹⁹I am a sojourner on earth;
hide not thy commandments from me!
²⁰My soul is consumed with longing
for thy ordinances at all times.

²¹Thou dost rebuke the insolent, accursed ones,
    who wander from thy commandments;
²²take away from me their scorn and contempt,
    for I have kept thy testimonies.
²³Even though princes sit plotting against me,
    thy servant will meditate on thy statutes.
²⁴Thy testimonies are my delight,
    they are my counselors.

²⁵My soul cleaves to the dust;
    revive me according to thy word!
²⁶When I told of my ways, thou didst answer me;
    teach me thy statutes!
²⁷Make me understand the way of thy precepts,
    and I will meditate on thy wondrous works.
²⁸My soul melts away for sorrow;
    strengthen me according to thy word!
²⁹Put false ways far from me;
    and graciously teach me thy law!
³⁰I have chosen the way of faithfulness,
    I set thy ordinances before me.
³¹I cleave to thy testimonies, O Lord;
    let me not be put to shame!
³²I will run in the way of thy commandments
    when thou enlargest my understanding!

³³Teach me, O Lord, the way of thy statutes;
    and I will keep it to the end.
³⁴Give me understanding, that I may keep thy law
    and observe it with my whole heart.
³⁵Lead me in the path of thy commandments,
    for I delight in it.
³⁶Incline my heart to thy testimonies,
    and not to gain!
³⁷Turn my eyes from looking at vanities;
    and give me life in thy ways.
³⁸Confirm to thy servant thy promise,
    which is for those who fear thee.
³⁹Turn away the reproach which I dread;
    for thy ordinances are good.
⁴⁰Behold, I long for thy precepts;
    in thy righteousness give me life!

⁴¹Let thy steadfast love come to me, O Lord,
  thy salvation according to thy promise;
⁴²then shall I have an answer for those who taunt me,
  for I trust in thy word.
⁴³And take not the word of truth utterly out of my mouth,
  for my hope is in thy ordinances.
⁴⁴I will keep thy law continually,
  for ever and ever;
⁴⁵and I shall walk at liberty,
  for I have sought thy precepts.
⁴⁶I will also speak of thy testimonies before kings,
  and shall not be put to shame;
⁴⁷for I find my delight in thy commandments, which I love.
⁴⁸I revere thy commandments, which I love,
  and I will meditate on thy statutes.

⁴⁹Remember thy word to thy servant,
  in which thou hast made me hope.
⁵⁰This is my comfort in my affliction
  that thy promise gives me life.
⁵¹Godless men utterly deride me,
  but I do not turn away from thy law.
⁵²When I think of thy ordinances from of old,
  I take comfort, O Lord.
⁵³Hot indignation seizes me because of the wicked,
  who forsake thy law.
⁵⁴Thy statutes have been my songs
  in the house of my pilgrimage.
⁵⁵I remember thy name in the night, O Lord,
  and keep thy law.
⁵⁶This blessing has fallen to me,
  that I have kept thy precepts.

⁵⁷The Lord is my portion;
  I promise to keep thy words.
⁵⁸I entreat thy favor with all my heart;
  be gracious to me according to thy promise.
⁵⁹When I think of thy ways,
  I turn my feet to thy testimonies;
⁶⁰I hasten and do not delay
  to keep thy commandments.

61Though the cords of the wicked ensnare me,
     I do not forget thy law.
62At midnight I rise to praise thee,
     because of thy righteous ordinances.
63I am a companion of all who fear thee,
     of those who keep thy precepts.
64The earth, O LORD, is full of thy steadfast love;
     teach me thy statutes!

65Thou hast dealt well with thy servant,
     O LORD, according to thy word.
66Teach me good judgment and knowledge,
     for I believe in thy commandments.
67Before I was afflicted I went astray;
     but now I keep thy word.
68Thou art good and doest good;
     teach me thy statutes.
69The godless besmear me with lies,
     but with my whole heart I keep thy precepts;
70their heart is gross like fat,
     but I delight in thy law.
71It is good for me that I was afflicted,
     that I might learn thy statutes.
72The law of thy mouth is better to me
     than thousands of gold and silver pieces.

73Thy hands have made and fashioned me;
     give me understanding that I may learn thy
          commandments.
74Those who fear thee shall see me and rejoice,
     because I have hoped in thy word.
75I know, O LORD, that thy judgments are right,
     and that in faithfulness thou hast afflicted me.
76Let thy steadfast love be ready to comfort me
     according to thy promise to thy servant,
77Let thy mercy come to me, that I may live;
     for thy law is my delight.
78Let the godless be put to shame,
     because they have subverted me with guile;
     as for me, I will meditate on thy precepts.
79Let those who fear thee turn to me,
     that they may know thy testimonies.
80May my heart be blameless in thy statutes,
     that I may not be put to shame!

⁸¹My soul languishes for thy salvation;
    I hope in thy word.
⁸²My eyes fail with watching for thy promise;
    I ask, "When wilt thou comfort me?"
⁸³For I have become like a wineskin in the smoke,
    yet I have not forgotten thy statutes.
⁸⁴How long must thy servant endure?
    When wilt thou judge those who persecute me?
⁸⁵Godless men have dug pitfalls for me,
    men who do not conform to thy law.
⁸⁶All thy commandments are sure;
    they persecute me with falsehood; help me!
⁸⁷They have almost made an end of me on earth;
    but I have not forsaken thy precepts.
⁸⁸In thy steadfast love spare my life,
    that I may keep the testimonies of thy mouth.

⁸⁹For ever, O Lord, thy word
    is firmly fixed in the heavens.
⁹⁰Thy faithfulness endures to all generations;
    thou hast established the earth, and it stands fast.
⁹¹By thy appointment they stand this day;
    for all things are thy servants.
⁹²If thy law had not been my delight,
    I should have perished in my affliction.
⁹³I will never forget thy precepts;
    for by them thou hast given me life.
⁹⁴I am thine, save me;
    for I have sought thy precepts.
⁹⁵The wicked lie in wait to destroy me;
    but I consider thy testimonies.
⁹⁶I have seen a limit to all perfection,
    but thy commandment is exceedingly broad.

⁹⁷Oh, how I love thy law!
    It is my meditation all the day.
⁹⁸Thy commandment makes me wiser than my enemies,
    for it is ever with me.
⁹⁹I have more understanding than all my teachers,
    for thy testimonies are my meditation.
¹⁰⁰I understand more than the aged,
    for I keep thy precepts.

101I hold back my feet from every evil way,
 in order to keep thy word.
102I do not turn aside from thy ordinances,
 for thou hast taught me.
103How sweet are thy words to my taste,
 sweeter than honey to my mouth!
104Through thy precepts I get understanding;
 therefore I hate every false way.

105Thy word is a lamp to my feet
 and a light to my path.
106I have sworn an oath and confirmed it,
 to observe thy righteous ordinances.
107I am sorely afflicted;
 give me life, O LORD, according to thy word!
108Accept my offerings of praise, O LORD,
 and teach me thy ordinances.
109I hold my life in my hand continually,
 but I do not forget thy law.
110The wicked have laid a snare for me,
 but I do not stray from thy precepts.
111Thy testimonies are my heritage for ever;
 yea, they are the joy of my heart.
112I incline my heart to perform thy statutes
 for ever, to the end.

113I hate double-minded men,
 but I love thy law.
114Thou art my hiding place and my shield;
 I hope in thy word.
115Depart from me, you evildoers,
 that I may keep the commandments of my God.
116Uphold me according to thy promise, that I may live,
 and let me not be put to shame in my hope!
117Hold me up, that I may be safe
 and have regard for thy statutes continually!
118Thou dost spurn all who go astray from thy statutes;
 yea, their cunning is in vain.
119All the wicked of the earth thou dost count as dross;
 therefore I love thy testimonies.
120My flesh trembles for fear of thee,
 and I am afraid of thy judgments.

¹²¹I have done what is just and right;
   do not leave me to my oppressors.
¹²²Be surety for thy servant for good;
   let not the godless oppress me.
¹²³My eyes fail with watching for thy salvation,
   and for the fulfilment of thy righteous promise.
¹²⁴Deal with thy servant according to thy steadfast love,
   and teach me thy statutes.
¹²⁵I am thy servant; give me understanding,
   that I may know thy testimonies!
¹²⁶It is time for the LORD to act,
   for thy law has been broken.
¹²⁷Therefore I love thy commandments
   above gold, above fine gold.
¹²⁸Therefore I direct my steps by all thy precepts;
   I hate every false way.

¹²⁹Thy testimonies are wonderful;
   therefore my soul keeps them.
¹³⁰The unfolding of thy words gives light;
   it imparts understanding to the simple.
¹³¹With open mouth I pant,
   because I long for thy commandments.
¹³²Turn to me and be gracious to me,
   as is thy wont toward those who love thy name.
¹³³Keep steady my steps according to thy promise,
   and let no iniquity get dominion over me.
¹³⁴Redeem me from man's oppression,
   that I may keep thy precepts.
¹³⁵Make thy face shine upon thy servant,
   and teach me thy statutes.
¹³⁶My eyes shed streams of tears,
   because men do not keep thy law.

¹³⁷Righteous art thou, O LORD,
   and right are thy judgments.
¹³⁸Thou hast appointed thy testimonies in righteousness
   and in all faithfulness.
¹³⁹My zeal consumes me,
   because my foes forget thy words.
¹⁴⁰Thy promise is well tried,
   and thy servant loves it.

141I am small and despised,
  yet I do not forget thy precepts.
142Thy righteousness is righteous for ever,
  and thy law is true.
143Trouble and anguish have come upon me,
  but thy commandments are my delight.
144Thy testimonies are righteous for ever;
  give me understanding that I may live.

145With my whole heart I cry; answer me, O LORD!
  I will keep thy statutes.
146I cry to thee; save me,
  that I may observe thy testimonies.
147I rise before dawn and cry for help;
  I hope in thy words.
148My eyes are awake before the watches of the night,
  that I may meditate upon thy promise.
149Hear my voice in thy steadfast love;
  O LORD, in thy justice preserve my life.
150They draw near who persecute me with evil purpose;
  they are far from thy law.
151But thou art near, O LORD,
  and all thy commandments are true.
152Long have I known from thy testimonies
  that thou hast founded them for ever.

153Look on my affliction and deliver me,
  for I do not forget thy law.
154Plead my cause and redeem me;
  give me life according to thy promise!
155Salvation is far from the wicked,
  for they do not seek thy statutes.
156Great is thy mercy, O LORD;
  give me life according to thy justice.
157Many are my persecutors and my adversaries,
  but I do not swerve from thy testimonies.
158I look at the faithless with disgust,
  because they do not keep thy commands.
159Consider how I love thy precepts!
  Preserve my life according to thy steadfast love.
160The sum of thy word is truth;
  and every one of thy righteous ordinances endures
   for ever.

¹⁶¹Princes persecute me without cause,
     but my heart stands in awe of thy words.
¹⁶²I rejoice at thy word
     like one who finds great spoil.
¹⁶³I hate and abhor falsehood,
     but I love thy law.
¹⁶⁴Seven times a day I praise thee
     for thy righteous ordinances.
¹⁶⁵Great peace have those who love thy law;
     nothing can make them stumble.
¹⁶⁶I hope for thy salvation, O Lord,
     and I do thy commandments.
¹⁶⁷My soul keeps thy testimonies;
     I love them exceedingly.
¹⁶⁸I keep thy precepts and testimonies,
     for all my ways are before thee.

¹⁶⁹Let my cry come before thee, O Lord;
     give me understanding according to thy word!
¹⁷⁰Let my supplication come before thee;
     deliver me according to thy word.
¹⁷¹My lips will pour forth praise
     that thou dost teach me thy statutes.
¹⁷²My tongue will sing of thy word,
     for all thy commandments are right.
¹⁷³Let thy hand be ready to help me,
     for I have chosen thy precepts.
¹⁷⁴I long for thy salvation, O Lord,
     and thy law is my delight.
¹⁷⁵Let me live, that I may praise thee,
     and let thy ordinances help me.
¹⁷⁶I have gone astray like a lost sheep; seek thy servant,
     for I do not forget thy commandments.

Love for God's Law

Like love, the law springs from the heart of God. Those who observe it with love will return to the heart of God. They are blessed who hear it, meditate on it, and keep it, for they share in the holiness of God. The Psalmist requires many terms to express such a comprehensive revelation: precepts, judgments, statutes, commands, ordinances, decrees, divine words, the way, promises. If created man has many

degrees of willing, the Creator has many more: direct orders, tolera-
tion, permissiveness, wishing, longing, and many more shadings of
each. By law the author means the total will of God revealed to man
for his religious and moral living. *Torah* is the old Hebrew word.

Couched in legal terms, the Psalm is anything but legalistic. Rather
it is full of intimate devotion, inner warmth, and loving thought of
God's will. To observe the known will of God is to love Him. And that
is happiness. This is by far the longest Psalm (176 verses, in acrostic
form, with a new letter at each strophe). There is much repetition,
for it is the record of "praying always." In our time it is much neglected, but the lover of God's will finds endless fresh food for meditation and contemplation. Because it reflects a liturgy of the Word
(there are almost no sacrifical cult references in it), we regard it as
coming from a foreign captivity of the Jews, where no Temple worship
was possible, but a type of synagogue service developed.

This Psalm expresses many familiar themes: seeking God, faith
and trust, praying at midnight and seven times a day, the pilgrim theme,
joyfulness in praise, suffering and contrition, humility and poverty,
opposition to enemies of the law, longing and human passion, pleas
for wisdom and discernment, and always the qualities and fear of God.
The law is truth (v. 160).

In His prayer life, Jesus reveals that God's gift of the law was His
delight. Because He was Truth, He was intimately one with the will
of God, even as He fulfilled it (Mt. 5:17). As Master of wisdom, He
came to do the Father's will (Jn. 8:29). He brought the new law of love
and held Himself up as the Way to follow (Jn. 14:6). "Come, follow
me." "Blessed are those who hear the word of God and keep it" (Lk.
11:28). Countless are the references to God's will expressed in the law
for right moral action. He, Lord and Teacher (Jn. 13:13), went ahead
with the example of obedience to all authority, even unjust (Phil. 2:8).
He showed that the law of love is the law of suffering (Mk. 14:36 and
Lk. 24:26, 44). In a day of hard legalistic literalism, His law brought
new light and refreshing liberty (see Mt. 11:28-30).

Be imitators of Him who gave the law of freedom (Eph. 5:1ff. and
Jas. 1:25). His divine will lives in His Church of the Holy Spirit, who
is the living Voice. There we have the certain and known will of God
for belief and action. His Body the Church claims to be the Home of
that light and law. If He promised opposition and suffering in following His law, then also peace and beatitude (Lk. 9:23). Let us read
this Psalm often, with the mind of Christ. The Church uses it daily at

noonday prayer (except Sundays), also on I Saturdays (lauds) and II Sundays (vespers).

Psalm 120 (119)

In my distress I cry to the LORD,
   that he may answer me:
2"Deliver me, O LORD,
   from lying lips,
   from a deceitful tongue."

3What shall be given to you?
   And what more shall be done to you,
   you deceitful tongue?
4A warrior's sharp arrows,
   with glowing coals of the broom tree!

5Woe is me, that I sojourn in Meshech,
   that I dwell among the tents of Kedar!
6Too long have I had my dwelling
   among those who hate peace.
7I am for peace;
   but when I speak,
   they are for war!

Prayer for Peace

In dialogue with God ("that he may answer me"), the faithful man begs for deliverance from lying lips, which no man can control. A sojourner away from home, the author dwells among people who foment war. There is no escape. Meshech and the tents of Kedar are real places, far apart, and there is no relief from the men of deceit, who cause dissension. With enemies seeking war for its own sake, the author lives in anguish and disagreement. The Psalm sets in high relief the man of peace who lives among infidels and pagans "who hate peace." Peace will come when lying lips are silent. God is the only and last recourse for help and judgment.

In human society there are pockets of evil and the ubiquitous underground where the enemies of peace thrive. Christ became the victim of such conspiring haters of peace. He came to bring peace and establish the new City of Peace for all pilgrims who are far away from home. He only reaped opposition and reproaches in return. "My peace I give to you; not as the world gives do I give to you" (Jn. 14:27). Every day we hear war cries and insurrection threats. Our warfare is not with arms and weapons, but with the instruments of the Spirit, the shield of faith, "with which you can quench all the flaming darts of the evil one" (Eph. 6:16).

Christ's yearning for peace lives on in the Church, and the popes repeatedly call for peace and harmony among nations and groups. In our Psalm, war proceeds from lying lips. Peace is God's gift, and the world would be at peace if all men took their laments to God. The Church uses this cry of Christ for peace often in her prayer life, namely, at noontide at the height of spiritual struggle, and we join the living Christ in His spiritual battle against enmity and the other causes of war.

Psalm 121 (120)

I lift up my eyes to the hills.
From whence does my help come?
²My help comes from the Lord,
who made heaven and earth.

³He will not let your foot be moved,
he who keeps you will not slumber.
⁴Behold, he who keeps Israel
will neither slumber nor sleep.

⁵The Lord is your keeper;
the Lord is your shade
on your right hand.
⁶The sun shall not smite you by day,
nor the moon by night.

⁷The Lord will keep you from all evil;
he will keep your life.
⁸The Lord will keep
your going out and your coming in
from this time forth and for evermore.

Trust on Life's Journey

Easy to understand but hard to realize, this Psalm of great simplicity stands ready for individuals and people who aspire to climb the mountain of God's revealed presence. It is a counterpart of Psalm 139, which tells us that we cannot ever travel out of God's sight. Why then is His help indispensable to attain His presence? It is indispensable because He is speaking of a special ascent and a search that entails obstacles on the path of life beset with hostile forces. We live constantly in the presence, yet it requires our best efforts to trust ourselves to Him.

The God who made heaven and earth is a kindly Father who watches our every step. If we sleep or doze, not so the Lord. When our feet slip on our way to salvation, He is there to rescue us. When the heat threatens to overcome us, He is our shade. Surely, this Psalm is a pilgrim's staff for going out and coming in and when we do not know the way.

In Christ Jesus we are speaking of the way to heaven. He is the Way. He is with us on our way. He promised His apostles, "I am with you always, to the close of the age" (Mt. 28:20). For our following of Christ this Psalm is important. He showed us the way. Never did He take His eyes off the Father. And with Him we pray, "My help comes from the Lord, who made heaven and earth." As He promised before His ascension, the Holy Spirit guides our steps so that our trust remains stable.

It is a decisive Psalm for one who aims at the constant presence of God and Christ, who dedicates every moment and breath, every heartbeat and step to Him, in the midst of many distractions. It means resting in the provident arms of the Father, instead of leaning on the false props of wealth, health, pleasure, and even work. Repeatedly praying this Psalm induces trust, right choice, and decisions because it is the prayer of Christ, who assured us: "I do not pray that thou shouldst take them out of the world, but that thou shouldst keep them from the evil one. . . . As thou didst send me into the world, so I have sent them into the world" (Jn. 17:15-18). "And no one shall snatch them out of my hand" (Jn. 10:28). With Him we walk the path of light and do not stumble (Jn. 11:9). We are at home everywhere.

This Psalm becomes most effective when the Church prays it in her liturgy worship with Christ present. Besides saying it at noon and vespers, the Church uses it for the departed (vespers) and on the Feast of the Transfiguration.

Psalm 122 (121)

I was glad when they said to me,
"Let us go to the house of the LORD!"
²Our feet have been standing
within your gates, O Jerusalem!

³Jerusalem, built as a city
which is bound firmly together,
⁴to which the tribes go up,
the tribes of the LORD,
as was decreed for Israel,
to give thanks to the name of the LORD.
⁵There thrones for judgment were set,
the thrones of the house of David.

⁶Pray for the peace of Jerusalem!
"May they prosper who love you!
⁷Peace be within your walls,
and security within your towers!"
⁸For my brethren and companions' sake
I will say, "Peace be within you!"
⁹For the sake of the house of the LORD our God,
I will seek your good.

Peace to the City of God

The pilgrim celebrates two moments in this true song of ascent
(a Gradual Psalm): first, when he hears the news of going to the Lord's
house, and then when he arrives in view of the Holy City and shouts
with enthusiasm, "Our feet have been standing within your gates, O
Jerusalem." Like Psalms 84 and 87 in spirit, this one gives us the very
heartbeat of Jewish piety. Now on the heights of Olivet, he breaks
forth in tears at the glorious sight of Sion before him, the goal of his
earthly longing, the Temple where the living God dwelt, the Ark and
Altar.

Jerusalem was built as a city, like no other city, for God had chosen
her and made Solomon's Temple one of the wonders of the world.
There was King David's palace, the great wall with its ramparts and
gates, and in it the judgment thrones which brought justice and peace
to the people. Here the tribes of the Lord assembled, milling in huge
crowds, singing the praises of their God, fulfilling their vows. It was

decreed for Israel to seek this face of God in the symbols of feasts, sacrifices, and gifts (Dt. 16:16f.). Here they had fellowship with God and each other, the source and goal of unity.

Even in the Old Testament the people believed that "the offering of a righteous man anoints [enriches] the altar, and its pleasing odor rises before the Most High" (Sir. 35:6). Each pilgrim contributed to the peace and happiness of all. In every sense the city was compactly built with the strong core of pride, joy, and brotherhood.

Jesus pilgrimaged to Jerusalem (Lk. 2:41ff.) and prayed our Psalm in an exalted sense. City, gates, walls, Temple, dwellings, Altar, thrones of justice and mercy, all typified Him. We pray it in His sense, applying it to the present Church and future, heavenly Jerusalem of peace. Greater than its thrones of justice are the new courts of forgiveness; greater than the old feasts is the new banqueting; greater than the old faith and praise are the hope and present goods of redemption, the brotherhood of charity and praise in union with Christ. All tribes and nations of the earth baptized into membership, after receiving the Good Gospel, form a great visible Body pilgrimaging to the New City. "Our feet are standing within your gates, O Jerusalem."

Think of your parish church and diocese, where you have fulness of redemption, with pride and gratitude. When you come to the house of the Lord, your festive joy abounds at the blessings and healing you take home with you. Do you pray, "Peace be within you! I will seek your good"? Even your home becomes a vestibule to heaven. Peace to your homes! "Do you not know that you are God's temple and that God's Spirit dwells in you?" (1 Cor. 3:16) Jesus comes in Communion to this temple. He is the New Mystery of God, the fulfillment of the old. Read Heb. 12:22-24.

The Church uses Psalm 122 not only at noon and in Sunday vespers, but at the dedication of a new church, and for feasts of the Virgin Mary, for virgins generally and all holy women, all who, like the women in Christ's following, are His sisters on the way and are joyfully sensitive to His will.

Psalm 123 (122)

To thee I lift up my eyes,
    O thou who art enthroned in the heavens!
²Behold, as the eyes of servants
    look to the hand of their master,
as the eyes of a maid
    to the hand of her mistress,
so our eyes look to the LORD our God,
    till he have mercy upon us.

³Have mercy upon us, O LORD, have mercy upon us,
    for we have had more than enough of contempt.
⁴Too long our soul has been sated
    with the scorn of those who are at ease,
    the contempt of the proud.

Daily Trust in God

Living in two worlds, a Christian will be "doing his own thing," till he learns the lesson of this poetic prayer. Keeping up a faith attitude while he lives in the midst of conflicting world forces demands a continual heavenward orientation of heart. The Psalm is both personal and communal prayer. It all begins with the season of Advent, when we train ourselves to raise eyes, hands, and hearts to the Lord God, while He comes with His redemption. He is enthroned in heaven, and our whole being must gravitate that way to final union with Him. The process will end with our resurrection.

Though short, the Psalm requires a lifetime of imitation till we are like the servant or handmaid who does not take his or her eyes off the master or mistress. "The contempt of the proud" will stand in the way and try to impede us. We will encounter a great deal of opposition in carrying out this Psalm. We complicate things for ourselves, as long as we serve two masters and lose sight of the Lord God.

The contrary attitudes of unbelief should call forth our instinctive contempt. Pride comes from a false secularism that despises the poor and identifies itself with contentment in riches. Secularism is insensitive to Christ's Sermon on the Mount, where He tells us that our Father in heaven provides for our every need. Keeping our eyes on Him is trust. To rely on our own power and wisdom would make us useless and helpless servants.

When we become humble and little in our own estimation, we can pray this Psalm with Christ, the Lord of prayer. He who is forever enthroned with the Father making intercession for us waits for us to raise our eyes and hands to Him. His faithful servants and handmaids do His will "till he have mercy on us." Then He extends the helping hand of His humanity. We become true pilgrims on Christ's way when we resist the appeals and tuggings of false love at our hearts, the love of the evil, unbelieving world.

The Church uses the Psalm at midday and for vespers.

Psalm 124 (123)

If it had not been the LORD
    who was on our side,
    let Israel now say—
²if it had not been the LORD who was on our side,
    when men rose up against us,
³then they would have swallowed us up alive,
    when their anger was kindled against us;
⁴then the flood would have swept us away,
    the torrent would have gone over us;
⁵then over us would have gone
    the raging waters.

⁶Blessed be the LORD,
    who has not given us
    as prey to their teeth!
⁷We have escaped as a bird
    from the snare of the fowlers;
the snare is broken,
    and we have escaped!

⁸Our help is in the name of the LORD,
    who made heaven and earth.

Gratitude in Crises

We continue our pilgrimage and thank God for the many times He rescued us in danger. Surrounded by personal and national enemies, the sacred writer uses three bold figures to describe threats along the way: 1) the teeth of wild animals, 2) overwhelming floods, and 3) the snares of hunters. Against all such odds the Lord delivered His people from violence and deceit. The word for thanks in Hebrew means the same as praise: "Blessed be the Lord!" While we are ignorant of the emergency or crisis underlying this prayer, it fits many a situation in Israel's history when they depended on the Lord.

The Psalm also suits many an occasion when we experience divine rescue from the lion's jaws, or when the Lord picked up the sinking Peter, or when hidden perils would trip us on our path to God. Jesus is in our midst no matter how great or sudden the danger that awaits us. Faith and trust are not the easy way out, but always the sure way. If we have faith like a mustard seed, we can stem any tide and break through any trap set for us. For the many times we are unaware of threats along the way, the Church gives us the closing verse of the Psalm: "Our help is in the name of the Lord, who made heaven and earth." This becomes a kind of official ejaculation that the Lord keeps ready for us in all emergencies.

When we experience God's help, our confidence is strengthened. We profit by praying this Psalm when we are helpless in the face of great social evils, when we would like to perform the physical and spiritual works of mercy and are hindered from doing so. May God deliver unborn infants from the snares of selfish pleasure-seeking and the profit motive of still others. May the Lord be on the side of the young who are unaware of the devil prowling like a lion to devour them. This Psalm is one of the Church's noon and evening prayers, times when the enemy of salvation is most active.

Psalm 125 (124)

Those who trust in the LORD are like Mount Zion,
    which cannot be moved, but abides for ever.
²As the mountains are round about Jerusalem,
    so the LORD is round about his people,
    from this time forth and for evermore.
³For the scepter of wickedness shall not rest
    upon the land allotted to the righteous,
lest the righteous put forth
    their hands to do wrong.

⁴Do good, O Lord, to those who are good,
  and to those who are upright in their hearts!
⁵But those who turn aside upon their crooked ways
  the Lord will lead away with evildoers!
  Peace be in Israel!

Mount Zion, Sign of Trust

Strong and firm, yet fervent and tender, the message of hope goes forth to the pilgrim as he approaches his goal. This Psalm is like a prophetic message that reanimates doubting spirits within reach of their final aim. Amid threats to their confidence, both nation and individuals welcome this divine Word of unshakable faith. It seems that the pilgrims already viewed Mount Zion and Jerusalem, built on a hill within a wider circle of higher mountains. Both stand for God and His immovable strength. God is like Mount Zion in the center of His people and God is like the mountains that encircle the city. He is within and He is without, a powerful motive for confidence that no force of evil can budge. Aside from their natural symbolism of firmness, these mountains are honored by God's revealed presence and promises "for evermore."

Righteous men must learn to trust God in the face of all obstacles. This Psalm presents no problems, except learning what forces of wickedness happened to threaten God's people at that hour. Whether it was an evil-minded king like Manasses, or more likely a foreign pagan power with its tempting idols, new trust in God was the answer to iniquity in power. These idols tempted even just men, but only as long as the people had no recourse to their God. Trust overcomes doubt, and the God who rested on the cherubim on the holy mountain would reward their prayer.

Human doubt still prospers, as when public polls and votes want to decide moral issues and make right and wrong depend on majority opinion. People weak in faith fall for "what everybody thinks and does." Even "the righteous put forth their hands to do wrong" (v. 3). When God takes action, He is in the majority! The least effort to trust Him puts us in His reward.

"Peace be in Israel!" must find an echo in our hearts. God and His people are one. All that does not lead to God is idolatry. Our adherence to the Lord brings peace to His City, the Church. True science and education follow Christ the Way; false science follows "crooked ways" and becomes the laughingstock of tomorrow. The house of pilgrims is built on rock, the new Mount Zion. Outside of this City stand the malefactors, the "barking dogs" (Rev. 22:15). Certainty and security stand on the side of God.

In the Church today we pray this Psalm for final perseverance (at noon and vespers). Christ promised that "the gates of hell would not prevail against" His Church (Mt. 16:18, Greek), and the days of trial will be shortened for the sake of the elect (Mt. 24:22).

Psalm 126 (125)

When the LORD restored the fortunes of Zion,
    we were like those who dream.
²Then our mouth was filled with laughter,
    and our tongue with shouts of joy;
then they said among the nations,
    "The LORD has done great things for them."
³The LORD has done great things for us;
    we are glad.

⁴Restore our fortunes, O LORD,
    like the watercourses in the Negeb!
⁵May those who sow in tears
    reap with shouts of joy!
⁶He that goes forth weeping,
    bearing the seed for sowing,
shall come home with shouts of joy,
    bringing his sheaves with him.

The Joy of Conversion

One can think of the return of the Jewish exiles from captivity as the situation which simultaneously called forth tears and laughter from those liberated. Added to this came the witness of the neighbors that God had done great things for His people. A rich harvest could evoke joy and sorrow, but it would hardly call forth special notice from other nations. The Lord God had reversed the earlier punishment (exile and destruction), and the entire nation rose in joyful praise. Like a dream come true, the chosen people were in a trance realized. The song of the homeward bound exiles has become the hymn of pilgrims on the way to heaven.

God does not leave things half done. He restores the fortunes of Israel, like the autumn rains change the dry wadis (river beds, valleys) of the South into swollen streams that bring fertility and life for man and beast alike. Both harvest and exile started with tears and labor and ended with joy and celebration. And the more so, since it was God's doing. These experiences of hard faith have given us the proverb: "Sowing in tears, reaping in laughter (or joy)." It also reminds us of the Pauline word: "I planted . . . but God gave the increase" (1 Cor. 3:6). A first step in restoring their fortunes was to grant them an abundant harvest, which required more than ordinary hard work.

Return from exile and the more sober joy of harvest becomes an image for the work in the Kingdom, the conversion of sinners.. It is a homecoming that costs tears and work and suffering and brings joy to angels and men. Conversion is also a pilgrimage process from one world to another, and the price is the suffering of Christ. Sorrow and pain according to God lead to rejoicing and love according to God (see 2 Cor. 2:1-10).

The Lord Himself will welcome the homecoming pilgrim with, "Well done, good and faithful servant. . . ." He promised His apostles tears and sorrow in His vineyard, but also joy that no one could steal (Jn. 16:22). The grain of wheat will die, but it brings forth much fruit (Jn. 12:24). We must do our part; the Holy Spirit will look out for the joy. When the day of reckoning comes, finally, all nations will proclaim the mighty deeds of the Lord (Rev. 15:3f.). The Virgin Mary gives us the same message: "He who is mighty has done great things for me" (Lk. 1:49). Let us sing this Psalm with her in the Church at noon and vespers, and again for vespers on the feast days of the apostles.

Psalm 127 (126)

> Unless the Lord builds the house,
>   those who build it labor in vain.
> Unless the Lord watches over the city,
>   the watchman stays awake in vain.
> ²It is in vain that you rise up early and go late to rest,
>   eating the bread of anxious toil;
>   for he gives to his beloved sleep.

³Lo, sons are a heritage from the LORD,
    the fruit of the womb a reward.
⁴Like arrows in the hand of a warrior
    are the sons of one's youth.
⁵Happy is the man who has
    his quiver full of them!
He shall not be put to shame
    when he speaks with his enemies in the gate.

Frustration Without God

This very ancient song of wisdom tells of man's basic religious conviction: that the natural world of man's effort and planning is carried by God. He not only created man and woman but also sustains their every action. And these actions must conform to His will. If we go our own ways, building a house is useless, guarding a city is in vain, rising early for feverish work is futile. Man constantly tries to do without the Creator. The simple work of building a home is not enough. God's care also extends to planning and enjoying a vacation. Without Him we build on sand. We use God's energy for every private and public activity. An easy Psalm with a hard message!

Think of all the men and women guarding their fortunes. Think of the armaments race with its potential for killing. Those who run governments cannot succeed unless they proceed according to God's known will. The God of heaven is the God of the poor on earth. Many people live and act as if there were no invisible God in the picture. This Psalm contains a difficult lesson for the worldling to learn: that he cannot go counter to the hand of God in his life.

The Creator has a leading role in all that happens. God works while man sleeps. Reason and revelation tell us so. Man thinks he is doing it all. God knows differently. The fruitfulness of labor and work depends on God's laws of justice. Earning one's bread by tilling the soil or driving a nail requires the same faith. The ancient city gates were places of assembly and courts of justice and business. There men transacted every community affair with their neighbors. God was invisibly there.

All fruitfulness is God's gift, human fruitfulness especially. "The fruit of the womb" is God's gift of life and His will is clear. All planning must follow His wisdom. Children are a natural blessing and a source of happiness to man and woman, not to mention the supernatural gifts that God has in store for them. "The enemies in the gate" are vicious, violent, and victorious, but they will be put to shame in the end before the whole world. God will stop the demons of race suicide and "put down the mighty from their thrones." The lives of the unborn are also in the Providence of the heavenly Father.

But without Christ we can do nothing. His wisdom is our rule of ascent in prayer. Psalm 127 comes to life most of all when the Church, in the Holy Spirit, prays it at noon and at vespers. The Church prays it also for the common of virgins and holy women, especially to honor the Virgin Mother Mary, all who realized spiritual fruitfulness in the Lord's way. They knew that the Creator of material gifts crowns His creation with still higher blessings.

Psalm 128 (127)

Blessed is every one who fears the LORD,
who walks in his ways!
²You shall eat the fruit of the labor of your hands;
you shall be happy, and it shall be well with you.

³Your wife will be like a fruitful vine
within your house;
your children will be like olive shoots
around your table.
⁴Lo, thus shall the man be blessed
who fears the LORD.

⁵The LORD bless you from Zion!
May you see the prosperity of Jerusalem
all the days of your life!
⁶May you see your children's children!
Peace be upon Israel!

The Happy Home

Ancient, short, happy, this Psalm fits with the preceding one. As a piece of Jewish wisdom and piety, it resembles Psalm 1 in pronouncing blessings on those who fear the Lord and walk in His ways. "Blessed" means both "happy" and "favored by God." Personal happiness and national harmony go together. The peace of Jerusalem depends on peace in the family, and vice versa. Normally, times of general prosperity bring contentment for the family and its members.

In a society that is malformed, harassed by an unjust economy, made up of families that are breaking up, victimized by a culture that works havoc on children, parents who fear the Lord and want to walk in His ways may regard this Psalm as unreal, "idealistic." For modern man it creates a problem in that he reaps none of the blessings held out to him here. The farmer and workman cannot "eat the fruit of the labor" of their own hands, as someone else eats their profits. The profit motive and the invasion of the home with dubious publicity, selfish standards and values, devilish suggestions compounds the inescapable force of the vicious circle. Yet this is a Psalm for today.

We have to learn anew the fear of the Lord and the piety of brotherly cooperation before social and family peace can exist. First, to restore God's will of justice for everyone is a prerequisite for walking in God's ways. Sharing the goods of this world, instead of hoarding and "hogging" them, means "tightening our belts" more than a little. If we spurn all divine and human laws regarding food, clothing, and shelter, praying this Psalm will be lip service of praise. The Savior's Sermon on the Mount is still valid: "But seek first his Kingdom and his righteousness, and all these things will be yours as well" (Mt. 6:33).

This Psalm does not stand alone, independent of other norms. They are blessed whom the Lord calls blessed. Transplanting this Word of God from another age to our hearts requires a living faith. That living faith includes belief in the Voice of Christ and His Spirit in the Church. We can be hankering after the fleshpots of Egypt (bounty, longevity, fecundity, comfort), when the cry is, "Pilgrims, wake up! The Lord is near! It is the high noon of crisis for the family! Prosperity is only a type of something greater!" Even now, uncounted blessings come to the family that tries to pray and live out this Psalm.

Union with Christ guarantees happiness to the family at every moment. Until we experience better days, we will not lose sight of the beloved home symbols of wife and children, of grandchildren and grandparents, of the round table of olive branches, all signs of peace at home and at the Table of the Lord. "Peace be upon Israel!"

Psalm 129 (128)

"Sorely have they afflicted me from my youth,"
    let Israel now say—
²"Sorely have they afflicted me from my youth,
    yet they have not prevailed against me.
³The plowers plowed upon my back;
    they made long their furrows."
⁴The Lord is righteous;
    he has cut the cords of the wicked.
⁵May all who hate Zion
    be put to shame and turned backward!
⁶Let them be like the grass on the housetops,
    which withers before it grows up,
⁷with which the reaper does not fill his hand
    or the binder of sheaves his bosom,
⁸while those who pass by do not say,
    "The blessing of the Lord be upon you!
    We bless you in the name of the Lord!"

Hope in Affliction

Part of the pilgrim's most necessary equipment is the divine message contained in this prayer for the defeat of his enemies and God's. Every follower of the Savior can match Israel's cry that the enemy "has afflicted me from my youth." The long history of God's people is that ceaseless affliction—"from my youth." When they were slaves in Egypt, bowed down under a heavy yoke, God snapped it. What the Psalmist calls "plowed furrows on my back" (v. 3), we still call a "harrowing" experience. The Psalmist classifies as God's enemies "all who hate Zion." God will shame them and turn them back.

The enemies of God are likened to grass on a roof that grows for a while, then fades for lack of moisture, and the reaper cannot use it. This receives an imprecation from the passerby, and no one has a blessing for them. While it was customary for harvesters and passersby to greet each other with a blessing ("The Lord be with you!" or "We bless you in the Name of the Lord!"), the enemies of Zion will hear no such benediction.

The new community of Zion, which is the Church of Christ, inherited this Psalm. As the Bride of Christ, she prays with Him for the conversion of the enemy and wants blessing to triumph over hatred and retribution. She calls down God's blessing on those who curse because "Mercy triumphs over judgment" (Jas. 2:13). Yet she, like the Savior, has no prayer for the reprobate, the forces of evil that are beyond redemption, but are active in the world. Deep trust in God sustains the Church from her earliest youth. The Lord predicted persecution and hatred coming from an unbelieving, sinful world.

This has left scars and "furrows" on Zion, the New like the old, just as the flagellation did on the Body of Christ. From ancient times till now, the people of God took seriously the hostility against themselves, which came from the "worship of the dragon" (Rev. 13:3f.). Faith senses that the dragon, the beast (Satan) still blasphemes against God (Rev. 13:6). That the Church cannot pray for this enemy, but against him, follows from reading 2 Thess. 2:3-10. That she will prevail was foretold by Christ in Mt. 16:18. God will vindicate the believer's hope.

Psalm 130 (129)

Out of the depths I cry to thee, O Lord!
2   Lord, hear my voice!
Let thy ears be attentive
      to the voice of my supplications!

³If thou, O Lord, shouldst mark iniquities,
      Lord, who could stand?
⁴But there is forgiveness with thee,
      that thou mayest be feared.

⁵I wait for the Lord, my soul waits,
      and in his word I hope;
⁶my soul waits for the Lord
      more than watchmen for the morning.
      more than watchmen for the morning.

⁷O Israel, hope in the Lord!
      For with the Lord there is steadfast love,
      and with him is plenteous redemption.
⁸And he will redeem Israel
      from all his iniquities.

De Profundis

This is the best-known title for this Psalm (Latin for its first words, "Out of the depths"). Rising from the depths of human sorrow, it comes from the heart of the sinner as well as from extreme physical suffering. The Church uses it for her departed ones. It is suitable for Confession as an act of contrition. Very properly the Church calls it one of her penitential Psalms.

The Church painfully recognizes the imperfections and sins of her members and knows that only God can forgive them. The sinner who prays it slowly and thoughtfully sees his own helplessness in sin and sickness. There is only God's mercy to wait for. Waiting for the Lord is its theme, and waiting is hard for the impatient sinner. As dawn is the sign of the new day, so the light of redemption and forgiveness is his only hope. The sentinels of the night mark off time with "watches" (the Jews had three, the Romans four). The sentinels hope for daybreak more than anything else. They know it is coming, but they must wait. The Psalmist repeats the hopeful cry: "My soul waits for the Lord more than watchmen for morning." Time drags on slowly for those who linger in the night of unbelief and evil.

Christ is the Sun of the new day of hope. He brought the new day of mercy, "plenteous redemption." The vast majority of mankind still awaits the Redeemer. In Him the redemption is accomplished, but the Good News must be broken to all for their acceptance in faith and forgiveness of sin. "That thou mayest be feared" refers to the fear of offending God. He keeps a "record" of sins unrepented ("mark iniquities"), but the poor man is now repentant and can hope. This fear is the "beginning of wisdom," as it leads to love.

Hope is divine when it is based on the revelation of faith. The promises of Christ are concerned precisely with mercy and readiness to forgive. He never refused a penitent man or woman forgiveness. God became man to confirm this truth and hope. All the sick sinners along the roadside called to Him, and He brought them forgiveness and health. The Son of God entered our sinful world to pray this Psalm for sinners. He still prays it with us from His place at the right hand of the Father. He showed His will to forgive by looking for the lost sheep and by the parable of the Prodigal Son. Now He reenacts His redeeming love in the sacraments of Penance and Holy Anointing. He is the Hand of mercy the Father holds out to all who are in the "depths" or have hit bottom.

The Church prays it especially on the Annunciation, Christmas, and on February 2 (see Lk. 2:38), also at compline on Wednesdays and IV Sunday vespers. We should also recommend it to the sleepless sick person, the night worker, the traveller, all who wait for the dawn, and tell them to give expression to their longing for Christ.

Psalm 131 (130)

> O LORD, my heart is not lifted up,
>> my eyes are not raised too high;
> I do not occupy myself with things
>> too great and too marvelous for me.
> ²But I have calmed and quieted my soul,
>> like a child quieted at its mother's breast;
>> like a child that is quieted is my soul.
>
> ³O Israel, hope in the LORD
>> from this time forth and for evermore.

Trusting Humility

This Psalm exalts humility, the hardest and most unpopular of all the virtues. Humility must come freely from within. It cannot be faked. No one can humiliate another person unless he accepts the humiliation. Sincerely accepting humiliation is humility. A saying has it that you cannot humiliate a humble person because he has already done so himself. "My heart is not lifted up." To say that honestly is humility.

No comparison could be more apt than that of a weaned child on its mother's lap, resting quietly in complete trust. Our security in God is even more sure than that of such an infant. Before God we are helpless infants, and that is salutary if we are quiet, silent, and without anxiety, because we "throw all our cares upon the Lord."

God raises up the humble and resists the proud, the "raised eyes" that look down on others. Humility is truth, that is, realizing our capacities and abiding within our limitations, not to meddle with "things too great." Ambition can be good or bad. When we strive to develop our God-given talents, it is a virtue. When our ambitions go beyond our potentialities, we are sinning. A "snob" has been described as "one who is educated beyond his intelligence." God has created us for just the right place, and humility keeps to its place. Knowing our place is truth; keeping it is humility.

Although unpopular because all the world urges us "to get ahead," humility is needed for living in society. It is necessary for obedience. Without it we are pretentious. The virtue of humility is part of the law of Christ, "Learn from me, for I am gentle and lowly of heart" (Mt. 11: 29). His human will lived in constant loving submission to the Father (Jn. 4:34). He declined the grandeur He had a right to claim, and He chose the way of the Cross (Phil. 2:7f.). He pronounced a blessing on the lowly (Mt. 5:5). He made childlike humility a condition for entering His Kingdom (Mt. 18:3). And He chose for His Mother the maiden of "low estate" (Lk. 1:48).

We pray this Psalm and descend by our humility, so that the Lord can raise us up. In His presence we want to be like the penitent publican, who kept his eyes lowered and for that went away justified (Lk. 18: 9-14). The Church helps us with this Psalm in her evening prayer (vespers) and on some Saturdays in honor of the humble Virgin.

Psalm 132 (131)

Remember, O Lord, in David's favor,
    all the hardships he endured;
²how he swore to the Lord
    and vowed to the Mighty One of Jacob,
³"I will not enter my house
    or get into my bed;
⁴I will not give sleep to my eyes
    or slumber to my eyelids,
⁵until I find a place for the Lord,
    a dwelling place for the Mighty One of Jacob."

⁶Lo, we heard of it in Ephrathah,
    we found it in the fields of Jaar.
⁷"Let us go to his dwelling place;
    let us worship at his footstool!"

[8]Arise, O Lord, and go to thy resting place,
    thou and the ark of thy might.
[9]Let thy priests be clothed with righteousness,
    and let thy saints shout for joy.
[10]For thy servant David's sake
    do not turn away the face of thy anointed one.

[11]The Lord swore to David a sure oath
    from which he will not turn back:
"One of the sons of your body
    I will set on your throne.
[12]If your sons keep my covenant
    and my testimonies which I shall teach them,
their sons also for ever
    shall sit upon your throne."

[13]For the Lord has chosen Zion;
    he has desired it for his habitation:
[14]"This is my resting place for ever;
    here I will dwell, for I have desired it.
[15]I will abundantly bless her provisions;
    I will satisfy her poor with bread.
[16]Her priests I will clothe with salvation,
    and her saints will shout for joy.
[17]There I will make a horn to sprout for David;
    I have prepared a lamp for my anointed.
[18]His enemies I will clothe with shame,
    but upon himself his crown will shed its luster."

Early Messianic Hope

To pray this Psalm intelligently, we must trace the origin of the pilgrim's faith in Zion. After David built his palace, the prophet Nathan praised him for the great things he had done for Jerusalem and the people, but said that God as yet had no home (resting place). That roused the king to a solemn oath to God (vv. 3-6) to provide for the Lord. Then followed the search for the Ark (Ephrathah and Jaar are uncertain places). The enemy Philistines had captured the Ark in battle, and it went from place to place till a certain Ebed-Edom obtained it. There they found it (1 Chr. 15). The levites and priests were readied by "sanctifying" themselves and clothing themselves with "righteousness."

All who came into the sacred presence, "worshipped at his footstool" before the Ark where God dwelt on His earthly footstool.

We hear David's voice again in verse 8 when the triumphal procession started; "Arise, O Lord, and go to thy resting place, thou and the Ark of thy might." The Psalmist adds the prayer: "For thy servant David's sake, do not turn away the face of thy anointed one." They proceeded to Jerusalem and to the installation of the Ark amid songs of joy, sacrifices, and festivity (1 Chr. 16:1-3). Here was the "resting place" of God until Solomon built the Temple (1 Chr. 6:16f.). The ancient promises of God to Abraham had come down in time and place to one visible sign, thus prefiguring the incarnation.

God's response was the inspiring oath to David and his house for all time to end in the glory of the Messiah (vv. 11-12). The language of this Psalm is very ancient, taking us back perhaps a thousand years before Christ. Verses 11-18 contain what God promised: the covenant with David and his dynasty, Zion as His chosen dwelling, bounty to all, to the poor, the priests, and faithful ones and glory in the end (1 Chr. 17:1-13).

That the final two verses are messianic, we have confirmed in Lk. 1:69, where Zechariah praised God, for He "has raised up a horn of salvation for us in the house of his servant David." Here is a new Zion with God incarnate present, new blessings of salvation, anointing with the horn of oil, the new King and Light of the world. All the grandeur and merits of David wane before this glorious reality. If it inspired ancient pilgrims to pray, the more so should it inspire us, who see His face always. We have found Him, not in the ancient Ark, but in the new Shrine of His humanity, full of blessings and feasting, of sacramental redemption and glory. Let us enthrone this last King of David's line in our hearts and in the world. To us His members He promised a royal share with Him: "Be faithful unto death and I will give you the crown of life" (Rev. 2:10).

Psalm 133 (132)

Behold, how good and pleasant it is
when brothers dwell in unity!
²It is like the precious oil upon the head,
running down upon the beard,
upon the beard of Aaron,
running down on the collar of his robes!
³It is like the dew of Hermon,
which falls on the mountains of Zion!
For there the LORD has commanded the blessing,
life for evermore.

Brotherly Love

The whole Christian life culminates in this Psalm and in the Lord's Word to love one another and St. Paul's "Love one another with brotherly affection" (Rom. 12:10). Although used only once officially (at noon prayer), Christians benefit by its daily use. There can be no doubt that the bond of fellowship, based on the divine life of grace, is what pilgrims have in common in the following of Christ.

Perhaps we have lost the joyous meaning of oil and ointment and fail to grasp the beauty and attractiveness of the great sacrament of Confirmation in which the sign of the Lord's presence is the fragrant, sweet-smelling chrism of the Gift of the Holy Spirit. We do not take the sacramental signs seriously. In the primitive Church, this led necessarily to brotherly love and community life, having all things in common, fulfilling each other's needs, celebrating the Eucharist together, eating one's food with gladness, finding favor with all the people, attracting new converts (Acts 2:44-47 and 4:32f.). The cause of joy was fraternal fellowship, love among the people of God.

Psalm 45 tells of the "oil of gladness" and compares it to heavy dew in the morning. This comparison of dew and rich oil is older than the Bible. The welcome, plentiful dew of Mount Hermon in the north descending on Mount Zion was held as a blessing from heaven and meant life, like eternal life. This is an old Psalm, as Psalms go, and clearly proclaims belief in immortality (dew is a sign of resurrection in Is. 26:19). No wonder that fragrance, dew from heaven and oil from the earth come together in the Genesis blessing (27:28f.).

It needed only moral wisdom to see all this in the anointing of Aaron as high priest with precious ointment to make this a favored

Psalm for brothers living in harmonious love and for pilgrims journeying peacefully to the place where the high priest ministered. Zion's Temple was the goal. There the high priest could always pray, "Thou hast poured over me fresh oil" (Psalm 92).

All this gave an attractive meaning to his high office: the oil was rich, plentiful, and fragrant. It flowed freely like perfume from head to garments. Like charity it was a broad mantle that covered all. Like brotherly and sisterly love, it is attractive, refreshing like dew, sweetening all life, joygiving, and peaceful.

Brothers in faith are brothers in Christ. Fraternal charity is their mother tongue. It comes from the joyful Baptism in Christ, who accepted the anointing from the sinner woman (Lk. 7:36-40; also Mk. 14: 3-9). He returns it in the Holy Spirit to all His members, and this fragrance fills the house of God and the Church through the centuries.

Psalm 134 (133)

> Come, bless the LORD,
>> all you servants of the LORD,
>> who stand by night in the house of the LORD!
> ²Lift up your hands to the holy place,
>> and bless the LORD!
>
> ³May the LORD bless you from Zion,
>> he who made heaven and earth!

A Night Blessing

After the day's work, God's work, in the Temple priests and people turn once more to God for a prayer of praise. They bless (praise) the Lord, and He in turn blesses them. He who made heaven and earth blesses them as a final act of their pilgrimage. All alike raise their hands to the holy place and bless the Lord.

It is a beautiful night prayer for Christians in their homes. They can turn to their parish church, or to a shrine at home, and parents can bless their children with this prayer. God's blessing never stops, day or night. The "servants of the Lord," who dwell in His house, keep watch over the people, so that even during "the watches of the night" the praise of God never ceases. On the Altar the fire of the Lord burns constantly as a sign of the divine acceptance of the people's prayers and gifts.

Psalm 135 (134)

Praise the LORD!
    Praise the name of the LORD,
    give praise, O servants of the LORD,
²you that stand in the house of the LORD,
    in the courts of the house of our God!
³Praise the LORD, for the LORD is good;
    sing to his name, for he is gracious!
⁴For the LORD has chosen Jacob for himself,
    Israel as his own possession.

⁵For I know that the LORD is great,
    and that our Lord is above all gods.
⁶Whatever the LORD pleases he does,
    in heaven and on earth,
    in the seas and all deeps.
⁷He it is who makes the clouds rise at the end of the earth,
    who makes lightnings for the rain
    and brings forth the wind from his storehouses.

⁸He it was who smote the first-born of Egypt,
    both of man and of beast;
⁹who in thy midst, O Egypt,
    sent signs and wonders
    against Pharaoh and all his servants;
¹⁰who smote many nations
    and slew mighty kings,
¹¹Sihon, king of the Amorites,
    and Og, king of Bashan,
    and all the kingdoms of Canaan,
¹²and gave their land as a heritage,
    a heritage to his people Israel.

¹³Thy name, O LORD, endures for ever,
    thy renown, O LORD, throughout all ages.
¹⁴For the LORD will vindicate his people,
    and have compassion on his servants.

¹⁵The idols of the nations are silver and gold,
    the work of men's hands.
¹⁶They have mouths, but they speak not,
    they have eyes, but they see not,
¹⁷they have ears, but they hear not,
    nor is there any breath in their mouths.
¹⁸Like them be those who make them!—
    yea, every one who trusts in them!

¹⁹O house of Israel, bless the LORD!
    O house of Aaron, bless the LORD!
²⁰O house of Levi, bless the LORD!
    You that fear the LORD, bless the LORD!
²¹Blessed be the LORD from Zion,
    he who dwells in Jerusalem!
Praise the LORD!

Praise God's Name Forever

The opening prayer formula and the end of this Psalm are the same: all who stand in the courts of the Lord unite in a chorus of praise. The reason is old yet ever new: first, God's greatness and goodness; second, His election of Israel and Sion as His earthly dwelling. His wondrous deeds helped to establish His supremacy over the idols of silver and gold, the work of men's hands. Since this is not an original Psalm, but composed of themes and formularies of other Psalms, it is a reminder of certain essentials for cult and piety.

God is Lord of creation and manifests His power in the phenomena of nature: storms, lightning, clouds, and rain. "Whatever the Lord pleases he does, in heaven and on earth" (v. 6), without being arbitrary or tyrannical like the gods of men. His special choice and works for His people are held up for the praise of generations. By contrast, the idols of the pagans are powerless and subhuman: they cannot speak, see, hear, or breathe. The inventors and devotees of such stupidities will become like them, idiots. This Psalm then was a constant reminder of the first and second commandments of God given on Sinai.

We of the New Testament can do vastly more to celebrate the God of creation and redemption, our God. God has come into our midst, not as of old, but incarnate as man, in the second Person of the Godhead, Jesus Christ. As Israel celebrated God, we celebrate Christ who is Heir to all of the divine prerogatives. This is the witness of Christianity and the power of our faith. Christ is the glorious Lord dwelling in His Body the Church, where He extends and spreads victories over Satan, sin, and death (Eph. 1:20-23) far greater than the old ones over Sihon and Og the giant. The "praise of his glory" ought to be the shout of all Christians (1 Pet. 2:9f.).

But strangely the contrary is often true. Instead of bending the knees at the holy Name of Jesus (Phil. 2:10), there is widespread irreverence and desecration by Christians. Instead of praying and blessing His Name, people abuse it, curse it, or make light of it. Nations who once were Christian at heart, who perhaps maintain a shell of Christ's revelation and religion, are the very countries where this takes place. How can the Name of Jesus, which stands for salvation and union with God, become a term of rejection of God? Are we dealing with something diabolical here, or plain insanity? Just as no one in the Holy Spirit say, "Jesus be cursed!" so no one says, "Jesus is Lord!" except in the Spirit (1 Cor. 12:3). By praying this Psalm, we are saying, "Blessed be Jesus Christ," and so make reparation for the angry scandal involved in this abuse. It is no credit to persons who defend it by saying, "People don't mean it." We pray this Psalm with the Church on Epiphany (vespers), on III Fridays (vespers), and IV Mondays (vv. 1-12 at noon).

Psalm 136 (135)

> O give thanks to the LORD, for he is good,
>> for his steadfast love endures for ever.
> ²O give thanks to the God of gods,
>> for his steadfast love endures for ever.
> ³O give thanks to the Lord of lords,
>> for his steadfast love endures for ever;

⁴to him who alone does great wonders,
    for his steadfast love endures for ever;
⁵to him who by understanding made the heavens,
    for his steadfast love endures for ever;
⁶to him who spread out the earth upon the waters,
    for his steadfast love endures for ever;
⁷to him who made the great lights,
    for his steadfast love endures for ever;
⁸the sun to rule over the day,
    for his steadfast love endures for ever;
⁹the moon and stars to rule over the night,
    for his steadfast love endures for ever;

¹⁰to him who smote the first-born of Egypt,
    for his steadfast love endures for ever;
¹¹and brought Israel out from among them,
    for his steadfast love endures for ever;
¹²with a strong hand and an outstretched arm,
    for his steadfast love endures for ever;
¹³to him who divided the Red Sea in sunder,
    for his steadfast love endures for ever;
¹⁴and made Israel pass through the midst of it,
    for his steadfast love endures for ever;
¹⁵but overthrew Pharaoh and his host in the Red Sea,
    for his steadfast love endures for ever;
¹⁶to him who led his people through the wilderness,
    for his steadfast love endures for ever;
¹⁷to him who smote great kings,
    for his steadfast love endures for ever;
¹⁸and slew famous kings,
    for his steadfast love endures for ever;
¹⁹Sihon, king of the Amorites,
    for his steadfast love endures for ever;
²⁰and Og, king of Bashan,
    for his steadfast love endures for ever;
²¹and gave their land as a heritage,
    for his steadfast love endures for ever;
²²a heritage to Israel his servant,
    for his steadfast love endures for ever.

²³It is he who remembered us in our low estate,
    for his steadfast love endures for ever;
²⁴and rescued us from our foes,
    for his steadfast love endures for ever;
²⁵he who gives food to all flesh,
    for his steadfast love endures for ever.

²⁶O give thanks to the God of heaven,
    for his steadfast love endures for ever.

His Love Is Everlasting

In later Jewish tradition, this Psalm, called the "Great Hallel" (song of praise), served the people of God at the annual Passover celebration to raise their voices and memory in thanks for their sacred history. It is a litany of praise in review of God's almighty deeds of creation and salvation. The people responded, "For his steadfast love endures forever." First is the acclamation of the God of gods, then follow many high spots of thanks in the nation's history.

Verses 5-9 single out some of the Genesis motives for the praise of the Creator, and verses 10 onward speak of God's intervention at the Exodus and at the Israelites' entry into the promised land. The events singled out are familiar from the story of Israel, from Egypt to Palestine, with the "strong hand" of Yahweh (the Name of God) always responsible for success and victory over powerful kings, such as the giant King Og of Bashan (Num. 21:21-35 and Dt. 3:1-11). Verse 25 is significant ("He who gives food to all flesh") as it reminds us of the desert manna and Christ's reference to it in Jn. 6:31: "He gave them bread from heaven to eat."

We pause to contemplate this verse, as the Lord used this Psalm with His disciples at the Last Supper, when He fulfilled it in the great eucharistic summary of salvation. There He gathered all the gratitude of sacred history and of His lifetime into one great action and immortalized it in the Sign of His sacrifice and glory. He had explained verse 25 at great length in Jn. 6, when the people asked Him how it was possible to give them bread from heaven and feed them with His Flesh and Blood. In answer He spoke of His ascension and glorified state (Jn. 6:62).

This Psalm is important for our life of prayer. Christians learn from it to count their favors and pray litanies of blessings received.

But above all they keep alive their proud baptismal memory, each one's sharing in the new Passover through the Red Sea and into the Promised Land. While historical events fade away into the past, the everlasting, steadfast love of God lives on into the future. God's Word in Christ will not pass away, and we are taken into the heavenly Mystery, of which those past events are typical. In Christ, memory is not dead and past, but living and present. With this in mind, we join the Church when she prays this Psalm on the Friday after Easter (office of readings), on IV Mondays (vespers), and on II Saturdays (office of readings). This prayer of the Church supports the eucharistic Mystery.

Psalm 137 (136)

By the waters of Babylon, there we sat down and wept,
    when we remembered Zion.
2On the willows there
    we hung up our lyres.
3For there our captors
    required of us songs,
and our tormentors, mirth, saying,
    "Sing us one of the songs of Zion!"

4How shall we sing the LORD's song
    in a foreign land?
5If I forget you, O Jerusalem,
    let my right hand wither!
6Let my tongue cleave to the roof of my mouth,
    if I do not remember you,
if I do not set Jerusalem
    above my highest joy!

7Remember, O LORD, against the Edomites
    the day of Jerusalem,
how they said, "Raze it, raze it!
    Down to its foundations!"
8O daughter of Babylon, you devastator!
    Happy shall he be who requites you
    with what you have done to us!
9Happy shall he be who takes your little ones
    and dashes them against the rock!

God Will Not Be Mocked

Beginning with the quiet pain of captives grieving for their home-land, far-off Sion, as a result of which they hung their silent harps on the willows near the streams of Babylon, the Psalm rises to great heights of just anger against Edom and Babylon, hereditary enemies who inflicted this grief on God's poor ones. The pendulum of passion swings from deep pathos to violent feelings because of the impudent provo-cations. The victorious captors cut into an open wound by asking the suffering captives to sing the beautiful songs (Psalms) of Zion to them in a pagan land.

Laboring in sorrow, the Jewish captives kept alive their faith in God and Jerusalem. It was torturing their memories, playing with their pain, to suggest that they sing with false joy and deny all that the God of Zion meant to them. If God were trying them with this captivity, they could not mock God and His great deeds by admitting that their God was powerless against the mighty Babylon. They longed not only for their beloved homes but also for God's presence on Zion. The provocation was too much.

The author calls on God to remember the fall of Jerusalem and Edom's treacherous part in it. Too long had this gone unpunished. First the sacred author promises that his tongue would cleave to his palate and his right hand be forgotten before he should ever forget Jerusalem or let some other joy come ahead of his happiness with the holy city. The request of the enemy was like saying, "Come, captives, amuse us with your happy songs of Zion, now that your God is dead." Instead of responding with a song, the author wishes fierce retribution on Babylon and her children. He prays that God may pay back the torturers' impudence and cruelty in kind because God is holy and just. May her offspring be dashed against the rock (Edom means "rock fortress"). Warfare in those days spared neither women nor children.

From all this we get insights into faith, for instance, that sadness cannot sing. But furthermore, this is not a pathetic and sweet poem "spoiled" by its final harsh note. There are those, children of a highly civilized Babylon or slaves of a literal sense, who cannot pray the final verse of this Psalm, as if they were sensitive to cruelty, yet they can tolerate the "scientific" slaying of millions of infants in the womb. There is a spiritual application of that verse, which is very real and necessary for our times.

The Psalm reminds us of the crude soldiers who blindfolded Christ and then played a game with Him by asking who had struck Him.

After His scourging and crowning with thorns, they made light of the King of heaven and earth, striking Him (Mt. 27:27ff.; Mk. 15:18ff.; Lk. 22:63ff.). Jesus had said, "Do not give dogs what is holy" (Mt. 7:6). To do so is a sacrilege. As we pray the Psalm with Christ, we leave justice to God, and no one is encouraged in violence, but in forgiveness and mercy. St. Benedict was right in requiring his monks to hurl their evil thoughts, while they were still young, against Christ, the Rock. This changes everything; the passionate anger is transferred to God's enemy Satan and his progeny, our evil thoughts and deeds. In the midst of an evil world, we are in exile, and heaven is our home (Phil. 3:20). All around us stands a seductive Edom and Babylon. Our top joy is Christ and Zion, as we join the Church in singing the Psalm on IV Tuesdays (vespers, vv. 1-6).

Psalm 138 (137)

I give thee thanks, O Lord, with my whole heart;
  before the gods I sing thy praise;
²I bow down toward thy holy temple
  and give thanks to thy name for thy steadfast love and
    thy faithfulness;
for thou hast exalted above everything
  thy name and thy word.
³On the day I called, thou didst answer me,
  my strength of soul thou didst increase.

⁴All the kings of the earth shall praise thee, O Lord,
  for they have heard the words of thy mouth;
⁵and they shall sing of the ways of the Lord,
  for great is the glory of the Lord.
⁶For though the Lord is high, he regards the lowly;
  but the haughty he knows from afar.

[7]Though I walk in the midst of trouble,
    thou dost preserve my life;
thou dost stretch out thy hand against the wrath of
    my enemies,
    and thy right hand delivers me.
[8]The LORD will fulfil his purpose for me;
    thy steadfast love, O LORD, endures for ever.
Do not forsake the work of thy hands.

Thanks With All My Heart

A royal Psalm from early days, this can only come from the heart of a God-fearing, public leader. He combines praise for past deeds of kindness and for favors yet to come. The author will worship in God's Temple in the presence of the whole assembly of believers and so give witness for the blessings and strength received in time of distress. Worship in the holy place is also in the sight of the angels ("before the gods" in the Hebrew may mean "pagan gods" and greater glory for the one true God's victory, but "angels" has more ready meaning for modern readers).

The Psalm is universal in tone, as it predicts that all the kings of the earth will hear the words of God and sing of the ways and glory of the Lord (vv. 4-5). This points to a future age, a time of fulfillment, which is clearly true of the era of Christ. Because the steadfast love of the Lord endures forever, He will bring to completion and perfection what He has begun and what He predicts. God's promises include continual help, grace, and strength for whatever tasks He assigns. We see divine Providence at work in this Psalm. Confidence in God is its counterpart. No one hopes in God in vain. In spite of His supremacy and primacy, He regards the lowly (v. 6).

There is no automatic salvation. It depends on free acceptance of the ways of the Lord. Just as haughtiness is freely willed, so too is humility and lowliness. St. Peter writes that God resists the proud and gives His grace to the humble (1 Pet. 5:5). The Mother of Christ gave voice to the same sentiments: "He has scattered the proud . . ." (Lk. 1: 51), and she is next to Christ for being "meek and humble of heart." Thanks too must come from the heart. Without it there can be no following of Christ.

If Christ lives in our midst, we experience in faith what the Lord predicted: worship in the sight of angels. "You will see heaven opened,

and the angels of God ascending and descending upon the Son of man"
(Jn. 1:51). Salvation is ongoing action of God in our midst. With Christ
as the fulfillment of the great promises to David, the work of God has
not ceased, but increased. On the day we call, He hears us (v. 3) and
never forsakes the work of His hands (v. 8). For this too we offer thanks
to the Father in Christ's Name. Victory against our enemies is the work
of His hand. Christ has truly brought to completion what God promised
in the Old Testament.

We can pray this Psalm with the Church to keep the foes of God
in check and to expand the mission of Christ in the world. We pray
it on the feast of the angels (September 29, vespers) and on II Tuesdays (vespers).

✓ **Psalm 139 (138)**

O Lord, thou hast searched me and known me!
²Thou knowest when I sit down and when I rise up;
thou discernest my thoughts from afar.
³Thou searchest out my path and my lying down,
and art acquainted with all my ways.
⁴Even before a word is on my tongue,
lo, O Lord, thou knowest it altogether.
⁵Thou dost beset me behind and before,
and layest thy hand upon me.
⁶Such knowledge is too wonderful for me;
it is high, I cannot attain it.

⁷Whither shall I go from thy Spirit?
Or whither shall I flee from thy presence?
⁸If I ascend to heaven, thou art there!
If I make my bed in Sheol, thou art there!
⁹If I take the wings of the morning
and dwell in the uttermost parts of the sea,
¹⁰even there thy hand shall lead me,
and thy right hand shall hold me.
¹¹If I say, "Let only darkness cover me,
and the light about me be night,"
¹²even the darkness is not dark to thee,
the night is bright as the day;
for darkness is as light with thee.

¹³For thou didst form my inward parts,
thou didst knit me together in my mother's womb.
¹⁴I praise thee, for thou art fearful and wonderful.
Wonderful are thy works!
Thou knowest me right well;
¹⁵   my frame was not hidden from thee,
when I was being made in secret,
intricately wrought in the depths of the earth.
¹⁶Thy eyes beheld my unformed substance;
in thy book were written, every one of them,
the days that were formed for me,
when as yet there was none of them.
¹⁷How precious to me are thy thoughts, O God!
How vast is the sum of them!
¹⁸If I would count them, they are more than the sand.
When I awake, I am still with thee.

¹⁹O that thou wouldst slay the wicked, O Gód,
and that men of blood would depart from me,
²⁰men who maliciously defy thee,
who lift themselves up against thee for evil!
²¹Do I not hate them that hate thee, O Lord?
And do I not loathe them that rise up against thee?
²²I hate them with perfect hatred;
I count them my enemies.
²³Search me, O God, and know my heart!
Try me and know my thoughts!
²⁴And see if there be any wicked way in me,
and lead me in the way everlasting!

God's All-Knowing Presence

Nowhere in the Psalms does the omniscience of God find such wonderful expression as in Psalm 139. His knowledge of man is also provident and omnipotent. We cannot grasp His foreknowledge of our days and actions, nor His memory of our past, written as it were in a book. The mystery lies in human freedom, how and why God lets man choose good or evil. Taken from earth's elements, woven in his mother's womb, man is the paragon of God's visible creation.

While touching on a profound secret in the world, this Psalm is easy to understand. No philosopher or theologian has expressed better how we are in God's hands. They quickly become abstract, sometimes abstruse, when they say how God is with us on our ways, present to our inmost thoughts, lending us His power when we try to escape. Day and night are all light for Him. God knows us better than we ourselves. Man cannot escape God.

To cultivate God's presence, then, means to awake to the fact that He is there and never forget that. God never forgets us; we forget Him. Then we are not there. But His personal presence and care remains. As we approach Him, our hatred for sin grows. The author's foes perhaps accused him of idolatry, an accusation that elicited passionate cries against the men of blood (19-22). Enemies of God, they are enemies of the psalmist. It was his way of liberating himself from false accusations.

This does not "spoil" the Psalm, as some would have it. Intimacy with God was the author's strength. The folly of sinners consists precisely in using darkness as a coverup for their sin, using God's energy to commit sin and run away from God. The more he runs away, the more he encounters God for his own ultimate destruction. Sin means striking God with His own power and gifts. Saint and sinner live on borrowed time and energy.

Christ refined the Old Testament way of prayer by loving the sinner and hating sin, by praying for those who persecuted Him. In this way He sublimates every Psalm, not by abolishing justice, but by exalting love and mercy. Because He loved sinners, He was falsely accused and put to death (Mk. 14:55ff.). The final judgment will bring justice to those hardened in sin, but mercy to the penitent. Meanwhile the good and the bad live side by side, and the sun shines on both. "Vengeance is mine; I will repay, says the Lord" (Rom. 12:19). Christ knew this Psalm (see the Sermon on the Mount).

On Easter the Church uses this Psalm for the Mass entry (Introit). It tells us that He is with us, that He knows His sheep individually (Jn. 10:14, 28f.; also Rev. 2-3). He holds them; He leads them on eternal paths (v. 24). Faith perfects our instincts of perceiving and responding, but we lack the language to express the redemptive presence of Christ, even the creative presence of God. Elevation to adoptive sonship says the most, but it needs this Psalm to make it credible.

Our search for God and the Savior, who knows us so well, will be rewarded by a better knowledge on our part if we pray the Psalm often, especially with the Church on IV Wednesdays (parts at vespers).

Psalm 140 (139)

Deliver me, O LORD, from evil men;
    preserve me from violent men,
²who plan evil things in their heart,
    and stir up wars continually.
³They make their tongue sharp as a serpent's,
    and under their lips is the poison of vipers.

⁴Guard me, O LORD, from the hands of the wicked;
    preserve me from violent men,
    who have planned to trip up my feet.
⁵Arrogant men have hidden a trap for me,
    and with cords they have spread a net,
    by the wayside they have set snares for me.

⁶I say to the LORD, Thou art my God;
    give ear to the voice of my supplications, O LORD!
⁷O LORD, my Lord, my strong deliverer,
    thou hast covered my head in the day of battle,
⁸Grant not, O LORD, the desires of the wicked;
    do not further his evil plot!

⁹Those who surround me lift up their head,
    let the mischief of their lips overwhelm them!
¹⁰Let burning coals fall upon them!
    Let them be cast into pits, no more to rise!
¹¹Let not the slanderer be established in the land;
    let evil hunt down the violent man speedily!

¹²I know that the LORD maintains the cause of the afflicted,
    and executes justice for the needy.
¹³Surely the righteous shall give thanks to thy name;
    the upright shall dwell in thy presence.

For the Evil Day

Reminiscent of many other Psalms, this one stresses the power
of the tongue as a killer and the powerlessness of man against the violent, lying devices of evil-intentioned enemies (e.g. Psalm 64). If they
are human foes, they are instruments of the foreign powers of evil,
invisible forces "of iniquity on high," the "ancient serpent," the "devil."
According to the familiar pattern of slanderous lying and violent hatred,

God's faithful believer adjusts his pattern of self-defense, which is reliance on divine help. This individual petition becomes the prayer of the many who share similar dangers and the same divine trust.

Wicked tongues have a poisonous power of stirring thought to action, violent action. Sins of speech are, like the demons, legion: calumny and slander, duplicity of words, deception, planning snares against the innocent and helpless, flattery and war-mongering. From the heart come evil designs and plots, violence with hand and weapon. In line with the Old Testament piety, the author invokes divine retribution on the opponents: may their planning defeat itself and the fire of Sodom and Gomorrah rain on them (compare Lk. 9:54f., where Jesus set the apostles right on quick punishment).

In the perspective of Jesus Christ, the believer has to reject evil as the Psalmist does, but take the Lord for his "helmet in the day of battle" (Eph. 6:11-18 and 1 Thess. 5:8), praying at all times in the Holy Spirit. The pattern of the Savior is the only way to end evil, by loving the sinner and showering on his head coals of kindness (Rom. 12:20) instead of revenge. Such is the love of Christ, atoning vicarious love. His resurrection is final proof that falsehood will not prevail. His lying enemies and blasphemous foes were finally overwhelmed and defeated, not by His retaliation, but by His dying and rising. His warning to us is not to fear those who kill the body, but Him who can assign both body and soul to hell (Mt. 10:28). Judgment and retribution are for God to carry out, not for us.

The life of the Church matches that of Christ. She constantly faces evil in the world. Sin is the opposite of redemption. Sin is hatred of Christ (Mt. 5:11 and 10:16ff.). The evil spirit does not rest, but incites individuals and nations to ever new hatred, sin and lying. The just will give thanks and abide forever in the Lord's presence and love. They should rejoice in this prospect, as they pray this Psalm with the Church (parts of it, on IV Fridays, at vespers).

Psalm 141 (140)

> I call upon thee, O Lord; make haste to me!
>> Give ear to my voice, when I call to thee!
> [2]Let my prayer be counted as incense before thee,
>> and the lifting up of my hands as an evening sacrifice!

³Set a guard over my mouth, O Lord,
    keep watch over the door of my lips!
⁴Incline not my heart to any evil,
    to busy myself with wicked deeds
  in company with men who work iniquity;
    and let me not eat of their dainties!

⁵Let a good man strike or rebuke me in kindness,
    but let the oil of the wicked never anoint my head;
    for my prayer is continually against their wicked deeds.
⁶When they are given over to those who shall condemn them,
    then they shall learn that the word of the Lord is true.
⁷As a rock which one cleaves and shatters on the land,
    so shall their bones be strewn at the mouth of Sheol.

⁸But my eyes are toward thee, O Lord God;
    in thee I seek refuge; leave me not defenseless!
⁹Keep me from the trap which they have laid for me,
    and from the snares of evildoers!
¹⁰Let the wicked together fall into their own nets,
    while I escape.

Lead Us Out of Temptation

God delivered the faithful person from evil when he lifted up his voice and hands in prayer. Apparently far away from the altar of sacrifice, his prayer was like the sacrificial incense that rose like a cloud heavenward, pleasing and acceptable to God. He was close in spirit to the Temple scene of worship.

His immediate prayer is that God may set a guard at "the door of my lips," lest he join the pagan crowd and go along with their sinful speech. In thought and speech we usually find the beginnings of sin, and the author responds to the divine guidance to resist evil in the very beginning. He knows clearly who are the evildoers and that the dainty banquets are the traps at which "the oil of the wicked" will anoint his head and lead him into wrong involvements. If God or a righteous man corrects him, that is kindness and salutary oil for his head. He accepts such reproof, even if it entails affliction. But evil judges and pagan leaders shall end in ruin (Sheol, the nether world). To be surrounded by them is a constant temptation the faithful man has to resist.

Only the Lord's Word and final judgment will mean salvation and escape from present snares.

These are the occasions of sin: the hospitality of the wicked world, the attraction to follow the crowd, and the appeal of a man's own excessive, dangerous appetites. They tug at his heart, draw him away from God and into traps of sin. Spiritual discernment must be the instrument of our counter-warfare.

The Lord has defined true liberty (Jn. 8:31-36) as freedom from sin and from the evil world that is manipulated by Satan. Our spiritual enemy wants to attach us to his dark world, and that is a trap of death. In his temptation of Christ, Satan offered him the whole world (Mt. 4:8-10) to rob God of worship. There is a further temptation in Jesus' life: to avoid the suffering that the Father had willed in atonement for the sins of the whole world. Even His disciples tried to dissuade Him from "unnecessary" suffering, and Gethsemane is the final struggle. The love of life and the love for the sinner threw Him to the ground in His battle for the will of the Father (Mt. 26:39). He did not pursue justice, but dealt out mercy. In resisting that trap of avoiding death, He freed us from the trap of eternal death (Jn. 12:31-33).

His prayer is to save us from the evil world (Jn. 15:19 and 17:14f.). We naturally love life and the good world, but in Baptism renounced the evil world and its traps. Jesus' prayer still rises like sacrificial incense, and the Father hears Him always (Jn. 11:41f.). At His reenactment of the Sacrifice-Banquet, He unites our prayer with His, as we pray against the devil and all his envoys, "Lead us not into temptation." We also offer this Psalm for help in setting a guard over our lips, "lifting up my hands as an evening sacrifice" in union with the Church (on I Sundays, vespers, vv. 1-9). Prayer rising like incense is a favorite theme in the Church (Rev. 5:8 and 8:4), a symbol of the soul rising to God from the crucible of fire and suffering.

Psalm 142 (141)

> I cry with my voice to the LORD,
>   with my voice I make supplication to the LORD,
> ²I pour out my complaint before him,
>   I tell my trouble before him.
> ³When my spirit is faint,
>   thou knowest my way!

In the path where I walk
    they have hidden a trap for me.
⁴I look to the right and watch,
    but there is none who takes notice of me;
no refuge remains to me,
    no man cares for me.

⁵I cry to thee, O LORD;
    I say, Thou art my refuge,
    my portion in the land of the living.
⁶Give heed to my cry;
    for I am brought very low!

Deliver me from my persecutors;
    for they are too strong for me!
⁷Bring me out of prison,
    that I may give thanks to thy name!
The righteous will surround me;
    for thou wilt deal bountifully with me.

Salvation in the Land of the Living

The just man is "brought very low" in spirit and body. Whether in prison facing a court trial or King David in the cave hunted down like an animal (1 Sam. 22:1ff.), the author's complaint is one of desperate agony. There is no human escape or help in sight for him, no chance for freedom or life, no ray of comfort from anyone; he spends his last energies hoping in the Lord. That is trust, confidence in divine Providence, hope overcoming human obstacles. God will raise him up in this agony of abandonment, and the faith in the living God balances out all his fears. This Psalm resembles Psalm 88.

St. Francis of Assisi died with the last verse on his lips, just as St. Paul counted death as a means of coming to Christ. The same spiritual desolation struck our Lord in the Garden and on the Cross before He entered "the land of the living," paradise. In the face of spiritual enemies, we are all in a hopeless situation unless we cry with our last strength to God. Actually, we are never alone when we trust, as we are in the communion of saints and angels who come to our rescue with God's eternal happiness. The Church gives us this comforting lesson.

Jesus cried with a loud voice in the Garden and on the Cross, "My

God, my God, why hast thou forsaken me?" (Mt. 27:46; Ps. 22:1; Heb. 5:7). His suffering and abandonment match this Psalm perfectly, as He went to the Father (Mt. 26:56), who heard His cry and delivered Him into glory. Just as He was brought low, so was He raised on high (Phil. 2:5-9) to show us the way to "the land of the living."

Today He still cries aloud in His countless poor and suffering members. All around us we hear their voices: prisoners, victims of war and injustice, those who have "hit bottom" of human weakness. Our common humanity should touch off sympathy for them, but especially the compassion of the redeemed in Christ should bring them comfort and the Word about "the land of the living." It is our Christian vocation, our discipleship of Christ, that must urge us forward to take their part, the poor for whom Christ divested Himself of glory in order to enrich them.

The glorified Savior is in our midst to give us hope. We must give hope to others and let the cry of Christ come to them, so that they may live (Jn. 5:25ff.). Faith now leads to glory hereafter. Our praise will lift others up in their hopelessness.

We pray this Psalm with the Church at vespers on I Sundays.

Psalm 143 (142)

Hear my prayer, O Lord; give ear to my supplications!
  In thy faithfulness answer me, in thy righteousness!
²Enter not into judgment with thy servant;
  for no man living is righteous before thee.

³For the enemy has pursued me;
  he has crushed my life to the ground;
  he has made me sit in darkness like those long dead.
⁴Therefore my spirit faints within me;
  my heart within me is appalled.

⁵I remember the days of old,
  I meditate on all that thou hast done;
  I muse on what thy hands have wrought.
⁶I stretch out my hands to thee;
  my soul thirsts for thee like a parched land.

⁷Make haste to answer me, O Lord!
　　My spirit fails!
Hide not thy face from me,
　　lest I be like those who go down to the Pit.
⁸Let me hear in the morning of thy steadfast love,
　　for in thee I put my trust.
Teach me the way I should go,
　　for to thee I lift up my soul.

⁹Deliver me, O Lord, from my enemies!
　　I have fled to thee for refuge!
¹⁰Teach me to do thy will,
　　for thou art my God!
Let thy good spirit lead me
　　on a level path!

¹¹For thy name's sake, O Lord, preserve my life!
　　In thy righteousness bring me out of trouble!
¹²And in thy steadfast love cut off my enemies,
　　and destroy all my adversaries,
　　for I am thy servant.

Darkness Without God

Penitential in character, this Psalm describes the condition of the believer who has fallen on evil days. Although crushed by human foes, the Psalmist has also incurred the enmity of God. "My soul thirsts for thee like a parched land" (v. 6), and he is seeking the face of God anew. "Enter not into judgment with thy servant" (v. 2) and "Teach me to do thy will, for thou art my God" point to more than physical affliction. The author humbly expects the gift of mercy and divine light because life without God is dark, and service of God means letting "thy good spirit lead me" (v. 10).

Couched in earthly images, the Psalm depicts the effects of sin, which leaves the sinner exposed to the enemies of God and of his own salvation. Not knowing his way, he fears the judgment of God, and his soul is like fruitless, parched land (see also Psalm 63). Light and life come from God's beneficent face. All is darkness without it. The character of this Psalm is to increase longing for God, and longing is aspiring love. Even the memory of God's past generosity and the neglected favors helps the penitent soul.

The author is insistent with his plea. He needs the guiding hand of God in order to lift up his spirits and walk straight in the ways of the Lord. The even path is the divine way of righteous living, doing God's will. In line with Old Testament spirituality, this includes separation from the enemy and his ways, all for the glory of God and His Name. And the more the converted believer perceives the light, the more impatient he becomes for the morning's dawn. Breaking away from sin is daybreak for the sinner. The penitent now moves in the power of God and the new spirit.

Jesus lived this Psalm vicariously, Himself without sin, yet He suffered for sinners and a sinful world (see also Psalms 22 and 88). During His suffering He prayed for us. Our sin threw Him into great darkness. Fidelity to the Father was His only light. He willed not the death of the sinner but that he be converted. The morning brought the dawn of a new day, the resurrection, and He holds out a share in it for us. In Baptism we rise to the new life, the daybreak of salvation, the straight, level path (Jn. 14:6).

The night is past; the day is here (Rom. 13:12). With arms outstretched, we pray for victory over the spiritual forces of wickedness, never for the personal ruin of our enemies. Mark how Jesus taught this lesson to His disciples, when the "sons of thunder" wanted to call down "fire from heaven" on the Samaritans (Lk. 9:52-55). If we walk with Christ, we walk in His Spirit (Gal. 5:16ff.). The Church prays our Psalm in the Spirit of Christ on Good Friday and Holy Saturday (vespers), on IV Thursdays (lauds), and Tuesdays (compline), omitting the final verse, lest people think of personal enemies.

Psalm 144 (143)

Blessed be the LORD, my rock,
who trains my hands for war,
    and my fingers for battle;
²my rock and my fortress,
    my stronghold and my deliverer,
my shield and he in whom I take refuge,
    who subdues the peoples under him.

³O Lord, what is man that thou dost regard him,
    or the son of man that thou dost think of him?
⁴Man is like a breath,
    his days are like a passing shadow.

⁵Bow thy heavens, O Lord, and come down!
    Touch the mountains that they smoke!
⁶Flash forth the lightning and scatter them,
    send out thy arrows and rout them!
⁷Stretch forth thy hand from on high,
    rescue me and deliver me from the many waters,
    from the hand of aliens,
⁸whose mouths speak lies,
    and whose right hand is a right hand of falsehood.

⁹I will sing a new song to thee, O God;
    upon a ten-stringed harp I will play to thee,
¹⁰who givest victory to kings,
    who rescuest David thy servant.
¹¹Rescue me from the cruel sword,
    and deliver me from the hand of aliens,
  whose mouths speak lies,
    and whose right hand is a right hand of falsehood.

¹²May our sons in their youth
    be like plants full grown,
  our daughters like corner pillars
    cut for the structure of a palace;
¹³may our garners be full,
    providing all manner of store;
  may our sheep bring forth thousands
    and ten thousands in our fields;
¹⁴may our cattle be heavy with young,
    suffering no mischance or failure in bearing;
  may there be no cry of distress in our streets!
¹⁵Happy the people to whom such blessings fall!
    Happy the people whose God is the Lord!

God Gives Victory

While God is a God of peace and not of war (see Ps. 46:9), He
destined Israel to conquer the promised land by force. Many times
He led their armies to victory against great odds to establish David's

kingdom of truth and justice, to punish nations for their wickedness, and to inspire faith in His revelation. The author of verses 1-11 may be David, whose schooling in warfare was protecting his flocks, the same that helped him to slay the giant Goliath with a slingshot. Trust in God was more effective than the sword. Israel was great in trusting God, not in stockpiling armaments.

If God has singled out a home for His chosen ones—a thing wonderful to contemplate—then no one will stand in His way and plan. What is man that God should single him out? A mere breath and passing shadow. The show of divine power increases the humility of man, as on Sinai. God's warfare also leads to praise, as the author takes his harp to "sing a new song to thee, O God." The fruit of God's battle is peace and praise.

With verse 12 we have a break in thought, a song of blessings in peace resulting from God's victory. The preceding verses repeat a theme from other Psalms, like 18. Prosperity and peace are the fruits of the Lord's warfare, gifts for doing His will. Strong youth, beautiful daughters, full granaries, abundant flocks, security and "no cry of distress in our streets" are all earthly benefits that God bestowed to train His people in His ways of faith and trust. They are a picture of greater riches to come.

The Psalm, if "it speaks of Christ" and His Church, holds out a richer yield for the new Kingdom. Jesus Christ, Son of God and Son of Mary, did spiritual battle against sin and Satan. God trained His hand for warfare, and it was the upraised hand of blessing (Lk. 24:50f.). Why this condescension of God in the incarnation? "What is man that thou dost regard him, or the son of man that thou dost think of him?" We stand without answer before this mystery of love and mercy. Man is created in God's image, and God always loves us first, always devises new victories of love. God blesses those who trust in Him, and we pray this Psalm in praise of messianic blessings and in no way for the craze for weapons and the commercials of prosperity.

Fruitful warfare is described in Eph. 6:11ff. for those who remain on the vine of Christ (Jn. 15:1ff.). The strength and beauty of youth and maidens is all spiritual. Christ educates them for victory by readying them in divine trust. The kingdom of David lives on (2 Sam. 7:16f.) in the Church, where we have plentiful redemption in Christ. We celebrate this great Psalm in worship when we pray it on IV Tuesdays (lauds, vv. 1-10) and on IV Thursdays (vespers, whole Psalm). "Happy the people whose God is the Lord!"

Psalm 145 (144)

I will extol thee, my God and King,
    and bless thy name for ever and ever.
²Every day I will bless thee,
    and praise thy name for ever and ever.
³Great is the LORD, and greatly to be praised,
    and his greatness is unsearchable.

⁴One generation shall laud thy works to another,
    and shall declare thy mighty acts.
⁵On the glorious splendor of thy majesty,
    and on thy wondrous works, I will meditate.
⁶Men shall proclaim the might of thy terrible acts,
    and I will declare thy greatness.
⁷They shall pour forth the fame of thy abundant goodness,
    and shall sing aloud of thy righteousness.

⁸The LORD is gracious and merciful,
    slow to anger and abounding in steadfast love.
⁹The LORD is good to all,
    and his compassion is over all that he has made.

¹⁰All thy works shall give thanks to thee, O LORD,
    and all thy saints shall bless thee!
¹¹They shall speak of the glory of thy kingdom,
    and tell of thy power,
¹²to make known to the sons of men thy mighty deeds,
    and the glorious splendor of thy kingdom.
¹³Thy kingdom is an everlasting kingdom,
    and thy dominion endures throughout all generations.

The LORD is faithful in all his words,
    and gracious in all his deeds.
¹⁴The LORD upholds all who are falling,
    and raises up all who are bowed down.
¹⁵The eyes of all look to thee,
    and thou givest them their food in due season.
¹⁶Thou openest thy hand,
    thou satisfiest the desire of every living thing.

¹⁷The Lord is just in all his ways,
  and kind in all his doings.
¹⁸The Lord is near to all who call upon him,
  to all who call upon him in truth.
¹⁹He fulfils the desire of all who fear him,
  he also hears their cry, and saves them.
²⁰The Lord preserves all who love him;
  but all the wicked he will destroy.

²¹My mouth will speak the praise of the Lord,
  and let all flesh bless his holy name for ever and ever.

Fullness of Praise

As a summary of praise, this Psalm will warm the hearts of all who
seek God in their deepening efforts to contemplate His perfections
and works. His deeds reflect the greatness of His Name and Nature.
His interventions in history, which climax in the incarnation, elicit
the fervent song of the Psalmist, who strives to enlist the whole human
family ("all flesh") in the sublimest of all human activities, loving
praise! As an alphabetic song (each verse starts with a new letter of
the alphabet), it gathers themes and phrases from other Psalms and
books of the Bible. We expect this from a prayer that extols God's greatness and Kingship.

Extolling the divine wonders will occupy us from generation to
generation into eternity where we will begin anew to spend ourselves
in this growing adventure. If God's works stagger us now, then the
future age will be inexhaustible. Even now we are blinded by His
glory and majesty, His justice and power. What attracts us most in our
present humble state is His mercy and goodness, His compassion with
fallen sinners, and His Providence over all. We need a Friend like this
who is all loyal, royal Love.

Praise leads to more praise. Our Psalm contains the old meal
prayer, "The eyes of all look to thee . . . ," to God who sustains what
He has created. He feeds His creature of the highest praise with the
greatest Food, the Eucharist. He wants His faithful ones to hunger
for Him ever more, for more praise and for the heavenly Banquet,
in order to prepare for the heavenly enjoyment of banqueting in the
Kingdom. This suggests the way in which our Savior completed the
first meaning of this Psalm.

He spent Himself praising the Father and doing good. His mission was to praise and teach us to praise (Eph. 1:3-14) and to reveal the inner life of the holy Trinity to man (Mt. 11:25-27). In Christ we learn the sublimity of our vocation to bless His Name. Those with better insight take a vow ever to praise God. Because of our sharing in the royalty of Christ (1 Pet. 2:9), a royalty which makes paupers out of human kings, we reenact the Lord's praise in the Church, proclaiming His power and goodness and mercy. All this we do in faith, for the things of faith are more real than those of the senses.

All must honor the Son, "For in him all the fulness of God was pleased to dwell" (Col. 1:19), even as all must honor the Father (Jn. 5:23). At the Name of Jesus, every knee must bend (Phil. 2:10f.). Jesus accepts this royal divine praise, even as He did in His lifetime. He opens His hand to feed His flock, as in the days when He made His royal claim (Jn. 6). Let us beg for the gift of praise (Mt. 21:22 and Jn. 14:13f.), so that more sheep may come to know their Shepherd. In the heavenly sheepfold, the Shepherd becomes the Lamb worthy of all praise, adoration, and blessing (Rev. 5:6-12). The Church uses this Psalm on Saturdays after Easter (office of readings), the feast of Christ the King (vespers), III Sundays (office of readings), and IV Fridays (vespers). It should also be a favorite Psalm for personal meditation and prayer.

Psalm 146 (145)

Praise the Lord!
Praise the Lord, O my soul!
²I will praise the Lord as long as I live;
I will sing praises to my God while I have being.

³Put not your trust in princes,
in a son of man, in whom there is no help.
⁴When his breath departs he returns to his earth;
on that very day his plans perish.

⁵Happy is he whose help is the God of Jacob,
  whose hope is in the LORD his God,
⁶who made heaven and earth,
  the sea, and all that is in them;
  who keeps faith for ever;
⁷   who executes justice for the oppressed;
  who gives food to the hungry.

The LORD sets the prisoners free;
⁸   the LORD opens the eyes of the blind.
The LORD lifts up those who are bowed down;
  the LORD loves the righteous.
⁹The LORD watches over the sojourners,
  he upholds the widow and the fatherless;
  but the way of the wicked he brings to ruin.

¹⁰The LORD will reign for ever,
  thy God, O Zion, to all generations.
Praise the LORD!

Blessed Trust in God

After the initial *Alleluia* and words of praise, this Psalm is all about
trust, true and false. False trust is dependence on man, who is powerless to save, even persons in power like princes. The futility of such
reliance comes from innate human fragility and perishability. In comparison with the power of God, the folly of trust in man is self-evident.
The infinite Creator is also the Savior, who helps all who are in need
and bowed down with affliction. Faith in God is the guarantee of peace
and trust.

The God of Jacob is the God of revelation, whose fidelity was
tried over many centuries. No other nation had a God like that, of justice and kindness, One who cared for the oppressed, the captives, the
blind, strangers who had no rights, the orphan and widow. Because
of Him Israel's laws of social justice and hospitality ranked above
those of pagan neighbor nations. The condition for help was always
simple: doing His will, believing in Him. The way of the wicked He
frustrated. Hope is the sustaining power of Israel.

Trust in God is a form of praise, something we need every day.
The Psalm was used as a Jewish morning prayer, and rightly so. Trust
in God is just as necessary today as in the Old Law. Christ taught us

the way. With faith more spiritual and less dependent on temporal success, our motives must be pure. Christ Himself is the Way of loving trust. All human dependence dropped out of His life. All props of security that people rely on, like power, wealth, pleasure, and friends, are out of His picture. By word and example, He advanced His promises and revelation. And His promises have all come true (except for His second glorious Coming).

Jesus was all heart for the sick, the lame, the blind, the helpless. He cured all who had faith and trust. He wanted His miracles to strengthen hope in forgiveness of sin. He had nowhere to lay His head. Mark His sympathy for a grieving widow (Lk. 7:11ff.), for the man born blind (Jn. 9:1ff.), or for the woman who was literally "bowed down" (Lk. 13:10ff.). Our confidence and trust in Christ is essentially the same as the Psalmist's.

When we lean on human props, they defeat themselves. Constantly the Church's voice urges us and proclaims to the community of believers and worshippers true reasons for trust. In the Holy Spirit of Christ we exercise the gift of fortitude, as we put our total confidence in Christ. The infant Church was strong in trust and therefore also in new miracles (e.g. Acts 4:8ff.). Peter and John boldly told the council that they must listen to God rather than to man (Acts 4:19). It cost them persecution and suffering (2 Cor. 6:4-10), but hope was alive. And we have inherited that hope and trust. We proclaim this Psalm in the liturgy of prayer on the feast of the Sacred Heart (vespers), on IV Wednesdays (lauds), in the commons of pastors and holy men (vespers), and in the office for the departed (lauds).

Psalm 147 (146-147)

Praise the LORD!
    For it is good to sing praises to our God;
    for he is gracious, and a song of praise is seemly.
²The LORD builds up Jerusalem;
    he gathers the outcasts of Israel.
³He heals the brokenhearted,
    and binds up their wounds.

⁴He determines the number of the stars,
    he gives to all of them their names.
⁵Great is our Lord, and abundant in power;
    his understanding is beyond measure.
⁶The Lord lifts up the downtrodden,
    he casts the wicked to the ground.

⁷Sing to the Lord with thanksgiving;
    make melody to our God upon the lyre!
⁸He covers the heavens with clouds,
    he prepares rain for the earth,
    he makes grass grow upon the hills.
⁹He gives to the beasts their food,
    and to the young ravens which cry.
¹⁰His delight is not in the strength of the horse,
    nor his pleasure in the legs of a man;
¹¹but the Lord takes pleasure in those who fear him,
    in those who hope in his steadfast love.

* * *

¹²Praise the Lord, O Jerusalem!
    Praise your God, O Zion!
¹³For he strengthens the bars of your gates;
    he blesses your sons within you.
¹⁴He makes peace in your borders;
    he fills you with the finest of the wheat.
¹⁵He sends forth his command to the earth;
    his word runs swiftly.
¹⁶He gives snow like wool;
    he scatters hoarfrost like ashes.
¹⁷He casts forth his ice like morsels;
    who can stand before his cold?
¹⁸He sends forth his word, and melts them;
    he makes his wind blow, and the waters flow.
¹⁹He declares his word to Jacob,
    his statutes and ordinances to Israel.
²⁰He has not dealt thus with any other nation;
    they do not know his ordinances.
Praise the Lord!

God's Bounty Seen in Faith

To express the meaning of this Psalm is to capture the spirit of the whole Old Testament, so rich yet so simple. Its themes occur elsewhere, like God's concern for the lowly and His kindness to those who love Him. Our comments will cover both Psalms, which in Hebrew are one with three parts (vv. 1-6, 7-11, 12-20), each starting with praise for God's goodness and power. The overall title is *Alleluia*, the call to praise.

It is a peace-time Psalm, soothing balm to the dispersed and injured, a blessing to those who fear God, new courage to all who face obstacles. The brokenhearted can trust anew; their needs are minimal to the God who names and numbers the stars. Restoring Jerusalem means restoring the whole nation. God's wisdom is sufficient reason for all who cannot see the reason for suffering. Just as God gathered His people and rebuilt Jerusalem, so He enlivens the individual believer. Everyone must read His signs.

Seeing with God's eyes is wisdom. The laws of nature still hold, but things are different when men of faith view the sky, watch things grow as food on the earth. Faith sees the strength of the steed and fleetness of man as God's gifts, not reasons for human boasting. All things that serve man must increase the praise of the bountiful Maker. The Lord of Zion is the Lord of nature. He who hears the awkward cry of the young raven is the one who makes Jerusalem strong. God's Word is a living power of love.

"His word runs swiftly." The bars of the gates, the blessing of children, the best of wheat are all His command. No sooner spoken than done! Snow, frost, hail and cold are His doing and undoing. The warm, melting winds follow His Word. The universe holds itself just where and as He wills. Science is far behind trying to catch up to His wisdom.

The same divine Word came to Jacob (Israel), His chosen ones by a special revelation. No other nation knew His Name. The light and the Word grew, waxed stronger, till the full Light appeared in the Sun of Justice at the incarnation of the Son of God (Jn. 1:14). God's Word became man and spoke to us, "spirit and life" (Jn. 6:63). The light of the Psalms also comes from Christ. He was "conceived" in them before He was conceived in the Virgin-Mother, by the same Holy Spirit. "You search the scriptures . . . , yet you refuse to come to me that you may have life" (Jn. 5:39f.).

The Word that shapes and guides all resources is the Word that reconstructed man in the salvation of Christ. The Spirit of love that feeds the birds (Mt. 6:26) also melts the frozen hearts of sinners and feeds them with the finest Wheat. Part 3 (12-20) fits the New Zion, the Church, perfectly. He who gathered the scattered and lost sheep (Jn. 11:51f. and Lk. 15:3ff.) calls each by name (Jn. 10:3) and invites them to praise.

After suffering, the Church renews herself in the normalcy of a happy, bounteous life, in using this Psalm (in part, usually at vespers) on Pentecost, Christmas, Corpus Christi, Good Friday (lauds), Trinity Sunday, Holy Cross (September 14), the Annunciation, All Saints, dedication of a church, commons of the Blessed Virgin, apostles, virgins and holy women, II and IV Fridays (noon, lauds), and IV Thursdays (lauds). Hearts who love God for His sake sing together, as it opens up new depths of God's goodness and graciousness.

Psalm 148

Praise the Lord!
Praise the Lord from the heavens,
praise him in the heights!
²Praise him, all his angels,
praise him, all his host!

³Praise him, sun and moon,
praise him, all you shining stars!
⁴Praise him, you highest heavens,
and you waters above the heavens!

⁵Let them praise the name of the Lord!
For he commanded and they were created.
⁶And he established them for ever and ever;
he fixed their bounds which cannot be passed.

⁷Praise the Lord from the earth,
you sea monsters and all deeps,
⁸fire and hail, snow and frost,
stormy wind fulfilling his command!

⁹Mountains and all hills,
   fruit trees and all cedars!
¹⁰Beasts and all cattle,
   creeping things and flying birds!

¹¹Kings of the earth and all peoples,
   princes and all rulers of the earth!
¹²Young men and maidens together,
   old men and children!

¹³Let them praise the name of the LORD,
   for his name alone is exalted;
   his glory is above earth and heaven.
¹⁴He has raised up a horn for his people,
   praise for all his saints,
   for the people of Israel who are near to him.
Praise the LORD!

Universal Command of Praise

All created things have voices and *Alleluia* is their song. In Genesis (1:26) God gave man dominion over visible creation to use things for His glory and man's benefit. Now the voice of the Psalmist goes further to enlist even the heavens and angels in the great symphony of praise to the Creator. Man, in the person of the Psalmist, occupies a key position in the universe with a responsibility to love and to engage all creatures in their order in praising with the voice God has given them. Here the two worlds, celestial and terrestrial, are one and man is their uniting link.

From this vision of faith flows the practical task. It was an ancient concept of created reality that dominates also this Psalm, an order known to the old pagan Egyptians and Babylonians. But the God of Israel lived beyond space and place. Modern man could perfect the list with his vast scientific insight, but it would not change the religious implications. Science cannot discover empirically the dwelling place of God. And it does not matter. He who by His Word created all things (Psalm 147) is beyond all of them, but still imposes on them a duty which shall not pass away. Even the nether world, about which we know so little, is not exempt from joining the chorus.

The wondrous God of a wonderful world outdoes Himself in the work of salvation to mankind, to Israel of old and now the New Israel, the People of God. Those who know His Name and revelation are living in faith and have a new insight into His majesty and love. They are the "people who are near to him" and have power to command praise, even to engage the heavenly hosts in the general voice of praise for His work of salvation.

The angels of heaven broke through and intoned the *Gloria* on earth when Christ was born (Lk. 2:13f.). Christ was the man who was also God and gave this Psalm an entirely new meaning. He took possession again of strayed humanity and brought it back once more to the key role of praise, to pick up the lost thread (see especially Rom. 8: 19-21). He laid down His life to restore the order of praise (Phil. 2:10f.) and to discover Christ in the Psalms (Lk. 24:44ff.). If we know the Psalms, we recognize His voice. He gathers in our praise (Col. 1:15-18). He triumphed over the nether world (Col. 2:15). In the Church He continues His work (Eph. 3:10f.; also 1:3ff.). It includes gathering the pagan voices, who will enrich the whole symphony (Rom. 15:8-12). In the light of this Psalm, He preached the Sermon on the Mount (Mt. 6:28ff.). He expects us not merely to answer "Present!" in the general roll call, but to extend ourselves and realize total, universal praise. Only then can we expect to share in the new creation of Rev. 21 and hear "every creature in heaven and on earth and under the earth" (Rev. 5:13) joining "the people who are near to him" praising the Lord! We join the living Voice of the Church in this Psalm on III Sundays, at lauds.

Psalm 149

> Praise the Lord!
>> Sing to the Lord a new song,
>> his praise in the assembly of the faithful!
> ²Let Israel be glad in his Maker,
>> let the sons of Zion rejoice in their King!
> ³Let them praise his name with dancing,
>> making melody to him with timbrel and lyre!
> ⁴For the Lord takes pleasure in his people;
>> he adorns the humble with victory.

⁵Let the faithful exult in glory;
    let them sing for joy on their couches.
⁶Let the high praises of God be in their throats
    and two-edged swords in their hands,
⁷to wreak vengeance on the nations
    and chastisement on the peoples,
⁸to bind their kings with chains
    and their nobles with fetters of iron,
⁹to execute on them the judgment written!
    This is glory for all his faithful ones.
Praise the Lord!

The Price of Praise

In this *Alleluia* Psalm, praise and warfare stand side by side. It reminds us of Neh. 4:6-17, when the people rebuilt their city walls and gates with one hand and fought off the enemy with a sword in the other. At one and the same time they sang with dancing, while they warded off the foe in battle. They celebrated God as King and Creator in festive cult, when simultaneously they took vengeance on earthly enemies according to God's decree. A common faith and purpose knit the assembly of Israel together. Their purpose was to make sacrificial praise possible for all in a strong, peaceful city. The situation has not changed.

All things serve to vindicate God as Lord and Master. He loved and protected His people, and they in turn responded with their total allegiance and service. Prayer and work, battle and suffering, were all one. Day and night echoed the same new song of praise. In the prophet Ezekiel, God promised vengeance on those who opposed the chosen nation (25:13ff.), so they could rest in joy on their couches. Such was God's verdict and reward for those who combined joyful song with courageous action for the Lord.

We are interested in the literal meaning of the Psalms insofar as this serves to describe Christ and His Kingdom. We seek seriously and enter the action of the Psalms in order to find Christ and His world. This Psalm invites us to "Sing to the Lord a new song," and we do so for Christ, the Lord. Every day of our lives we have reason for new song in His holy Assembly. And we go beyond the literal sword and battle and vengeance to celebrate our victory in Christ. His life was a battle, but a spiritual one, more fierce than any warfare, against the ancient enemy of mankind and God.

Swords are turned into ploughshares as we fight evil with goodness. Now it is true that the two-edged sword of justice is the "sword
of the Spirit" (Eph. 6:17), and the "sword of God" is His Word (Heb.
4:12). In this Psalm as in so many others, we are engaged in the Lord's
spiritual battle, which is constant. As we cast our anxieties on the Lord
(1 Pet. 5:7ff.), we are at peace and sing on our couches. Christ promised
to be always with His Church and members, because the praise and
warfare are continuous (Rom. 8:36 and Mt. 28:20). The heroes of glory
are the martyrs of His Kingdom, who sing untiringly the new canticle
of immortality. We sing it in the Church on I Sundays (at noon).

Psalm 150

> Praise the Lord!
> > Praise God in his sanctuary;
> > praise him in his mighty firmament!
> [2]Praise him for his mighty deeds;
> > praise him according to his exceeding greatness!
>
> [3]Praise him with trumpet sound;
> > praise him with lute and harp!
> [4]Praise him with timbrel and dance;
> > praise him with strings and pipe!
> [5]Praise him with sounding cymbals;
> > praise him with loud clashing cymbals!
> [6]Let everything that breathes praise the Lord!
> Praise the Lord!

Alleluia Amen!

The final word is praise! The conclusion to the whole Psalter is
another appeal for all-out praise of God and His deeds. Giving glory
to Him gives unison and harmony to all that has spirit and voice. Ten
times does the *Alleluia* of love resound in this Psalm. It is a fitting summary of all, and it means doing the best thing in the best way, with
all possible talent of music, voice, and instrument. When man puts
his best talents to work in a high human and cultural performance of
this duty, he is loving God with all his heart and strength. Spiritual
culture, like good music, makes for good worship of the Creator and
Savior.

What seems to be the end becomes a new beginning. Just as the *Amen* continues in heaven, so does the *Alleluia*. Referring to the *Amen* as the end of things is a kind of human insight without faith, for faith sees the *Amen* as the new beginning, in creation and in re-creation by Jesus Christ, whose very Name is *Amen* (Rev. 3:14). The Psalmist invites all living creatures to join the Assembly in never-ending praise.

When we think that we have mastered the art of praise, we can begin over again. The origin of praise is not man's sole effort, but a gift of the Holy Spirit of Christ, who leads us "from glory to glory." In heaven it will not be a "duty," but a mystic encounter with the Blessed Trinity, never ceasing in its ever more profound experience of God. The work of Christ in His chosen assembly (Heb. 2:12) is more than the spirit of man can fathom. Now we speak to each other in songs and Psalms to prepare ourselves for this community action and final consummation (Eph. 5:19f.).

The elders of heaven teach the juniors of earth by falling down and worshipping God with *Amen* and *Alleluia!* There are also elders on earth, the bishops of the Church, who guide the prayer-tradition for us. Mother Church leads us by the hand when she uses the Psalms. It is for us to surrender ourselves to their message, which is union with God in our daily affairs, our worries and sufferings and our joys. The Psalms are sacramentals of divine fulness, which have the power to raise us up and sustain us on high, always in Christ.

The Church prays this Psalm on Holy Saturday, on II and IV Sundays, and in the liturgy for the departed, always at lauds.

The *Magnificat*

"My soul magnifies the Lord,
and my spirit rejoices in God my Savior,
for he has regarded the low estate of his handmaiden.
For behold, henceforth all generations will call me blessed;
for he who is mighty has done great things for me,
and holy is his name.
And his mercy is on those who fear him
from generation to generation.
He has shown strength with his arm,
he has scattered the proud in the imagination of their hearts,
he has put down the mighty from their thrones,
and exalted those of low degree;

> he has filled the hungry with good things,
> and the rich he has sent empty away.
> He has helped his servant Israel,
> in remembrance of his mercy,
> as he spoke to our fathers,
> to Abraham and to his posterity for ever."
>
> (Lk. 1:46-55)

Blessed Among Women

This perfect Psalm and "precious canticle" (Luther) is Mary's response to the incarnation, written down probably by Zachary after the visitation. It mirrors the simple humility of the Mother of God and her unparalleled holiness. Following the greeting of Elizabeth, who hailed her as the Ark of the indwelling Lord, the infant John the Baptist leaped for joy in his mother's womb. Mary revealed her soul in this song, which captures the spirit of all the Psalms, resembles Hannah's canticle (1 Sam. 2:1-10) and welcomes Christ, the fulfillment of the Old Testament Psalms.

We know the authoress and the occasion. Coming from her who abounded in the wisdom of the Holy Spirit, this song was long in preparation. God prepared her immaculate holiness, her precocious wisdom in the will to virginity and her readiness to accept God's will in faith. Fittingly, she received first the revelation of the holy Trinity (Lk. 1:35). Her infinite delicacy and beauty was of the Holy Spirit, who made her the Daughter in faith of her Son, before she became His Mother (Dante). The greater the gifts, the deeper the humility. The divine Motherhood is the greatest gift to mankind and makes all subsequent salvation possible.

Mary lived in faith. "Blessed is she who believed" (Lk. 1:45). Therefore, "All generations will call me blessed." We would expect her to refer to the incarnation, and she does. "He who is mighty has done great things for me" says it all. God did not leave her ignorant of His plan. God has shown mercy "to Abraham and to his posterity for ever." She received more than just "some inkling" and was more than an unwitting instrument. She praises the Almighty for scattering the proud and mighty, for exalting the lowly and poor. Her words embody the expectations of all the poor of God.

God is almighty, holy, merciful, the God of Old Testament piety. Mary's first thought is of Him, whom she praises for His own sake, for His promises and works, His truth and fidelity. Christ praised her as one of those "who hear the word of God and keep it" (Lk. 11:27f.). St. Luke is the evangelist of Mary. She, who offered hospitality to God as her Son, contemplated all He said and did in her motherly heart (Lk. 2:19). It does not surprise us that her prayer contains judgment and retribution for God's enemies, as she echoes the will of God fully. In her the hour of God has struck.

Christ came to her, as He comes to us. Our lives will echo her *Magnificat* if we join all generations in blessing her faith and glory. As we acknowledge God's great gifts to us, this song becomes the masterpiece of our Psalmody. Like her, we must become "the harp of the Holy Spirit" first. She became the new Eve, becoming the Mother of all mankind, of the redeemed (Jn. 19:27). She is there for Christ and for us, as we climax vespers daily with the greatest act of devotion to her, incensing the Altar during her *Magnificat*. The Altar is Christ in consecrated symbolism. Christian tradition has ever regarded Mary as the type of the Church. As we surround the Altar in the sight of God and the angels, our song rises like the sweet incense of prayer, in her words, "Holy is his Name."

The *Benedictus*

"Blessed be the Lord God of Israel,
for he has visited and redeemed his people,
and has raised up a horn of salvation for us
in the house of his servant David,
as he spoke by the mouth of his holy prophets from of old,
that we should be saved from our enemies,
and from the hand of all who hate us;
to perform the mercy promised to our fathers,
and to remember his holy covenant,
the oath which he swore to our father Abraham, to grant us
that we, being delivered from the hand of our enemies,
might serve him without fear,
in holiness and righteousness before him all the days of our life.
And you, child, will be called the prophet of the Most High;
for you will go before the Lord to prepare his ways,
to give knowledge of salvation to his people
in the forgiveness of their sins,

through the tender mercy of our God,
when the day shall dawn upon us from on high
to give light to those who sit in darkness and in the shadow
    of death,
to guide our feet into the way of peace."

(Lk. 1:68-79)

The Benedictus: The Dawn From on High

In the morning of the new Day of salvation, the priest Zechariah, "filled with the Holy Spirit," sang this canticle of high praise. The infant John had just brought joy to him and Elizabeth late in their lives. In the presence of the Mother of God and a circle of relatives and friends they celebrated the dawn of redemption, which terminated the long, long waiting and preparation we call the Old Testament. Many a generation of Jews lived and died in the hope that was now realized. God was faithful to His promises in a wonderful way, one that called forth another great Psalm, as it brought Mary's *Magnificat* from her holy heart.

Jesus is the "mighty savior" and John the Baptist was His forerunner. The *Benedictus* is prophetic. In its literal meaning it welcomes "the horn of salvation" (the strong Messiah). He clearly foretells that John will prepare the way of the Lord, and He also reveals that the work of salvation consists in God's compassionate forgiveness of sins. What the prophets and writers of old had spoken was the same as God had sworn in oath to Abraham: freedom from their powerful, transcendent enemies: sin, Satan, and death. Such is the joyous dawn that suddenly broke after the long night of darkness.

The whole story is told in Lk. 1:39-80. We presume that Zechariah, well versed in the law and Old Testament, recorded this canticle as well as Mary's *Magnificat*. This chapter stands off from Luke's Greek style with a strongly Semitic quality. From doubt and dumbness, Zechariah's tongue became loose and eloquent for the Son who had come into the world to enlighten every man (Jn. 1:9). Jesus called Himself the Light of the world (Jn. 8:12). Whosoever walks in the light of Christ is redeemed from darkness and from the "hand of all who hate us," the enemy who operates in darkness. This canticle is altogether fitting as a morning prayer. The Church uses it daily at early lauds, and she makes God's intervention two thousand years ago contemporary and present to us.

God is "visiting" us daily in the liturgical renewal, in the eucharistic Sign and its surrounding prayer of the Church, where the total redemption becomes present reality. At that "hour" this messianic song of welcome climaxes each morning prayer, as we stand in joyful expectation of His second Coming, another hailing of His final Coming. He now stands at the door and knocks (Rev. 3:20). We stand on tiptoe as we await Christ's breakthrough, now in the sacramental Signs and Psalmody, then in His glorious Coming. If we appreciate this canticle, we must be up and giving "knowledge of salvation to his people." As we become forerunners of His second Coming, we sound the horn and become God's prophets and instruments of light, joy, and salvation to the rest of humanity. Two-thirds of the race still sit "in darkness and in the shadow of death," awaiting the message of this song.

Nunc Dimittis

"Lord, now lettest thou thy servant depart in peace,
according to thy word;
For mine eyes have seen thy salvation
which thou hast prepared in the presence of all peoples,
A light for revelation to the Gentiles,
and for glory to thy people Israel."

(Lk. 2:29-32)

Welcoming Christ

Here the aged Simeon chants his final praise to God as he holds in his venerable hands the Christ child, presented by His Mother and St. Joseph. In the Temple, in the presence of God's people, he stands in humble gratitude that he received this singular grace to see with his bodily eyes and with faith, to hold in his very hands, the Messiah, the fulfillment of all ancient hopes.

Not only is Christ Jesus the glory of His people Israel, but He is the light revealed to the Gentiles, to us. Used by the Church as an evening prayer (compline) and for the departed (lauds), this canticle represents all the Psalms in their fulfillment ("mine eyes have seen . . ."). We stand in the Temple of God, embracing the glorified, real, personal Lord as we chant the divine praises.

Suggested Psalms for Various Occasions

The Psalms are relevant, in whole or in part, for many other intentions, seasons, and feasts (*see* the official Liturgy of the Hours).

Thanksgiving and praise
Psalms 8, 9, 16, 18, 19, 21, 28, 30, 34, 40, 45, 47, 48, 65, 66, 92, 93, 96–100, 103–105, 111, 113, 115, 116, 117, 118, 136, 138, 143, 145–150

Petition
Psalms 70, 86, 88, 101, 104, 120, 122, 130, 143, 145

Blessings on marriage, the home, children
Psalms 33, 34, 45, 80, 103, 112, 121, 123, 126, 127, 128, 133, 145, 148

For the missions, catechetics
Psalms 19, 22(vv. 22ff.), 67, 96, 98, 117, 119

For the night
Psalms 3, 4, 91, 134

Penitential
Psalms 6, 25, 32, 38, 51, 102, 103; thanks for forgiveness: 130, 143

Perseverance, strength
Psalms 25, 27, 34, 42–43, 63, 66, 89, 119, 125, 126

For the poor and helpless
Psalms 8, 22, 35, 44, 59, 72, 88, 90, 107, 112, 113, 134, 140, 145

For the homeless, exiles, prisoners, displaced persons
Psalms 2, 3, 17, 19, 27, 57, 102, 107, 121, 123, 124; victims of corruption: 14, 43

For rain, crops, weather
Psalms 65, 67, 85, 104, 144; in famine: 22, 107, 112

In sickness
Psalms 6, 8, 30, 38, 39, 41, 102, 119; for the aging: 61, 71, 90, 91, 102; for a happy death: 22, 31, 40, 51, 88, 103, 130

For the departed
Psalms 23, 25, 42, 148 (infants); 16, 23, 25, 27, 42–43, 63, 103, 116, 122, 130, 141, 143 (adults)

In temptation
Psalms 26, 70, 73, 77, 91, 119, 139, 141

Trust in God
Psalms 4, 14, 17, 27, 40, 42–43, 46, 55, 60, 62, 63, 68, 81, 91, 96, 125, 131, 132, 142, 146

For union
Psalms 23, 100, 117, 118, 122, 133

Blessings on work
Psalms 44, 80, 90, 104, 127, 128

To know one's vocation
Psalms 16, 22, 23, 24, 27, 33, 34, 40, 45, 60, 63, 84, 100, 110

In danger of war
Psalms 46, 72, 85, 122

In any need, emergency
Psalms 67, 70, 80, 85, 123, 134

Safe in Joseph's Arms

I have learned to rely on the man who taught Jesus.

by Dorothy Garrity Ranaghan

My eldest brother died last year . . .

. . . and I became the last surviving member of my immediate family. It was a sobering moment. The consolation came from knowing that I can take great joy in my own progeny: six grown children and fifteen grandchildren.

It was with some nostalgia, therefore, that I began to sort through some very old photos. I found one of my favorites, a faded black and white picture of my dad holding my two-month-old twin sister and me. He holds one of us in each arm. In the picture, my sister is sound asleep. But I am awake and smiling up at him, and he is beaming back at me.

The tender affection and strong security of my father's arms were a constant in my childhood. His death when he was only fifty-one and I was twelve years old was a crushing loss. But the foundation of love and trust in my father enabled me to love and put trust in God the Father, and it is the solid foundation on which my prayer life rests to this day.

St. Paul of the Cross, the founder of the Passionists, believed that the essence of prayer was to "remain like a child on the bosom of the Divine Father." Those of us who have known comfort and security in our human fathers find that easy to understand. Amazingly, Jesus, the incarnate Son of God, became man and learned to live in the bosom of his divine Father in the same way I did. He was wrapped in the arms of his strong, humble, faith-filled foster father, Joseph. Because of that, Joseph has always been my favorite saint, a model for my prayer life, and, since the death of my father, he has become someone I have looked to as *my* foster father.

A Mentor for Prayer. The impact of Joseph on my prayer life comes primarily from imitation. Like any good Jewish father, Joseph would have taught Jesus not only to work and to honor his mother but also to pray and to read Scripture. I can almost hear Joseph teaching Jesus to pray to God the Father and to recite the psalms both at home and in the Temple. If it was good enough for Jesus, it's more than good enough for me!

When we hear Jesus speak in the Gospels, he is often quoting the psalms. "Blessed is he who comes in the name of the LORD." "The stone the builders rejected has become the cornerstone." Even at the hour of his death, the oh so comforting and

The foundation of love and trust in my father enabled me to love and put trust in God the Father.

familiar words of the psalms formed on his lips. "My God, my God, why have you abandoned me?"

For more than forty years, my favorite way to pray has been using the Divine Office, the prayer of the Church. Its primary content consists of the same psalms that Joseph and Jesus must have prayed.

Within our family, my husband led us in Morning Prayer every day. Before school, before play, before anything else, the word of the Lord was heard and recited. The repetition day by day, month by month, year by year, lodges deep within. Without intending memorization, memorization happens.

There is a psalm for every mood of my day—jubilation, sorrow, frustration, and anger. Snippets of those memorized psalms keep me aware of the presence of God in all things. Surely the conversations in the home

of Nazareth were sprinkled with such reminders as well. On rough days I have only to recall that the Lord is a "shield around me." The wisdom of the psalms can turn crushing sorrow into joy. "Those who sow in tears will reap with cries of joy!" When prayers are answered favorably and the good times come, praise comes easily. "Our mouths were filled with laughter; our tongues sang for joy."

A Strong and Vigorous Father.

Jesus called Joseph *Abba* long before he taught us to say "Our Father." I have a sense that when we look at Jesus, we not only see God the Father but a little bit of Joseph as well. Not biologically of course, but in the way that familiarity and discipleship produce a strong image. It makes me smile to watch my own son and his father. Though they are very different, there are moments when a gesture or mannerism, a way of speaking or mode of conversation makes the resemblance striking.

I have never cared for the artwork that portrays Joseph as an old man with a grey beard. It seems to demean the strength of his chastity by assuming it was the result of old age. An apocryphal tradition held that Joseph was a widower who married Mary at an older age. It seemed to answer the problem posed by the Scripture that refers to the "brothers" of Jesus. In this view they are the children of Joseph's earlier marriage. But St. Jerome believed the word used more properly meant cousin. And I am of that belief. Since Jewish custom at the time was to marry young, that is how I see St. Joseph—a strong, young, vigorous man holding the child Jesus close to his heart.

St. Joseph teaches me to hear the Lord, whether in thoughts, in words, or in dreams, and then to obey what he says, even if it means the wrench of changing my mind. Joseph did it after he had decided not to break it off with Mary, accepting the responsibilities of fatherhood for a child who was not his own. He did it again when told to flee into Egypt. This decision could not have been easy. But with great faith, he accepted God's will and plan, even though it meant traveling through the scorching sands of Egypt to go live in pagan surroundings.

Humility and Love. Joseph also teaches me the joy to be found in silence and humility. Pride and wordiness are more my style. But Scripture doesn't record any word that Joseph ever spoke. That's downright convicting. If one who is humble doesn't consider himself more than he is, but also not less than he is, then Joseph's acceptance of his authority in the family of Nazareth personifies humility. As Blessed Pope John Paul II said, it was Joseph "into whose custody God entrusted his most precious treasures."

St. Joseph was the first to love Mary, and with him I come to know and love her better. How much she must have trusted in his strong and gentle presence! As John Lynch says so eloquently in *A Woman Wrapped in Silence,* when Joseph and Mary and their infant child were far from home in a strange land, Joseph knew that "he was a homeland for her heart."

Saint Joseph was also the first, with Mary, to love Jesus. Learning to pray was for me as simple as "seeing" how Joseph talked with Jesus:

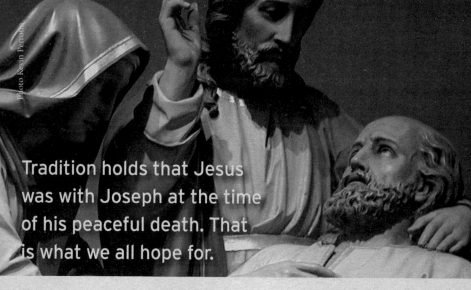

Tradition holds that Jesus was with Joseph at the time of his peaceful death. That is what we all hope for.

directly, naturally, familiarly, confidently, tenderly, and no doubt with humor.

Resting with His Son.
Decades after John XXIII placed the name of Joseph in the Roman Canon, Pope Francis has cleared the way for him to be named in the Mass in Eucharistic Prayers II, III and IV in the third edition of the Roman Missal. It's about time. Next to Mary, Joseph may well be the "greatest saint." As such, it is truly "right and just."

It was death that got me thinking along these lines, and it is reassuring to me in my seventh decade to remember that St. Joseph is the patron of a happy death. Tradition holds that Jesus was with Joseph at the time of his peaceful death. That is what we all hope for. In death it was Joseph's time to rest in the bosom of the Son who is ever "at the Father's side." (John 1:18)

And so I make my own this ancient prayer to St. Joseph.

Oh, St. Joseph, I never weary of contemplating you and Jesus asleep in your arms; I dare not approach while he reposes near your heart. Press him in my name and kiss his fine head for me and ask him to return the kiss when I draw my dying breath. St. Joseph, Patron of Departing Souls, pray for me. ■

Dorothy Garrity Ranaghan lives in South Bend, Indiana. Her latest book is Blind Spot: War and Christian Identity, *available from New City Press.*

DAVID TAUGHT ME

Praying with King David

The psalms keep me focused on the Lord.

HOW TO PRAY. Well, not exactly.

I learned to pray using words attributed to David—the psalms. And over the past five decades, the psalms have not only shaped my prayer; they have shaped my understanding of God and of life.

I bumped into David when I was a nineteen-year-old sophomore at Duquesne University. I had accepted the invitation of a friend to join her and several other students and teachers for early morning prayer. They introduced me to a layperson's version of the Liturgy of the Hours. That's where I met David. During that year his songs captivated my heart, and I have prayed with them ever since.

Finding the One True God.

The psalms showed me who God is and what he is like. They flooded my mind with images that revealed his greatness. I prayed to the God who "counts out the number of the stars, and gives each one of them a name" (Psalm 147:4). I conversed with the God whose thoughts, if I had an eternity to count them, would total more than all the grains of sand on every shore (139:18). Psalm 103 and others like it declared why God deserved my praise and thanks, and gave me the words to do it:

Yahweh is tenderness and pity,
slow to anger and rich in faithful
    love;
his indignation does not last
    for ever,
nor his resentment remain for all
    time;
he does not treat us as our sins
    deserve,
nor repay us as befits our
    offences.
As the height of heaven above
    earth,
so strong is his faithful love for
    those who fear him.
As the distance of east from west,
so far from us does he put our
    faults. (Psalm 103:8-12)

Praying with the psalms has helped me thwart a temptation described in C. S. Lewis's wonderful book, *The Screwtape Letters*. This little story showed me how Satan is

The psalms invite me every day to spend time adoring the true God, who is eternal, infinite, and almighty.

always tempting me to make God into someone he isn't—and in so doing, keep me from God.

In the book, the master devil, Screwtape, instructs a demon trainee to tempt his victim to pray to a god that he imagines in his own mind and thus not to God at all. Screwtape says that this kind of temptation will have the effect of separating the victim from God's presence.

Screwtape warns his apprentice devil that if the victim ever consciously directs his prayers to God as he reveals himself instead of this imagined god, then all their efforts will become nearly impossible: "Once all his [incorrect] thoughts and images have been flung aside . . . and the man trusts himself to the completely real, external, invisible Presence, there with him in the room . . . then the incalculable may occur." And what is "the incalculable"? It's that the man actually meets the Lord and finds his life changed by God's love.

So praying the psalms has prevented me from worshiping a god that I might have created in my imagination—perhaps a cruel, vengeful god or a distant, uncaring one. Immersing myself in the psalms causes me to worship God as he is. They invite me every day to spend time adoring the true God, who is eternal, infinite, and almighty: "Come, let us . . . kneel before Yahweh who made us" (Psalm 95:6).

Praying with David. David's songs have also taught me how to respond to God, who initiates all prayer. They trained me in dispositions of thanksgiving, repentance, and intercession.

Thanksgiving. Praying the psalms has made giving thanks a theme of my prayer. "Let us come into his presence with thanksgiving," says Psalm 95, "acclaim him with music"(Psalm 95:2). When I come across verses like this one, I stop midpsalm to spend time expressing gratitude for all the Lord has done for me. I thank him for creating me; for giving me a human nature; for Christ's passion, death and resurrection; for the sacraments; for granting me a share in his divine life; for Mary Lou, my wife, and our children; for my friends; for providing all my material needs; and, most of all, for forgiving my many sins. This spirit of thankfulness has kept my prayer fresh and lively.

Repentance. Psalm 51, David's prayer of repentance, holds a high place among my favorite psalms. I pray it often because, as you might guess, I sin often. It helps me ask forgiveness for such things as fits of irritability when things cross me and

speaking unkindly to my wife. I take comfort in verses like these:

> Have mercy on me, O God,
>   in your faithful love,
> in your great tenderness wipe
>   away my offences;
> wash me clean from my guilt,
> purify me from my sin"
>   (Psalm 51:1-2)

This Psalm also helps me fight temptation. Frequently throughout the day I find myself praying,

> God, create in me a clean heart,
>   renew within me a resolute
>   spirit.
>   (51:10)

I have no way of telling for sure, but I think this little practice may keep me from indulging in some of my bad inclinations.

Intercession. The psalms have given me a heart for intercession because they encourage me to expect God to answer my prayers. For example, Psalm 145 declares that God

> fulfils the desires of all
>   who fear him,
> he hears their cry and he saves
>   them.   (Psalm 145:19)

Notice the condition that the Lord only listens to intercessors who "fear" him, that is, those who surrender their lives to him. Submission to God's will does not guarantee his yes to a request, but it is a good ground to stand on when asking him for something. I intercede for a long list of relatives and friends at my morning prayer time. And I trust the Lord for his best answer, which may be "Yes," "Wait," or "I've got something better."

A Remedy for All My Cares.

For more than fifty years, David's songs have encouraged and strengthened me. Even in hard times, praying the psalms has lifted my heart and kept me on an even keel. For example, I have prayed Psalm 116 so often that these reassuring verses are locked in my memory:

My heart, be at peace once again,
    for Yahweh has treated you
        generously.
He has rescued me from death,
    my eyes from tears,
        and my feet from stumbling.
I shall pass my life in the
presence of Yahweh,
    in the land of the living.
                    (Psalm 116:7-9)

St. Basil the Great (329–379) describes the Book of Psalms as the complete prayer book, proclaiming all truth, directing every aspect of life, and meeting every need:

The Holy Spirit composed the Scriptures so that in them, as in a pharmacy open to all souls, we might each of us be able to find the medicine suited to our own particular illness. . . . But the Book of Psalms contains everything useful that the others have. It predicts the future, it recalls the past, it gives directions for living, it suggests the right behavior to adopt. It is, in short, a jewel case in which have been collected all the valid teachings in such a way that individuals find remedies just right for their cares. (*Homily on Psalm 1*)

That's what praying with David's songs does for me. ∎

Bert Ghezzi's most recent book is The Power of Daily Prayer (*The Word Among Us Press*). *He and Mary Lou, his wife, pray the psalms at their home in Winter Park, Florida. Scripture quotations in this article are taken from the New Jerusalem Bible.*

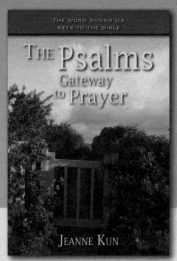

THE WORD AMONG US
KEYS TO THE BIBLE

THE Psalms
Gateway
to Prayer

JEANNE KUN

"It's Poetry, Stupid!"

How a book on the psalms has helped expand my prayer.

by Paul Harvey

I first picked up a guitar nearly thirty years ago, when I was seventeen and just coming to know Jesus in a personal way. From the outset, I wanted to write and play Christian songs. Since then, I have played my guitar and sung to the Lord in all sorts of places—churches, prayer meetings, classrooms, coffee houses, and even market squares, and Metro stations. Many of my "mountaintop moments" have taken place as I worshipped God in song, and writing songs about the Lord is one of my greatest pleasures. I love using his gift of creativity to present his truth. I love, too, the work of honing music and lyrics till they express just what is on my heart.

For all the creativity God has given me, though, I have felt somewhat stilted when addressing myself to him directly. I've had this feeling that for my prayer to be genuine, it should be somewhat plain. With good reason, I think, I wince at songs and prayers that seem too flowery or "touchy-feely." But at the same time, I've asked myself, "Shouldn't there be a place for musical and poetic creativity in worship and private prayer?" Or would God just say, "For goodness sake, speak plainly, man!"

It's with these questions about the role of creativity in prayer that I began using Jeanne Kun's new Bible discussion guide, *The Psalms: Gateway to Prayer*. Going through it, I have come to see that my fellow songwriters, the psalmists, enjoyed great freedom in how they expressed themselves to the Lord.

Helps and Hindrances. To be honest, I have had something of a love-struggle relationship with the psalms. On the one hand, these prayers have played an important role in my work of writing Christian music. A number of my best songs are near word-for-word renditions of psalms. I've always found them tremendously satisfying to write, like collaborating with an ancient lyricist!

I have loved the psalms, too, because they provide powerful words that have become part of my personal prayer over the years: "Shout with joy to God all the earth!" "Why are you so sad, my soul? Put your hope in God, for I will yet praise him." "Teach me your ways, lead me in your paths." "My soul thirsts for you." "I, by your great mercy, will come into your house." As Jeanne Kun says in her introduction, the psalms "teach us how to pray, for they give us a rich vocabulary."

On the other hand, I have found the psalms frustrating and even irritating. So many of them seem meandering and stream-of-consciousness. Why can't they keep to one point? Why do they repeat things multiple times in only slightly different ways? And what about those psalms that speak a language I can't relate to—about crushing enemies, hating evildoers, and having led a "blameless" life?

Experiencing this tension as I do, I was glad to discover that this Bible study didn't sidestep my questions. Certainly, the book helped me grow in my love for the psalms in general. But it also gave me tools and information for tackling the specific psalms and styles that I have struggled with.

"Talk to Me! Here's How." Given my questions about creativity and its place in prayer and worship, I especially relished the section titled "The Poetic Artistry of the Hebrew Psalms." Learning about the literary styles and techniques used by these ancient authors—who were themselves poets and musicians—opened my eyes to appreciate the psalms *as poetry*. It has been something of a breakthrough to reread familiar psalms as pieces of creative writing. The repetition I struggled with in the past? Now I know: "It's poetry, stupid!"—part of the artistry I wasn't able to see before.

This book has also helped me see the psalms as an answer to the question, "If I want to deepen my relationship with God, how should I speak with him?" With all their different moods and modes, the psalms are like an invitation from God. It's as if he's telling us, "I want us to have a real relationship. So come on! Here's how you can talk to me." And so, these prayers are real:

They are emotional and raw. The psalms express heights of joy, depths of despair, and everything in between. Many of them read more like spontaneous outpourings of the heart than highly polished works of literature. This tells me that I can speak to God from my heart as well, expressing all that I feel without worrying about using just the right words!

They are intimate. There's nothing distant or cold about the psalms. They are not formal recitations to a distant deity, but deeply personal words between a people and their God. Through them, God is inviting me to turn to him in the same way—to be intimate with him, to draw near and know his friendship.

They are honest, yet proclaim the truth. The psalmists don't fake anything; they say it like it is. They sometimes complain and at times even wallow. They can even be melodramatic—"I drench my bed with tears!" Likewise, God asks me to be genuine and not to fake anything when I address him.

But the psalmists proclaim the truth about God, along with how they feel. "You are a shield around me." "I will not fear the tens of thousands drawn up against me on every side." Did they always *feel* as confident as they sound? I don't think so. Yet they knew the truth, took their stand on it, and declared it in their prayer. I'm called to do the same, however I may feel.

> The psalms are not formal recitations to a distant deity, but **deeply personal words** between a people and their God.

Ancient yet Alive. Perhaps the test of a good book is whether its message continues to affect you *after* you've finished reading it. *The Psalms: Gateway to Prayer* has left its impact.

Since going through it, I find myself turning to God in ways that are more expressive and free. I am also reintroducing myself to the psalms one by one—reading and rereading them, taking notes, writing them in my own words, basing new songs on them, and learning anew how to pray with them. These ancient but living prayers are expanding the vocabulary and creativity of my prayer life. ■

Paul Harvey lives in Urbana, Maryland, with his wife, two children, and a few guitars.

The Psalms: Gateway to Prayer, by Jeanne Kun (softcover, 128 pp.), is available from The Word Among Us at 1-800-775-9673 or online at www.wau.org. To read an excerpt, visit our website, and click on "Books."

Daily Mass Readings
January 1–February 12, 2013

Below are the daily Scripture readings from the Roman Catholic liturgical calendar as adapted for use in the United States. Celebration of solemnities, feasts, memorials, or other observances particular to your country, diocese, or parish may result in some variation.

Sunday

6
Is 60:1-6
Ps 72:1-2,7-8,10-13
Eph 3:2-3,5-6
Mt 2:1-12

13
Is 42:1-4,6-7
Ps 29:1-4,9-10
Acts 10:34-38
Lk 3:15-16,21-22

20
Is 62:1-5
Ps 96:1-3,7-10
1 Cor 12:4-11
Jn 2:1-11

27
Neh 8:2-6,8-10
Ps 19:8-10,15
1 Cor 12:12-30
Lk 1:1-4; 4:14-21

3
Jer 1:4-5,17-19
Ps 71:1-6,15-17
1 Cor 12:31–13:13
Lk 4:21-30

10
Is 6:1-8
Ps 138:1-5,7-8
1 Cor 15:1-11
Lk 5:1-11

Monday

7
1 Jn 3:22–4:6
Ps 2:7-8,10-12
Mt 4:12-17,23-25

14
Heb 1:1-6
Ps 97:1-2,6-7,9
Mk 1:14-20

21
Heb 5:1-10
Ps 110:1-4
Mk 2:18-22

28
Heb 9:15,24-28
Ps 98:1-6
Mk 3:22-30

4
Heb 11:32-40
Ps 31:20-24
Mk 5:1-20

11
Gn 1:1-19
Ps 104:1-2,5-6,10,
12,24,35
Mk 6:53-56

Tuesday

January 1
Nm 6:22-27
Ps 67:2-3,5-6,8
Gal 4:4-7
Lk 2:16-21

8
1 Jn 4:7-10
Ps 72:1-4,7-8
Mk 6:34-44

15
Heb 2:5-12
Ps 8:2,5-9
Mk 1:21-28

22
Heb 6:10-20
Ps 111:1-2,4-5,9-10
Mk 2:23-28

29
Heb 10:1-10
Ps 40:2,4,7-8,10-11
Mk 3:31-35

5
Heb 12:1-4
Ps 22:26-28,30-32
Mk 5:21-43

12
Gn 1:20–2:4
Ps 8:4-9
Mk 7:1-13

Wednesday

2
1 Jn 2:22-28
Ps 98:1-4
Jn 1:19-28

9
1 Jn 4:11-18
Ps 72:1-2,10,12-13
Mk 6:45-52

16
Heb 2:14-18
Ps 105:1-4,6-9
Mk 1:29-39

23
Heb 7:1-3,15-17
Ps 110:1-4
Mk 3:1-6

30
Heb 10:11-18
Ps 110:1-4
Mk 4:1-20

6
Heb 12:4-7,11-15
Ps 103:1-2,13-14,17-18
Mk 6:1-6

Thursday

3
1 Jn 2:29–3:6
Ps 98:1,3-6
Jn 1:29-34

10
1 Jn 4:19–5:4
Ps 72:1-2,14-15,17
Lk 4:14-22

17
Heb 3:7-14
Ps 95:6-11
Mk 1:40-45

24
Heb 7:25–8:6
Ps 40:7-10,17
Mk 3:7-12

31
Heb 10:19-25
Ps 24:1-6
Mk 4:21-25

7
Heb 12:18-19,21-24
Ps 48:2-4,9-11
Mk 6:7-13

Friday

4
1 Jn 3:7-10
Ps 98:1,7-9
Jn 1:35-42

11
1 Jn 5:5-13
Ps 147:12-15,19-20
Lk 5:12-16

18
Heb 4:1-5,11
Ps 78:3-4,6-8
Mk 2:1-12

25
Acts 22:3-16
Ps 117:1-2
Mk 16:15-18

February 1
Heb 10:32-39
Ps 37:3-6,23-24,39-40
Mk 4:26-34

8
Heb 13:1-8
Ps 27:1,3,5,8-9
Mk 6:14-29

Saturday

5
1 Jn 3:11-21
Ps 100:1-5
Jn 1:43-51

12
1 Jn 5:14-21
Ps 149:1-6,9
Jn 3:22-30

19
Heb 4:12-16
Ps 19:8-10,15
Mk 2:13-17

26
2 Tm 1:1-8
Ps 96:1-3,7-8,10
Mk 3:20-21

2
Mal 3:1-4
Ps 24:7-10
Heb 2:14-18
Lk 2:22-40

9
Heb 13:15-17,20-21
Ps 23:1-6
Mk 6:30-34

When Your Worst Fear

The Old Testament Book of Ruth tells the story of a young woman who left her home, her family, and her traditions out of loyalty to her widowed mother-in-law. After her husband—Naomi's son—died, Ruth could have stayed in Moab to find another husband from among her own people. But she decided instead to stay with Naomi and make sure the older woman was cared for.

When Naomi tried to convince her to choose the greater security of a life in Moab, Ruth replied with words that are often identified with the vows couples make to one another at their wedding: "Wherever you go I will go, wherever you lodge I will lodge. Your people shall be my people and your God, my God. Where you die I will die, and there be buried." (Ruth 1:16-17).

What did Naomi have to offer Ruth? She herself admitted there was nothing she could do for her daughter-in-law. But Ruth wasn't trying to get something from Naomi. She saw a friend in need and decided to support her. So she joined Naomi in Bethlehem and took up menial work in order to provide for both of them.

Ruth's hard work and unselfish care for Naomi attracted the attention of Boaz, a wealthy distant relative of Naomi. Boaz fell in love with Ruth and took her as his wife. The story ends with Naomi holding Ruth's infant son in her arms and joining the women of Bethlehem in blessing the Lord for caring for her so well through the love and commitment of Ruth.

Is a friend going through a difficult time—perhaps a painful illness, financial trouble, or a death in the family? Is someone you know struggling with disappointment or betrayal by another person? Take Ruth as your model, and show that person covenant love! Support him or her in any way you can. Remember, too, how faithful Jesus has been to you, and try to be just as faithful to your friend. Jesus didn't "gain" anything by covenanting himself to you; he did it simply because he loves you. Ask him to give you that same love for the people in your life. Know that as you remain loyal, you will become a minister of Jesus' peace, hope, and healing. ■

I can't think.
I can
hardly pray.
But I can

My first big clue that something was very wrong came in February 2009. I was on a Christian mission trip to Costa Rica, meeting with a small group of women. Suddenly I couldn't understand a word they were saying.

I didn't let on, but I was totally at a loss. All I could do was make a comment every now and then so people thought it was all right. I got some puzzled looks, but somehow I made it through the next hour. Afterward, how I made it through to normal.

Becomes Reality by Myriam Torres

Things weren't normal, though, when I got back home. I cried all the time without knowing why. In my job as a high-level statistician, I found myself struggling to analyze data and needing to delegate my work to other analysts.

"Could be menopause," a friend suggested. I was fifty-six and had already gone through that stage, so it didn't seem likely. "Stress," thought someone else. I took a month off from work, but things only got worse.

A nurse practitioner urged me to see a doctor, and so began two years of medical tests. Early on, after a psychological test revealed "significant" mental impairments, one specialist noted: "probably Alzheimer's disease." If I ever read his comment, I dismissed it right away.

That diagnosis wasn't confirmed until May 2011. By that time, because of my increasing confusion and forgetfulness, I had left the job I loved. And I was wrestling with God in a very serious way.

But I'm Your Bride! For most of my adult life, I've lived "single for the Lord" as part of an ecumenical group of women who have chosen not to marry in order to dedicate ourselves to a life of prayer and Christian service. And so, though we work at various professions and don't take religious vows, I see myself as a bride of Christ, deeply loved and deeply in love with Jesus.

Every day before work, I used to get up to spend an hour with him. I loved it. I'd praise and worship God—singing, reading Scripture, reflecting, and writing down things that struck me. But as I felt myself declining, I became very angry with the Lord.

"Is this the way you treat your bride?" I'd ask him. But he was silent.

Deep down, I knew that if I refused to choose "your way, not mine," I was the one who was going to be the loser. Still, for nearly two years I fought happening tried to denied what was cover up. used to discuss I W all my heart I wanted to believe that my problem was sleep dep stress, or even depression—anything but Alzheimer's.

This wrestling went on and on, but at least I kept talking to the Lord. Then one day, during my prayer time, he gave me an unexpected grace. I suddenly realized that I could really trust him with my future. "I accept this," I told Jesus very simply.

The peace I felt got me through the final medical consultation, which left no doubt that I have progressive dementia: Alzheimer's disease, according to one last test. Sherry, a close friend who is also single for the Lord, was with me as I got the bad news.

"Myriam, you're too quiet," she said, when we were back in the car. "What are you thinking?"

"I'm okay. I worked it out with God last night. And I told him it's okay, whatever it is."

Sherry couldn't believe what she was hearing. I could hardly believe it myself. It was pure grace—and so

freeing to be able to admit what was happening and to talk about it.

Loved and Loving. After a couple of weeks, I felt like the Lord was asking something more: Thank me. Again I prayed, Accepting my situation had been hard enough. Did I really have to do that truly gra I saw in myself. "I'm relating to people differently, in a softer, more loving way. Thank you, Jesus, for this opportunity." And as I prayed, I sensed a call to go deeper—not just to accept and give thanks, but to embrace the journey with trust in God's love and wisdom. This time my response came easily: I embraced it like a gift from heaven.

This may sound strange, but even as I'm losing my abilities, I'm seeing the "gift" side of what's happening. More and more, all I can do is love and be loved. And I feel so much love from so many people! They're praying for me, telling me what I mean to them, thanking me for ways I've helped them.

And God is still using me to speak words that people need to hear. When women I've counseled over the years call and ask my advice, I usually know what to say. I say it more directly, too, because along

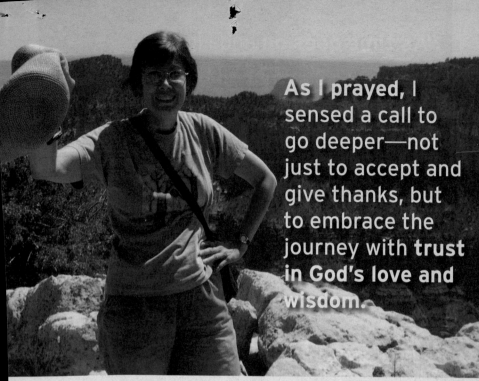

As I prayed, I sensed a call to go deeper—not just to accept and give thanks, but to embrace the journey with **trust in God's love and wisdom.**

Myriam Torres fulfilled her dream of visiting the Grand Canyon last year.

with Alzheimer's comes a lessening of inhibitions! I noticed this recently, when a woman in my Zumba exercise class said how worried she was that her husband might have dementia. Not only did I tell her how to get medical help, but right there, with other people listening in, I prayed with her. "I feel so much better now," she said afterwards.

Suffering Servants. Don't get me wrong, though. Embracing this journey isn't the same as embracing the disease. I'm doing all I can to stay fit and slow my decline—speech therapy, exercise, social contacts, a good diet. If God chooses to heal me, I'll be ecstatic. And although I've arrived at a basic peace, there are still struggles and tears.

I loved being a statistician, being savvy and capable. Now I can't even count. I can't tell time without a lot of effort. If people talk fast, I can't understand what they say. I have a hard time focusing to pray. It's hard to accept help, too, hard to let go.

An experience I had at the airport last year drove home this sense of loss and helplessness. I was traveling with Sherry, but she went through security just ahead of me, so she couldn't help when I got confused

> ## "As time goes on and I lose all I have, I see that all this is making me more like Jesus, the suffering servant."

at the guards' directions. I couldn't understand where they wanted me to place my luggage. I didn't know which hand they wanted me to raise. "Don't you know one from the other?" one guard jeered.

I stumbled out of the checkpoint crying. I felt so humiliated. "This is what's coming," I was thinking. "This is the way I'm going to be—all the time." Explaining it to Sherry later, I could only say I'd had a taste of what it was like for Jesus, when he was stripped of everything and people were mocking him. I take comfort in the fact that I am being conformed to him. As I wrote in my journal, "As time goes on and I lose all I have—the ability to communicate, my memory, being able to do my daily functions—I see that all this is making me more like Jesus, the suffering servant."

St. Ignatius Loyola put it more eloquently in words that I now pray from the heart:

Take, O Lord, and receive all my liberty, my memory, my understanding, and my will, all that I have and possess.

You have given all these things to me. To you, Lord, I return them. All are yours. Do with them what you will.

Give me only your love and your grace, for that is enough for me. ∎

Myriam Torres is a lay pastoral worker and founding member of Bethany Association, an ecumenical group of women living single for the Lord. She told her story with a little help from her friends. For Myriam's practical tips for people with memory loss, see the online version of this article at www.wau.org.

Do you have a story about how God has worked in your life? Send it to us at editor@wau.org.